The New Poetics in Canada and Quebec:
From Concretism to Post-Modernism

THE NEW POETICS
IN CANADA
AND QUEBEC
From Concretism to
Post-Modernism

Caroline Bayard

UNIVERSITY OF TORONTO PRESS

Toronto Buffalo London

© University of Toronto Press 1989
Toronto Buffalo London
Printed in Canada

ISBN 0-8020-5726-8

Printed on acid-free paper

Canadian Cataloguing in Publication Data

Bayard, Caroline, 1947–
 The new poetics in Canada and Quebec

 Bibliography: p.
 Includes index.
 ISBN 0–8020–5726–8

 1. Canadian poetry (English) – 20th century –
 History and criticism.* 2. Canadian poetry
 (French) – Quebec (Province) – History and criticism.*
 3. Canadian poetry (French) – 20th century – History
 and criticism.* 4. Literature, Experimental – Canada
 – History and criticism. 5. Literature, Experimental
 Quebec (Province) – History and criticism. 6. Poetics.
 I. Title.

 PS8155.B37 1989   C811'.54   C89-093564-5   PR9190.5.B37 1989

To Ruth and Marvin Sackner

This book has been published with the help of a grant from the Canadian
Federation for the Humanities, using funds provided by the Social
Sciences and Humanities Research Council of Canada.

Contents

Acknowledgments

I would like to express my gratitude to the various individuals and institutions who have made this book possible, especially to Marvin Sackner for generously granting me unlimited access to his marvellous collection of concrete and post-modern artefacts. Without such direct, visual, and hands-on contact with concrete and deconstructed items, I would have known them only abstractly and have missed an irreplaceable experience. I would also like to express my appreciation to SSHRC for enabling me to travel across the Americas to research the primary theoretical background for this work; as well, I am greatly indebted to the McMaster Arts Research Board for its generous support in facilitating my research in Europe as well as the investigations which carried me through the last chapter.

I will always be grateful to the poets whose imaginative constructs inspired me to undertake this work over these past years. If there is any merit to this endeavour the rewards should be theirs, not mine.

I would particularly like to pay homage to the memory of bpNichol, whose presence will be with us for years to come and whose figure looms large over the pages which follow. As well, I pay special tribute to the memory of Robert Zend, whose humorous constructivist meditations brought us treasures of irony, defiance, and tenderness from his Hungarian/East European heritage. I am most grateful for the contributions of Judy Copithorne and bill bissett to the visual and political explorations of our time – they alerted me to the richness and complexities of our West Coast culture – and I cannot miss the opportunity of thanking the gentle ancestor of Canadian concretism, Earle Birney, whose reputation lent credibility to the young marginals of the 1960s. I was an attentive witness to the immense creativity of Daphne Marlatt and Lola Lemire Tostevin, and I greet their reaching out to Québécois feminist poetics with delight. After watching the rich cross-cultural exchange in which they and Nicole Brossard, France Théoret, Madeleine Gagnon, Louise Dupré, and France Mongeau participated, I would suggest that cultural solitudes belong to our past, however tangible our differences and distances will always be.

Finally, I want to thank all the writers and explorers who have expanded the limitations and delineations of poetics in the last decades: David UU, Gerry Gilbert, Steve McCaffery, and Michael Dutton for having eased the constrictions of avant-garde writing and ushered us into post-modernism; France Mongeau, Normand de Bellefeuille, André Roy, Hughes Corriveau, Denys Vanier, Josée Yvon, Roger des Roches, and André Beaudet for having taken us beyond the expectations of our theory-conscious decade and onto a stage where performances or 'représentations' do take place; and Paul Chamberland, Claude Beausoleil, Yolande Villemaire, and Philippe Haeck for reminding us of the importance of fictions in our private and public lives.

The New Poetics in Canada and Quebec:
From Concretism to Post-Modernism

Introduction

Most scholars and critics have looked upon avant-garde poetics in the two Canadas as peripheral at best or irreverently gimmicky at worst. While such perceptions reflect some of the truisms cherished by the general public about most avant-garde movements – at any given moment and at virtually any place – such a collective mistrust coming both from the niches of academia and from journalistic criticism provoked me to re-examine specific moments of contemporary poetics which have been ignored in our two cultures.

The term *avant-garde* was my basic and very broad departure point. As it turned out, however, it was inappropriate to define the position where I was to end my inquiry. The 1980s had witnessed serious questioning of its relevance to contemporary forms of art.

If one had to condense the long history of this locution,[1] one could say that the term *avant-garde* was first used in a military context at the end of the eighteenth century and then about 1820 became a political concept current among utopian socialists.[2] Its third acceptation in the second half of the nineteenth century is the one that I concerned myself with, namely that of an aesthetic metaphor commonly used to identify writers and artists intent on establishing their own formal conventions in opposition to the dominant academic and popular taste. The radically disruptive writings of Lautréamont and Rimbaud were to give birth to the literary avant-garde of the late 1860s, while in the 1870s art critics were to use the term to refer to the innovations of the early French Impressionists. The high point of the avant-garde has usually been considered the following seventy years, particularly the 1910–30 period when expressionism, futurism, dadaism, surrealism, and constructivism were to generate antagonistic and visionary impulses which signalled a vital tradition of social radicalism and social innovation.

During the 1950s and 1960s the post-war re-emergence of self-conscious stylistic innovation in the arts led a number of critics to speak of a neo–avant-garde in the wake of strong criticism of the academicism of the old avant-garde. The work of writers as diverse as Julio Cortázar, Thomas Pynchon, Donald Barthelme, Günter Grass, Alain Robbe-Grillet, and Peter Handke, however, was soon to be grouped under another historical category – post-modernism – which maintained the concepts of a self-reflexive formal orientation but set them – as Charles Russell put it in *The Avant-Garde Today* (1982) – within a context of liberal, diffusive pluralism. Only three years later Guy Scarpetta argued for the need to take stock of the avant-garde, its excesses, its stereotypes, its limits, and put forward post-modernism as the persuasive act of impurity, the 'métissage' which moves us away from the strictures of the 1920s avant-garde, from the postulates of modernism, of Theodor Adorno in particular, and to a certain degree from Jean-François Lyotard's perspectives. Post-modernism, delineated from Scarpetta's starting points – and I must admit that I find them extremely persuasive – transforms and perverts the function of the avant-garde, reroutes its directionalities away from the utopian myths of artistic progress, 'tabula rasa,' and artistic breakthrough. To be post-modern, in Scarpetta's understanding of the term, has little to do with breaking semantic or syntactical rules, with minimalizing the referential aspects of art. Rather it is an attitude: the capacity to fuse and celebrate what had been previously separated; that is, narrative from textual process, pleasure from scientifically established assertions, representations from non-representational elements.

It would be unfair to pretend that Scarpetta was a newcomer to the area. From John Barth's 1967 and 1980 articles to Jean-François Lyotard's numerous writings on this problematic,[3] post-modernism as a theoretical axis has had a short but eventful history. Scarpetta's contribution – one which I have clearly availed myself of – has been to set a distance between the purist avant-garde (from Mallarmé onwards), whose textual premises were outlined by Julia Kristeva in *Révolution du langage poétique*, and the impure and ambiguously hybridized aesthetic approaches which were to emerge in the late 1970s.

Looking at the two Canadas of the past twenty years and specifically at the concrete movement, at sound poetry performances, and at the deconstructed texts of the late 1970s and early 1980s, I realized that the concepts the theoreticians and practitioners of the avant-garde and of post-modernism had struggled with had also been part of our collective experience. Admittedly we never had a dada movement in the 1920s, but the 1960s and 1970s certainly witnessed serious experiment with these concepts. bpNichol's consideration on this whole problematic, on the amnesia he as an English Canadian had to come out of, was particularly significant for me. I felt that a specific terrain had to be explored, and Quebec's struggling with its own amnesia (and I am thinking here of Claude Gauvreau's fiercely isolated experiments in the 1950s, of Paul-Marie Lapointe's 1948 *Le Vierge incendié*, which was to surface into the public's consciousness only years later) had to be scrutinized and interrogated before any conclusions about radical poetics per se in this country could be reached.

While there had been important critical forays into specific areas (Stephen Scobie's remarkable work on bpNichol, Douglas Barbour's research on sound poets, Ken Norris' perceptive reading of modernist and concrete developments, Clement Moisan's comparative studies of contemporary Canadian and Québécois poets, Gilles Marcotte's earlier analyses of Raoul Duguay's experiments, not to mention Richard Giguère's special *Ellipse* issue on concretism in both Canadas), it still became obvious to me that we had yet to develop a global perspective, a comprehensive vision of these experiments. They needed to be explored both from a national standpoint (these two avant-gardes, their neo- and trans-successors) and from an international one (how were these movements situated in relation to others around the world?). My own contribution to the formulation of this problematic could start there: how could one attempt to define radical poetics in this country and still try to relate them to a wider ensemble? In the course of this process one of Jonathan Culler's reflections was to haunt me. Namely, that to engage in the study of literature is not to produce yet another interpretation of *King Lear* but to advance one's under-standing of the conventions and operations of a mode of discourse.[4] It was this specific mode of discourse which for better or for worse critics have referred to as avant-garde and post-modern that I wanted to observe and re-situate in the context of other literary and non-literary discourses.

Once these objectives were defined some difficult choices had to be made about the working hypotheses and the methodology I was willing to work with. Did I only want to write a literary history of radical poetics in our two cultures? Or did I feel the need to provide textual analyses of the productions in question and if so what angle of observation was the most suitable? What had previously frustrated me in my investigation of avant-garde poetics and more specifically of the international concrete movement was the talkativeness, the effusiveness, of the authors when launched on literary historical paths, the abundance of unearthed influences and ancestors, and their simultaneous reluctance to formulate analytical premises, to define the nature of their departure base.

I decided that if I had to begin to delineate the basic patterns of the discourse I was dealing with I would have to connect them to the premises laid by the philosophers of language from Plato's *Kratylus* to Heidegger's reflections on poetics. This specific focus was also to constrain me and inevitably lead me to pass over other aspects which will deserve to be examined at another time. I was well aware that the documents I was scrutinizing were also the manifestation, the product of and participants in, a certain moment of history. The growing number of magistral studies in the area of interdiscursivity which were to follow the now seemingly remote foundation texts laid by Michel Foucault in *Les Mots et les choses* and *L'Archéologie du savoir*, by both American and Canadian authors such as Fred Jameson, Timothy Reiss, and Marc Angenot, opened large vistas for me. I soon became aware that the very nature of the theoretical questions raised by the poetic texts I was examining, as well as the approach I was using, tipped the scale in specific directions. The problematic in which my corpus engaged me was overdetermined by what I would call the linguistic/formalist fold. Two theoretical texts were specifically instrumental in directing my focus: Gérard Genette's *Mimologiques* and Paul Ricoeur's *The Rule of Metaphor* (and particularly his study no. 5). These works, as well as the momentous shadow of Plato's *Kratylus* looming in the distance, stressed for me the necessity of scrutinizing the aural, typographical, and syntactical functions of the texts I was examining. Inevitably, I came to privilege the functioning of signifier over signified. The historical and ideological premises and implications of contemporary poetics do nevertheless warrant an analysis of the latter. The vitality of historically oriented semiotics in Quebec specifically points in that direction. The type of research initiated by Jacques Pelletier in *L'Avant-garde culturelle et littéraire des années 70 au Québec* (1986) as well as Yvan Lamonde's and Esther Trépanier's *L'Avènement de la modernité culturelle au Québec* (1986) or the important work of Jean Fisette in the area of cultural semiotics have certainly been laying down the foundations of such a critical inquiry.

It did not escape my attention that the texts I was dealing with took place and developed within a specific historical context and that their language was irretrievably part of that history. I realized that it would be a misguided fallacy to suggest that avant-garde and post-modern texts – to use Scarpetta's oppositional terms – operated strictly within the precincts of a literary canon and were unrelated to the larger fabric of a general interdiscursivity. In more than one way I am too indebted to the perspectives developed in the analyses of Jean-François Lyotard, Jean Baudrillard, or Timothy Reiss to deny the key role they played in determining my own focus.[5] I realize the necessity to situate texts within a linguistic as well as civilizational context. But, because I was looking at language constructs and because these experiments[6] were situated within the precincts of language, I determined that my first and primary responsibility was to the prosodic and linguistic components of the texts in question. This has not been without regrets: critical attention to the ideological implications of concrete and post-modern texts is very much warranted at this time, particularly when our two literatures are being examined in the context of a wider interdiscursivity, and when semioticians and hermeneutists alike are leading the way towards new and exciting avenues of knowledge.

While I might work in that direction in a not-so-distant future, I must for the time being accept the restrictions I have chosen and hope that these premises will well serve my limited goals. If the crisis of language which I will investigate in the next chapter ushered in the reign of the signifier, I might be excused for focusing primarily on that signifier.

FROM CLOSURE TO SEMIOTIC MONISM:
THE BATTLE RAGES IN THE PRISON-HOUSE OF LANGUAGE

> Heidegger provides the premise according to which poetry may be freed from the slavery of referent, from its subjection to the purely representative concept of sign which has dominated the representational attitude of metaphysics. Because of the assumption of the language-reality relation as a representational relation, traditional aesthetics has always had the problem of specifically qualifying poetic language either in terms of certain kinds of content (for example the emotions) or of certain purely formal characteristics (verse). Twentieth century poetics has definitively destroyed these perspectives; ... it has ... adopted a perspective which denies the representational dependence of language in relation to things.
>
> Gianni Vattimo, 'From *On the Way to Silence*
> *(Heidegger and the Poetic Word)'* in *Open Letter*, 5th ser., no. 1 (Winter 1982), 48

Ainsi, si l'on accepte le principe de l'isomorphisme entre les syllabes et les énoncés sémantiques, les considérations relatives à la construction et aux possibilités combinatoires des syllabes seront chaque fois valables pour la compréhension de la structure sémantique prise au même niveau d'articulation.

A.J. Greimas, *Du sens*, 41

The end of the nineteenth century witnessed the emergence and the convulsions of a language in crisis. From Gertrude Stein's facetiously serious eccentricities to dadaist antics, from the subjective ruptures of lettrist furores to more recent concrete/pop developments, self-consciousness, ambiguity, and destructiveness have raged in the prison-house of language.[7] This crisis has been scrutinized and dissected by various critics, philosophers, and theoreticians. It reached far beyond the confines of literature and affected the visual arts, philosophy, linguistics, and even the realm of political economy. One need only glance at the deconstruction theories of Jacques Derrida, the politico-linguistic analysis of Jean Baudrillard, or the reflections of Jean-François Lyotard on the deconstruction of artistic forms between 1890 and 1920 to grasp the range and intensity of this crisis of language.[8] To bring in a justificatory network of causes and consequences would be a lengthy and possibly even fruitless enterprise, but a brief examination of the changes which affected linguistics as a science might yield some clues as to what happened to the critical discourse on literature and to literature itself. Ferdinand de Saussure's *Cours de linguistique générale*, published in 1915, marks an important date for the study of linguistic discourse. Its definition of the linguistic sign as a two-fold entity composed of a signifier and a signified and the radical separation it demarcated between the latter and ontological reality – the sign thus referring to itself and not to any external object – ushered in what has since been called the famous 'closure.' The sign was defined as uniting not a thing and a word but a concept (signified or sd) and an acoustic image (signifier or sr). In a way – as Fred Jameson put it – the Saussurean conception was to strike down the most archaic theory of all, regularly revived by the poetic imagination, that of the indissoluble link between words and things. This link was perceived from that time on as no longer intrinsic.

Saussure decided to refer to language as a semiology: 'un système de signes exprimant des idées, et par là comparable à l'écriture, à l'alphabet des sourds-muets, aux rites symboliques, aux formes de politesse, aux signaux militaires etc. Elle est simplement le plus important de ces systèmes.'[9] Semiology was thus looked upon by the Genevan linguist as a science capable of teaching us what signs are all about, which laws regulate them, which functions they hold within the fabric of social life. The *Cours* inaugurated both a break from seventeenth-century rhetoric, in which the word was based upon its correlation with an idea, and a closure: the sign itself became the fundamental entity. Objective reality was excluded and a semiotic monism thus instituted.

Why should this closure be singled out as such a momentous moment in the history of language? It could be argued that all Saussure did was to move from a realist concept of language to a mentalist one. Indeed, he himself was quite aware of the potential problems raised by his definitions of the signified.[10] But the important move here was that by positing the sign as a unit value, he defined the signified and signifier as purely relational elements whose identity would stem from the configuration of the linguistic system and from the opposition networks articulating it.[11] Excluded from consideration was the 'thing itself,' the object of reference in the 'real world.' This declaration of independence of linguistics from any purely semantic concerns was more than a shift: it was a disconnection or, to use Jameson's terminology again, a 'bracketing off.'[12]

When reusing the structural postulates of Saussurean linguistics, most contextual semanticists endorsed the by-then famous closure. Gottlob Frege, in his often-quoted article 'Uber Sein und Bedeutung,'[13] developed the differences between sense and reference, between the information contained within a word and the object it refers to, and reminded his readers that

1. An expression may mean something and not refer to anything which exists objectively (unicorns, sirens, etc.)
2. One word may have a clear meaning without our having an exact and precise knowledge of its referent (the German walfish)
3. Some expressions may have different meanings and refer back to the same object (morning star/evening star).

Frege's distinction between immanent sense on the one hand and external reference on the other (what is said versus that of which one speaks) was to facilitate a dual approach to the study of textual meaning. On the one hand there was to be semantics, a science which could take language outside itself, to the thing denoted; on the other, semiotics, exclusively concerned with intra-linguistic relations, with signs which refer to other signs within the same system.[14] The impact of Fregean and Saussurean reflections upon literary criticism was considerable. Its effects were particularly noticeable throughout the emergence of New Criticism, which suspended the motion between sense and reference, split the first from the second, and focused literary scrutiny on the first: 'words do not refer back to things or ideas but back to other words.'[15] While a logician like Frege or a linguist like Emile Benveniste had been careful to introduce a distinction between *discourse* (which relates to ontological reality and belongs to semantics) and *semiotics* (the level upon which language signifies), the New Critics, especially Monroe Beardsley after I.A. Richards, moved their whole attention from reference to sense: 'words are the things to consider first.'[16] During the 1960s and the 1970s the rise of the New Rhetoric in Europe reinforced these postulates. What it did – as Paul Ricoeur puts it – was to take semantics to its highest degree of structural radicalism and elevate its Saussurean postulate to a sort of 'crystalline purity.'[17] The Belgian μ group thus shifted the focus of structural semantics from word to seme (the units each word can be decomposed into) and concentrated its operations on that level (focusing for instance upon the binary oppositions and hierarchies of disjunctions which gave the form of a tree to all the repertories language may offer on a linguistic level). Ricoeur notes the elimination from such analyses of the speech-related consciousness of either receiver or sender. He stresses that semantics was from that point on fitted into the framework of linguistic semiotics for which all units of language were varieties of the sign (negative/differential/oppositional entities) and all of whose relations were immanent within the sign itself. The relation between signifier and signified was held to be sui generis, and the latter was decomposed into semantic atoms.[18]

The rise of semiology, or semiotics,[19] during the 1960s and 1970s was an important comment upon contemporary discourse – in all its various artistic, literary, political, or psychoanalytical developments. Semiotics was deemed to be an approach to every phenomenon of signification and communication. While it did not pretend to encompass all phenomena, still it proposed to study those which could be defined as sign-functions,[20] thus placing signification squarely within linguistic or, more specifically, Saussurean parameters.

Ricoeur has expressed his concern about a linguistics which would have 'events vanish while systems remain.'[21] The relation between event and meaning, which he describes as one of dialectical unity, appears to him to be severely weakened by a linguistics essentially applied to the structure of systems, and he focuses somewhat sternly on the dangers inherent in such a reductively abstracting approach: 'An act of discourse is not merely transitory and vanishing, however. It may be identified and reidentified as the same so that we may say it again or in other words. We may even say it in another language or translate it from one language into another. Through all these transformations it preserves an identity of its own which can be called the propositional content, the "said as such." '[22]

Shoshana Felman has also brought interesting new insights into this bracketing of the referent. I shall come back to this later when I examine the psychoanalytic inflexions of some deconstructionist theories, but I should say for the time being that she points to this move as a change in the status of *the referent as such* whereby language ceases to be looked upon as a simple reflection of the referent or its mimetic representation.[23]

The effect of such a determination was to turn the code into the instance of absolute reference. By making it refer to its own logic, by divorcing it from a subjective and objective reality, this approach abolished both signified and referent to the sole profit of the signifier. The signifier became its own referent.[24]

It is worthwhile to look at a semiotician's and a logician's triangles on form and representation to perceive the radical changes which affected the perception of the three elements involved:

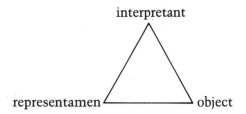

C.S. Peirce defines the process of semiosis as the action or influence which involves the cooperation of three subjects such as a sign (or representamen), its object, and its interpretant.[25] This triadic relation does not have a referential function but an interpretive one. Meaning = signification, not reference, and the object of a sign cannot be conceived of as an object of reference.[26] The interpretant (one should not confuse it with an interpret*er*, as Charles Morris did) is conceived of as a mediator, or that which mediates the character of the sign and guarantees its validity. The interpretant can be a sign translating and interpreting another sign. In Peirce's terms, 'it is nothing but another representation to which the torch of truth is handed along; and as representation it has its interpretant again. Lo, another infinite series.'[27] Turning to Frege's representation of the same problem, one finds the following:

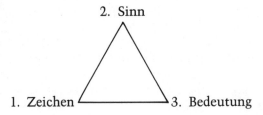

With Frege, objects can be considered only within the framework of a narrow reading. Only (3) is understood as the actual object to which the sign refers. But (3) is more frequently regarded as a *class* of actual objects, thus akin to content and to be studied by a theory of interpretants. If, as Peirce points out, a sign can only be explained through another sign, then the manifest result of this process is that (3) is grasped through a series of its (2) and not vice versa. Or, more explicitly, the semiotic object of a semantic is *not* the referent – as previously thought – but a content which is a cultural unit, a code.

The critical developments previously mentioned from the New Critics to A.J. Greimas may be graphically summarized in the same triangle:

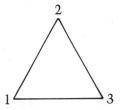

Umberto Eco estimates the impact of such developments in the following manner:

1. One ceases to be concerned with objects as real things.
2. Every attempt to establish what the referent of a sign is forces us to

define the referent in terms of an abstract entity, which, moreover is
a cultural convention.[28]

Explicit here is the shrinkage of (3) from an object-status (partially
granted by Frege) to an abstraction, cautiously introduced by Peirce[29]
and confirmed by Greimas. In mathematical terms (3) has shrunk into
(2), and (2) is only related to (1). Readers are left, at the end of this
reduction process, with a product emptied of its substance, of its
history, and reduced to a function of difference within a system of
differences – a sign-object, a sign function. Not only has (3) been
abolished, but (2) also. The signifier has become the absolute reference,
the all-powerful monad upon which the whole signification system is
resting.[30] As Baudrillard dramatically states it: 'The signifier's ghost
shadow is thus cast upon the world.'[31]

The effects of such developments may be observed in the literature
of the past century. From Mallarmé onwards the obliteration of the
Bedeutung never ceased to be felt. Not only is the ontological world
removed from the senses, but letters, linguistic matter, are viewed as
possessing an autonomy of their own. As Julia Kristeva aptly puts it:
'Mallarmé designates this internal semiosis within language, ... a
rhythm ... a space underlying language, uncontrollable, irreducible to
an intelligent verbal translation ... held back by one guarantee only:
syntax.'[32] She is referring here to 'Mystères dans les lettres,' but one
could as easily designate the famous 'Un coup de dés' (1897) as an
instance of this concentration upon the signifier's powers.[33] She
suggests that words are the condensation of pulsions, the carriers of
signification made possible by recurring patterns on the lexemic and
graphic levels.[34] Only a decade or two later the futurist texts
proclaimed a similar conviction, namely that a word's pictorial design
must be as active as its semantic charge, that there existed a deep
interdependence among the graphic form of the letter-symbol, its
sound, and its signification impact. To the constructivists of revolutionary Russia the shape of each letter was equally as important, being
able to convey a definite mood to the reader independently from the
words being used.[35] The fact that the futurists were essentially literary
people and the constructivists graphic designers does not alter their
relevance to this contemporary perception of meaning and sense. What
they did was to usher in modernity, the reign of the signifier, dada and
Gertrude Stein. With them, more than ever, the left side of the triangle,
the *Zeichen-Sinn* ties, became the focus of concern to the detriment of
the *Bedeutung*. The *Zeichen* was endowed with an autonomy of its

own: both pulsions and structures were enshrined within it, and only *it* retained creative power.[36]

Dada expanded upon these convictions and took them well beyond their initial confines. Tristan Tzara's 'On the Situation of Poetry' – written in the 1920s but not published until 1931 in a magazine – discards poetry 'as a means of expression' to replace it as 'an activity of the mind ... a performance.'[37] If the futurists had already introduced the idea of provocation in art and had abundantly practised it in their own performances, the dadaists, who started their concert performances at the Cabaret Voltaire in 1916, challenged all the preconceptions their spectators might have ever harboured about poetry. Not only did they abandon the line, metaphorical discourse, and discursive meaning in favour of sounds, onomatopoeia, and dancing patterns but they also made use of simultaneity (shouting/whistling/speaking/singing) as an organic concept.[38] One of dada's commentators deemed this simultaneous poetry an activity designed to create 'nonsensical yet sonorous effect.'[39] It might be worth noting here that the obviously unrelated texts which were read simultaneously were also in different languages. Since the final product was to be a sound-object, signification and coherence mattered very little. The concept of automatism, the idea that thought is produced in the mouth, appears to confirm the absolute autonomy of the signifier from other factors as well as its dominance in the functioning of form and representation. Indeed, representation becomes form. Period.

Lettrism, in spite of the polemical disputes it entertained with dada, essentially corroborated the same founding postulates.[40] Phonetic matter was irretrievably divorced from recognizable words, from any decodable anchor in meaning. One could substantially argue here that nonsense as a literary mode did not wait for the dadaists or the lettrists to make its impact upon the literary imagination. As early as the Middle Ages with the 'Grands Rhétoriqueurs,'[41] who abundantly used puns, alliterations, and cacophonies, and as late as *Alice in Wonderland*, whose Humpty Dumpty revels in such games, to say nothing of nursery rhymes, which are older than any of the latter, nonsense has been a prominent literary mode. But what is significant here is that neither the medieval troubadours nor Lewis Carroll ever systematized these operations into a conceptual apparatus. None of them said that meaning was born in the mouth – even though their literary products would convince us that they suspected that much. Indeed they left it to linguistics and nascent semiotics to allow the radical separation of the three sign-compounds and the enshrining of the first. One moved from imaginative experimentation to a systematic analysis of the very systems of discourse.

To undertake a scrutiny of contemporary literary works based upon similar research postulates would demand the attention of more than one well-intentioned researcher. Suffice it to say that the typographical explosion of E.E. Cummings,[42] which showed how vital to the touch words were, the Imagist dictum 'not in ideas but in things,'[43] which signalled a departure from earlier poetics, and the objectivist statement 'a line must be as warped, as clean as wood is'[44] all concur to point out a move from signified to signifier within literature itself.

The overall sociological effects of this radical switch have been analysed by numerous post-modern thinkers.[45] The effects of this hierarchical relationship between a dominating form and a dominated one, the loss of the symbolic to the advantage of the semiotic,[46] pose questions which overstep the boundaries of literature. But this closure constitutes more than a background or even a context: truly it defines the terms of the world in which concretism, in particular, and the avant-garde and post-modernism, in general, emerged and produced texts.

More specifically a number of these tensions are echoed throughout concretist manifestos. One should not suggest that they were either resolved or clarified there. One faction of the concrete movement endorsed the Saussurean closure and its Peircian developments. But the other attempted a radical return to the world of objects, to ontological reality, by introducing the concept of isomorphism: the fusion of sign and object, the merging of representation and reality. While epistemologists are entitled to have their reservations about the latter move, as they find it both naïve and confused, this division reflects an old contention, which began in Plato's *Kratylus* and followed various circumvolutions throughout the centuries to the present. The now famous closure, as I will show, may have been considerably older than Saussure, and it is possible that post-modern developments have found an exemplary spokesman in the Hermogenes of Plato's dialogue.

1 Theoretical Background of a Crisis

Don Quichotte dessine le négatif du monde de la Renaissance; l'écriture a cessé d'être la prose du monde; les ressemblances et les signes ont dénoué leur vieille entente ... *Don Quichotte* est la première des oeuvres modernes ... puisque le langage y rompt sa vieille parenté avec les choses ... [Mais] sous les signes établis, et malgré eux, [le poète] entend un autre discours, plus profond, qui rappelle le temps où les mots scintillaient dans la ressemblance universelle des choses ...

Michel Foucault, *Les Mots et les choses*, 61–3

WHAT IS CONCRETE POETRY: A BRIEF SURVEY OF ITS MEANDERINGS IN EUROPE AND LATIN AMERICA

Today, 'Concrete Poetry' is the general term which includes a large number of poetic-linguistic experiments characterized by conscious study of the material and its structure ... I find it wisest to stay with the word, even with the usual meanings of the word ... The purpose of reduced language is not the reduction of language itself but the achievement of greater flexibility and freedom of communication.

Eugen Gomringer, 'The Poem as a Functional Object'
[Foreword to *33 Konstellationen*], in Mary Ellen Solt, *Concrete Poetry: A World View*, 69

The beguiling simplicity of a concrete poem should not mislead us into the assumption that it represents mere typographical fiddling. We must remember its origins in the hidden knowledge of ages past. It preserves a persistent connotation that names are integral parts of images and objects, though the modern alphabet of Phoenician invention to expedite trade and commerce has almost lost this attribution.

Yet today, concrete poetry continues to revitalize older embodiments of hidden power, transforming the consonant *M*, for example, into a nocturnal owl or altering other letters such as *A* from its status as vowel and article into the soaring diurnal eagle, all partners in an endless passage.

John McAuley, 'Concrete Poetry: The Story of a Further Journey,' in Ken Norris and Peter Van Toorn, eds., *The Insecurity of Art: Essays on Poetics*, 90

The first natural queries of the reader will be: but what is concrete poetry, when did it begin and where? who first used the term? and why? is it possible to determine the antecedents of concretism and what are the grounds to do this?

Before attempting to define this complex – and often contradictory term – it might be worthwhile to look at its fluctuating fortunes in the realm of literature and fine arts. One of the first persons to use it with an adjectival function was the Dutch painter Theo Van Doesburg in April 1930.[1] Van Doesburg wanted to substitute it for the term *abstract art*, an expression which he found wholly inadequate. He was not alone in seeing the need for a prompt substitution and the artist-poet Hans Arp was quick to explain the reasons why: 'We do not want to copy nature, we do not want to reproduce, we want to produce directly and not through interpretation as there is not the slightest trace of abstraction in this art: we call it concrete art.'[2] Another graphic artist, the Swiss concrete painter Max Bill, was to complete this definition by adding: 'The term concrete art refers ... to works *that bear no relation to external phenomena* and are not the result of any kind of abstraction.'[3]

When one turns to musicography and to its developments in the 1950s, one can see that composers did in their turn borrow and use this word. Pierre Schaeffer, the French composer, summarizes their understanding of it: 'La musique concrète est le son à l'état natif, tel que le fournit la nature, le fixent les machines, le transforment leurs manipulations.'[4] And he illustrated in two columns the differences between traditional music and concrete music:

Musique habituelle (dite abstraite)	Musique nouvelle (dite concrète)
Phase I conception (montable)	Phase I matériaux (fabrication)

Phase II	Phase II
expression (chiffrée)	expérimentation
Phase III	Phase III
exécution (instrumentale)	composition (matérielle)[5]

The graphic arts and music conferred upon this term a common core of concerns: the rejection of mental abstraction processes and the elimination of mimetic interest in outside phenomena, in favour of concentration upon what was viewed as *matter*: graphs and sounds respectively. (But who could pretend that *matter* was *not* an outside phenomenon?)

The first writer to use the term *concrete* was Ernest Fenollosa in 1908. Though he did not give it the same materialist twist that Brazilian, French, or Swiss concretists did years later, his perceptions are not devoid of relevance and one detects here a powerful nostalgic yearning for the ideogrammatic suggestiveness lost to an alphabetic culture:

> In Chinese the chief verb for 'is' not only means actively 'to have,'
> but shows by its derivation that it expresses something even more con-
> crete, namely 'to snatch from the
>
> moon with the hand.'   Here the baldest symbol
>
> of prosaic analysis is transformed by magic into a splendid flash of *con-
> crete poetry*.[6]

What Fenollosa did was to equate concrete poetry – in his terms of course – with ideogrammatic texts. He reactivates here what Jacques Derrida will refer to as the 'Chinese prejudice,'[7] namely the perception of a universal script and language as embodied in this specific model. His comments unwittingly point to the specific problems which were going to plague and divide concretists half a century later: was the concrete poem to become the representational graph of an object or – if objects there were not – of a fragment of our ontological universe? or had it to be looked upon as an arbitrary, conventionalized, algebraic system? The history of writing, traced by linguists, anthropologists, and philosophers, would seem to indicate a move from graphic representationality to arbitrariness. Writing functions so as to signify the world rather than to be a visual mirroring of it. Michel Foucault's analysis of the different epistemes of the pre- and post-Renaissance period certainly point in this direction.[8] The linguist E.A. Llorach's tripartite division of the history of writing into an ideographic, a semiographic, and a phonographic period also gives credibility to this theory about the history of writing.[9] And Jean Piaget lends further plausibility to this analysis by viewing writing as an evolution from imaged symbol to analytic sign.[10] The issue of the figurativeness of language at its 'source,' in its ancient 'origins,' has preoccupied philosophers for many centuries. William Warburton in eighteenth-century England, focused on this specific issue.[11] While the 'representativity' of language in the cradle of its origins is not ascertained to be as obvious as it once appeared to be,[12] the accepted 'doxa,' the commonly held opinion up to the twentieth century, was that indeed ideogrammatic writing could be considered to be figurative. Hence the reference to the 'Chinese prejudice' (Derrida) and the often-quoted concretist approbation of the Pound–Fenollosa perception of this phenomenon.[13]

The first concrete theoretician – or the first to apply the term *concrete* to poetry – turned out to be a Swede whose 1953 manifesto, ignored for years, had to await the emergence of a movement to be drawn out of obscurity.[14] Oyvind Fahlstrom's proposal was quite simple. Describing himself as disgusted with romantic, surrealist, and psychoanalytic aesthetics, he argued that poetry should be created *and* experienced as concrete material. Visuality and rhythm: such was the field of poetry, nothing more, nothing less.[15] Fahlstrom's radical premise is the same which will later underlie all subsequent literature on this subject: a materialistic emphasis of language, which is 'that which poems are made of.' It becomes the creative impulse, *the* energy source of imaginative production. Matter sings and speaks by itself. In order to revolutionize tired, old norms, one can only explore visuality and rhythm. Spatially one can introduce diagonal, mirrored, and simultaneous readings, break stanzas into vertical, parallel, or framed forms, or introduce kernel words which can be read from right to left and bottom to top. Rhythmically the possibilities are even larger: one may create onomatopoeic phrases, homonymic ones. What Fahlstrom calls in Swedish 'Zuegmabinding'[16] undermines the reader's security and suggests that conventional meanings are as arbitrary as the newly suggested ones.

The experiments of concrete music – sound reversals, pitch modifications, and sound atomizations – carried out by Pierre Schaeffer in France are direct-line descendants of the Swedish writer's premonitions, and one could evidently argue that in 1953 this obscure Swedish theoretician was both ahead of his time and totally isolated.[17] While his manifesto prefigures the dual direction of concretism – visual and auditive – it is curious to see how he overlooked the rich field of European medieval literature which had centuries before him exemplified the principles he was enunciating. A good deal of his premonitions concerning reading order, words hidden beneath words, and kernel words had been the routine staple of many troubadours from the ninth to the fourteenth centuries.[18] Though he makes a passing reference to the 'Grands Rhétoriqueurs' as 'language kneaders of all times,'[19] one is inclined to wonder how fully he was aware of their practices.

In the area of visual experiments the Swiss and the Germans brought out the most articulate statements.[20] Eugen Gomringer, who in 1953 had never heard of Fahlstrom, in 1964 published his 'From Line to Constellation'; the graphic artists Diter Ross and Marcel Wyss, the members of the Darmstadt Circle in the late 1950s,[21] and Max Bense, H. Mayer, and Franz Mon in Stuttgart all stressed the graphic and typographical possibilities of concretism, matter of visually alive and vibrant objects.

Max Bense, one of the most prolific thinkers on the subject of concretism, emphasizes the materialist, nothing-but-itself approach: '[concrete] to be understood positively, as in Hegel, [is] the opposite of the term abstract. The concrete is the non-abstract. Everything that is abstract is based on something from which certain characteristics have been abstracted. Everything concrete, on the other hand, is nothing but itself.'[22]

This will justifiably raise eyebrows. What *is* this itself? Bense would answer: what one sees and hears. Notwithstanding the truism that different readers hear and see differently, the 'literalism' proposed by Bense presents several difficulties. Disposed of conveniently here is the entire question of the signified, its structural composition and complexity, as well as the relative competence and possible performance of the receiver of the said signified. Not only the stark monism but also the simplistic nature of this definition was bound to have repercussions upon later poetic developments. Incidentally, though not accidentally, Bense happened to be a semiotician thoroughly grounded in Peircian theories and actively engaged in semiotic research. In his own tripartite division of signs he used the ensemble theory to articulate as precisely as possible the differences between these three elements.[23] Revealing in this area was the positive connotation attached to the term *symbol* and the negative one applied to the term *icon*. It appears that Bense upheld the independence of the symbol (that is, its high degree of semioticity as the most convention-alized of all three signs) to the detriment of the icon's figurativeness (that is, low degree of semioticity). Perusing Bense's semiotic research allows us a better understanding of his concrete theory. For him semantics do not exist, and words are not used as carriers of meaning but as material of construction. The concrete poem is constructivist.[24]

Perhaps more stimulating and exploratory was the notion of *Denkgegenstanddenkspiel* ('play activity') expounded by Gomringer, which he viewed both as information and communication. The poet invents new rules for the game and incites the reader to become involved in the play: a mental area of possibilities is opened for the reader to enter and join in.[25] The focus here is slightly displaced from linguistic components to the reader, producer and decoder – a heretofore ignored element. One recurring preoccupation, common to all German writers, should finally be noted: the need for formal simplification, concentration, and economy. This ascetic yearning for an 'abbreviated, restricted form'[26] was partially an outgrowth of these media artists' daily encounter with advertisements, signs, and slogans, the recognition of immediate linguistic changes. But more important-ly it was a signal that poetry wanted an 'organic function in society' and not the superfluous niceties of a decorative adjunct. Gomringer wanted the public to use poems as daily objects, to remove aesthetic distance and replace it with a 'utilitarian relationship.' But one should note here that the *Denkgegenstanddenkspiel*[27] was not only a play activity but also a pleasure principle (a great catchword of French literary theorists in the late 1960s and early 1970s, who, however, gave it a Freudian inflexion which Gomringer's manifestos were thorough-ly void of).[28]

Explicit in the whole German movement was the same division which was to split the international movement. On the one hand there were those writers who preconized the fusion of typography and semantics (Gomringer and Mayer, whose sign-characters were de-signed to be unravelled by readers); on the other, those who rejected this iconicity and along with it semantic accountability to emphasize pure visuality, the text as texture, and the constructivist possibilities of words.[29] The same demarcation line separated the French (of a constructivist bent) from the Brazilians who tried to devise a system integrating semantics and signs. Indeed the latter wanted to cover *the entire perceptual field* and not the mere components of language, an endeavour acutely reflected in their coining of the suggestive expression 'verbivocovisual' as applied to concrete experiments.

THE MYTH OF A UNIVERSAL LANGUAGE, THE ICONIC FALLACY, AND ONE OF ITS CONTEMPORARY AVATARS, ISOMORPHISM

> This sort of plan would at the same time yield a sort of universal script, which would have the advantages of the Chinese script, for each person would understand it in his own language, but which would infinitely surpass the Chinese, in that it would be teachable in a few weeks, having characters perfectly linked according to the order and connection of things, whereas, since Chinese script has an infinite number of characters according to the variety of things, it takes the Chinese a lifetime to learn their script adequately.

> Leibniz, quoted in Jacques Derrida, *Of Grammatology*, 79–80

> In spite of all the differences that separate the projects of universal language or writing at this time (notably with respect to history and language), the concept of the simple absolute is always necessarily and indispensably involved. It would be easy to show that it always leads to an infinitist theology and to the logos or the infinite understanding of God ... Within a certain historical epoch, there is a profound unity among infinitist theology, logocentrism, and a certain technicism.

> Jacques Derrida, *Of Grammatology*, 78–9

The historian of concrete poetry would look upon Brazilian theoretical texts as the richest and most articulate contribution to concretism. The coining of the term itself was theirs, and the Swiss poet Eugen Gomringer, whose 'Constellations' had emerged in the early 1950s, immediately endorsed it. Key to the elaboration of the main body of theoretical texts was the 'Plano Piloto para Poesia Concreta'[30] and the three Sao Paulo poets Haroldo de Campos, Augusto de Campos, and Decio Pignatari. Their Noigandres[31] group also involved avant-garde musicians and artists, all engaged in research which culminated in the publication of this synthesis, the famous Pilot Plan, which was to come back in the writings of numerous concretists during the following decade. Concrete poetry was posited, in this manifesto, as a verbi-voco-visual manifestation, solidly entrenched upon the concept of isomorphism. What this term referred to was an identity relationship within the sound/visual form/semantic charge triad. Signifier(1) +

signifier(2) + signified were firmly based upon this cornerstone principle, which seems to have been derived from linguistics. While L. Hjemslev is never mentioned in *Teoria da Poesia Concreta*, it would appear that a great deal of his research was utilized – as well as modified at some points beyond recognition – by the new concrete movement. In his *Prolegomena to a Theory of Language* the Danish linguist had established the two levels of the sign-function: the expression-form and the content-form. The Brazilians capitalized on this practical distinction as the foundation for their concept of isomorphism. To them the well-constructed concrete poem *had to* equate graphic-typographical form with semantic function. Or as they aptly put it: content-form = form-content. There is no doubt that this particular formula fitted their need at the time for an overall synthesis. The possibility of casting – at once and forever – in the same mould, linguistic matter and content, phonemes and semantics, signifier and signified must have been very tempting. That it fulfilled their creative purposes while simultaneously endorsing a Kratylian function for language is explicit enough.[32] What needs to be scrutinized more closely, however, is the use and interpretation of the Hjemslevian schema. To the Brazilians the equation of content and form was *prescriptive*. A good concrete poem must communicate – auditively or visually – its *estructura-conteudo* ('content-structure').[33] They did grudgingly admit that this process would take place in two stages: the first would be *fisiognomia*, a state in which the isomorphic tension between form and content tends to be resolved by a simplistic imitation of natural appearance, for which they used the English term *motion*. During the second stage isomorphism would resolve itself into *em puro movimiento estructural*, which they translated themselves as *movement*. In this second stage geometric forms and the mathematics of composition should prevail.

If one returns to the *Prolegomena to a Theory of Language*, the conceptual gap between Hjemslev's analyses and the Brazilian manifestos appears more clearly. Besides the obvious polemical and prescriptive nature of the latter, it is curious to see the use the original linguistic text was put to. The Danish linguist had explicitly stated the *solidarity* of the expression-form and the content-form, the fact that they *necessarily* presuppose each other. Except by artificial isolation, specifies Hjemslev, there can be no content without an expression, nor expression without a content.[34] But nowhere in the *Prolegomena* is there a mention of a homology, or even of a similarity, between the two functives. Indeed this text is quite explicit as to the nature of the relationship the functives entertain with one another: 'They are defined only oppositively and relatively as mutually opposed functives of one and the same function.'[35] Elsewhere Hjemslev uses the terms *correlation*, *common principle*, and *interplay*.[36] However, he never suggests the possibility of a fusion of one with the other. He even explicitly articulates his opposition to such a confusion: 'The necessity of operating with two planes must be that the two planes ... cannot be shown to have the same structure throughout, with a one-to-one relation between the functives of one plane and the functives of the other. The two planes *must not be conformal.*'[37]

What the Brazilians were prescribing, in fact, was a fusion of expression and content. It is noteworthy that this strived-for structural similitude was decomposed into two successive stages. The first one, *fisiognomia*, was to imitate an object's 'natural appearance.' In this case no mention was made of content or of signified. If a search was on, it was for the object, in all its sensual, physical presence. It was only during the second stage that concretists would attain the merging of text and signified and that both structures were fused.

The process at work here would seem to fall into a category which Umberto Eco – at another time and in another context –termed the iconic fallacy.[38] This particular problem might be made clearer through the examination of a specific poem; for example, one of Gomringer's early constellations. The poem titled 'silencio' could be, and has been, looked upon as an exemplification of the first stage. 'Silencio' (see Fig. 1) imitates a certain 'natural appearance,' that of the absence of speech, noise, or sound, by using a five-by-three rectangle with the central *silencio* missing.

If one now turns to Eco's critique of the naïvety of iconism, one realizes that for the Italian semiotician an iconic fallacy is based upon the conviction that a sign has the same properties as its object and is simultaneously similar to, analogous to, and motivated by its object.[39] Once these links are more carefully thought out it appears that 'silencio' does not have the same 'properties' as the term *silence*, that it is in no way similar to it (how could the absence of sound present a similitude[40] with a plane surface?). If one is accustomed to associate the idea of iconism with an visual relationship between similar *spatial* properties, the suggestion that Gomringer's poem is similar to a *perception* of silence seems somewhat whimsical. *Analogous* presents more serious difficulties. If the term is taken as a synonym for 'unspeakable,' that is, in its 'most vague and metaphorical sense,'[41] then indeed one could think of a vague resemblance between the idea of silence and this particular text. But 'analogy' should be taken as a 'proportional relationship,' and within such a definition the connection between concept and text does not make sense. Eco suggests that if icons are thought of as *surrogate stimuli*, then this does not imply that they possess the same properties as their objects.

The iconic fallacy which the Brazilians appear to have fallen into – at this first stage of their program – should not detract us from examining their second step, the 'pure structural movement,' which makes no reference to any object but draws attention to expression and content. An illustration of it could be given through 'sem um numero,' a poem dedicated to Brazilian peasants, which is built upon the slow, diagonal decomposition of the poem's title *0*, or zero (see Fig. 2). One observes a dual movement here: *0* is on the middle point of the diagonal line, which can be read either from the top down or from the bottom up. Thus no visual escape is allowed from the zero, from nothingness and the outcome of destruction, by having the *0* squeezed between the two parts of the linguistic equation, 'sem um numero' and 'um sem numero.'

What matters here is the nature of the content-form. This content-form delineates the features of a devastating material and psychological alienation. The Brazilian peasant, no matter which way one chooses to look, is irretrievably brought back to a zero point. The content is the zero. What this poem did was to use graphic convention in order to transform the conceptual and perceptual conventions which motivated the sign. *Parts* of the content-form were related to *parts* of the expression-form: for instance, the concept of nothingness was linked to the graphism of *0*. But there was no absolute fusion between *all* the elements of the content-form and *all* the elements of the expression-form. A selection was made and it was coded; there was a transformation by which the *x* factor of the content model was made to correspond to the *x* factor of the expression model. This transformation should not suggest the idea of a natural appearance but seems rather to be the consequence of rules and artifice.[42] *0* in other cultures might denote different content-types. But in Brazil – as in any Western culture – it is perceived as being equated to nothingness.

And this raises another issue, different from the iconic fallacy but implicit in a number of concretist writings: the wishful contention that concretism, just like some semiotic codes, could be viewed as a universal language. Gomringer entertained this thought, as did – though through a conventionalized, arbitrary system – some of the young Brazilian semiotists.[43] The Swiss theoretician and his Latin

American counterparts were adopting different premises here. Gomringer was suggesting a 'natural,' 'spontaneous' universalism, while the Brazilians were proceeding from a conventionalized, designed system, but with a common objective: the construction of an idiom theoretically understandable by all. In this sense both were proceeding from a shared horizon, and the infinitist theology of the first shared a profound complicity with the technicism of the latter.[44]

The problem dismissed by both Gomringer and the Brazilian theoreticians was that of the content – incongruences between languages. To choose a well-known example, Hjemslev's schematic summary of the boundary distinctions of the colour spectrum by different European languages is explicit on this point. Portions of the same colour-continuum are divided differently and arbitrarily by different cultures.[45] What his graph stunningly summarizes is the fact that different linguistic cultures create non-concomitant perceptual structures. And even if there were such a thing as 'scientific truth' codable into a poem, it could not be universally perceived and scientifically decoded. Gomringer's and Pignatari and Pinto's texts show affinities with the school of structural semantics which presumes that every sign refers to a univocal position in the universal semantic system because of the existence of a single code. They are therefore not exactly alone in this: a universal semantics, as an *objective*, has held a prominent place in linguistic research.[46] But as a creative theory endowed with a peculiar dogmatic connotation (namely, that the concrete poem *must* be universal), it presents unsurmountable difficulties.

The dividing line which separated the German movement into two distinct factions can be found again between the French and the Brazilians: the believers in isomorphism, on the one hand, and the overthrowers of semantics, on the other. Pierre Garnier in France clearly sided with the latter. He emphasized the autonomous power of language, its lonely and formidable richness, and viewed concretism as the dawn of a new era, of a radically altered relationship between reader and text:

Les mots regardent l'homme et l'homme leur rend leur regard ... les relations ... d'exploiteur à exploité sont dissoutes. Des relations d'amour, de compréhension mutuelle, d'éclairage réciproque peuvent désormais s'établir entre l'homme et le mot.

Peu à peu la langue-réalisation prend le dessus ... Saussure, Victoria Welby et Peirce créent la semiologie au début du siècle; depuis un

considérable travail d'éclaircissement a été fait, la théorie de l'information et la théorie du texte ont été créés et les poètes concrets et
spatialistes doivent beaucoup aux Wittgenstein, Abraham Moles et
Max Bense qui ont su découvrir les structures sur lesquelles se fonde
aujourd'hui notre poésie.[47]

Explicit in Garnier's writings is his need to liberate language from
'sense,' to allow it to be 'what it was before literature,' to vibrate
through its signs, letters, and articulations as a sensitive totality.[48] He
sketches a theory of reader's participation by suggesting a reversal of
conventional roles. The reader becomes a maker, the audience a
performing artist.

Such concepts were not new among European semioticians during
the early 1960s. Umberto Eco had published *Opera aperta* in 1962,[49]
but Garnier never elaborated upon such theories. He was content to
refer to them in didactic and prophetic fashion throughout his various
manifestos. The same lack of inquisitiveness may be found in his use
of multidimensionality as a creative concept. For instance, he advocated the use of neon lights, signs, screens, slides, and wall paper,
particularly in the area of performance, but never investigated these
possibilities in greater detail. He was more thorough on the issue of
syntactical destruction, of its necessity in the context of a new
poetry.[50] His suggestion that all grammatical usage should be thrown
to the winds, adjectival gender agreements rejected, and all verbal
modes discarded, with the exception of the infinitive, was particularly
tantalizing.

Garnier's practices lead, for instance, to the following word-noun
associations:

il corps	elle estomac
il tête	elle ventre
il coeur	elle coeur[51]

The poet would thus rid himself of syntax, grammar, and metre. As for
the sentence, it was looked upon as the epitome of an old, structured,
hierarchized order: 'Quelle différence entre le tigre sur les rives vient
boire et le mot seul: TIGRE! La phrase précise un tableau fade et
rassurant: le mot déclenche tout le psychisme – il introduit l'orage.'[52]
The time had come for the word-object, the word matter.

If the word was Garnier's salvation goal, his compatriot Henri
Chopin went one step further by altogether rejecting it and pleading for

a return to buccal sound, to a human sound, a 'signifier'[53] deprived of
any reference and depending solely upon mouths, throats, and bodies
for its existence. The result was deemed to be an 'art suggestif,' a
medium capable of animating human bodies, allowing them to open up
their own biological, physical capacities. In his hymn to the primitive
powers of the body ('Why I Am the Author of Sound and Free Poetry'),
Chopin chooses sound over word, cry over written idea, impulse over
meaning. It remains one of the most extreme theoretical statements
ever written on phonic poetry even though it substantially articulates
the aspirations of a number of concretists. The experiments conducted
by bill bissett on the West Coast, and by the Horsemen and Owen
Sound in Toronto, owe much to Chopin's radical ideas about sound,
semantics, and language.

The Belgian Paul de Vree only reinforced Chopin's position with his
exhortation that 'one must do away with lexicality since all predication is an assault upon the freedom of Man'[54] and look upon phonic
poetry as a modulation, a shout, a whisper. De Vree went as far as
challenging the written poem as a non-existent entity – 'le non-poème'
to be obliterated from human memory. The rift between the believers
in isomorphism and the overthrowers of semantics was, by the late
1960s, clearly operative. The myth of a universal language had been
seriously shaken, and the logocentric model of Western civilization
was coming under severe attacks from various quarters.

WESTERN CONSCIOUSNESS AND THE KRATYLIAN CONTROVERSY:
WHAT HAPPENS WHEN POETS INVEST AN AREA
VACATED BY PHILOLOGISTS

Speculating on the origins of language is not a particularly recent
phenomenon, nor is it uniquely a preoccupation of our times. Its
formidable 'dossier,' to use Paul Claudel's metaphor,[55] can be traced
back to Kratylus and because of those origins has often be referred to as
'Kratylism'[56] after Roland Barthes, who coined the term and synthe-
sized it as 'this great secular myth according to which language
imitates ideas and – contrary to the precisions of linguistics – signs are
motivated.'[57] One might recall the problem at issue here: Kratylus
affirms that each object received a correct denomination, determined
according to its natural appearance, while Hermogenes maintains that
names are simply the result of an agreement and convention regulated
by use and usage and therefore wholly artificial. Socrates seems to be on
the side of Kratylus at the beginning of the dialogue but progressively

drifts towards that of Hermogenes. Yet some commentators have been quick to point out that Socrates' position was not contradictory but conciliatory: his final choice being neither viewpoint but the suggestions that some words may be badly chosen, or badly formed, that the guilty culprit here was the 'word artificer' [onomaturge],[58] that language was never perfectly formed, and that there has been an original or congenital defect about words.[59] This interpretation would turn Socrates into a disappointed Kratylus and prefigure the famous Mallarméan ire about the perverse couples such as jour/nuit ('day/ night') and ombre/ténèbres ('shadow/darkness') being inadequate to express their respective objects.[60] While the Greek philosopher appears to prefer his own disappointment to some facile potential compensation and wishes good luck to both his protagonists, the temptation to choose one or the other side could not have ended here. More specifically, the compulsion to compensate for the mimetic imperfections of language turned out to have a long and convoluted history. Gérard Genette coined an original term to refer to such a need, mimologism or secondary Kratylism, which seemed eloquent enough to be retained in this study.[61]

While Hermogenes can be looked upon as the obdurate – if not always articulate – ancestor of Saussure, Kratylus in one form or another had more followers than one could have surmised from Socrates' laconic farewell. It appears now that the Greek text had indeed articulated a hiatus between a direct and an indirect motivation for words.[62]

The first motivation could be referred to as phonetic mimeticism: the essence of each object being imitated through letters and syllables.[63] (Here Plato refers us to the first known systematization of a phonetic symbolism.)[64] As for the other motivation, the indirect one, it is strictly etymological[65] and poses the question in the following way: does the search for the actual origins of a word salvage the motivation of the sign?[66] It is worthwhile to note that this search for a motivation is based upon nouns [onomata], not upon verbs, a choice neither explained nor justified but which can be paralleled with the concretist preference for substantives over verbs. But Socrates, who had attempted to found this search for the potential motivation of nouns upon that of names (proper names), is led to the conclusion that such a process is circular, each word being referred to the next and so on until one comes back around to the first word. The last word refers back to the first and this first is a moneme beyond which one will only find sound and letters.[67] But the impossibility of extracting any proof from this procedure has been pointed out earlier, thus justifying Socrates' abandonment of the Kratylian thesis.

What is extremely suggestive here is the fact that both procedures – direct[68] and indirect[69] – had their various followers and contenders in the course of history. In fact concretism can only be *partially* looked upon as a Kratylian development: that faction of the movement which rejected isomorphism and semantics and was to usher in the deconstructed text as well as post-modernism could not have been less concerned with the coincidence between signifier and signified, between word and object, and would radically exempt itself from any involvement with such a philosophy. But in the eyes of those who believed in the fusions sound/sense and graph/sense, the indirect motivation (etymological) has occasionally presented some advantages,[70] while the direct one (the correspondence sound/sense) has operated as the cornerstone of their entire system.

Looking at Genette's fastidious research on this topic, one surmises that this debate had a lasting impact upon philosophical as well as philological thought from Socrates' time to the present. And literary minds did not exempt themselves from active participation in this polemic either. If one follows the chronological order of its avatars, it appears that few periods in history, if any, showed indifference to this issue. Early Christian scholastics were inquisitive about such matters. Isidore de Seville used hermeneutic etymology for demonstrative exegetical purposes, while Saint Augustine, who professes his mistrust of Stoic thought upon the origins of words, ends up synthesizing their theories with great astuteness.[71] This Christian scholar intimates an oblique mimesis: never alluding to a direct imitation of sound by sense guarantees a 'more or less' direct relation between signifier and signified. Indubitably Saint Augustine's attitude is replete with ambiguities for while subtly distancing himself from a clear ontological link, he moves to an analogical procedure: things resemble one another and this allows us to derive the name of one from that of the other.[72] *Similitude* is the key term here and eschews any rupture from the mimetic sphere.[73]

Following scholastic scrutiny, philosophical thought focused its attention on such matters with Locke (*Essays concerning Human Understanding*) and Leibniz (*New Essays*). The distance taken from mimetic theories is immediately apparent in each discourse. Locke does not believe that there could be a natural link between articulated sounds and ideas and that if a word was made the sign of a specific idea it was mainly through an arbitrary decision. Leibniz does not refute the conventionality of the sign but suggests that not all languages need be looked upon as purely artificial. In fact, apart from Chinese and the divine language of its origins,[74] he suggests that other idioms could have a natural motivation and that it is likely that 'languages emerged out of a natural human tendency to adjust sounds upon affections.'[75] Yet Leibniz regrets this motivation and could gladly exchange it, he assures us, for a purely arbitrary language. In his eyes language could only benefit from absolute arbitrariness and one must reform it in that direction, or at least invent a language that would satisfy such exigencies. Curiously, for Leibniz conventionality and artificiality are the obvious manifestation of intellectual superiority. Onomatopoeias were within the reach of the 'primitive mind,' while artificiality demanded the intervention of a divine or at least intelligent mind. What Leibniz is yearning for is a philosophical algebraic language, a rational organization of signifieds which would select rigorously arbitrary signifiers to establish its operations and denominational procedures.[76]

To simplify this complex philosophical as well as philological debate, I would conclude that some writers have favoured graphic mimesis (that is, letters imitating an object's natural appearance),[77] while others focused their attention on phonic mimesis (that is, each letter being the visual analogue of a phoneme).[78] I should also specify here that in the theoretician's view phonic mimesis operates in a cumulative fashion. A phoneme imitates a letter, which in its turn imitates an object.[79] The massive number of treatises written in both areas testifies to the vigour of Kratylian obsessions from the eighteenth century on. Divergences are all the more interesting because they reveal a slow but irrepressible movement from Kratylism as an unshakeable premise to Kratylism as a sought-after, pined-after objective. While Court de Gebelin defines writing as painting and the alphabet as an ideogram,[80] with Charles de Brosses[81] phonic elements have long lost their mimetic virtue and it is up to a new hieroglyphic alphabet to attenuate this deficiency.[82] With Charles Nodier this sliding motion is taken one step further and his critical analysis of the French alphabet prefigures Saussure's course in general linguistics, with all concepts of writing as painting resolutely effaced in favour of phonic mimesis: only the vocal organs can attempt to represent and imitate.[83] The old premise of a primitive universal language, so dear to eighteenth-century thought, was discarded in favour of a Babylonian 'mimologism':[84] languages are multiple and diverse because they reflect the world's diversity. With the development of comparative

philology at the beginning of the nineteenth century came the
death-knell of semantic concordances between different languages and
the concept of a necessary relationship between sound and sense.[85]
The Saussurean closure further undermined the Kratylian concept of a
unity of all languages. Should one conclude in favour of the humiliat-
ing defeat of mimologism? Genette suggests a strategic displacement
instead and implies that the debate was transferred from the area of
scientific inquiry to that of literature.[86] Poets invested the field
vacated by philologists and attempted to recoup the losses. What
could not be affirmed as truth was henceforth searched after as a
compensation, a correction of deficiencies, the re-establishing of a
utopian state when things and signs not only coincided but were fused
into one.

This peculiar resistance against the imperfections of everyday,
ordinary discourse found ample support in Mallarmé's and Valéry's
writings.[87] To the first the phonic elements of language had very nearly
lost all their mimetic faculties, English being *the* exception. With his
Petite Philologie à l'usage des classes et du monde, les mots anglais
(1877), Mallarmé recognizes that languages are sadly doomed to be
imperfect, that discourse fails to represent objects, and that ultimately
it is the task of poetic verse to restore this justness which phonemes
are capable of and which has been betrayed by words. Genette's graph
of Mallarméan mimologism synthesizes the whole issue very accurately:

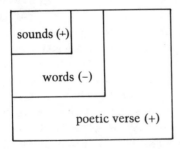

(*Mimologiques*, 275)

What his position emphasizes is a scission between everyday idiom,
the 'universal reportage,'[88] which can only narrate, teach, and describe,
and poetic language, which is alone capable of reconstructing a perfect,
supreme, divine language.

Valéry's position later introduced complex nuances into the issue.
Saussure's course might have borne fruit with Valéry, for the arbitrariness of the sign is fully accepted by the poet ('each word is the

instantaneous assembling of a sound and sense which bear no relation to one another').[89] Mimeticism therefore will only be the product of an illusion, a well-wrought one of course, but still a chimera: no text is ever unmodifiable and no formal necessities are ever perfect. Aware of the contradiction lying at the core of modern poetics between a conventionalist reality and a hereditary reflex keen on enhancing mimeticism, Valéry chooses poetry over prose, dancing over walking.[90]

With Claudel the testimony of grammarians and philologists had become so monumental that he is careful not to touch upon their demonstration of the sign's arbitrariness. Rather, he cunningly be- haves as if graphic mimesis were an unchallenged truth in the absence of which he could not even begin to talk. After Fenollosa and Pound – but contrary to Leibniz – Claudel casts the Chinese ideogram as the confirming myth, the exotic guarantee,[91] a role which in fact hiero- glyphic writing had already played before Champollion.[92] Hence his developing thesis: that the Western alphabet is to be viewed as an ideogram endowed with the power of representing the object it signifies. Claudel's development here, one must hasten to say, is not based upon linguistic knowledge but rather upon wishful poetic thinking. Nor is he projecting future concrete developments, since he never points to the *text* as an entity endowed with an ideogrammatic function, but rather to the letters of any word, those of the alphabet. But this move brings his definition of the poem rather unexpectedly close to concrete perimeters: each letter being endowed with a will and an impulsion of its own. This radical move back to the components of language brings us squarely within Garnier's and Bense's territory. One specific example brings out vividly both the common resonances and the differences: Claudel's analysis of the word *vol* ('flight'), in which he analyses each letter (*v* the two wings of the bird, *o* the circle it flies, *l* the bird which comes and goes).[93] But to Claudel the order of words is indifferent: *vol* could as easily be read as *lvo* or *lov*, the whole word not functioning in an isomorphic way, but simply as a con- glomerate whose component units only are descriptive. One is quite far here from the well-wrought urns of Gomringer or de Campos, but it is possible to recognize, as Genette puts it, a 'primary Kratylism'; that is, a perspective for which 'letters represent value-contents, tools, mechanical parts, interchangeable but specialized in this vast general store, always ready to serve God's creation.'[94]

To cut a long mythical quest short, the Kratylian dossier from early scholastics to Francis Ponge[95] and Michel Leiris,[96] only confirms suspicions that the issue of linguistic figurativeness never ceased to

haunt Western consciousness. Notwithstanding the fact that hiero-
glyphs and ideograms have loomed at a distance – either lending
credibility and a commodious point of origin to those dreams, or
operating as the exact antithesis for the Kratylian ideal – it appears
that the whole history of writing, and of literature in its wake, has
searched for a satisfactory solution to the problematic posed in ancient
Greece. Neither the intended death-blow brought by linguistics to this
issue, nor the insistence of semiotics to get burial arrangements over
with, has disposed of the problem. It is tempting to perceive concretism as the latest – though in all probability not the last – resurgence of
the Kratylian controversy. But what partially undermines this simplification and makes it questionable is the fact that concretists were
split into two camps, one which reinterpreted the basic Kratylian
premise and another which rejected it but did not side with Hermogenes either. For to affirm that there is no natural bond between
external reality and words is quite different from stating that words do
not produce ideas and just are, in and by themselves, a living texture
devoid of meaning (except that which the reader will choose to invest
it with). While a large number of the issues debated in the dialogue can
be traced throughout a twenty-year span of manifestos, it would be
inaccurate to suggest concrete poets all sided with Kratylus on this
issue.

This rift was followed by others. While some indirectly admitted the
cognitive and ideological values of the poem, others repudiated them:
the poem, devoid of any scientific-cognitive value, was defined as an
object which aroused a set of varied responses in its audience. But one
concept shared by all was that of the role of the audience/listener/
reader. It is significant that the public's participation was deemed an
essential part of the poem, even though referred to in different
manners: Gomringer stressing its play-activity, Garnier its energy-
giving quality, and Chopin its bodily value. The other common
denominator was the introduction of technology into the making of
the poem. Electronics, computers, sound systems, and complex
printing systems made their entrance into the creative process and
became part of the actual structuring of the work of art.

When the Canadians and the Québécois finally acceded to the
international concrete movement, they came into a complex and
divided camp, but the fact that they reached it many years after its
beginnings gave them an unforeseen advantage: the time to observe
the effects of the movement's contradictions on the writings it had
generated.

FROM MIMESIS TO DECONSTRUCTION

> Deconstruction is a constant reminder of the etymological link be-
> tween crisis and criticism. It makes manifest the fact that any radical
> shift of interpretative thought must always come up against the
> limits of seeming absurdity ... Deconstruction works at the same giddy
> limit, suspending all that we take for granted about language, experi-
> ence and the 'normal' possibilities of human communication.

Christopher Norris, *Deconstruction: Theory and Practice*, xi, xii

> One of the major projects of Deconstruction in philosophy has been to
> challenge severely the privilege of an *original* in language, superior
> to what is borne away (translata) from it.

Jonathan Arac, Introd., *The Yale Critics: Deconstruction in America*, x

The Philosophical and Critical Implications of Deconstruction

Deconstructive theory was to reflect upon the question of mimesis and
representation in a substantially new way: the fresh insights it brought
to bear on this subject deserve more than a passing glance for they put
in a different and broader context literary developments of the 1970s
and the 1980s.

The most significant contribution was that of Jacques Derrida. This
French philosopher scrutinized hierarchical oppositions between
object and representation, between originals and imitations, from a
novel angle. Two of his texts, 'Economimesis'[97] and *La Dissémination*, were to address specifically this issue of the different values
attributed to mimesis in the Platonic tradition, wherein it was
condemned as sheer duplication, praised for reproducing an original, or
described as neutral with the value of representation depending upon
the value of the original. Later aesthetic traditions, as Derrida noted,
even allowed imitations to be superior to their originals *if* the artist
imitated the creativity of God or Nature. But as he pointedly
comments, in all these cases 'the absolute discernibility of the
imitated and of the imitation is maintained. There is a metaphysical
stake in maintaining this distinction between the representation and
what is represented and the priority of what is represented to its
representation.'[98] Two key elements stand out in Derrida's analysis of
this question. The first is that truth can be conceived either as (1)
aletheia, the unveiling, the making present of what has been hidden,

the doubling which presents something to itself, or as (2) homoiosis, namely an adequation, a correspondence. (Both processes, as I will show later, can be retraced throughout the concrete poetry movement.) But equally important is the notion that mimesis must follow the process of truth. Its norm, its rule, its law, is the presence of the present.[99] The instability of this logocentric system, its doubling of imitations of imitations ad infinitum therefore nourishes an endless proliferation as well as upholds the plenitude of an origin, the plenitude of a divine, absolute original. And it is the privilege of this point of origin, of this centre, of this absolute Godhead, which Derrida and the deconstructionists determined to challenge radically.

A careful observer of avant-garde and post-modern movements cannot fail to note the definitional parallels between mimesis (1) or aletheia (or the isomorphic mode among concretists) and mimesis (2) or homoiosis (or the constructivist aesthetic). Both modes of representation proceed from Platonic premises. Their ideal would normally have been to contemplate thought or numen directly. Since this was not deemed possible, the best one could hope for was a language as transparent as possible. The rejection of the signifier was the rejection of a writing viewed as always necessarily defective, faulty, inadequate. And there commenced the terrible longing for a *presence* or, in Derrida's words, the metaphysics of presence. As he puts it in another text, *Writing and Difference*: 'all names related to fundamentals, to principles, or to the center have always designated the center of a presence.'[100] From this viewpoint writing inexorably becomes a distortion of speech and the above account of the Kratylian controversy shows what literary forms this longing for the lost innocence of voice and speech has created. As far back as the *Phaedrus* writing was condemned as a bastardized form of communication, consisting of physical marks and cut off from the speaker, a technical device to represent speech yet primarily a distortion of it. Moreover, being separated from the Father (that is, the moment of origin), it was perceived as giving rise to all sorts of misunderstandings. The continuity between Plato and Saussure is remarkable, the intensity of the ethical anxiety being as strong in the Greek philosophers as in the Genevan linguist. The latter spoke of writing as a derivative and parasitic form of speech, whose pathological errors would infect and corrupt natural spoken forms.[101]

Analysts of the history of discourse and of its successive epistemic developments have commented on these *breaks* in the history of writing (others have preferred to refer to them as *transitions*). Michel

Foucault, as I have mentioned previously, pointed to the seventeenth century as a demarcation line between a mimetic discourse articulated around analogical bonds and a Cartesian one which substituted analogies with identities. Elsewhere Timothy Reiss has elaborated upon this epistemological transition, between what he calls a discourse of patterning (which refuses to recognize differences between objects and signs, interior and exterior, but perceives them both as signs of the same totality) and Cartesian discourse or, as he puts it, 'the analytico-referential.'[102] Whether one keeps the classical terminology (aletheia/homoiosis) used by Jonathan Culler,[103] or that of Timothy Reiss, or that of the theoreticians of concrete poetry (isomorphism versus constructivism), one finds oneself within similar perimeters. What unites and binds these two discourses is a hankering after an authentic origin, a primeval ground almost lost beyond recall through the multiplied errors of linguistic figuration. Jacques Derrida, and in his wake the American deconstructionists, have illustrated what they describe as the symptoms of a recurrent delusion, a nostalgic mystique of origins complicit with the history of Western metaphysics.[104] Both traditions for this French philosopher intrinsically pertain to the massive tradition of logocentrism, and both can be defined by the craving of self-presence, which confirms the 'natural' priority of speech.

But is it in fact possible to define the deconstructionist undertaking? It would appear that any effort at delineating the nature of an epistemological questioning which precisely challenges this very possibility seems hopelessly doomed from the start. What one can attempt to do – with a sense of the contradictions and traps lying ahead – is to retrace, albeit schematically, the processes whereby deconstruction irrupted into the intellectual apparatus of the last two decades, and in this process to try also to retrace the gap which separates avant-garde productions such as concrete texts from the post-modern, disseminated textual practices of the later period.

Most commentators would concur with Christopher Norris and Jonathan Culler that to present deconstruction as if it were a fixed body of ideas is to falsify it and lay oneself open to charges of reductive misunderstanding.[105] Others would risk oversimplification in the hope of clarifying a complex and ambiguous question. Frank Lentricchia does not hesitate to run such risks when he optimistically asserts:

> Sometime in the early 1970s we awoke from the dogmatic slumber
> of our phenomenological sleep to find that a new presence had taken

absolute hold over our avant-garde critical imagination: Jacques Derrida. Somewhat startingly, we learned that, despite a number of loose
characterizations to the contrary, he brought not structuralism but
something that would be called 'post-structuralism.' The shift to post-
structuralist direction and polemic in the intellectual careers of Paul
de Man, J. Hillis Miller, Geoffrey Hartman, Edward Said, and Joseph
Riddel – all of whom were fascinated in the 1960s by strains of
phenomenology – tells the whole story.[106]

Such an over-schematization entices Culler to quote it and to add
precipitously that this is not the whole story. He admits (with
beguiling pragmatism) that Lentricchia's 'mythification' does help us
to focus on a number of problems – on structuralism versus post-
structuralism, on poetics versus interpretation, and on readers versus
critical metalanguages – and in doing so facilitates a confrontation in
the relations of deconstruction to other critical languages. Norris
himself titles the first chapter of his *Deconstruction: Theory and
Practice*: 'Roots: Structuralism and New Criticism,' so that, willy
nilly, the elements of a genealogy are indeed put into place. The whole
organization of that chapter – (a) From Kant to Saussure: The
Prison-House of Concepts, (b) New Critic into Structuralist?, (c)
Roland Barthes, (d) Beyond New Criticism – demonstrates a temporal
progression, a process. Its author posits deconstruction as post-
structuralist in its refusal to accept the idea of structure as in any sense
given or objectively there in a text. But this is not its only rejection;
there could be others, possibly even more fundamental, which the
attentive reader will retrace. Key among these are the specific
distinctions traditionally maintained by philosophy – from Plato on
the Sophists to John Searle on Derrida – when it establishes strong
demarcation lines between (a) serious philosophy aimed at the one
authoritative truth and (b) a rhetoric which exploits its own irreduc-
ibly figurative status.[107] What Derrida's texts proclaim is the liberation of rhetoric, or writing, from this subjugation at the hands of
philosophic reason and the rejection of a firm disciplinary line between
poem and commentary, between primary (elective) and secondary
(critical) texts. Norris half facetiously implies that deconstructionists
have practically made it a virtue to cross that line wherever possible
and even in some cases (Geoffrey Hartman's in this instance) to push
this new-found freedom to the point of dissolving putative distinctions
between literature, criticism, and theory.[108] But what he more seriously suggests, in effect, is that to the old structuralist dream of a science

of literature has succeeded the post-structuralist contention that theory is one variety of text among others, that the notional line between commentary and text has been systematically blurred by the two-way traffic of interpretative sense which flows across it.[109]

Would it be a gross misrepresentation to suggest that deconstruction constituted a break with New Criticism? Norris does not seem to think so and strongly implies that there was a shift of awareness which in a parallel way affected both structuralist activity and the foundations of American New Criticism. While he is careful not to want to see this parallel pushed too far, both his book and his article 'Some Versions of Rhetoric' seem to indicate that he strongly leans in this direction.[110]

The prison-house of language demarcated by Saussurean linguistics[111] is an obsession which the deconstructionists skilfully and also desperately try to circumvent. J. Hillis Miller summarizes this venture when he declares that such critics attempt 'to escape from the labyrinth of words, an attempt guided not only by the Apollonian thread of logic but by Ariadne's thread as she might be imagined to have rescued it.'[112] What Miller notes here is a logic which is not a logic, a thread which is not a thread. Such processes have been described by Ronald Schleifer and Robert Con Davis as a radical subjunctive, a word and a mode, inscribed in an ambiguous *temporality* (I will come back to this later), which both assert and deny authority. In Hartman's words it is 'an interpretation which no longer aims at the reconciliation or unification of warring truths.'[113] What such a *mise en abyme* does (in Derrida's texts and in those of his American followers) is to stage an unstoppable linguistic regression, the drama of language falling away to reveal other languages, flexible and expandable enough to envelop all varieties of paradox and contradiction, chiasmus and catachresis, metaphor and metonymy, original and replica, error and truth.[114] It should thus be clear by now that deconstructionism is neither a method nor a set of discursive procedures but rather a questioning of the codes which have been inherited from philosophy, ethics, and politics. It dares to suggest that this yearned-for centre may have been displaced, or, more ambiguously, that there may never have been one. Readers therefore are going to have to search for the rifts, the gaps, at the heart of the draft,[115] to look for differences or *différances* (namely, that which de-fers, de-lays, dis-tances). For meaning is always deferred by the play of signification. *Différance* designates not only this theme but offers, in its own unstable meaning, a graphic example of the process at work (that is, of the move from difference to deferment, the one shading into the other). If there are two interpretations of interpretation, one of these will always be deferred and thus conceptual closure or reduction to an ultimate meaning always be deferred. One will always dream of deciphering a truth, an origin; the other will turn away from the latter to affirm play only. Derrida is engaging us not to choose between one or the other but to live them as simultaneously irreconcilable and reconciled in an obscure economy.[116] Deconstructive readings will both stem from and identify paradoxical situations. More simply, 'deconstruction has no better theory of truth. It is a practice of reading and writing attuned to the aporias that arise in telling the truth'[117] (an aporia being an impasse, the impossibility of choosing between two alternatives and the resulting acceptance of their conflicting realities, that is, of a reading which in Paul de Man's terms is unthinkable in terms of a logic dominated by truth and error).

What are the effects of deconstructionist practice? Norris strongly suggests that such practice provokes a sharp continuing discomfort because it allies a disciplined rigour of argument with the seemingly irrational conclusions to which this argument leads. Norris particularly singles out Derrida and de Man here and contrasts New Critical containment of paradox, irony, and other 'safely accommodating tropes' with *their* flagrant transgression, their refusal to separate the logic of commentary from 'that other, less answerable logic of poetic figuration.'[118] While the assumption of the New Critics was that poetic texts are paradoxical and ambiguous *because* this is the way literary language works as distinct from ordinary, rational discourse, Derrida and de Man suggest that all texts are figural and that no refuge can be found outside the apparently distant territory of poetic figuration. Consider as a specific example de Man's discussion of Yeats' line from 'Among School Children': 'How can we know the dancer from the dance?' De Man notes that the two meanings engendered by this grammatical pattern are mutually exclusive. What Yeats does, in his view, is to ask to know the difference *and* to deny rhetorically that such knowledge is possible. It is not that questions of logical accountability can simply be suspended here or even that the poem has two meanings which exist side by side, but rather that 'the two readings have to engage each other in direct confrontation since the one reading is precisely the error denounced by the other and has to be undone by it. Nor can we in any way make any decision as to which of the readings can be given priority over the other; none can exist in the other's absence.'[119] To the deconstructionist critic the possibility of reaching a totalized, integrated whole by adding up the sum of a text's parts or meanings is infinitely deferred. As Barbara Johnson states it, a text's difference is not its uniqueness, its special identity, but its way of differing from itself.[120]

One could, to summarize deconstructionist processes, suggest therefore that to deconstruct an opposition (such as philosophy/ literature, speech/writing, presence/absence, central/marginal) is not to destroy it but rather to undo it, to displace it, to situate it differently.[121] Culler stresses that the distinction between the literal and the figurative works differently when deconstructive reversal identifies literal language as figures whose figurality has been forgotten, instead of treating figures as deviations from proper, normal literality (as a full-fledged structuralist like Jean Cohen has done, for instance). Deconstruction is also an attempt to identify grafts in the texts it analyses, the points of function and stress where one line of argument interesects with another. Derrida examines in Rousseau the graft of logocentric versus anti-logocentric arguments and in Kant the chain of motifs which stretch back to Plato and Aristotle as well as, woven in with them, other sequences inadmissible within a Platonic and Aristotelian politics of art: 'But it is not enough to sort or measure length. Folded into a new system, the long sequences are displaced: their sense and function change.'[122]

The Political Stakes: Deconstruction vis-à-vis Feminism, Psychoanalytic Theory, and Marxism

The deconstructionists' defiance of hierarchies, binary oppositions, and centripetal systems obviously begs the question of their relationship to politics in general (in the sense of power exerted from a centre towards a periphery), to history, to Marxism in particular (as a specific analysis of power and history), to psychoanalysis (as a means of exerting power on other people), and to feminism (one of the major systemic challenges to notions of power defined as logocentrism or phallogocentrism).

While Derrida addressed these questions in a variety of contexts, one example clearly stands out as a specific articulation of the links and responsibilities he saw as binding deconstruction and the exercise of power:

> What is somewhat hastily called deconstruction is not, if it is of any consequence, a specialized set of discursive procedures, still less the

rules of a new hermeneutic method that works on texts or utterances in the shelter of a given and stable institution. It is also, at the very least, a way of taking a position, in its work of analysis, concerning the political and institutional structures that make possible and govern our practices, our competencies, our performances. Precisely because it is never concerned only with signified content, deconstruction should not be separable from this politico-institutional problematic and should seek a new investigation of responsibility, an investigation which questions the codes inherited from ethics and politics. This means that, too political for some, it will seem paralyzing to those who only recognize politics by the most familiar road signs. Deconstruction is neither a methodological reform that should reassure the organization in place nor a flourish of irresponsible and irresponsible-making destruction, whose most certain effect would be to leave everything as it is and to consolidate the most immobile forces within the university.[123]

While some commentators have persuasively argued about the ways in which deconstruction might be harnessed to political ends (most notably Michael Ryan in his *Marxism and Deconstruction*),[124] others have severely put it under attack for misreading Marxist texts or failing to do what it proposed to achieve.[125] Most critics tend to differentiate between Derrida,[126] who might bear the torch of a truly revolutionary program, and the Yale deconstructionists, who to some would turn out to be traditionalism's last formalist buttress.[127] Barbara Foley's critique, in the special issue of *Genre* dedicated to deconstruction, is of particular interest because it manages to rebut both the Yale deconstructionists (for what is described as a patrician disregard for the world beyond literary discourse) and Derrida (for what she perceives as 'a fundamental misreading of Marxist texts well rooted in antipathy to Leninist epistemology and politics').[128]

Foley's questioning of deconstruction's claims to an oppositional status, to a liberatory philosophy, rests upon what she views as Derrida's re-fetishization of what he had taken such pains to overturn. From her perspective, while he had proposed to overturn and transgress binary oppositons, the rhetorical operations generated by such a dualism can do nothing but 'perpetuate the adjunction of a real interior in contradiction to a false, derivative exterior.'[129] In other words the margins have simply replaced the centre. Derrida's rejection of a 'third term,' potentially capable of transcending these oppositions, is what separates him from Marx and Lenin. To elevate undecidability to 'the status of the historical subject' cannot be identified with proposing to overturn and transgress the binary oppositions of wage labour/capital – in Foley's view the essence of the Marxist project.

While Foley's critique deserves to be noted, it seems to me that she conveniently dismisses a number of pointers very much present in Derrida's own texts which would set this whole problematic in a substantially different context. For instance, Derrida stresses – leaning I also believe against Althusser's testimony – that Marx's and Engels' texts may not be read as finished products containing a finished signified hidden beneath the textual surface, but rather through a transformational process.[130] Also, in Derrida's view the texts of Marx, Lenin, or Engels cannot be given the privileged status – any more than any other texts – of homogeneous critiques. Like other texts they operate within a textual economy and therefore reflect and formulate differentiated structures. Homogeneity, 'the theological motif par excellence,'[131] cannot be invoked on their behalf any more than for Freud's and Saussure's texts.

In any case the question of deconstruction's putative alignment or non-alignment with Marxist analysis *and* liberatory movements is a complex question which – however important – cannot be fully discussed here. Of more direct concern at present are the relationships of deconstruction to literary criticism and to feminist theory and psychoanalysis (two conceptual apparatus which were to have a remarkable impact upon both Canadian and Québécois textual productions, but most notably upon the latter). Two of deconstruction's moves become relevant in this area: (a) if literary cure and disease are cast in the dynamics of textual error and textual error is a function of any narrative, then the perception of sickness and cure must be reconsidered: for if language is afflicted by a sickness unto death, how can it be capable of healing also? and (b) alertness to anything in a text which counters authoritative interpretation or subverts presuppositions necessarily involves attention to the marginal and identifies exclusions on which hierarchies depend (and this certainly is a practice which feminists as well as deconstructionists – the two not being necessarily concomitant – have brought to our attention in the last two decades).

Both (a) and (b), as challenges, point as much to the relevance of deconstruction to psychoanalysis as to its links with feminist criticism. In the case of (a) the deconstruction of the traditional hierarchical opposition conscious/unconscious argued by Freud showed that the second term presented not an undesirable direction but rather a condition for understanding the suposedly prior term.[132] As a deconstruction of the humanistic and Cartesian tradition, it both revealed the determining force of unconscious motives and pointed to consciousness as a derivative instance of unconscious processes.

But subsequent deconstructions of the Freudian text itself by other theorists bring forth different challenges. Shoshana Felman's and Sarah Kofman's immediately come to one's mind. But if I may bracket them off for a moment and deal with them in a later context, I would like to draw the reader's attention to Derrida's analysis of the irreducibility of the effect of deferral. What the French philosopher designates as Freud's discovery is specifically this effect. What he sees as being challenged in this locus is a lot more than hierarchical oppositions or specific series of binary structures. More specifically and more dramatically it is the idea of cure itself. The attempt to pose a therapeutic movement from disease to health, from inauthentic to authentic, or from error to truth is unmasked here as another instance of Freud's 'jargon of authenticity,' and Derrida stresses that there can be no triumph of the therapeutic precisely because language itself is affected by a sickness unto death.

The applicability of these figures of disease and health to the opposition of error and corresponding truth is most relevant to literary criticism. Western tradition has identified nominational curing with the concentrated language of poetry. As Robert Con Davis puts it, 'poetry names as a kind of healing';[133] it does not destroy experience in repression, but in naming it alters it.

Some Yale deconstructionists have attempted to strike a middle ground between this traditional perspective and Derrida's radical questioning. J. Hillis Miller, for instance, suggests that if poetry is the impossible cure of experience, criticism is the impossible cure of literature.[134] One can attempt to cure by naming, by nurturing and covering over the wounds, and thus fit into the category which Miller names the 'canny critics,' or the Socratic critics, who are committed to the rational ordering of literary study. Or one can admit to seeing in literary studies prominent regions that are alogical and absurd, and confess that sooner or later one's analysis will lead to an aporia, or impasse; such would be the perspective of the 'uncanny critics.'[135] Miller admits that there are degrees of uncanniness and that the division is problematic since Socratic procedures themselves, if carried far enough, lead to uncanny conclusions.

The very *constitutive instability* which Miller designates as deriving from a text's function is manifest, and I dare say even blatant, in his own criticism. In his 'Stevens' Rock and Criticism as Cure' each sentence keeps swerving from what it had previously established, each clause veers from its own meaning in order to posit a new meaning which in turn will be decentred. In contrast, others like Shoshana Felman have used the speech-act perspective of J.L. Austin and, in utilizing the concept of the unclosable gap between constative and performative, have pointed to the failure of language as principally indicating its disjunctive and self-referential qualities. In *Le Scandale du corps parlant* Felman illustrates this doubleness of language, its always being referential and yet failing at referentiality: the scandal being that of a language radically in error. She shows how Molière's Don Juan promises ad infinitum but never has to act in a marriage ceremony (the *activity* of language as saying nearly obliterates its *validity* as saying); just as J.L. Austin, in his fundamental gesture, substituted the criterion of *satisfaction* for the criterion of truth in replacing his early constative/performative distinction with a performance theory based on the notion of illocutionary force. In Felman's view Austin's subsequent interweaving and overlapping of the constative and performative showed him to be in fact a linguistic performer, like Don Juan. What is of utmost importance here is the impossible matching of utterance and statement, the inevitable excess, as Austin himself shows, of utterance over statement, the manner in which a doing always overshoots its intention and 'dictates that infelicity is an ill to which all acts are heir.'[136] Thus, if no performance escapes error, this notion of infelicity, of perennial error, reveals the productive imbalance in language, the dynamic principle that continually drives it towards a repetition of difference.[137] This postulation of error as the function of all texts (literary or non-literary) positions them within psychoanalysis and specifically within the discourse of Jacques Lacan. For such a scandal is truly a psychoanalytic scandal since it is psychoanalysis which addresses the terms of word and body, of a language-producing body, of a being who continually makes promises that cannot be kept and lives in a linguistic/bodily scandal.

The same dynamic principle should – in Felman's eyes – be at work in the relationship between psychoanalysis and literature. Neither should have mastery over the other,[138] yet their dialogue in the context of the questioning of authority – an essential feminist effort in the words of Jane Gallop – may be invaluable for a feminist rethinking of power. And this is precisely the point where French feminists demarcate themselves from American feminists. While the latter tend to dismiss psychoanalysis as another patriarchal discourse, French psychoanalysts have attempted to uncover the functioning upon and within us of patriarchy as discourse.[139] Jane Gallop explains how for pragmatic and political reasons there has been a history of resistance to the concept of difference in North America, while in France the same question was posited against a provocative background: that of a Lacanian interpretation of Freud and of a deconstruction of Lacan by his ex-disciples (Luce Irigaray, in this case).[140] The French perspective thus alters the ways in which the self is conceptualized: (a) it emphasizes Freud's subversive view of the unconscious (that which undermines the subject's coherence as a self-determined actor in its own affairs, as Gallop puts it);[141] and (b) it explores Lacan's analysis of language as a model for the structure of the unconscious (if we are constituted by language or rather by the many cultural languages of our own society, we thus internalize the laws of the world and along with them the reflections of patriarchal power). Rather than focusing on the development of ego-strength and social adaptation, French psychoanalysis allows us to raise the question of 'the powers of the unconscious as potentially revolutionary.'[142] This is where French women theorists enter and draw on this tradition. Julia Kristeva, Luce Irigaray, and Hélène Cixous centre their whole approach on difference as the pivotal point at which sexuality may be delineated, a sexuality which they refer to as an economy of differences.

On this particular terrain the term *difference* raises political and philosophical issues which are emotionally overcharged, and although they are very much linked to exegetical concerns (recall Barbara Johnson's perception of difference as textual specificity and her reference to a text's difference as 'its way of differing from itself'),[143] they also go beyond textual politics. *Difference* as a key term and a theme has been integral to modern feminist thought since Simone de Beauvoir's *The Second Sex* (1948, English translation 1953) and since the rebirth of the women's movement in the late 1960s. Hester Eisenstein and Alice Jardine recall that while the first current of feminist thought (Kate Millet, Elisabeth Janeway) demonstrated that difference had been exaggerated and could be reduced, and that biological sex was not coextensive with social gender, with the 1970s there was a considerable shift in emphasis and a change of attitude towards the value of women's difference from men.[144] They recall, too, that it is not so much difference in itself that has been dangerous to women but the political uses to which this concept has been put and its linkage to a certain use of power. If the naming of differences is replaced with, or at least challenged by, the reclaiming of differences and individuality, then a step has been taken along the road to liberation.[145]

When one looks at the writings of contemporary French feminists (Kristeva, Cixous, Irigaray), one cannot help observing that the premise underlying their works proceeds from Lacanian analysis. Within these premises repression does not exist merely in economic and social structures: it is embedded in the Logos, in the vast text which in the history of Western thought has been founded on the structure of the binary, on the old dichotomies of male versus female, rationality versus emotionality, activity versus passivity, presence versus absence. And it is only by deconstructing this Logos that we can hope to transform the real in a fundamental way. Hélène Cixous focuses on this question in *La Jeune Née*: 'Everything is word, everything is only word ... we must grab culture by the word, as it seizes us in its word, in its language ... Indeed, as soon as we are, we are born into language and language speaks us, language dictates its law, which is a law of death ... you will thus understand why I believe that political thought cannot do without thought on language, work on language.'[146]

If one chose to oversimplify an extremely rich and contrasted cluster of activity, one could reductively point to three major and systematic deconstructionist processes at work in France in the late 1970s. All the previously mentioned theorists articulated these processes in different ways and proceeded from departure points which were both dissimilar *and* bound with one another by their urgency to undermine traditional logocentric discourse.[147] How did they conduct these processes? Irigaray challenged the Platonic metaphors which she saw as dominating the whole of Western discourse. She described these metaphors as forces positing the principle of identity (conceived as masculine sameness or male presence) and continuing their domination throughout twenty centuries right into Freudian discourse (albeit in a more ambiguous way since Freud was found to undermine the concepts of presence and identity through his delineation of the unconscious).[148] But in Irigaray's view Freudian discourse still defined sexual difference in terms of an a priori sameness – the male phallus – and consigned female sexuality to absence, lack, deficiency.[149] Irigaray calls for a radical convulsion of this system of thought, of the old Logos, if woman is going to exist as subject, the subject of her difference.

Kristeva deconstructs the Western notion of the subject from slightly different departure points: Aristotle's syllogistic logic, which secures the position of the subject, and Hegel's consciousness of self, which posits the knowing subject as unity and envisions it as passing from one transcendent act of cognition after another. To what she views as a phallic conception of the subject Kristeva opposes an ungraspable one capable of transforming the real in allowing the semiotic (the female principle) to erupt into the symbolic (the Law and Logos of the Father), giving free rein to difference and heterogeneous meaning and subverting the existing system of signification.[150] Such an eruption introduces what she calls 'negativity'[151] and operates as an act of subversion, as a dissidence. It is somewhat disconcerting that in *Révolution du langage poétique* Kristeva's selected examples for such an activity, a female praxis, are exclusively male nineteenth-century avant-garde writers (Lautréamont, Mallarmé) and avant-garde twentieth-century theoreticians (Artaud, Bataille). While she establishes an analogy between poetic language and women's writing,[152] it is nevertheless curious that she does not distinguish between the female impulse's subversion of the Logos and the polymorphous manifestation of dissidence. She differs in this from a number of French women writers who have focused on the need to articulate a female language, to allow for its passage through the lacks and interstices in the syntax and grammar of male language. Marguerite Duras and Xavière Gauthier's *Les Parleuses* (1974), Annie Leclerc's *Parole de femme* (1974), and Claudine Hermann's *Les Voleuses de langue* (1976) testify to such needs. In contrast with Cixous it has been said of Kristeva that she 'recuperates'[153] archaeologically and formulaically a potential originary space situated before the sign, while Cixous displaces. Indeed, of all three Cixous is the one who stresses the most violently the revolutionary power of *l'écriture féminine*. Contrasting speech (as overdetermined by the dominant system of discourse) and writing (as the springboard, the precursory movement of a transformation of social and cultural structures), she points to the need for women to write as they fly/rob ['écrire comme voler'], that is, take over every symbolic system, every political process.[154] More specifically the effort to speak female sexuality, her *jouissance* in all its forbidden aspects, pervades both Cixous' and Irigaray's writings (see *Le Nom d'Oedipe* [1978] by Cixous and *Ce Sexe qui n'en est pas un* by Irigaray [1977], as well as works by Madeleine Gagnon, and Nicole Brossard on this side of the Atlantic).[155]

The contrast between French and Anglo-American feminism is nowhere as clearly displayed as in Cixous' preface to the translation of Phyllis Chesler's *Women and Madness* (Paris: Payot 1975). To Cixous promoting women's liberation by practising a language which relies on binary thinking is doomed from the start; the battleground is language, discourse, and the way to undermine it is to valorize the female's difference, her otherness, as the repressed, the missing signification. This disconnection between the American pragmatic empiricist preoccupation, on the one hand, and the French obsession with the subversion of occidental discourse, on the other, has also been lucidly focused on by Toril Moi.[156]

By now it cannot have escaped the reader that deconstruction puts forward a questioning of the Western concept of knowledge, of its logocentric principles. It must also be evident that deconstruction not only challenges specific linguistic and political structures founded on the principles of identity and resemblance but also provides a re-evaluation of other concepts, namely heterogeneity, alterity, and difference.[157] The contribution of many French feminists and critics to this problematic has been crucial in several respects. The issue which Kristeva, Cixous, and Irigaray raise is that difference cannot be eternally perceived as an inverted magic double, a repressed self or absence, but rather as multiplicity, as that which cannot be defined. They also remind us that at stake in women's struggles is a lot more than economic equality and legal or contraceptive rights (while recognizing the necessity of such gains).[158] At stake is nothing less than the human subject as entity, as truth, as desiring subject as well as subject of knowledge. In interrogating this concept of difference women are thus reinscribing their heterogeneity (rather than re-instituting an anti-system which would be the oppressive reverse of the old one) and introducing the prospect of a plurality of possibilities. The reluctance to define, to mould definite structures and specific positions, is nowhere so explicit as in Kristeva's writings, which refer to woman as 'that which cannot be represented, cannot be told because it hovers on the ambiguous fringe of a "not that," of a "not yet."'[159] Not all French feminists share this perception – Catherine Clément and Monica Wittig, in particular, have expressed their misgivings about such a systematic dissidence.[160] Yet such contrasts should not blur from view the fact that there is a problematic common to all French theorists: that of the subject as a function of difference, and of language as the bedrock upon which the whole problematic lies. The contrast between French and Anglo-American feminist theories is indeed as pervasive on the terrain of literary criticism as it is on the subject of psychoanalysis. While cultural and thematic concerns have been at the forefront of the latter,[161] the focus among francophone feminist writers has been to move away from masterly constructs and didactic ('male') fiction. Feminist writings in their view can be summarized as 'open, non-linear, unfinished, exploded, fragmented, polysemic ... [they are writings that would] incorporate the simultaneity of life as opposed to or clearly different from logical, non-ambiguous, so-called transparent or functional language.'[162] Female writings are thus biographical in the sense that they primarily write 'the body.' As Chantal Chawaf puts it, 'Writing is to push the beginning farther back, because in language nothing of the body, nothing of the woman has as yet been integrated ... everything starts from the body and from the living, from our senses, our desires, our imagination.'[163]

It has of course been noted that such a theory of feminity is dangerously close to repeating in deconstructive language the traditional assumptions about women and feminity.[164] Such a perception of difference (that is, difference in the relation of women to language) has been described as narrowly based upon Freudian postulates which describe the symbolic (law, language, social order) as *necessarily* functioning on the basis of the repression of women's bodies, so that the corollary here is the feminine will thus be referred to as that which is undefinable, unspeakable, or silent. Another corollary, this time an extremely pragmatic one, is that by identifying discourse with power and then rejecting both, women will choose silence and non-speech. As Makward puts it, 'The speech of the other will then swallow them up, will speak for them and instead of them. Nothing will have taken place but a displacement of the feminine.'[165]

Some have chosen – as an alternative to this impasse of silence – a return to the initial postulate of bisexuality. To speak as a woman would thus be to speak as a gynandrous being or an androgynous one. Such an undertaking would neither denounce nor obliterate the contradictions which exist within feminist discourse but rather go beyond them, pass through the impasse, or fly-jump over them as Hélène Cixous puts it in 'The Laughter of the Medusa.'

What this brief inquiry into French feminist theories testifies to is the overdetermined impossibility of expressing the concept of difference in a unified way. But out of these conflicting perspectives emerges a core of specific concerns. I have stressed the central preoccupation with language and its positioning as the strategic locus where stakes can be stacked, lost, or displaced.[166] But there also are other concerns which have been masterfully singled out by Anglo-American critics as cultural/historical issues (such as the intersections between postmodernism and feminity) as well as literary/ critical ones (how does feminity translate itself into critical practice?). These 'others' are essential to an understanding of contemporary poetics and of the shifting critical tools which were put in place after the successive dismantlings of the New Critical and structuralist apparatus.

How do deconstructive practices fare in the face of disseminated texts? One author's focus on these issues appears to me to be remarkably helpful. The way Alice Jardine's *Gynesis* (1985) illuminates the intersections between the post-modern gesture and feminism,[167] as well as the questions raised by these intersections in the area of literary criticism, I have found to be both comprehensive and exacting. The challenges posed by post-modernism to the bedrock of literary critical practice have been immense. By questioning the very concept of intentionality,[168] destroying the teleology of narrative, undermining the very definitions of characters (who end up with little more than proper name functions), by turning the image/icon into an unrecognizable object, and by dismantling the framework of sexual identity, such post-modern challenges are shown by Jardine to intersect with the fundamental feminist gesture. She convincingly exemplifies the systematic undermining of the self, of a secure stable identity, by psychoanalysis, and she also swiftly demonstrates the feminist concerns about (a) the Western notion of the self (one of the foundations of Western metaphysics) and (b) the status of truth and representation. In the case of the latter she shows that one of the radical questions asked by the post-modern stance has been that of the status of truth in fiction. The constant foregrounding of the fictional process in contemporary productions provokes in her view new kinds of crises in legitimation between discourse and reality. She notes that such a questioning intersects with the feminist impulse in that truth and reality necessarily have to be problematized by feminist readers.

The question of who defines reality and for whom has been in the forefront of feminist inquiry for much longer than the past two decades. Yet Jardine also admits that however 'irresistibly linked'[169] the two projects might be, they also are resistant to each other, and their intersections are difficult to negotiate. The theorists who participate in the deconstructive, post-modern effort may articulate their entire conceptual apparatus around woman, but seldom around women. Jardine regretfully recognizes that a survey of disparate but logically related writers in this respect (Cixous, Irigaray, Kristeva, Lacan, Derrida, Deleuze) yields few references to women writers.[170]

The post-modern stance has directed us towards a questioning (to borrow Jean-François Lyotard's formula) of master narratives.[171] Such a crisis in legitimation concerns not only the status of knowledge but also that of the social contract itself within patriarchal culture. If as critics we follow Lyotard's gesture and challenge such legitimacies, proposing new logics and 'temporary pacts' rather than 'universal social contracts,' we could then attempt the re-working 'on the basis of non-centrism, non-finality'[172] of a new future. Hélène Cixous views such a deconstruction as a total transformation of the social body:

> What would become of logocentrism, of the great philosophical systems, of world order, if the rock upon which they founded their church were to crumble? If it were to come out ... that the logocentric project had always undeniably existed to found [fund] phallocentrism, to insure for masculine order a rationale equal to history itself? Then all the stories would have to be told differently, the future would be incalculable, the historical forces would, will, change hands, bodies, another thinking as yet unthinkable, will transform the functioning of all society.[173]

When one attempts to put avant-garde and post-modern productions in the context of a general interdiscursivity and to situate them in a certain synchronicity, several points come to the fore. The discourses on language in general, from traditional philology to Saussurean and post-Saussurean linguistics, as well as the discourses of the social sciences (Marxism and post-Marxist theories),[174] provide a perspective on such manifestations which literary history in and by itself cannot really furnish. The concept of break, or rupture, between these two phases then takes on a different meaning. It becomes not so much the rejection of a certain aesthetics (after all, literary history is full of such claims), but rather the expression of a totally new perception of reality, of a new ontology. It ceases to be a particular way to look at or to produce art, within the narrow confines of taste/style or formal expectations, and it becomes a different way of relating to language, to the discursive processes which affect our lives (and to our lives as they affect such discursive processes).

Concretism in its two phases (isomorphism/constructivism) appears then to be not only the manifestation of avant-garde aesthetics but also part of Kratylian history. Such a history, from Plato's dialogues throughout the next twenty centuries, is very much a part of Western discourse. It points to the yearning for a lost presence, to either the unveiling (aletheia) or the homoiosis (adequation/correspondence) of such a presence, and the possibility of coming to be in touch with it. Whether this takes the form of a pre-Babelian language or of a numinous linguistic life does not matter as much as the continuity of the search throughout different moments of history.[175]

The concrete texts published in Europe and both Americas in the 1950s and the 1960s were replaced in the later part of the second decade by productions which showed anagrammatic dispersion and affirmed only the de-centring of all systems, the rejection of truth, origin, nostalgia and guilt.[176] Canada and Quebec did not fare differently. The only substantial differences would be in their respective reactions to deconstructionism. If one were to look at their specific situations in relation to one another and no longer in the context of Western civilization, it would appear that in Canada there was a measure of resistance to a total dispersion of the elements involved (typographical, semantic, visual). Steve McCaffery's and bpNichol's perceptions of the reader as logotherapist or logotect are eloquent on that score. Moreover, the redemptive elements (and the term should be taken here in its full religious and ethical implications) outlined by Nichol in Book III of *The Martyrology* cannot be discarded from the total picture. But in Quebec redemption was defined in radically different terms: as freedom from reference, from theological binarism, as a signifier degree zero, as dizziness, vertigo even. André Roy summed it up in his quasi incantation 'je ne crois plus': 'I do not believe any more, not to believe, such a joy, not to believe in militarism, in terrorism, in politics, in society, in art, such a joy, such a joy.'[177]

The disseminations of François Charron's paintings (see Figs. 70, 71) may also be defined as logotherapies. But if the cures are comparable, the ills are not. Nichol and Charron are attempting to free their audiences from substantially different pitfalls. In the Canadian situation the search for a centre, a focusing point, an Adamic beginning, is a continuous claim. It really matters little whether such a quest is defined along native Indian reference points (Palongwahoya) or Judeo-Christian ones.[178] What is remarkable, rather, is the continuity of the search amidst chaos. The Québécois reflexes and needs were markedly different. 'Freeing oneself from the great patriarchal night,' to use François Charron's striking formula, referred not only to a history of the Logos, to Derrida's 'theological prejudice,'[179] but also to the specific history of 'la nuit patriarcale' in Quebec.[180] Post-modern texts in Quebec explicitly posited the conviction that there were many ways to free oneself from logocentrism and hierarchical structures, that turning them upside down might not be the only answer, but setting them askew and playing with them might offer different possibilities. Such a weariness of binary oppositions points the way to Philippe

Haeck's metaphors about post-modern texts in Quebec: 'Mallarmé's shawl' and 'Brecht's cigar,' which would be to the 1970s and the 1980s what the isomorphic explorations of sound and sense had been to the 1960s.

2 How Theory Suggests New Roles: The Canadian and Québécois Experiences

When I began aleatoric verbal composition, I thought of the works as being 'concrete' ... as I saw it then, the attention of the perceiver is directed to each word and/or string in turn, rather than to anything outside themselves. Later, in the early 70s, when John Cage used chance operations to compose a long four-part poem made up of language elements drawn from H.D. Thoreau's *Journals*, he called it *Empty Words*, implying that these words, etc., have no 'content.'

But ... the very fact that these works are composed of language elements that have intrinsic references precludes their being completely empty. Even disjunct or collaged phonemes remind us of words in which they may occur. Similarly, words and phrases inevitably lead the perceiver's mind to possible sentences in which they might be occurring, and sentences at least *connote* larger discourses.

The fact that there may be no such sentences in the works themselves ... does not prevent the perceiver's mind from 'semiconsciously' constructing larger wholes of which the given language elements are parts. The mind moves beyond the language elements themselves, impelled by a complex melange of denotations and connotations and of remembered language experiences and life experiences. That some perceivers are *moved* by some works of this kind is adequate proof of this.

Some writers of the type being discussed may consciously form their works to secure such an effect – some may even have an underlying subject-matter. Others may not. But in almost all cases, in varying degrees, the *perceiver* becomes the center – the *meaning-finder*.

Whatever the intention of the authors, if the perceivers give serious attention to the works, they will – at some 'level' – be finding meanings. This is what arouses and sustains their interest and sometimes moves them emotionally.

Thus it may be most correct to call such verbal works *'perceiver-centered'* rather than 'language-centered' (and certainly rather than 'nonreferential'). Whatever the degree of guidance given by the authors, all or the larger part of the work of giving or finding meaning devolves upon the perceivers. The works are indeed 'perceiver-centered.'

Jackson MacLow, 'Language-Centered,' *Open Letter*, 5th ser., no. 1 (Winter 1982), 25–6

CONCRETE THEORY IN CANADA: FROM PALONGWAHOYA TO
ARTAUD: THE CLEANSING OF PRIVATE HELLS AND THE
RETURN TO A PRIMEVAL WORLD

What did Canadians contribute to an already massive and complex theoretical edifice? Research in this area demonstrates the energy and the creativity of the Canadian poet-researchers. The individuals who made the most consistent contributions were bill bissett, bpNichol, and Steve McCaffery. The Horsemen and Owen Sound – two Toronto-based sound-poetry groups – and the Véhicule Gallery poets – anglophone Montrealers – also brought new insights into concrete theory and deconstructive practices.

But not all poets take pleasure in elaborating manifestos. Some find it against their grain and, more generally, most North Americans prefer to integrate their conceptual framework within creative texts. Thus to try to separate theory from practice can lead to curious pitfalls. Particularly in the anglophone world, which favours pragmaticism over theory, empiricism over conceptualization, such a division can lead to artificial boundaries.

One of the very first to concentrate upon this area of concern, in the early 1960s, was bill bissett. He was also the one who was the least inclined to separate theory from practice. His pronouncements on language are to be found throughout the books, records, and collages which form the body of his work. Even though his trajectory and Nichol's or McCaffery's occasionally meet, he never chose a specifically critical space to express his thoughts the way the other two did.[1]

The first idiosyncrasy of bissett's relationship to concretism is his spelling of it. The title page of *Stardust* announces that this is a 'picture book uv molecular *konkreet* pome collages.'[2] Nothing could be more foreign to him than the didacticism and the dogmatism of other theoreticians. He is not suggesting that everyone should write concrete but simply that konkreet is

> one uv th many flames
>   uv th trew
>   fire[3]

This concept of fire, spirit, or energy recurs throughout his texts. The spirit is within language as well as within the natural, elemental world. Essential to an understanding of bissett's theoretical framework, but puzzling to an eye and ear trained in the materialist vein of European concretism, is bissett's belief in phonemes as spiritual elements. This conviction cuts a deep demarcation line between this West Coast poet and his European as well as Latin American predecessors.

It is no accident that several critics have commented on his affinities with the English poet William Blake. To bissett the energy which speaks through the poet's voice comes not only from the picture inside the word but from the soul. References to the Great Spirit abound in all of his writings, so that his universe is suffused with an animistic metaphysic. The spirit is everywhere and within everything:

> our body is th earth is into th earth th opening
> our body is flowr mushroom[4]

Several of the 'soul' poems published in the same volume as the above quotation are also revealing of his ontological perceptions. Some use a mirroring device: each typewritten set of letters being reflected onto another, which in turn reflects itself onto a third set, thus suggesting a fusing motion, a chain of communication from one level to the next, from one soul to another. The word *soul* is also used to reproduce a West Coast native Indian drawing of the Great Bird, thus affirming the poet's close identification with native beliefs and religious practices.

How does this philosophical framework affect his writing theory? One only needs to look at the program he outlines for himself in the first pages of *Ice*:

> Spelling – mainly phonetic
> Syntax – mainly expressive or musical rather than grammatic
> Visual form – apprehension of th spirit shape of the pome rather than
>   stanzaic nd rectangular
> Major theme – search fr harmony
> Characteristic stylistic device – elipse [sic]
> General source – there is nly one ... i don't feel th I, i e ME writes but that I
>   transcribe indications of flow mused spheres sound[5]

If the narrating i expresses the music of the spheres, does it mean that readers are dealing with a sacred semantic universe which they are to accept as an unalterable truth? The answer is a resounding no. As bissett suggests in *Pass th Food*: 'words can also be non-directory, non-commanding, non-structuring, non-picturing. objects, fleshy perceptual flashes, all-directions, away from the conscious death-sentence, ... spread . space . enter . give.' The last four verbs suggest the magnitude of changes which he would like to witness among readers. This statement goes beyond a plea for participation – one of the favourite keywords of the 1960s aesthetics – and also beyond game-playing:[6] it asserts bissett's own rejection of all rules, and it strongly urges readers to do the same. Readers should let the spirit's voice speak to them through words, objects, and elements and interpret it *as they please*. bissett's affinities are just as mystical as anarchistic. His theoretical basis is a long string of exhortations for freedom. They can be read as a list of rejections and a plea for throwing off all shackles:

> so yu dont need th sentence
> yu dont need correct spelling
> yu dont need correct grammar
> yu dont need th margins
> yu dont need regulation use of capital nd lower case
>
> yu dont need sense or skill
> yu dont need this
> what dw yu need[7]

Semantic freedom (for writer and reader) is equated here with political liberation. The 'allegiance to th ruling class of meaning'[8] is what bissett abandons and wants his readers also to give up in order to feel the energy of words. To refer to his writing as 'theoretical' is to operate within a paradox. For didacticism, strict definitions, and rigid positions are precisely the pitfalls which he is denouncing and the title of one of his books, *What Fuckan Theory*, speaks eloquently to that effect.[9] The only precept here would be the 'u cin dew it too'[10] which recurs over and over in his poems.

His readers too can suspend, change, alternate, or recreate meanings, forget or suspend rules. One revealing dialectical tension in bissett's conceptual framework is his belief in the diffuseness of meaning as well as his need for unity, wholeness, oneness. Just as the 'Spirit' is *one* and everywhere, meaning equates the soul *and* everything *or* anything his readers might wish it to be, so that they should simultaneously 'let / th pomes / speek fr them / selvs' and reject 'th imperialism uv seman-tiks'[11] – a difficult program for even moderate rationalists.

Though a practising sound poet, bissett did not contribute any strikingly new theories to the performance aspects of that area. But his premises are unique: sound and breath are viewed as the way for 'speaking tongues to pass'[12] through and among individuals. Implicit here is the link between breath and soul, breathing rhythm and Great Spirit. For a while individuals become one with it; then it leaves them, after having brought 'food and energy.'[13] These metaphysics of sound single bissett out, especially in comparison with his European counter-parts, yet in North America in the context of Jerome Rothenberg's research on Indian myths and sound,[14] in that of Raoul Duguay's, and the Horsemen's and Owen Sound's clearly formulated convictions about the mystical and healing properties of sound, they are not so astonishing. What is unique, however, is his deeply seated conviction about a spiritual universe which transmits messages to us through 'speaking tongues.'

In view of bissett's total mistrust of industrial technology, political institutions, conventions, and rules of any kind, it is worthwhile to examine his predilection for the typewriter and his quasi-total reliance upon its mechanical means. To him the typewriter means a democrat-ic access to the printed page, and autonomy for small presses and the individual poet who can thus proceed with production without depending upon a publishing house.[15] There are also formal and stylistic reasons for this preference: the typewriter allows a more conscious and controlled use of the page-space. Typographical setting and blanks have always played an important role in concrete poetry. This awareness of one's textual spatiality is precisely what bissett is after:

> the typewritr is amazing how it
> meens . . . . [that]
> yu can place th words on th page wher
> th moovment rhythm sound change happins use th
> space inbtween th words
> > Experience that space as th molecular shapes uv language in ur
> writing[16]

Few writings could set a more definite contrast with bissett's theories than bpNichol's and Steve McCaffery's. A first look at the writings of the Toronto Research Group (hereafter referred to as the TRG)[17] seems to suggest that Nichol's and McCaffrey's intellectual sophistication – which has its occasional facetious lapses into teasing pedantry – could not be further removed from bissett's simplistic belief in the Word which speaks through the Great Spirit. In comparison with them the West Coast poet speaks as a visionary making innocent and prophetic announcements from the primeval Rockies. One would look in vain for scholarly references to the great thinkers of the past – or of our times – in *What Fuckan Theory*. But bissett's lack of interest in Saussure or Heidegger does not necessarily imply a lack of awareness about theoretical questions. Nor does it imply that he leaves no imprint on Canadian theory. The only differences are that he only mockingly refers to 'theory' and that he does not attempt to relate his to someone else's interpretive framework.

The TRG operates in a diametrically opposed way. Nichol's and McCaffery's framework of reference is thoroughly grounded in post-modernist writings. It includes James Joyce's and Gertrude Stein's forays into new textual possibilities[18] and also all of the Brazilian, French, and German concrete texts. More recently, in the early 1970s, it turned towards the experience of the American poets of the *L-A-N-G-U-A-G-E Review*, such as Clark Coolidge, Bruce Andrews, Ray di Palma, Barbara Barracks, and Ron Silliman, and drew on their experience.[19] (One derives from these exchanges between *Open Letter* and *L-A-N-G-U-A-G-E* magazine the sense of a new North American community of post-modernists, of a different generational phenomenon.) It seems equally safe to assume that Nichol and McCaffery have often crossed paths with Ponge, Merleau-Ponty, Robbe-Grillet, and Derrida.

Their association has the peculiar quality of being a tightly structured text in which neither contributor is identifiable – not a dialogue, but a search, a quest, for new modes of interpretation, new approaches to writing. It is obvious that the manifesto approach did not satisfy them since they quickly abandoned it after two attempts.[20] The first problem they set out to highlight is that of the function and limitations of theory: 'all theory is transient and after the fact of writing.'[21] But it quickly becomes evident that to them it still functions as an indispensable tool for the charting of linguistic and civilizational changes. In order to understand the house we dwell in (read: our language), we must grasp the alterations made by what they paradoxically refer to as 'the avant-garde tradition.'[22] And if this 'tradition' goes back to the 1930s and the 1940s, in Canada no one knew anything about it until the 1960s. If the TRG appears to be 'regurgitating' so much of the history of twentieth-century writing, it is in order to go beyond it, thus proceeding the way an amnesiac does when he tries to regain an awareness of his past.[23]

Theory therefore is a recognition of the past as well as the urge to research the directions, goals, and impulses of the new writing. Again they use the house/body as a metaphor. Our memories are complex composites which contain heterogeneously mixed elements: primeval screams, childhood onomatopoeia, Edwardian speech modes, electronic voice manipulations, just as our abodes often belong to another era while existing in highly technologized cities.[24] Theory is to make us bridge the gap. Nichol and McCaffery want to discuss both the premises of such changes and the consequences they have for our relationship to texts,[25] and being careful pragmatists, they scrutinize those comic strips, semiotic poems, and collages which best exemplify their theories.

McCaffery's and Nichol's epistemological premises are clearly framed around post-Hegelian, Husserlian ontological concepts. Meaning is not an essence, does not have an existence of its own, and can only be derived from experience, from the act of experiencing, of perceiving, of seeing an object. While they are aware of numerous shifts in the literary past – particularly the move to bring signifier and signified together into a visual instantiation of an object-event[26] – they would like to take this process one step further. What they propose is a demystification of the 'fetishistic referent' which disguises and excludes the actual labour process of the text. In order to reach this goal they short-circuit the loop from signifier to signified. Signification becomes a centripetal energy: a force which does not point outwards towards a concept or an object outside the text, but which thrusts inwards towards its sign-grapheme.

Instead of consuming the text, instead of absorbing meaning, 'this surplus commodity,' readers are to bring meaning into the evacuated sign. While the TRG is not in bad company here – Franz Mon in Germany and the lettrists in France having chosen before them the path to non-referentiality[27] – one must also recognize that the Canadian writers are elaborating a new, systematic, and political analysis, a different lexicology. How? First of all they are delineating new roles for reader, text, and sign. The reader becomes producer, the text turns into a labour process, and the sign into a relational configuration. The audacious all-out extremism of this system should not be construed as an interpretive assumption valid for all texts. A great deal of the literature they refer to does not operate exclusively through evacuated signs, but as writers they manifest a move in that direction. One realization which grows, as one moves through ten years of theoretical writings,[28] is that both Nichol and McCaffery want to evacuate, to pre-empty, the sign but feel caught in a net of contradictions. In the light of their original premise they find it almost impossible to remove memory discharges from the sign. One case in point is their fine examination of intertextual procedures and of what they call 'a secondary system of referentiation which becomes operative when a text thrusts outward to other texts.' Not only do they not guard their readers from this filling-in of the sign, but they actually encourage it as 'the instinctive drive towards a reassertion of context.'[29]

But judging from these reports it seems that this-never-quite successful evacuation of the sign has one pragmatic value: it deconstructs a certain power structure, that of the old hierarchy writer-producer/words-meaning-producer/reader-recipient-consumer of words. And because it brings with it the dismissal of the writer as Godhead, it reveals new processes whereby the single isolated text is 'always *lacunaire.*'[30]

But how long is this text going to remain *lacunaire*, empty, void of any semantic echo? The TRG recognizes two possible movements here: (1) the reader will accept the 'semantic cipher' as a pure density, as an event; or (2) he will choose to augment and complete the text, thus becoming a 'logotherapist' or a 'logotect.'[31] The key problem with this hermeneutic approach is the 'cipher.' It is defined here as an emptied sign, less an active sign than one 'removed from function ... to be observed and experienced as event per se.'[32] But ontologically this evacuation poses serious problems to the sign. As Derrida warns in *Writing and Difference*, when we erase the opposition between signifier and signified we destroy one of the terms of this opposition, thereby reducing the other to a purely metaphysical concept:

> ... as soon as one seeks to demonstrate in this way that there is no transcendental or privileged signified and that the domain or play of signification henceforth has no limit, one must reject even the concept and word 'sign' itself – which is precisely what cannot be done. For the signification 'sign' has always been understood and determined, in its meaning, as sign-of, a signifier referring to a signified, a signifier different from its signified. If one erases the radical difference between signifier and signified, it is the word 'signifier' itself which must be abandoned as a metaphysical concept.[33]

And also:

> The concept of the sign, in each of its aspects, has been determined
> by this opposition throughout the totality of its history. It has lived
> only on this opposition and its system. But we cannot do without
> the concept of the sign, for we cannot give up this metaphysical com-
> plicity without also giving up the critique we are directing against
> this complicity, or without the risk of erasing difference in the self-
> identity of a signified reducing its signifier into itself or, amounting
> to the same thing, simply expelling its signifier outside itself.[34]

But this violence against the ontology of the sign which has preoccupied many linguists and philosophers turns out to be a political choice
here. For McCaffery the deconstruction of the sign (in Derrida's terms,
its reduction to a metaphysical concept) implies a deconstruction of
the word, of the sentence, of the 'whole functioning of linearized,
serialized, capitalized society.'[35]

In fact there are two different ways of eliminating this difference
between signifier and signified. The first is to put the sign within the
controlling powers of the mind (the preference of conventionalists of
all times from Hermogenes to Locke). But the second, the TRG's in
this case, is a signifier which does not *have to* signify anything.[36] And
Nichol and McCaffery promptly add to this: *precisely* it can signify
everything or anything the reader may choose, so that their way out of
the evacuated-sign trap is a reader who replenishes its depleted
structure. Left in a semantic universe devoid of absolutes, the reader
discovers a new function for herself: meaning-producer. The old
dichotomies crumble down and reading = writing. Operationally the
two are strictly identical and are defined as the foregrounding activity
of specific elements. What remains on the axis of the possible – the
words a writer could have chosen / the texts a reader could have read –
is a non-narrative. What is selected for realignment on the axis of the
chosen enters the domain of the narrative.[37] What these choices point
to is a different approach to literary texts. One is now on deconstructionist territory whereby the perceiver becomes, in almost all cases
and in varying degrees, the meaning-finder. Jackson MacLow suggests
that rather than language-centred or non-referential, one should call
these texts *perceiver-centred*.[38]

But the TRG does not limit itself to this realignment of roles; in fact,
it introduces another very new concept of the text. The reading
performance is referred to as a geomantic act and the reader's task as

the 'reorganization of energy patterns perceived in literature.'[39] Even though this is never acknowledged, what we are witnessing is a qualitative jump from one contemporary thought system (from a deconstructionist perspective which rejects the fetishism of reference) to an animistic one (wherein divination is practised in order to interpret signs derived from the earth: topographies, soils, hills, and rivers – geomancy being the reading of the natural alignment of signs).[40] If the literary text is to be described as a complex of *energies* or of *energy patterns*, it seems clear that we are dealing with a completely new element here. We are being taken beyond/beneath the signs themselves and brought into the presence of a radically new substance – totally unmentioned in previous reports – that of energy.

The critic encounters here the combination of three hermeneutic systems. The first one looks upon texts as conglomerates of 'necessary signs'[41] which 'speak for themselves.'[42] The second is Marxist-derived: poetry becomes the prototype for revolution and the poem the deconstruction of an old power structure. Linguistic revolution becomes 'root revolution.'[43] New, language-centred writing illuminates the 'fetishistic displacement'[44] of reference and reinstates the object-quality of the text as well as its labour processes.[45] Last, but not least, comes a third hermeneutic system: geomancy and a spiritual, mystical concept of language: the Word is energy and carrier of healing processes.[46]

The cross-breeding of these three TRG approaches has various repercussions. One is the destruction of the master-minded text and the suggestion that the old categories of readers (passable, good, best) have become just as obsolete as the notion of one single acceptable reading: the writer cannot know the entire macrosyntactic context from which his readers will draw. All readings will be different.[47] Another is the delineation of the reader as producer and the text as a labour process. A third is the elaboration of a new lexical system which points back to the primeval origins of words.

If the poem (concrete or deconstructed) becomes a strategic place for change, it necessarily follows that a new lexical system must be elaborated: the functions of literary terms have shifted. Or is it that one is taken back to their first recorded functions? There is a strong suggestion throughout the TRG reports that the *new* functions of lexical terms can be traced back to their etymological definitions, an explicit Kratylian approach. Consider, for instance, the term *book*. The two theoreticians suggest that the key link to its *new* function relates to its ancient meaning: 'the tree, the beech' (the basic

Indo-European root being *bhag*).[48] From this same root derives the Gothic *boka* or, as the TRG explains, 'a letter of the alphabet with its plural *bokos*, i.e., document.'[49] Etymologically, therefore, one traces two semantic leanings within the same term: first that of an organic object that preserves knowledge; secondly, that of a single sign, signifier, or document holding secret, non-communicative information.

The TRG makes two analogical borrowings from geomantic cultures: it highlights a sense of language as landscape, as organic living cells. Also it reacts to this earth-boundedness with an interchange of dimensions: if words are worlds, then worlds become words and the way to affect the world order is to modify the word order.[50] This sense of language as an environmental construct, a vertical support for organic growth, is reinforced by numerous other references.[51] But the central notion here is that of text as an energy field holding together a number of parts. Within this conceptual framework, the terms *form* and *content* find a new functionality. Form becomes the movement and relation of textual parts existing within the text: a lateral movement across a surface. Content, in contrast, is a frontal movement off a plane surface. It operates as a referential thrust connecting one text with others, building up a complex intertextual network, referring out to other texts which then enter the sphere of our actual reading.[52]

But all these lexical shifts[53] do not in fact bring the reader into a closed system. The TRG's hermeneutics do not set up rigid interpretative structures. Theirs is a research process, a cross-breeding of philosophical and linguistic systems. Implicit in the choice of their name (Toronto *Research* Group) is openness to new forays, to other quests. Exemplifications of this new reading/writing praxis can be found in three types of texts: new comic strips,[54] collages, and semiotic poetry. Comics are of interest to the TRG for the simple reason that they operate in a reverse process to 'regular language.'[55] In the latter one notices two opposite movements: (1) words go out to their referents; and (2) words go inwards to their own constitution. In comics, where the frame functions both as syntactic unit and receptacle of content, both movements are inverted: (1) words go inwards (inside the frame) to their referents; and (2) words go outwards to their syntactic constituency (one frame alongside other frames). The structural dynamics derived from this examination is that conventional language is endoskeletal while comic strips are exoskeletal and reflect the general tendency of contemporary writing. The text becomes the externalized bone-structure of the book.

It seems now that one has gone full-circle back to the evacuated sign, the empty sign. A deadlock? Not really because Nichol and McCaffery use the reader-logotherapist to get themselves out of this tautology. The text is *lacunaire*, but the reader will reassert a context, will place the text into a vast macrosyntactic structure, thus giving it back its true function of language as movement, as polysemous energy.[56]

It is inescapable here that Nichol and McCaffery make two strong didactic suggestions in the course of their argument. The first is that in order to come to a 'truer' definition of words, we must go back to their roots – which suggests our ancestors (primeval human beings) knew better than us. The second points to the present exoskeletal push of the deconstructionists, which is also a 'desire to understand the nature of writing,'[57] a 'rebalance of energies,' an 'eradication of misleading dualities,' and a 'substitution of more totalizing concepts.'[58]

Collages in their view operate in a similar way. One witnesses here according to Nichol and McCaffery: (1) a decontextualizing of linguistic groupings; (2) a re-contextualizing of all annexed materials through an alteration of context. The collage-assemblage, like the comic strip, provokes the dissolution of autonomous writers, abolishes the poem as property, and 'states a past present in a present lacunaire.'[59] Here, too, the need to establish a link-up with the past is explicit. McCaffery suggests that collages are comparable and often tantamount to eighteenth-century poetic imitations of classical forms, in which the text was conceived as an area for 'collecting and maintaining prior energies.'[60] Forms and genres were adopted for their quality as vehicular transparencies through which the voices of the past could 'sound through authoritative resonances into the present context.'[61]

These analogies make one wonder whether the earlier distinctions – for all their simplistic nature – between conventional and contemporary writings are still worthwhile working hypotheses. If each new shift is tantamount to another in the past, is it really a shift? Even if the history of literary forms is but a series of shifts, interlocking and related, the alterations they create in the course of their movement have to be clearly demarcated from each other. Otherwise the very concept of shift is trapped in another tautological circle. This is a problem which is never satisfactorily resolved in the TRG writings.

As for semiotic poems they regroup all of the activities mentioned above: presentation of sign as truncated materiality; decontextualization of language elements; and inward movement of signifier towards the centre of its own form. The best illustrations of semiotic poems can be found in McCaffery's own *Transitions to the Beast* (1970). The practice here precedes the theory by some eight years. The poems are built around a single letter which, as a 'non-specific sign,' functions within and for a 'non-lexical sign language.'[62] In 1970 this move signalled an abhorence, as well as a brave rejection, of any lexical key whatsoever. The Brazilians had explored these conceptual possibilities extensively a few years before.[63] However, as has already been described, the TRG did not confine itself to this strict definition and eventually broke out of the *lacunaire* sign to suggest new functions for the reader and new dimensions for the word.

The key one, which has been already discussed, was that of energy. In fact it is essential to an understanding of almost all Canadian concrete theory. Explicit in bissett's texts, this concept recurs in the TRG reports, and later one finds it in the Horsemen's writings and later still in Owen Sound's.[64] But more particularly it intervenes in the elaboration of sound poetry concepts.

Clearly the concept of energy is not the exclusive property of sound poetry. In fact it could stand as a defining feature for any text: 'a configuration of discharges, graphic or semantic, arising from a reader's engagement with a text.'[65] But it seems that the history of this concept and its development have been best highlighted by that of sound poetry.[66] Indeed, it appears that the ability to transfer energy, and therefore its therapeutic value, are the exclusive property of concrete texts destined to be performed. One of the four Horsemen, Paul Dutton, makes references to this function in a brief essay.[67] To him sound poems actualize the unearthing and the awareness of unconscious dynamics. The first is the performer's job. The second that of the audience's. Together they participate in a therapeutic process which is both personal and societal. By purifying the individual, the sound performer heals the community. The structure of this process must be communal: it can only happen in contact with others.

McCaffery explains how the sharing of awareness is embedded in *écouture*: a developed expertise in the aural.[68] The Horsemen – in his words – have trained themselves to be sensitive barometers to each other by becoming each other's text, performers, and audience. Their relationship is both metonymic and synecdochal: they are both the parts and the whole. And one can quickly see how these tensions concretize an ethical as well as therapeutic dialectic. As McCaffery puts it, it connects 'an anthropology and a semiotics': 'The operating notion of 'whole' is ... a juxtapositional whole ... entering into relationship with the parts but in no way dominating them ... what this structure homologizes are certain human states: the movement from isolation into community, the problematics of community ... the collectivisation of the self.'[69] It seems that in concrete sound the politics of the referent do not merge into a vacated sign, but rather into the self (the unearthing) and out of the self: the actualization of one's terrors. The awareness which Dutton refers to takes place after the completion of these two processes. Their end result is a healing, the act of seeing and being free from what one has seen.

Indubitably the Horsemen confer upon the performance a specific and irreducible value: what a reading cannot achieve may be produced by a performance. Such a process touches a realm of experience to which visuality has no access. In the light of their theories it is of interest to read in Derrida's essay on the theatre of cruelty his quotations from Antonin Artaud. Artaud's angry pronouncements take on an added dimension in the presence of Canadian sound performances:

> ... the kind of diffuse poetry which we identify with natural and
> spontaneous energy ... must find its integral expression, its purest, shar-
> pest and most truly separated expression, in the theater.[70]

Still quoting Artaud, Derrida comments that Artaud proposes to make use of speech 'in a concrete and spatial sense' in order to 'manipulate it like a solid object, one which overturns and disturbs things,' and explains that in this new theatrical language gesture and speech are not yet separated by a logic of representation.[71] He quotes Artaud as follows:

> I am adding another language to the spoken language, and I am trying to
> restore to the language of speech its old magic, its essential spell-
> binding power, for its mysterious possibilities have been forgotten.
> When I say I will perform no written play, I mean that I will perform no
> play based on writing and speech, that in the spectacles I produce there
> will be a preponderant physical share which could not be captured and
> written down in the customary language of words, and that even the
> spoken and written portions will be spoken and written in a new sense.[72]

One could make the mistake of interpreting Artaud's theories (or for that matter the Horsemen's practice) as a psychoanalytic session. It is not the desacralization of dreams which is aimed at here. The performance is not a vicarious act, a skilful substitution, but the access to a new awareness:

> The theater of cruelty thus would not be a theater of the unconscious.
> Almost the contrary. Cruelty is consciousness, is exposed lucidity.
> 'There is no cruelty without consciousness and without the
> application of consciousness.'[73]

If Artaud had no heirs and if the concept of a literary legacy from him to
the Horsemen seems absurd, it still remains that coincidences of
concern exist between this French drama theorist and the Toronto
sound poets: particularly a belief in a living, unrepeatable, and unique
vocal act which recovers forgotten primeval powers.[74]

Artaud, like the Horsemen, believed in the rejection of rigid scores.
The Toronto performers justify this choice with the comment that
sound pieces are by definition of a transient nature. Their 'energy
gestalt'[75] varies with each reading. Just as the actual duration of a poem
is indeterminate, its energy flows are not to be chronologized. It is
curious to see here how their sound theory recoups their visual one.
This rejection of chronology and strict duration brings the sound poem
back to the quest for a non-narrative prose.[76] The sound poem becomes
a kinetic narrative, a motion of particles in unspecified time-frames.
The performers know when a destination is reached through their
écouture. We are both what we say and what we hear. And simultaneously. At the same instant.[77]

Another peculiarity of Canadian sound performers is their apparent
distrust of – or lack of interest in – the electronic machinery which has
held the French and Swedish poets' attention for more than two
decades. It is indeed a curious reversal of the facile stereotyping of
technological attitudes – avid North Americans versus technology-
weary Europeans. While Henri Chopin in France uses tapes and their
multiple array of manipulatory devices, and the Swedes have been
notorious for utilizing the human voice as a departure point into
electronic signals, Canadians have relied upon their own vocal chords,
their physical presence on the set, and their contact gestalt with their
audience. This reliance on both performers' and listeners' bodies, this
need to implicate them into the actual performance, explicitly
underlines a cathartic intent. It also indicates the importance of the
praxis of sound versus its written theory. Many Canadian sound
theories have actually been researched and documented in the course
of performances. One such is the 'intermedia'[78] aspect of sound
performances, or as Canadian musician Murray Schafer calls it, their
'confluence.'[79] In this, the extent to which Canadians break away from
their European counterparts (British performer Bob Cobbing and

French poet Henri Chopin, in particular) is obvious. To the Horsemen, Owen Sound, or poet Sean O'Huigin[80] sound performances should not be limited to the use of sound. When needed, composers may introduce objects, lighting, props, and other media components. One of Owen Sound's pieces is a case in point. 'Children's Toys' includes an assortment of thirty children's accessories used phonetically and dramatically in the course of the performance. It is easy to see how these rattles, drums, whistles, jolly apples, and clackers use a polysemous texture: not just pure sounds, but a series of chain reactions related to the audience's memory and private referential field. Other Owen Sound pieces have included video elements and blended them into sound. Steve Smith refers to them as 'sound sculptures,'[81] and this term has also been used by Murray Schafer about his own compositions.[82] This move towards a contextualization of sound within spacial, tactile, visual, and olfactory textures is not the Canadians' only; the Québécois have also developed it. But it signals a rejection of the didactic precepts of their European friends. Schafer sought after this contextualization process for more than fifteen years. One of his earlier pieces, 'Loving,' was defined by him as an audio-visual poem, devoid of plot and inhabiting an unreal time-space in which 'questions may be answered before they are asked.'[83] The drama about love between a man and a woman is expressed in two different languages (the man speaks French and the woman English), and the two characters are surrounded by singers who speak many other idioms: 'languages we do not understand ... listened to purely as musical sounds.'[84] The weaving of its ambiguous visual and sound textures reflects the concerns of Canadian sound writers today.[85] Other pieces by Schafer present the rare distinction of being concrete poems written by a musician. Their scores reveal mirroring techniques, non-linear readings, scripts merging in and out of run-on sentences, nonsense, and semantic implosions. Other parts of their score are scripted as concrete music. The blending of the two produces some unique effects,[86] but more importantly it indicates Canadian concrete sound as a continuously evolving form and also one that rejects systematic principles. An open praxis seems to be the sound poets' preference in this area.

According to French theoretician Bernard Heidsieck, four currents can be distinguished in sound poetry: these flow neither parallel nor opposite, but with distinct borders and superimposed trajectories.[87] They range from (1) mainly phonetic to (2) the voice-as-the-main-centre-approach to (3) the electro-acoustic mode and (4) pure electronics with no spoken word (the text being devoured here by the machine).

Canadians have explored the whole range, but in my opinion they have favoured (1), (2), and (3).

A brief consideration of bpNichol's *The Martyrology* must be added to complete this survey of Canadian theory.[88] This work looms over the complete body of other theoretical writings with the lofty distance which sets metaphysics and mythologies apart from other works. All four of its books may be looked upon as a long prayer, as a geography of time (Book III) and of the dead Logos: God, the Father, whose disappearance is grieved by the narrator from the very beginning of Book I. *The Martyrology* is indeed about metaphysics and myth. It focuses its entire attention on what founded our existence: the Logos, which we are now deprived of. What we are left with is a substitute language, a 'prototype / perfect model of the robot run amuck' (Book I), a dead speech because we have lost the gift of tongues. Yet we have one hope: our words, the saints who will attempt to bring us redemption. They play the role of intermediaries between the Logos and ourselves. They have left heaven (Book III) and though they have never felt at home upon the earth (Book III), they have come to help us reclaim our heritage, the mythology which founded our very existence. This experience binds us all to one another since we all are implicated, tied to one another through using the same language. Redemption is a collective process – just as *écouture* and the cathartic experience of sound poetry[89] – and the saints are going to intervene on our behalf to bring about 'the cleansing of speech' (Book III) and the end to our private hells.

The Martyrology clearly provides us with a mythology and a gospel. In doing so it fuses two traditions: the Platonic one, of the Father-Logos forever removed from common mortals;[90] and native Indian metaphysics, that of the God Palongwahoya, whose function was to sing the praise of the creator by vibrating in tune with the vibratory axis of the cosmos until humans started to use speech as a way to isolate themselves from each other thus destroying the harmony and the fusion of humanity and cosmological sound. *The Martyrology* explicitly looks for this God-Sound:

> How can i live who cannot be without you
> ...
> only the skies empty my tears
> hell i could fill the space with moaning
> oh you are gone & i am left
> lonely father   ('Friends as Footnotes,' Book II)

Just as in the Palongwahoya legend humans have stopped vibrating with the cosmos and lost *sound* in order to develop speech, *The Martyrology*'s narrator has lost the Logos and is left with words: 'a substitution' which ruins humans' lives. But this text goes beyond a documentation and explanation of a distant past (the mythology). It also suggests the coming of a new age, a redemption, a healing process:

> Speech is a holy act
> linking as it does the whole body
> ...
> Father
> i seek that speech cleanses
>   address you
>   as is your due
> ...
> we set the axis in motion father
> holy sound to bring death's bird down   (Book III)

From a theoretical angle *The Martyrology* sets high goals for the poetic text: the regaining of our birthright or, to use native terminology, the recovery of our ancient cosmological powers. Yet in doing so it only confirms and completes all of bissett's and most of Owen Sound's, the Horsemen's, and Schafer's writings. These theoreticians believe and constantly assert the metaphysics of sound, both from a therapeutic and philosophical viewpoint.

The TRG, however, does not completely fit into this picture. There are contradictions between the metaphysics of concrete and the materialistic assumptions of some, not all, of the TRG's reports. These contradictions are never resolved or even actually debated, but coexist in a quiet complicity as if no one should, or would, ever wonder about them. As a deconstructionist body of theories, the TRG reports are explicit about their diversity and diffuse in their intents/contents.

THE EMERGENCE OF PERFORMANCE THEORY IN A POST-MODERN ERA

> Nearly two years ago in an essay called 'Pictures' ... I first found it useful to employ the term *Postmodernism* ... I wrote at that time that the aesthetic mode that was exemplary during the seventies was performance, all those works that were constituted in a specific situation and for a specific duration; works for which it could be said literally that you had to be there.
>
> Douglas Crimp, 'The Photographic Activity in Postmodernism,' in Pontbriand, ed., *Performance*, 70

Douglas Crimp was not the only one to find performances 'the exemplary art' of the 1970s. Bruce Barber and many others concur on this point.[91] Indeed the 1970s saw the emergence of a large body of theoretical works on this subject, which also demonstrated the ambiguities of its definitional spectrum.

Just as the concrete manifestations of the 1950s and 1960s had introduced a variety of artistic media, performances during the 1970s interwove graphic and pictorial designs, phonic and musical elements. But this time the media spectrum was even wider, technological means more diversified, and theoretical stands very much grounded within a multi-media perspective. By the late 1970s it became evident that performances as art-forms represented a vast area which had attracted both critical credibility and researchers' scrutiny. There had been since the mid-1970s a general consensus that performances be considered under the complex category of post-modernism.[92] This does not necessarily help to understand them better, but it situates them within a larger framework.

The first difficulty that needs to be confronted is of course the choice of the term itself. Are performances really new and unique phenomena? Were there not after all such artistic and aesthetic manifestations gravitating around the Cabaret Voltaire in 1915 or around the Italian futurists during the 1920s? Some critics, such as Rose Lee Goldberg, have indeed insisted that it was in the practice and experimentation of performance that dadaists, futurists, and surreal-ists found their roots and not – as suggested by art historians – in the creation of art objects. It was thus 'in performance that they tested these ideas only later expressing them in the form of objects.'[93] Other more recent phenomena, for instance, the agit-prop theatre and the 1960s happenings, also come to mind, so that one is justified in raising the question: is performance art a new art-form rejecting the conceptu-alizations which determine other art-forms, or does it function within specific generic boundaries?[94] Chantal Pontbriand focuses her atten-tion on this issue when she recognizes that what artists and critics have done is to create a sort of 'history in reverse' for lack of a better solution.[95] In doing so, they have invoked Marcel Duchamp's ready-mades, used Walter Benjamin's texts on cinema and theatre, quoted minimal art explorations from the 1950s, and utilized John Austin's concepts of performative acts as well as German reception theory. In her view such a history is one of the paradoxes of post-modernism. The *post* of *post-modernism* does not refer to what would normally be expected – the period which succeeds modernism – but, quite the contrary, to a new attitude which specifically challenges linear historical concepts, defies notions of evolution or progress, and questions the logocentric project of Western thought. Her choice therefore is to enter performances under the generalized deconstruction code which appears to be one of the agreed common denominators of post-modernism.

Pontbriand's perceptions are confirmed by a number of other critics who self-consciously reject the dangerously linear premises of 'tradition' and prefer instead to thrust forward into the vast and uncertain territory of post-modernism. Thierry de Duve clearly summarizes this intention when he notes, 'We are gathered here to bring into the world an object which does not pre-exist to its name; its construction rules are too uncertain and varied to be specific; in other words, it is without tradition.'[96] And Birgit Pelzer echoes, 'I have chosen to regress back to a elementary and minimal level ... to perform is less "un dire qu'un faire";[97] while Daniel Charles reminds us that the 'doing' of performances is not overdetermined by a calculating objectifying episteme, that it is not the product of traditional Western thinking, so keen on viewing man as a 'logon echon' – a being who controls and utilizes language as a tool in his transactions. But, on the contrary, such 'doing' is a return to the narrativity, to the Saga, which overdetermines human beings rather than the opposite.[98] It is true that in the basic dictionary sense *performance* means the interpretive enactment of a play script or a musical score. John Austin's theory, as we know it, has allowed us to think beyond such categories as re-enactment and representation of the 'thing' done in the performance itself. Another factor has also since intervened, and in Jean-François Lyotard's view it is an essential one: the presence of a body which moves, sings, or speaks. 'It is this transcribing on and for bodies,' Lyotard claims, which singles out performances among other artistic creations: 'it is linked to the idea of inscription on the body.'[99] It thus seems inescapable that performances contain within themselves not only the sense of a physical act, of a corporal accomplishment, but also of a 'carrying out.'[100] Many artists therefore insist that a performance is not a purely aesthetic act, but also a community act, a celebration of what is being brought to experiential fullness through performance. To perform a text is not only to say something, but, as Richard Palmer notes, 'to do something.' And he quickly adds that we also need to reflect more deeply on 'that doing.'[101]

Yet there is a radical difference between Austin's definition of *performance* and the contemporary use of the term. In speech-act theory human beings are still 'logon echon' (that is, creatures who possess and overdetermine language in their transactions with one another). Their speech acts therefore are moves accomplished by a centred subjectivity. In such circumstances, as de Duve stresses, 'man remains the rational animal; language the instrument of his rationality.'[102] But post-modernists have specifically chosen to challenge this Austinian sense of the instrumentality of language and the Logos. Lyotard, for instance, reminds us that it is narratives which carry forth human beings, and not the other way around, while Jacques Lacan notes that it is not we who are speaking a language but rather that we are spoken by it.

Performances appear to proceed from such premises. The decentring paradox which underlies their operations is that such acts both are *performative acts* (in that they transform a situation, have a *force* not a truth value like Austin's speech acts) and are *radically different* (in that to be performances they necessarily *have to* be infelicitous and need not offer what they seem to be about to give).[103] It is these infelicities which by lingering in the viewer as a delay, difficulty, or resistance allow such acts to come into being.[104] Performances therefore place us onto what Pelzer calls a slippery path. And because this noncoincidence opens up what she refers to as 'un espace voyou aux codes tous confondus ... un espace multiple, dépliable et postulant ... le règne de l'interférence [la performance] engendre ainsi un univers de la batardise et de la fraude ... en recourant simultanément au triple principe de l'équivalence, de la substitution infinie et de l'absence de relation d'ordre.'[105]

But such a radical heteronomy (an act which lets itself be seen and therefore misunderstood) is not meaningless. For Pelzer it is the symptom of the destruction of a certain social fabric, the crumbling down of social units which used to be stable, clear, and transparent. But she stresses that it does not 'represent,' that representations or reproductions are a function of the past, that mimetical operations are obsolete. What performances do is to coexist with, let us glimpse at, the liquidation of both a heritage and a future. Their aesthetics are thus a strange mixture of amnesia and memory: they simultaneously confront us with archival inventories *and* deny the presence of such genealogies. From some quarters such choices have provoked strong criticism. Bruce Barber, for instance, sees them as very much related to what he perceives as the narcissistic and hedonistic culture of ·

advanced capitalism.[106] Peter Frank is even more scathing and refers to such manifestations as acts of self-indulgence bordering on self-exhibitionism and valorizing not only one's autobiography but also one's narcissim.[107] Yet for Barber one cannot divorce from such manifestations their instrumentality (that is, their potential for function). Contrary to de Duve and Pelzer, he stresses that such gestures must do or mean something, and his attendant judgment is that such acts confront us with our historical impasse, an impasse which in his terms 'can allow us to describe the postmodern era as an era without a vector.'[108]

Confrontation *is* representation here, and the presence of a body performing an act is also a sign of something else, an index or an icon pointing in another direction. Performance theory is clearly divided: for some, like Chantal Pontbriand, Thierry de Duve, and, to a certain extent, Birgit Pelzer, performance is pure manifestation, sheer trace;[109] for others, like Bruce Barber and James Hougan,[110] while performance challenges the logocentric temptations of Western thought, it cannot avoid being part of a certain societal system and therefore mirroring its demise, its archival decomposition.

Craig Owens, the American art critic and theoretician, attempts to find ways out of the 'historical impasse,' that is, the dysfunctional mode which performances have got themselves into. While recognizing that weaving one's way out of the labyrinths of signs (specifically in this case Laurie Anderson's performances) is highly problematic, he pleads for a new perspective on the problem of interpretation. Such a novel approach is warranted – or so Owens suggests – by the elocutionary shift in emphasis which one notices in post-modern writings. Such a shift is comparable to what Emile Benveniste refers to as the transition from third-person narration (the impersonal address of the historical mode) to second-person narration (direct address, exhortative discourse, or simple discourse).[111]

The latter mode is directed at the reader in an attempt to modify his behaviour, and its messages, as Owens puts it,[112] are exhortative and account for the centrality which post-modern art assigns to the reader-spectator. According to Owens, in contrast with a 'traditional' picture or photograph, which addresses no one in particular and maintains its own relationship to its author independently from its audience, performances or post-modern productions 'take the form of a directive *to* someone, a directive that exists in the space of confrontation between sign and emblem and the one who views it.'[113] The angle which Owens provides on this question is different from both Barber's serious political criticism and de Duve's justification of the art-form on the grounds of its decentring impulse. Owens, in fact, insists that performances have little to do with modernist strategies, that they do not bracket or suspend reference nor suggest that an art object, for instance, can be metaphorically substituted for its referent. The difference between modernist and post-modernist strategies is that when the 'postmodernist work speaks of itself it is no longer to proclaim its autonomy, its self-sufficiency, its transcendence but rather [it is] to narrate its own contingency, insufficiency, lack of transcendence.'[114] To this art critic such manifestations can only tell of desires which are perpetually frustrated, of ambitions that can only be forever deferred. Thus it is not only contemporary myths and political expectations which performances seek to deconstruct but, more to the point, the symbolic totalizing impulse which characterizes modern art. In this context Owens quotes Roland Barthes' *Image, Music, Text*, where we were reminded that the artist's strategy is not to change or purify symbols, but to undermine the sign itself.[115]

The questions raised by Canadian, European, and American performance theories might be summarized by two general questions. The first one deals with the relationship(s) of performances both to history and the subject: do these relationships function as an apparatus capable of producing transformations, or are they a simple invitation to share narcissistic impulses? The second has to do with performances' alleged identity (that is, deconstructed acts) and simultaneously with their relationship to the concept of presence: is it tenable to aim at an hermeneutic disclosure when one posits deconstructed acts?

The relationship of performances to both history and the subject is deeply problematical. Both concepts simultaneously challenge the identity and stated purpose of this art-form. To a large number of observers performances have become the art of the self, of a self as text grounded in the presence of a body (usually of one, sometimes of several), of a voice, of a fetishistic desire, and of the figuration of this desire.[116] The defensiveness of other theoreticians is symptomatic of a deep uneasiness about the role of the subject in this particular process. René Payant, for instance, cautions that performances do not signal a return to subjectivity, but rather, challenge the audience, trying to implicate it within the work and to incite it to be a component of the process. Is it not tantalizing that Payant would see fit to warn us away from the dangers of subjectivity with such convincingness? That he would deem it necessary to remind us that neither humanist thought nor facile emotionalism is the order of the day here?[117] Might it be that performances risk loosing their artistic credentials, that we may remain unaware of their potential 'to lay open the rules of artistic institutions'?[118]

Such entreaties surely are prone to arouse our suspicions, to make us wonder whether this 'subject' is not in fact a furtive player, a dissimulated ace. When the urge to expell it from the pack turns to an obsession, might not such cautions be a backlash to the Austinian premises of performance theory – however modified, however transformed? The legacy of Austin, whose stated purpose was to approach the total speech act in the total speech situation, was also in its time a reaction to the formalism and abstractness of much modern literary criticism.[119] Richard Palmer is less guarded about such matters than his Quebec counterpart. As he bluntly puts it, 'Performance is not just an aesthetic but a moral act, a community, a celebration ... it does not just say something, it does something and we need to reflect more deeply on that doing.'[120]

For Palmer performative acts reject the rationalist-humanist view of man as the measure and measurer of all things, in control of the world, definer of a perspectival sense of space, and conceiver of linear time. History from such a rationalist perspective could only be conceived as a straight line that never circles back on itself, as progress, as scientific reason capable of controlling nature and thus transforming the world.[121] What post-modernist impulses have done is to take us beyond this anthropology of secularized man as a tool-using animal to a new hermeneutical situation. The event of interpretive mediation is now located in a different place: feminine, shamanistic, intuitive. The post-modern work is multi-perspectival; it works through us, it transforms us, it 'heals the soul.'[122]

Jerome Rothenberg has been the keenest formulator of such choices and their relationship to history. As a performer and theorist, he explains that performances do not deny history, are involved with it, but proceed from a model or a vision that has shifted. The old paradigm of Western civilization is no longer viable.[123] The new paradigm is *both* an obvious disdain for paradigms per se *and* a transformational form, a visionary experience which *does* something involving an action or a process, not through propagandist overtones (or undertones for that matter), nor from a functional viewpoint, since such operational modes belong to the old civilizational paradigm (culture as progress), but through a participatory process that is non-commanding, non-directive, and non-hierarchical: a co-creation of performance and audience 'in which the one-time viewer/listener himself becomes the maker.'[124]

In Canada, while the Horsemen and Owen Sound explicitly share Rothenberg's 'vision,' not all performers can be said to partake of such a non-secular and mystical project: specifically, not Tom Konyves among the Montreal Véhicule poets and not General Idea, another prominent Toronto performance group. Richard Palmer is aware of such differences. But his position is that an explicitly secular position does not really enter into the post-modern experience, that in fact such a position is simply a continuation of the humanist trajectory.[125] I would suggest that it is hazardous to risk a delineation of performance theory which does not strike a balance between these two polar opposites; between, that is, Palmer's and Rothenberg's definitions, clearly anchored within a certain metaphysics, on the one hand, and Lyotard's, Scarpetta's, and Payant's deconstructive twists, on the other (modernity in the last decade of this century is just this: there is nothing to replace; no holding on to any locus is legitimate, or they all are; replacements, and therefore meaning, is only a substitute for displacement).[126]

History therefore, like reality, is a place for questioning, a questioning which comes from the performer but also from the spectator.[127] Performances expose, display, these relationships. While I do agree that 'secure discourse' is a paradigm of the past, that 'there is no such situation where subjects are present to themselves,' I think – contrary to Bruce Barber – that performance is not a predominantly narcissistic and hedonistic manifestation, or one 'that beckons a step closer to a stock market of human relations,'[128] even though I will concede that it sometimes partakes of these features, especially in the perception of it projected by the press.[129] But to me its main investments are predominantly geared towards a displacement of old models and not a reinforcement of their prerogatives.

The most convincing summary of performance's accomplishment is articulated by Birgit Pelzer when she suggests that performances do not transgress (an instinctual drive of the avant-garde movement) but rather digress (the post-modern preference); the issue therefore is not to challenge paradigms but rather to 'disadapt meaning.'[130] And this brings me to the second set of questions: Are performances deconstructed acts? Or do they embody a certain presence? Do they disclose anything for us?

Looking at the critical literature on performances it is overwhelmingly obvious that they are referred to in deconstructive terms.

Commentators might disagree about a number of problems, but all seem to converge in this single direction. Performances primarily concern themselves with the 'deconstruction of information by atomizing the discursive elements which [they play] against one another.'[131] It is impossible to extract coherent, monological messages from them, and attempts to decipher such works testify only to their failure.[132] While they do not reject narration, even manifest an increased interest in it, homogeneity and continuity have disappeared, the great Western narrative continuum has dissolved, and their main organizational modes are superimposition, multi-layering, quotation, repetition, and aleatory arrangement.[133] Their deconstructive language is not only 'a strong impulse.'[134] It is trace, not sign; it does not represent, it presents; and the body it uses is also not a sign, but a trace.[135]

How do such manifestations deal with the whole problem of presence? On the one hand performances proceed from a very basic premise; as de Duve puts it, they are 'an art of the here and now, [which] implies the co-presence in real space-time of the performer and his public.'[136] But de Duve himself admits that there is nothing more suspect in our contemporary context than the idea of presence: 'From Husserl to Derrida, from Heidegger to Wittgenstein, presence has been questioned, put in doubt, deconstructed. This century has discovered that re-presentation was hiding even in the most immediate being-there; it no longer has faith in the nature of presence.'[137] The fall of Kantian transcendality is not put in question here, but more to the point 'presence' takes on neither the Kantian sense of nostalgia for an a-priori space time[138] nor Walter Benjamin's sense of yearning for the artistic aura.[139] This new concept of presence implies the intervention of a reproduction system. As de Duve puts it, it is not the presence of Elton John which matters to 200,000 teenagers in Central Park (in fact, without amplification systems, video terminals, and microphones, not a soul would have been there for the concert). But what matters in such a society 'in which symbolic manifestations are treated not as signs but as signals in a perpetual transcoding is that the *presence*, the effective being-there of ordinary man, goes continuously through these *indifferent mediations*, these *transcoding machines*.'[140]

De Duve distinguishes three types of performances: communions or participations in the Grotowski or Kaprow sense, and he might have included Rothenberg here; minimalist performances; and those – the greatest number in his view – which rely on the mediation of the reproduction-systems mentioned earlier.[141] His preference for the latter is not really relevant here, but what is at issue is this new perception of 'presence' in our media-conscious, simulacra-creating age. Definitions have shifted, concepts do not have the same currency, and ultimately the Western obsession for presence operates in a universe where meanings have been displaced, where a media-image has more 'presence' than the flesh and blood of a physical body.

The power of simulacra challenges both representation as a concept and disclosure as a hermeneutic expectation. Can performances disclose anything? What can they possibly bring to the surface if all they are involved in is to superimpose narrative layers, to displace and multiply speaking subjects and voice sources (the work of Joan La Barbara on voice and reading machines is particularly relevant here)?[142] Could one venture to say that performances are very much akin to therapeutic processes? Indeed the occasional emergence of a secret drama whose object is to bring back a distant past, obliterated memories, would convince us that they partake of such impulses. The work of the American performer Leony Sacks, for instance, especially her performance 'The Survivor and the Translator,' which is modelled upon 'one of performance's constitutive elements, that of the translation metaphor,'[143] would tend to prove that much. Leony Sacks goes back and forth, into and out of her past, and into and out of different generations, desperately trying to track and assemble an impossible memory, that of a holocaust she hasn't experienced and which operates as an immense vacuum within her life.

There are, within most performances, elements of a reached-for transformation – not in the sense of information to be decoded, but rather of energy to be transmuted. The frequent references to Artaud certainly imply that much.[144] They suggest that the nihilistic question of absence and negativity posed by the famous French theoretician is very much relevant to modern performance artists.[145] Durand tells us that Artaud, as does post-modernism, transformed 'each spectacle into an event';[146] such events do aspire to a re-creation, a projection of inner conflicts. Artaud's scenographies and modern performance's scenographies have substituted – de facto if not in principle – ritualistic modes for narratives, indetermination for causality, and variability for planned hysteria.[147] The concept of 'acting out,' which brings performances into an area strongly overdetermined by psychoanalysis, is far from being foreign to Artaud, except that performance artists have foregrounded it openly, bluntly even. As one artist put it, 'It is a means of expression; it gestures at a deaf person to whom it addresses itself.'[148] Durand's references to Shoshana Felman's *Le*

Scandale du corps parlant are self-explanatory here; performances manifest, foreground, such processes. They are a ritual enactment of desire,[149] a description which allows us to focus better on the undecidable nature of performative acts, which hover between real and symbolic ones. As Durand puts it, signs are but 'un lieu de passage, un lieu de transaction de deux désirs et l'esquisse d'une réponse qui ne cesse pas de se faire entendre, dans les deux sens.'[150] I am reminded here of Maria Bicocchi's and Fulvio Salvadori's thoughts on this matter, that 'while Performance itself is beyond history, it happens in that time without time where personal and collective memory touch, an event which can take place only in privileged instants.'[151]

Both Canadian and Québécois performance artists and theorists have testified to this. Both their experiments and their writings on this subject have determinedly selected these options. While in the area of literary creativity differences have been substantial, particularly in their respective visions of post-modernism, performance artists in Canada and Quebec have faced the various issues which confront this art-form in a remarkably similar fashion. I do not mean to suggest that performances have presented a homogeneous front – certainly the divisiveness around the issue of the secularism of avant-garde art versus its post-modern shamanistic forms has been very much present in this country. But our two cultures have reflected upon this issue in ways which are very similar. Basing one's judgment upon Chantal Pontbriand's 1981 *Performance*, A.A. Bronson's and Peggy Gale's *Performance by Artists* (1979), or René Payant's *Vidéo* (1986), it appears to be explicitly clear that performance artists in Montreal, Toronto, Calgary, or Vancouver are confronting similar problems which they deal with in not very dissimilar ways; there are no bi-cultural boundaries here, and differentiations spring from aesthetic principles which have little to do with linguistic or national identities.

Yet the reception which these theories found in Europe, on the one hand, and in North America, on the other, has been different. As Renée Baert points out in *Vidéo*, the context in which such works were exhibited in Canada (video installations/performances) was primarily the context in which they were produced. While the existence of artist-run centres, which grew substantially since the inception of the earliest models, gave Canadian artists 'generous latitude to shape the discourse of their work ... this network operates both in practice and in metaphor within a closed circuit environment, in which one has not succeeded in allowing a body of work critically engaged with social, political and aesthetic issues a convincing participation in a wider cultural milieu.'[152] And this may be the key difference between performance theory and practice in this country and its development in Europe and the rest of North America. There was a degree of marginalization or ghettoization which Canadian and Quebec performers had not quite grown out of by the middle and late 1980s.

CONCRETE AND POST-MODERN THEORY IN QUEBEC:
THE BURSTING OUT OF A DEFINITIONAL BASIS

Act I: Fusing, Celebrating, Calligraphing

> There is the joy of seeking a total language, one which encompasses all styles, which aims at the spontaneous harmony of the inner and outer worlds, at once continuous and discontinuous, like the law of matter and its transformation into spirit. The attempt to return to the simplicity of the decivilized humanized primitive.
>
> When I write, I find myself very aware of the shape of the letters, their visual dimensions, their geometrical arrangements, the straight lines, the curves, the movement of the lines, etc. Then, on the level of sound, I carry my investigations even farther. For example, the frequency of a particular vowel in conjunction with another, palatals, labials, dentals, all the phonetic particulars. I investigate these very deeply in order to discover the relations between sounds.
>
> Raoul Duguay, 'Poetry is Yrteop,' *Ellipse*, no. 17 (1975), 80

From the mid-1960s on, Quebec appears to have been an ideal ground for experimental writing theories to grow in. While English-Canadian poets and critics somewhat uniformly agreed upon the term *concrete* as an adequate definition, their French-speaking counterparts did not. In Quebec one witnesses an explosion of definitions, a terminological pluralism. Such varied references as 'art sensoriel,' 'poésie matérialiste,' 'poésie visuelle,' 'objective,' 'spatiale,' and 'mise en question du langage' appeared as early as 1967 in Cécile Cloutier's article on 'la nouvelle poésie.'[153] Soon after, Clément Moisan, a comparatist of the two national literatures, equated concretism with 'poésie infra': 'Le concrétisme comme on l'appelle au Canada anglais ou la poésie infra comme on la nomme au Canada français est sans doute la forme la plus avancée en poésie.'[154] Raoul Duguay, a sound performer and theoretician, chose a grouping of terms: 'le stéréo-poème-audio-visuel.'[155]

Indubitably this richness of terms complicates the critic's task. It threatens the validity of any strict definition of terms and suggests that one is facing a movement of great amplitude whose ramifications may well go beyond what had been called concrete. Which criteria should we use to select our body of theoretical texts?

For clarity's sake it may be simpler to isolate those which start from a concretist premise (whether it is explicitly acknowledged or not). As was pointed out earlier, concretism demands that the attention of poet and reader-listener be focused on the material components of the poem. It is the interrelationship of these elements and their perfect coincidence with the semantic message which produce a concrete poem both in time (performance) and space (on the page). I have also commented on the temptation of nonsense, or, as Henri Chopin prefers to call it, the 'return to a pure sound, a signifier deprived of any reference.'[156] By focusing on texts which display these traits, whether or not they make explicit reference to the term *concrete*, it will be possible to examine the Québécois' practice and see in what way they used, expanded on, or even broke away from these specific premises.

One of the first manifestos which appears to warrant critical attention is Claude Péloquin's *Manifeste infra*, which Moisan suggested was directly related to concretism.[157] One excerpt from the *Manifeste* might be useful to test for the premises stated above:

> INFRA: processus d'agir et de penser conçu et exigé pour raison de conscience. Pénétration des couches infra-réelles; pour toucher la réalité existante tant dans les dessous du réel que dans ses dehors cosmiques. Mise en place des pouvoirs occultes d'un langage de l'esprit, d'un réel d'attente, face à l'Ailleurs.[158]

A close reading of this theoretical project reveals that the narrator's focus is not on word-objects, on language matter, on syllables and phonemes, but on the human conscience and the human mind. In fact, what Péloquin is striving for here is much more akin to surrealist explorations of creativity (through dreams, drugs, or explorations of the individual as well as collective subconscious) and not anywhere close to the materialistic premises of concretists.

But the examinations above of bill bissett's *What Fuckan Theory* or bpNichol's *Martyrology* have shown that some Canadian writers believe in the effects of a Spirit-Logos upon phonemes. Belief in the magical powers of the word is not, in itself, a concrete premise (if anything, it is a rather curious deviation from concretism's original aesthetics). It is primarily because of bissett's pronouncements in *Ice* (on grammar, spelling, and visual form), in *Pass th Food* (on words as non-directory, perceptual flashes), and in *What Fuckan Theory* (on the overthrowing of sense), as well as Nichol's tight charting of the fortunes and misfortunes of concretism through the TRG reports, that one recognizes these writers' specific concretist concerns.

But concentration upon the matter which texts are made of never emerges in Péloquin's works. Thus Moisan's judgment of Péloquin's work as concrete does not rest on sufficient evidence to be convincing. Conversely, however, lack of reference to concretism in a poet's theoretical reflections should not be construed as excluding him/her from that field. Quebec's terminological pluralism calls for a higher degree of discrimination on the reader's part.

Raoul Duguay's writings are directly related to concrete experiments. Gilles Marcotte once referred to his earlier works, *Ruts* (1966) and *Or le cycle du sang dure donc* (1967), as an attempt 'to handle words the way one would play with objects.'[159] His theoretical writings confirm Marcotte's judgment. Indeed their primary concern is sound and phonic poetry. One of his first articles in this area starts with a definition which could have been written by American projectionist Charles Olson: 'Donc il est manifeste que l'essentiel c'est le souffle ... le souffle est la respiration de la vie ... ainsi toute métaphysique du langage doit se ressourcer dans l'émotion primitive, physique, viscérale.'[160]

It does not take long to realize that in fact Duguay's definition of poetry is much more an outgrowth of phenomenological theory than a development of existing phonic theories (Henri Chopin's or Paul de Vree's). It is uncertain whether or not the latter were known to him in 1967, but there is no doubt whatsoever about his interest in, and his identification with, French phenomenologist Mikel Dufresne in the area of sound and meaning. He quotes the French philosopher – '... le son est tout entier dans le sens'[161] – and proposes a definition of the poem which Dufresne could entirely subscribe to: 'Ainsi [sic] la définition du poème est dans l'équation suivante: tout son (toute image) est substrat de sens. Tout sens: attribut d'un son (d'une image).'[162] Duguay's position vis-à-vis semantics is far less radical than Chopin's or even de Vree's. While the Europeans have rejected all semantic luggage of the word as obsolete, he maintains an equation between sound and meaning, a tension between pure emotion and semantic intentionality: 'Ouvrir la voie de l'âme par la voix du corps. Assigner à l'émotion une intentionalité. Une structuration à base bilabiodentale, fricative, scande les rythmes intérieurs.'[163] In 1967

Duguay's refusal to abandon the semantic elements of the word may have stemmed from cultural-political needs. His *Quoi* statement was written at a time when his political stand was an integral part of his work. To him, at that particular moment, the poetic text had a pragmatic and political function: 'Le cri du poème est le plus authentique pouvoir dont je dispose pour m'identifier à la profondeur de l'inconscient collectif québécois ... ce cri est action.'[164]

From the viewpoint of phonic theory this 1967 article presents a triple interest. First, it establishes an organic relationship between orality and visuality – 'l'oralité transparait déjà dans l'écriture,'[165] a concept totally foreign to European phonic theoreticians. Secondly, it proposes a structuring of the visual text that will be capable of conveying new rhythms, new breathing techniques, through specific breaks, ruptures, and permutations. Thirdly, he openly confesses having borrowed these techniques from concrete or serial music and from jazz composers: '... j'ai été influencé par les musiques atonales dodécaphonique et expérimentale (concrète et électronique), par le jazz expérimental et free ... la technique sérielle m'a fait découvrir la possibilité de fractionner à l'infini un intervalle considéré ... comme le plus petit dénominateur chromatique.'[166]

Duguay articulates with great precision, and to a greater degree than Chopin or de Vree, the extent of his borrowings from musical theory: 'J'emprunte à la musique contemporaine certaines notions applicables aux sonorités des mots comme: timbre. percussion. durée. dynamique. hauteur. tempo. intensité. tessiture. densité.'[167] Thus he creates a new terminology based upon two key concepts: the participatory role of his public; and the different effects produced by phonemes upon the human ear: 'J'invente le poétron ... dans un poème qui appelle la participation du public auditeur ... et le divise en acoustron et articulatron ... l'acoustron est le temps acoustique ... caracterisé par la discontinuité et la momentanéité signifiées par des consonnes oclusives ou explosives bilabiales dentales et vélaires (p. b. m. t. d. n. gn. k. g.). L'articulatron est caracterisé par la continuité, l'irradiation ... des consonnes fricatives (f. v. s. z. l. ch. j. y. r.).'[168] This terminology is unique to him. No other Québécois phonic poet has ever attempted to borrow from it. But his ideas about the applicability of serial music techniques to poetry are not unique. The poet Luc Racine, who also collaborated on *Quoi*, expanded upon the transposition of serial notions from music to poetry, and his theories come very close indeed to Chopin's. Only the terminology is different.

Racine, in order to define the transformations he introduces within a text, uses serial music terms. In fact, Racine's transformations (permutations and combinations) of different units of sound (rhythmical and metrical) and the way he combines them ('renversement et non-renversement de l'ordre de succession des unités: synonymie et antonymie')[169] bring him close to his European counterparts. But he, like Duguay, does not reject semantics, which he conceives of as another unit system, parallel to the metrical and rhythmical systems, and capable of various transformations. But exactly how he envisions semantics remains vague. One regrets his lack of exploration in this area because it would have challenged the Europeans' assumptions about sound and meaning.

Another interesting foray into creative theory was Duguay's reinterpretation of the stimuli-receptor principle established by Mike Weaver in 1964 and later developed by the French and the Brazilians. Duguay did not challenge this classification system but advanced it by proposing a synthesis of all sensory stimuli in order to create 'le stéréo-poème-audio-visuel.'[170] In fact, he does not use the word *synthesis* but suggests another term, *synergie*, to emphasize the dynamic nature of the grouping. The multi-dimensionality of the work, according to him, is based first upon the use of all sensory stimuli (visual, tactile, auditive, olfactory, gustatory) but also upon the use of different levels of language, of different socio-linguistic layers of speech.

These tantalizing propositions are briefly sketched at the end of 'Or Art (Poésie) total du cri au chant au' and elaborated in greater detail in 'Le Stéréo-poème-audio-visuel.'[171] Two adjectives which recur in the latter article – *total* and *global* – both illustrate, not only his vision of the work of art, but also the basic aesthetic premises of most concrete shows produced in Quebec during the 1966–80 period. The fusion of all modes of sensory perception as well as the necessity to allow for a wide range of interpretations were recurring landmarks of the times: 'Une oeuvre totale doit comporter une configuration de stimuli et placer le récepteur dans un champ de possibilités interprétatives.'[172] In writing this Duguay provided other Québécois with a solid theoretical ground for staging multi-media shows.[173] He also challenged an important concretist assumption; namely, that a concrete poem relies on one, or at the most, three modes of sensory perception. Instead he proposed that all five senses should be included to produce a multi-dimensional work.

Another important concept touched on by Duguay, and certainly essential to any discussion about experimental literature, is one he called 'transgression' or the rejection of grammatical and spelling rules. Many concretists were tempted by rejections of old codes (generic/syntactic, etc.), but few defined their specific implications.[174] Duguay did not operate in a substantially different way. The humour of the title of his article 'La Transe et la Gression' does not compensate for the basic lack of development of the notions discussed in the article itself. The central concept is thus circumscribed:

TRANSGRESSER

... c'est désobéir aux lois de l'écriture mais en transmettant un nouveau code de langage.[175]

But what mutations does Duguay propose to introduce? What elements are going to undergo a rhythmic, syntactical, or spelling change? What are the immediate effects of such transgressions? Unfortunately he leaves the concept at the general level of 'dépassement' or 'la faculté de sauter des lignes, des frontières verbales,'[176] instead of looking at the practical effects of improvisations, inversions, and permutations. Similarly, in various interviews, when asked why he had abandoned linear writing and what he would replace it with, he would mention the three devices indicated above but would refuse to elaborate any further.[177] Thus the task of exploring the linguistic, political, and sexual impact of transgression fell upon the poets of the next decade (Nicole Brossard, Madeleine Gagnon, François Charron, Claude Beausoleil).

Duguay's most comprehensive statement was *Le Manifeste de l'infonie*. In spite of its title, it was not a manifesto in the conventional sense of the word, but a book of poems where each text becomes the enactment of a specific musical structure. Its projected aim was the achievement of a symbiosis between music and poetry, semantics and cry, meaning and elemental sound. Some of its author's principles about phonology, phonetics, and sound follow a strict concretist tradition – the return to the smallest possible unit, the phoneme, as a necessary step for the poet-composer: 'L'écriture poétique doit s'alchimier, la langage étant morcelé jusqu'au monosyllabe, jusqu'aux sons précisément frottés et vibrés que sont F-V-S-Z-W-L-CH-J-R-Y, consonnes fricatives et vélaires ventileuses de souffle continu.'[178]

Part of that period's idealization of science (and of its so-called saving powers and objectivity) can be retraced here in Duguay's insistence that the poetic text is none other than a mathematical construction, the resolution of a series of operations structured into time schemes:

```
i a u e o
a u e o i
u e o i a
e o i a u
o i a u e
```

Les 5 voyelles correspondant aux 5 voix, ce schéma représente une durée de 15 secondes qui peuvent être remplies par 15 sons (12 de la série et 3 aléatoires), par chaque voix qui chante pendant ces 15 secondes. Pour en comprendre la complexité, multipliez les possibilitées de composition autant de fois qu'il y a de lignes verticales horizontales et transversales et vous obtiendrez les sons possibles en une seconde, c'est à dire 15 fois 5 fois le chiffre obtenu par seconde.[179]

Judging from the text itself and more particularly from its layout, it seems that Duguay, like Chopin in France, or bissett and Nichol in Canada, was interested in breaking sentences, taking them apart and reassembling them. *Le Manifeste de l'infonie* provides us with specific examples of this concrete technique referred to as '24 phrases percutées.'[180] Commenting on this experiment and its effect upon each sentence, each syntactical unit, he writes: 'Segmentées, désarticulées, démontées, elles sont difficilement audibles à travers l'enregistrement, mais elles sont là et chacune de leurs particules est catapultée de tous bords tous côtés. La désintégration du langage est accomplie.'[181]

The careful reader quickly decodes Duguay's main writing techniques. The first is the breaking down of sentences and words into atomized units. The second is his use of simultaneity – words or phonemes being projected at the same time, by different voices, from different places. The third is the search for a notation system, a score – words being placed on bars with annotations which indicate measure, tonality, and length. In effect, the poem becomes a musical score, the notes being either words or phonemes. The fourth is the need for a visual presentation, one which, however, has little to do with visual concrete principles. Most of his poems present a typography similar to that of old illuminated texts. Graphic designs form the background, words the foreground. Some are pure pattern poetry, very similar to seventeenth-century pattern poems or to Apollinaire's calligrammes, shaped in the form of a cross. Few could be defined as visual concrete.

On the whole, Duguay's contribution to international concrete theory is his exploration in the areas of sound, phonetics, and phonology. One interview with Nichol, three years after the publication of *Le Manifeste de l'infonie*, is a case in point. Nichol's questions (which reveal more about Nichol than about Duguay) revolve around the value of alphabetic characters and the realignment of traditional spelling and syntax. Duguay evaded most of them and concentrated instead upon the importance of vowels and consonants, the effect of different combinations, and the impact of phonemes upon the human ear. While Nichol focuses all his attention on concrete *visual* theory, Duguay centred his on concrete *sound* theory.[182]

All of Duguay's statements are consistent, both in approach and in focus. As a theoretician he changed remarkably little between 1967 and the end of the next decade. His commitment to sound, to the human voice, underlies his whole career as a composer-performer: 'For myself I essentially explore sound areas. I research the human voice. The voice is my first instrument.'[183] His basic disagreement with European sound theoreticians in the area of semantics never changed with time. In 1967 he stated that one should assign 'une intentionalité à l'émotion' and open 'la voix de l'âme par la voix du corps.'[184] In 1975 he reiterated this stand and when asked whether he would consider discarding referentiality replied, 'I want to be ideological, I have ideas.'[185] In 1978, when confronted with the many changes which altered his contemporaries' perceptions of language, he stated: 'Je ne crois pas à la force matérielle des mots, je crois à leur force psychique ... les mots pour les mots ne valent rien. Les mots insufflés d'esprit contiennent une charge d'énergie.'[186] One could hardly find a more explicit rejection of the materialistic premises so central to concretism. But Duguay was far from being representative of Quebec textual developments after 1970. One might even perceive his position, looking at the subsequent wave of formalist and Marxist-derived movements of the early 1970s, as one of increasing marginality.

Yet his position, like that of Paul Chamberland, is more than a niche cut in the ephemeral facade of the Quebec counter-culture. If one looks briefly at Paul Chamberland's textual experiments, in the period which starts with *Eclats* and continues throughout the decade (particularly at statements such as *Terre souveraine*, published during the Quebec referendum campaign), the general theoretical context of Chamberland's thought becomes explicit. The lesson of non-power, of non-domination, enunciated in his writings spanning these eleven years, is abundantly evident. The 'anthrope,' the community, a collectivity in a state of communication,[187] is the bedrock of Chamberland's utopian vision. Such a bedrock was a reality easily communicable in the particularly exuberant years of the counter-culture. In the subsequent decade it did not enter into the mainstream discourse. Like Duguay's it became a marginal reality, respected because it came from a well-known writer but nonetheless kept at a distance, deterritorialized in a sense.

Act II: De la modernité au post-modernisme

Donc revenir au texte.

Y revenir mais ne point se méprendre sur sa conjoncture. Car ce qui peut être dit de la femme qui écrit et de son écriture agit forcément dans le sens de la multiplication des vides, des creux. Nous entrons par l'écriture dans un terrain vaste et vague où le tout luit et se reflète.

Nicole Brossard, 'e muet mutant,' in Double impression: poèmes et textes 1967–1984, 58

Ecrire, pour retrouver l'objet, tous les objets, des plus visibles aux plus cachés, objets réels, objets rêvés, écrire pour trouver l'adéquation entre mots et objets, les concomitances, les opalescences, écrire pour trouver la distance aussi, l'inadéquation du mot à l'objet, leurs liens contingents, leurs rencontres basardeuses, leurs noces accidentelles. L'écriture serait peut-être cette approximation (proximité dans l'à peu près) de l'aléatoire, cette diction de tous les accidents de parcours de la chose à l'objet et aux mots.

Madeleine Gagnon, Préface, Autographie I: fictions, 9

Par rapport à cette image du Père, à cette dictée de lois et d'interdictions, nous avançons l'hypothèse que l'expérience littéraire ne peut se vivre, dans ses manifestations les plus novatrices, les plus radicales, qu'en refusant et émiettant le roc de la régulation sociale, roc qui cerne et enferme les sujets au sein des familles, des groupes, des idéologies. Autrement dit, la littérature n'a pu et ne peut surgir dans sa dissymetrie dépaysante qu'à la condition de risquer la perte insoutenable du sens et de la face paternelle, qu'à la condition de maintenir cette tension constante entre sens et non-sens. C'est ainsi qu'une déraison et une jouissance questionnent les multiples directions que prend l'existence de chacun et de tous.

François Charron. La Passion d'autonomie, 19

Au moindre petit choc, la bande palimpseste vie-texte, ultra-sensible, se remet en marche. Il peut suffire que je me trouve dans le métro Champ-de-Mars un mardi jour de la guerre et peur d'être en retard pour être déportée. Jusqu'à gamma de la Grande Ourse par exemple ... Maintenant, quand je tombe sur un feu rouge, au lieu de tomber au point mort, je le regarde en pleine face et la couleur s'efface. Apparaissent alors les taches noires qui me laissent passer.

Dans un tel silence, on voit les ponts. C'est de nouveau relié: on sait que lire, c'est lier. On lit mieux encore: on voit que le pont est une trame de cordons infernaux. On voit la chaîne aussi. On peut choisir de sauter, sauter, toujours plus haut, sur le pont, pour le défoncer.

Et quand ça défonce, on rit *zen*, on rit comme avant d'avoir oublié ce qu'est le rire. On tombe dans un autre étage du réel. On tourne, derviche tourneur, dans un autre monde.

Yolande Villemaire, *Adrénaline*, 92–3

La pensée se fait dans la bouche.

Tristan Tzara

There was a surge of collective efforts – starting with *La Barre du Jour* in 1965, continuing with *Les Herbes Rouges* in 1968, but really gaining momentum in the post-1970 period –which attacked a certain ideology of the text: namely writers' trust in the semantic ballast of the sentence. Clearly it was not Duguay only who was attacked,[188] but a whole conception of literature. This radical rejection of the referentiality of the text found its first collective formulation and media exposure through 'Les Dix Propositions,' a manifesto published in the Saturday edition of Montreal's big daily *La Presse*. As a polemical statement – 'nous refusons ... nous accusons ... marquons notre désaccord le plus formel'[189] – the ten propositions were a key document because they interpreted the theoretical assumptions underlying the writings of *La Barre du Jour* between the mid-1960s and 1975. As France Théoret put it, ten years later, this manifesto intended to fill up a theoretical gap and to explicate a certain practice of the literary text.[190] The categories which the group denounced were numerous. Let me mention four main ones. The first was that of poetry as the expression of a social, personal, and perceptual reality: 'rite par la parole signifiante prétend coincider avec la parole signifiée.'[191] The second was the subjectivity of the author, to be destroyed at all costs. The third was the rapport author-reader. The fourth, the function and nature of the text, which must cease to be the expression of the author's truth and personal world and become impersonal by modelling itself on scientific experiments: 'La poésie est science, déconstruction des évidences mortes ... celle du coeur, de l'âme, de la patrie et de l'homme.' And later: 'poésie critique ... révolutionnaire ... travail impersonnel comme tout procès de production.'[192]

The decade which followed this statement developed, expanded upon, but also rejected parts of these initial propositions. Indeed the trajectory between this first landmark and the 1980 colloquium on new writing (= *la nouvelle écriture*) reveals many deviations and significant departures from the course projected by the 1970 propositions.

In order to trace these ten years of theory one needs to look at specific texts. *La Barre du Jour*, which in 1977 became *La Nouvelle Barre du Jour*, provides us with the best documentation on the switch from formalist/structuralist theories to feminist texts. Let us examine a few illustrative texts. In 1968 Claude Bertrand posed the problem of representation, that of the world through and via the text.[193] In his terms the concept of rupture, or fissure, announces the crumbling down of symbolist thought and the closure of meaning. Three years later François Charron and Roger des Roches dealt with the same issue in slightly different terms: they *rejected* the text as a representation, as a reflection of the material world, and urged readers to refute the idealism of the creative act as a pure myth:

> Ce qu'on nous transmet en réalité ne sont que les figurations motrices d'une idéologie dominante: justement ce pauvre reflet des choses, cette photographie qui n'explique en rien le processus des données concrètes du monde ... on nous a subtilement imposé la poésie comme un acte essentiellement idéaliste. On a donné l'illusion au poète, en tant que 'sujet conscient' du pouvoir, par ses idées personnelles, avoir une action déterminante sur le réel extérieur (la matière). On a désiré entretenir le mythe d'une vérité que chaque individu possède en propre, vérité du poème devenu fétiche.
> ...
> Donc une nouvelle écriture (écriture matérialiste ... va dénoncer cette idéologie du texte-miroir ... accorder la primauté à la matérialité des mots (production du signifiant).[194]

The mid-1970s must be referred to as a turning point, not only at *La Barre du Jour*, but also on the intellectual terrain of Quebec's women writers. The year 1974 was to mark the publication in France of *La Venue à l'écriture*, by Annie Leclerc, Hélène Cixous, and Madeleine Gagnon, and 1977, that of Nicole Brossard's *L'Amèr*. Such texts, and others, announced a radical change in the area of theory and put forward a new vision, not only of language this time but specifically and purportedly of the culture and civilization language was inevitably bound to. The arid protectionism of the 1970 'Dix Propositions' gave way from then on. Language was perceived as an intrinsic part of social constructs, of sexual constraints, of the physical as well as political texture of the writer's and her readers' existence.

It would be deeply misleading to suggest that the feminist texts published in Quebec during the mid-1970s provided a unified or even partly homogeneous vision. But what is peculiarly striking about the two texts mentioned above and others (*Retailles*, by Denise Boucher and Madeleine Gagnon, 'Le Cortex exubérant,' by Nicole Brossard, published in book form in 1978 as *Le Centre blanc*, and *Autographie I*, by Madeleine Gagnon) is their need to rethink history as well as the place women occupy in that history. All address that need and confer upon the text a responsibility which is much different from that perceived in 1970 by the signatories of the ten propositions. For instance, Madeleine Gagnon and Denise Boucher write: 'L'écriture, contrairement au reportage supposément fidèle à la réalité nous conduit à tout autre fidélité; celle de nos vérités respectives, les seules pouvant accéder à la vérité d'une histoire dont nous manqueront toujours celles qui ne furent pas dites.'[195]

To facilitate access to a history they have been excluded from means therefore for writers to inscribe all the simple, quotidian, humble references which have been thrown into the garbage bins of history. For instance, in *Retailles*, Xantippe, Socrates' wife, is evoked along with an imagined worn-out little notebook which she might have carried with her through the Agora and which will never be recovered (see *Retailles*, cover page). What is left for the authors to do? To imagine what she might have scribbled and to pray that other women do not despise the frail, personal, quotidian components of their lives, nor feel devoured by tasks which seem to go nowhere and produce nothing. Madeleine Gagnon's focusing on this self-consuming process is particularly intense: 'A force de produire du travail invisible, à force de fabriquer des choses qui n'ont pas l'air de produits, j'ai l'impression ... de grignoter indéfiniment et invariablement des parcelles de vie qui se consument et se dévorent d'elles mêmes.'[196]

Retailles' very construction is a testimony to that concern. As a text written by two very different writers, it functions as a patchwork which brings side by side as well as sewn together the little fragments of two women's lives, their political complaints, as the subtitle puts it, and also the rich subterranean ground of their fears, dreams, nightmares, and daylight terrors. They raised many questions both in the form they chose (a non-sequential, non-continuous, and openly hazardous wandering into their own private lives and others') and in their style (Boucher often uses popular idioms and joual inflexions, while Gagnon moves from intense political overtones – 'Nous avons trahi dites vous la révolution' – to the idiosyncratic speech patterns of a frightened hospital patient – 'vous le recouserez [sic] mon ventre, docteur, est-ce possible').[197] Some of these questions are theoretical, others infinitely more practical. To name the first – since this section is primarily concerned with such problems – the issues Boucher and Gagnon brought to our attention had to do with the relevancy and the responsibility of textual constructs to women's lives.

Texts could be looked upon as therapeutic confessions, as practical devices, or as historical documents, but their common denominator was certainly a focus on the signified. Such a concern was in contrast with what had taken place during the late 1960s and early 1970s, and it ushered in a perception of the existential and political responsibility of textual activitity which *Les Herbes Rouges* writers were going to pursue throughout the 1970s.[198]

But Nicole Brossard's *L'Amèr* signalled a different direction in feminist theory. While certainly addressing the issue of a history never reconstituted by women, as well as a history that never seriously took them into consideration, it also situated the feminist problematic from a lesbian viewpoint. In doing so it reoriented several initial premises (about the function of motherhood/reproduction, about a woman's relationship to other women, about men as individuals and as institutions, that is, patriarchy). It was not so much a question for Brossard of retrieving a lost history (compare Xantippe as evoked by Gagnon/Boucher) as necessarily putting an end to the perception which a collectivity had had of its own history until then. The references to an end – 'mettant ainsi fin à l'Histoire'[199] or 'Histoire. Elle ne peut que la faire éclater' (23) – bring to the fore the notion that a clause, a first and essential clause, needs to be modified. Such a clause is the instrument of re-production, woman's key instrument, her only tool ('son seul outil' [25]). In the meantime, as long as the writer operates within history, all she can do is to modify, disturb, the symbolic field ('troubler le champ symbolique' [25]). How does a lesbian viewpoint transform so totally the writer's perspective vis-à-vis the world? The whole section of *L'Amèr* which is titled 'l'état de la différence' deals with this issue, with the ideological deadweight of the argument of difference, of its enormous impact on all relationships (from the exoticism of difference to its biological rhetoric, reproduction thus determining power relationships between men and women). To abolish a difference which men have chosen to accentuate thus becomes not only a temptation but also a way to free the imaginary, the symbolic, field, to rewrite fiction, to rewrite woman, 'the mutilated little girl who resists woman' (79, translation mine).

The relationship to history, to the remaking of history, is more complex here than in *Retailles*. On the one hand there is a definite 'separatist' pulsion in *L'Amèr*, the desire to opt out, walk out, tune out. On the other, the imaginary or the symbolic field, the fictional, is described as the locus which can preserve the best of the human species' code ('Que l'imaginaire constitue un lieu où se préserve à son meilleur le code de l'espèce' [92]). In more than one way such statements are paradoxical. Is 'preservation' a goal women should strive for? Are imaginary constructs sufficiently powerful to modify the said species? Or are they mere preservative devices? The very last sentence of the book would definitely favour the first option: 'je veux en effet voir s'organiser la forme des femmes dans la trajectoire de l'espèce' (99). But Brossard remains, by choice, on a terrain which is far more theoretical than Boucher's or Gagnon's, especially the Gagnon of *Autographie* and *Poélitique*, texts which envision a global change not only on a symbolic level but also in the everyday political fabric of women's lives. But such choices are not purely accidental. Gagnon was very much bound to the generation of *Les Herbes Rouges* writers, and the reader who moves from the feminist discourse of *La Barre du Jour* in the 1970s to that of the young Marxologists of *Les Herbes Rouges* encounters significantly different ontological perceptions.

Among the latter the free signifier is still celebrated, the transgression of grammatical/syntactical rules is still an essential part of new writing's processes, but the concerns have become markedly political, enriched with strong Marxist references. Reference points here are less to Roland Barthes or Julia Kristeva (as they had been in *La Barre du Jour*) than to Marx, Mao Tse Tung, Lenin, Althusser, and Mayakovsky.[200] It is not, as François Charron explained in 1981, that *Les Herbes Rouges* writers wished to reject the concepts of pleasure and production, of textual structure experienced as libido, but rather that they wished to both take advantage of them and distance themselves from them.[201] With Gagnon and Charron poetics and politics in the early and mid-1970s are fused in a totalizing impulse: the poem manifesto.

But it is important to stress that at this point transparency and mimetic modes had long been banished. And this is perhaps where *La Barre du Jour* and *Les Herbes Rouges* show substantial complicities. The absolutism of meaning (meaning as a clear, tangible, monodimensional entity) is not to be retrieved – we are not dealing here with a subtle nostalgia for socio-realism. As Normand de Bellefeuille, another *Herbes Rouges* author, reminds us, referentiality, clarity, and indubitable meanings must be bypassed. We are thus warned against: 'l'intention lisible,'[202] 'le pari du lisible,'[203] and 'le caca et le lisible.'[204] All of these are depicted as alternatively theological or opportunistically populist, but always crudely expedient.[205]

Les Herbes Rouges writers were equally mistrustful of Quebec's literary ecclesiastical tradition[206] and of its nationalistic proclivities (la terre, le patrimoine, la femme –all favourite themes of the 1960s). To de Bellefeuille and Charron, to be a radical writer (read one who upholds progressive and/or leftist values) within a readable text is *not* political. Radical politics are the deconstruction of a certain power-structure. In order to be a practitioner of *la nouvelle écriture,* one must participate in the destruction of the old order, the order of meaning, theology's last refuge.[207] Their tools are: 'l'illogique, le polyvalent, le contradictoire.'[208] Their method: 'la réorganisation des déchets et des restes, le recyclage.'[209] Their goal: 'une écriture fulgurante, fugitive, indéchiffrable, en croissance, déplacement dans le quotidien';[210] as well as 'un objet textuel [qui] se matérialise inscrit les préoccupations de son inscription.'[211] The obstacle is the reader's sense of security and self-confidence, which must be challenged at all costs so that he/she is placed in front of a text which is 'insécurisant, écrit du côté du risque.'[212] As Charron puts it: 'Ecrire un texte parfaitement clair, c'est se taire.'[213]

Indeed, at this point the writers of *Les Herbes Rouges* cross paths with *La Nouvelle Barre du Jour*'s and *Cul Q*'s writers, though the freedom of the signifier is celebrated in different terms and proceeds from different motivations. It is enlightening to bring side by side Paul-Marie Lapointe's perceptions on this issue –

> Ecrire dans l'écriture. Sans autre référent au monde que les mots. Les mots mêmes. Dégagés de leurs gangues, de leurs usages imposés, de leurs significations connues ... de leur rôle de serviteurs de la pensée

... L'écriture refuse. Le poème ne parle plus cette langue là. Le poème ne
veut plus rien dire. Le poème dé-parle. Parle seul.[214]

– and François Charron's views on *la nouvelle écriture* as a freeing
process from the old theology of meaning, from an absolute monothe-
ism (one God – one meaning). His celebration is both an assertion of
the powers of matter –'Il y a le signifiant incompréhensible ... il y a
l'incommunicable beauté de la matière qui chante et qui pense' – as
well as a plea for a non-theological perception of writing: 'La nouvelle
écriture désamorce le rapport où le fils se croit engendré par le Père.'[215]

While for Nichol the Logos was a lost kingdom he felt forever bonded
to, for Charron the loss of meaning – 'la destructuration du reflet
spéculaire'[216] – was a splendid discovery, one for which he would
never shed tears because it aroused delight, surprise, relief, jubila-
tion.[217] Hieroglyph-drawing, writing, and painting stood there as a
reaffirmation of this freshly discovered freedom: 'Vous êtes en train de
vous réveiller dans la grande nuit patriarcale et monothéiste ... vous
vous mettez à barbouiller, à griffonner, à danser, à fredonner.'[218]

What was referred to as theology, the absolutism of meaning, was
the target which the Québécois wanted to hit and destroy at all costs.
Normand de Bellefeuille stressed the same point with a passion which
borders on obssession. His 'intention lisible,' 'pari du lisible,' and 'caca
et le lisible' were depicted as traps with a conviction which is not
without parallels in other North American texts of the same period.[219]

The shades/switches/nuances from the materiality/productivity/
scientificity of the text (the ten propositions), to textual-libido and
later feminism (*La Barre du Jour*), to feminism and political transgression (*Les Herbes Rouges*) were never linear. Intersections and inter-
connections were frequent and numerous. While such writers never
converge towards unified centre points, they all share certain perceptions. In their view the text ceases to be a consumable object and
becomes an incentive: it incites *us* to displace the old production
structure from author to text to reader. In fact the dynamics depicted
here are similar to those described by the TRG: reading = writing =
a/any/production/deconstruction process. As Paul Chamberland puts
it: 'Toulmonde est écrivain, Toulmonde parle'[220]; 'La lecture n'est plus
représentation, elle est mouvement'; and 'Ce qui compte ce n'est pas le
produit en tant que tel, c'est le processus.'[221]

While in the 1980s writing theories in Quebec increasingly moved
towards deconstructionism, towards texts (whether critical, poetic, or
fictive) viewed as a dissemination process, it is important to note that

such pulsions had originated some ten years previously with Chamberland's Fabrike d'Ekriture in the blossoming of the counter-culture. Such theories of writing viewed texts as a series of grafts collaged alongside, over, and beneath one another. Interestingly the Fabrike had happened as a collective experience, with far-reaching social ramifications. Individuals who never before had been interested in writing came to his Fabrike. The principles underlying this process are what are at issue here, and basically they were a de-conditioning of the writing experience and one which *de-theorized* writing. Poetry was thus moved onto an experiential, pragmatic field away from the power-structures of knowledge,[222] skill, and competence and open to the social strata which had been most excluded from it (children, minorities, marginalized individuals).

The use of discarded materials, recycled refuse, was very much part of the skills thus put forward by Chamberland. The 'arte povera' movement in Italy had theorized and practised such choices. Another method that was often commented upon was the utilization of newspaper cuttings in a manner comparable to bissett's approach, except that here it took on collective features and a more distinctly articulated intention. The concept of intertextuality, of history itself as part of this body of texts, is very much at the core of deconstructive thinking in Quebec. Chamberland himself explicated these choices by describing how the juxtaposition of two newspaper cut-outs (one reporting the tortures inflicted upon a Chilean priest during the Pinochet regime, the other a description of the alchemist's obscure toilings, of the black matter, and of the gold emerging out of it) produced what he called the 'contagion effect' – one tortured body thus becoming a metaphor for 'l'oeuvre au noir.'[223] This notion of the Great Text, of the vast text, was indubitably present among dadaists, but nowhere, not even with William Burroughs in the late 1950s, did collages take on this prophetic tone. Chamberland referred to himself as a 'generator-relay for a utopian community.'[224] By destroying old associative processes, 'neurological imprints,' he proposed an opening to new potentialities. He perceived the need to move from paranoia (a condition abundantly illustrated by Burrough's collages) to 'metanoia' – a mental state which would reverse the old conditioning and heal, as well as create, along imaginative modes remote from the old fossilized ones. (Interestingly enough, given his previous *Parti Pris* involvements, Chamberland put Marxism in the latter category.) Such positions and choices are abundantly explicated in *Le Recommencement du monde: méditations sur le processus apocalyptique*. The sense of an end of civilization, of the degradation of the planet, and of the desperate need to move towards a possible utopia are explicitly present in this text:

> Par rapport à ce qui n'est plus que du vide, je fais le vide. J'évalue froidement l'étendue des ruines. Je pars. Je n'aurai pas un regard en arrière. Entre ce qui bientôt ne sera plus et ce qui n'est pas encore, en ce cruel hiatus d'à-présent, je veux un partage net. J'apprends à trancher. Au plus dense de la nuit, j'affûte le couperet de l'aube.
>
> J'ai gagné la lisière du désert grandissant. Je suis un étranger. Mon visage s'imprègne de couleurs inconnues, des lueurs du temps d'*après*. Je peux me dire saisi et possédé par la vision. Je sais comment je renaîtrai *là-bas*, et accueilli par quels peuples, associé à quel recommencement du monde.[225]

From the times of La Fabrike d'Ekriture, when he was positing fiction as a potentially therapeutic activity, to those of *Le Recommencement du monde*, Chamberland has shown writing theories much akin to bpNichol's and Steve McCaffery's. The merging of the personal self and of the collective body was a specific concern of the early 1970s and one that played a major role in the experimentalism throughout the decade both in Canada and Quebec. Three magazines brought forward most of the theorizing about dissemination / deconstruction / and therapeutic metanoia: *Hobo-Québec*, *Main Mise*, and *Cul Q*. But the conclusive synthesis of the decade is to be found in *La Nouvelle Barre du Jour*'s colloquium on new writing in May 1980.

What are the common assumptions that one derives from these twenty years of contradictory theorizing? A number of indications emerge. Gone is any secureness about/with/in front of texts; gone also self-evident convictions, clear meanings. The new theoreticians want texts to drift, to whirl around in circles, to deprive us of oxygen: 'suggérer à la fois l'excès, le cercle et le vide'; 'tourner en rond par un glissement de sens allant de l'excès au délire, du cercle à la spirale et du vide à l'ouverture.'[226] They constitute a libidinal territory: 'écriture lit de procuration érotique'; 'd'où l'écriture donc le lit'; 'écriture extension de la libido'; 'd'où l'écriture comme activité masturbatoire'; 'd'où la lecture comme temps analogue de l'acte sexuel: ça va, ça vient, on entre, on sort: le désir circule, la jouissance remplit'; 'd'où la lecture copie conforme à l'acte sexuel.'[227]

This sexual dimension is more diffuse in Canadian concrete and post-modern texts. bissett, for instance, certainly used the libido as a creative concept[228] but never strived to develop it into a reading/writing theory.[229] Daphne Marlatt elaborated textual strategies which emphasized both her feminity and her libidinal choices as a woman and a writer. *Touch to My Tongue* (1984) specifically examined language's links with the writer's body, her physicality. Similarly Lola Lemire Tostevin, with *Color of Her Speech* (1982) and *Gynotext* (1983), brought the experience of writing into a clearly libidinal territory. But such a grounding of texts, while significant, was not in Canada the overwhelming expression of a collective will as it had been in Quebec during the previous decade. While the single most striking phenomenon of the 1970s in Quebec had been the feminist orientation of such post-modern texts, it would be inaccurate to put forward a similar judgment about Canada. There were individuals who made a number of moves in that direction, but no concerted collective will emerged that was intent on manifesting the politics of the text from a woman's or a lesbian's viewpoint. In contrast, the orientation of feminist texts in Quebec signalled a linguistic drifting from patriarchal strategies,[230] the rejection of an old code to the benefit of new ones, of different semiotics. Such choices were inextricably tied to a different perception of the politics of the text,[231] to a revolutionary intent which was dissimilar from the old nationalist and radical dream of the 1960s. Post-modernism pointed to a feminist reinterpretation of creativity, of writing, and imaginary constructs: 'les femmes renouvellent l'idée même de révolution'; 'nouvelle écriture, ouverture à la différance ... non-solidaire de causalités à sens unique.'[232]

Male writers also participated in this process. Writing in the feminine mode was a practice which the male writers of both *La Nouvelle Barre du Jour* and *Les Herbes Rouges* very easily wove themselves into. Theirs was also, though not totally, a response to a repressed libidinal urge, in this case the restoring of a feminine repressed libido.

The pluralism which had been the hallmark of concretism in its incipient beginnings (mid-1960s) was prolonged by the *nouvelle écriture's* multi-dimensional theorizing. The uniqueness of these texts, their pragmatic originality, stems from the fact that as early as about the mid-1970s they diffracted away from the visual/isomorphic core of concerns so dear to their Canadian counterparts, burst out of the boundary line so obsessively covered by the TRG (sound/sense, signifier/ied, semantic cipher), and in the post-modern era collectively confronted sexual and political issues.

The other major difference pivots around the nexus of metaphysics so central to Canadian theory, so inherently tied to the Great Spirit (with bissett), with the Father Logos (with Nichol). Neither native Indian cults nor animism entered the Québécois' ontology. While Duguay and Chamberland distanced themselves from their contemporaries' theoretical allegiances,[233] on the whole it could be said that in the post-modern era *Les Herbes Rouges'* indebtedness to Marxist materialism was an important component of its writers' conceptual trajectory. In the same light the feminist perspective of *La Nouvelle Barre du Jour's* writers, that of Nicole Brossard most notably, was a secular one. If there was a dividing line between the two cultures, it lay there. And while there may have been some timidly rebellious signals against the authority of such secular perspectives[234] there was no clear collective determination to challenge them.

THREE DECADES OF EXPERIMENTS: A BRIEF LITERARY HISTORY (CANADA/QUEBEC)

Canada

> ... when I started doing this stuff [concrete] like there was *nobody*, and I mean but *nobody* who was doing it. I really felt sort of crazy; why was I doing it? ... From 1965–67 it was really vital that I have that European–South American connection because it was really the only place from which I got feedback input that propelled me on.

> 'Interview with bpNichol,' *Essays on Canadian Writing*, no. 12 (Fall 1978), 250

> ... that twentieth century writing has gone through an unacknowledged present; that is, there is a whole tradition which we can call the avant-garde tradition, for lack of a better word, which is Stein, which is Dada, which is the Russian futurists like Klebnikov and so on ... There's a whole tradition that went through, which up until very recently, up until the last five or six years, was literally undocumented. I mean the stuff existed, but in private libraries all over the place; it was not accessible. Therefore, we were operating much like amnesiacs would. That is to say, we were operating out of a necessity to first of all regurgitate the history of twentieth century writing in order to get beyond it.

> 'Interview/bpNichol,' *Capilano Review*, nos. 8–9 (Fall 1975–Spring 1976), 333

The Visual Sixties

The Canadian concrete phenomenon differs from the international one in that it was not a reality here before 1963. October 1963 marks the publication of the first Canadian magazine, *Blew Ointment*, to include such texts, mostly collages and graphs, the whole edited by bill bissett, Gerry Gilbert, and John Newlove. The latter two were to drop out of the venture altogether, and bissett was to singlehandedly manage the fortunes of *Blew Ointment* as well as those of the press which bore the same name. The fact that this was taking place on the West Coast was not purely accidental. The Tish group, which gravitated about Robert Creeley and Warren Tallman at the University of British Columbia, had already started a magazine of its own in the early 1960s. There seems to be some evidence that the three Vancouver poets who went off to produce *Blew Ointment* had expressed reluctance to work with a group in which they perceived 'the academy in new fangled garb,' as Roger Seamon was later to put it.[235]

But the presence of the Tish group on the edges of nascent Canadian concretism was not irrelevant. There were a number of issues raised by this American-Canadian community which were to find deep echoes among concretists. Tish had grown out of the Imagist and Black Mountain tradition. The presence of William Carlos Williams, Ezra Pound, Robert Creeley, and Charles Olson always loomed large over its developments.[236] Two specific preoccupations were to be carried on by bill bissett and bpNichol. The first was the whole question of the vocality or orality of the poem. Charles Olson had defined the poem as auditive energy, vocal energy. His insistence upon breath, mouth, and lungs was significant. Furthermore, in Olson's view, meaning and breath were inseparable, and meaning could only emerge out of adequate breathing rhythms: 'Each line is a progression of both the meaning and the breathing forward ... a projective poet will go to that place where breath came from, where meaning came from.'[237] Indeed this concept of the poem as phonic energy, energy-gift, or 'energy-discharge,'[238] which became very much a part of the Tish editorial focus, had equally been on the forefront of the international concrete movement. When one reads an editorial statement by Jamie Reid in a 1964 issue of *Tish* magazine – '... a poem detones. It explodes and sets up a structure of tone. It is pure action. It lives in the verb, in the naked verb. A poem ... is the discharge of unretainable energy'[239] – one could as well be reading Pierre Garnier:

Le poème fut jusqu'alors le lieu d'internement des mots. Ne les rendez pas esclaves des phrases: quelle différence entre le tigre sur les rives vient boire et le mot seul: TIGRE! La phrase précise un tableau fade et rassurant: le mot déclenche tout le psychisme – il introduit l'orage ... Le mot lu n'effleure que le psychisme du lecteur, le mot perçu par contre, ou reçu, déclenche dans ce psychisme une chaîne de réactions.[240]

The other conceptual kinship between the Tish group and concretism had to do with space, with the poem as a figure of visual contact, and the need, felt as an imperative by the poet, to fuse into the poem's typography or visuality both its rhythm and duration. Lionel Kearns, one of the founders of the *Tish* magazine, went as far as to devise a system, 'stacked verse,' which was a method to transcribe into the poem the inflexions of each syllable as well as control the duration of the metrical line through means of graphic and temporal measure. Stacked-verse was intended to serve as a score, to indicate how the poem was to be read aloud by emphasizing all of its stresses. The stress present in the stack-foot was indicated by a vertical stack-axis along which the feet and lines of the poems were laid out. Not surprisingly it never satisfactorily worked for anyone but Kearns (and not very long even for him). But as an integrative effort of typographical and rhythmic components, it was symptomatic of the obsessions of concretists during the 1950s and 1960s. A rapid glance at back issues of *Tish* discloses clusters of coincidental concerns and recurring analyses. William Choy's preoccupation with the white space of the page and intervals between words – which he relates to the concept of Tao[241] – finds an echo in Nichol's analysis of the white areas between words, of the role of their phenomenological impulsions: 'areas of stress in which the brain strains to make the imaginative jump and fill in the gaps.'[242]

The Tish group, composed of George Bowering, Jamie Reid, Frank Davey, Lionel Kearns, and Warren Tallman, began to discuss aesthetic issues around the late 1950s. The Black Mountain school (and through it Imagism, Pound, and Williams)[243] as well Donald Allen's seminal anthology *The New American Poetry* have been viewed as having a monolithic influence upon the Tish group.[244] It would seem to me more accurate to suggest that what Tish inherited was a sense of place, of 'locus' as Olson would have put it, a sense of the crucial relations among themselves, their community, and their language. As Frank Davey articulated it, fifteen years later:

> It is the sense of *belonging* that is projected by *Tish* magazine ... that
> has been most incomprehensible ... to writers and critics in other prov-
> inces ... No one will ever fully understand *Tish* ... who does not
> understand this concept of community. This concept assumes that
> man must find his place in the cosmos, in the physical geography of
> his place, in the social fabric of his human settlement, in the rhythmic
> and syntactic patterns of his language ... The act of writing becomes
> a 'poetics of dwelling.'[245]

According to Warren Tallman the beginnings of Tish are to be dated
in February 1961, when Robert Duncan appeared at the Festival of
Contemporary Arts in Vancouver.[246] Later that spring George Bowering, David Dawson, Lionel Kearns, Jamie Reid, Frank Davey, and Fred
Wah formed a study group to discuss the works that Duncan had
introduced them to: Olson's *Maximus Poems*, Duncan's *The Opening
of the Field*, and works by Robert Creeley and Denise Levertov. The
gain – as stressed by Tallman – was not simply in the awareness of
individual authors, but in the awareness of American modernism.[247]
Finally in August 1961 and under Duncan's impulsion the magazine
Tish (phonemic inversion of the word s-h-i-t) came into being. More
than a periodical, it was designed to be a record of on-going activity
'that preserved every roughness, insight, and stupidity that this
activity enclosed.'[248]

The Tish group preceded Canadian concretists by less than half a
decade; more importantly, they unconsciously provided a conceptual
apparatus which the *Blew Ointment* and *Ganglia* poets were to use for
their own purposes. Cross-fertilization phenomena are to be expected
in any generation of poets.[249] The breaking point here between Frank
Davey and George Bowering, on the one hand, and bpNichol and bill
bissett, on the other, is more tantalizing to define than their common
concerns. It has to do with the need to push the demands made upon a
text; an extremism in two directions: rupturing semantic and phonological order as well as pressuring words into isomorphic functions.
The latter appears to have been the breaking edge here, the cut-off
point between Tish and concretism.

But George Bowering, who had refused to publish Nichol's poems in
Imago, put him in touch with the European underground of concrete:
Cavan McCarthy and Bob Cobbing in England, Ian Hamilton Finlay in
Scotland, and through them Pierre Garnier and Henri Chopin on the
Continent. Bob Cobbing was the first to publish Nichol's visual

poems, so that most of the cross-fertilization took place far away from
the West Coast, definitely outside Canada. What is more interesting,
in diachronic terms, was the gap, the vacuum, that had been left in the
area of Canadian avant-garde poetics in the 1920s, the undocumented
dadaist, futurist, and constructivist periods, the inaccessibilty of
them, an issue which Nichol almost obsessively goes back to over and
over.[250] His haphazard access to this level of experimentation was
through Fenollosa, Japanese haikus, chinese poetry, Kenneth Patchen
and his poem-drawings, Apollinaire, and dada. These tentative meanderings were conducted in Toronto and were wholly unconnected to
Tish.

In Vancouver bissett's initial impulse seems to have come from
painting and graphics, which were part of his training. From his early
graphic works he went on to character writing around 1961–2. As Ken
Norris reports, bissett was then living with a community of artists –
who included Martina Clinton and Lance Farrell – and the images he
was employing slowly merged into letters as he began writing visual
poems.[251] Bissett himself describes this process as a breakthrough, a
discovery of the poem as sound/picture breaking up words.[252] The link
with the international movement was a post-facto phenomenon for
bissett. His explorations were essentially pragmatic, empirical, diffuse, and explicit models from the tradition were never a reality for
him. The real bonds were with his own artistic community (among
whom one should also include Judith Copithorne), with Nichol in
Toronto, and D.A. Levy (an American expatriate from Ohio who died
in 1968). Nonetheless, the point which bissett does not make, but
which remains to be stressed, is that *Tish* opened up a number of
aesthetic possibilities, a new sense of notation (albeit in the range of a
recognizable printed text), thus making it feasible for bissett to view
the poem as an organic process, rather than a perfected text, an
opportunity for breaking through the restrictions of clearly defined
spelling rules, linear lay-outs, and syntactical correctness.

An examination of this first period, from the early 1960s to the later
part of the decade, shows bissett and Nichol as distant sailing
companions, peers with no teachers – or only remote and almost
metaphysical ones – who invested a vacant field, long left fallow.
Nichol's description of this vacuum has the vulnerable inflexions of a
process of intellectual and emotional loneliness. Stephen Scobie's
summary of this early part of concretism's literary history is extremely
accurate in this respect;[253] the origins of concretism in Canada sprung
from specific cultural needs very much defined by a geographical

locus, just as they had in Brazil with Pignatari,[254] and yet writers also reached out for previous and different experiments when they developed their own formal features.

There are two rich sources which are essential to an investigation of concretism in the 1960s: *Ganglia/Gronk* in Toronto, *Blew Ointment* in Vancouver. Both functioned as magazines and publishing houses. The key difference between them was that Nichol's *Ganglia/Gronk* was a wide-open window to what was happening in the rest of the world while *Blew Ointment* was West-centred (as a magazine) and self-centred (around bissett, as a publishing house). Yet both give us an invaluable reading as to what the cross-breeding grounds between Canadian concretists and the rest of the world actually were.

The 'Alphabet of Blood' by Pierre Coupey (published in *Delta* no. 19 in 1964) was said to have made a deep impression on Nichol. Both this poem and the first issues of bissett's *Blew Ointment* functioned as accidental founding texts for him. He read them while still in Vancouver on a brief vacation and when he returned to Toronto in 1965 he was motivated to start publishing his own concrete magazine. *Ganglia* was thus in 1965 the first timid founding of avant-garde poetics in the East. Its original impetus, according to Nichol, was to publish little-known West Coast writers who were receiving no attention back East (George Bowering, Judith Copithorne, and bill bissett). Later issues included British concretists Ian Hamilton Finlay and John Furnival, and the French theoretician Pierre Garnier. Hardly a magazine, one could more accurately call it a pamphlet or mimeo-sheet. It gave its name to Ganglia press, which put out limited editions of 'series,' so that the distinction between magazine and press productions was blurred from the outset. *Ganglia* became *Gronk* in 1967. The appearance of the latter coincides with a greater awareness on Nichol's part of the European experimental scene. *Gronk* was launched in lieu of the never-to-appear sixth issue of *Ganglia*. It was to have a sequence of sixty-four issues (see index in the sixty-third one), followed by an intermediate series of twenty-four issues, each of which was composed entirely of the works of a single author. From its beginnings *Gronk* was part of an international exchange. 'Manuscripts concerned with concrete sound/kinetic and related borderblur poetry welcome' is the prescriptive note to be found on the cover of *Gronk's* first issue, and as Ken Norris notes, the contents of *Gronk* were to immediately reflect such prescriptions. In this first issue one finds typewriter concrete focusing on word-atomizaton (by David Harris and Rob Smith), mixed-media creation by D.A. Levy (typewritten sections / handwritten ones, illustrative iconography), a computer piece by Pierre Garnier, a calligraphic text by bissett, and a concrete one by Nichol, who focuses on individual letters, random words, as well as non-language visual signs.

For all of its strong Canadian base *Gronk* retained its international vocation: issue no. 3 (March 1967) featured the work of D.A. Levy (u.s.a.), nos. 6–7 (June–July 1967), that of Hansjorg Mayer (Germany), Brown Miller (u.s.a.), and Jiri Valoch (Czechoslovakia). Later issues such as no. 8 of the fifth series featured French writer Julien Blaine, while the combined issue nos. 6–7 of the same series was an anthology of Czech concrete. One should nevertheless add that for all his editorial openness, Nichol was unexplainably closed to Québécois experiments during this period. While one *Gronk* series had a French issue called 'Regardez la révolution en marche,' no one at the time seems to have thought of giving some space to North American francophones.

An important aspect of *Gronk* was its publication of book-length collections by young Canadian experimental writers. Books by Nichol himself and John Riddell appeared as part of the second series; books by Gerry Gilbert, Nelson Ball, Nichol, and Riddell as part of the third series; books by David UU and Hart Broudy, Earle Birney's *Pnomes Jukollages and Other Stunzas* (Birney's first collection of visual work), and books by David Aylward, Judith Copithorne, Andrew Suknaski, and Stephen Scobie, as part of the fourth series; by Steve McCaffery, Aylward, and Martina Clinton, in the fifth series; by McCaffery in the sixth; David UU and Hart Broudy in the seventh; and by Nichol and bissett in the eighth. This provided first publication, or close to it, for many of these young writers and served as the only organized and available front for much experimental work of this kind.

The merits of *Gronk/Ganglia* were considerable. First of all they provided a sense of community for the avant-garde: a forum where events, readings, exhibitions, and listings were modestly and unassumingly offered in the small, uncapitalized letters of Nichol's mimeo-sheet newsletter. Obviously designed for a small circle of friends and fellow concretists, they nevertheless provided their readers with a unique source of information. Secondly, by devoting either entire or partial issues to developments in other parts of the world, they put Canadian experimenters in touch with what was going on in Germany, Czechoslovakia, Brazil, Japan, and France. The originality of such choices was that for the first time one could observe European and Canadian texts co-existing side by side. Cross-breeding it never was, probably because one was not really dealing here with exchanges between communities or individuals, but rather, through mimeo-sheets, with a spectrum of examples meant to exemplify what was being done the world over, as well as right here in Canada.

Blew Ointment fared quite differently under bissett's direction. Its first (deceptive) feature was to avoid giving a name to the experiments printed in it. No conceptual or systemic moves at work here, no effort to relate anything to the international movement or to more broadly defined issues (from linguistics to politics). Yet it is difficult not to see the overall effect as delusive because there was a common denominator at work, both from a linguistic and ideological viewpoint. But it was diffusely, pragmatically revealed, rather than conceptually articulated. There was a free-flowing spirit of anarchy streaming through these gestetnered, stapled sheets. The only visible non-Canadians were Americans (Barbara O'Connelly and D.A. Levy): as far as bissett was concerned, Czech, Brazilian, or French concretists might as well not have existed. The general diffuseness of his editorial preferences also meant an undifferentiated acceptance of both well-established lyric poetry (Al Purdy's, Raymond Souster's, Margaret Atwood's) and concrete and post-modern explorations (Nichol's, Steve McCaffery's, Earle Birney's, and bissett's own). *Blew Ointment* ushered in what Jean Baudrillard would call quite a few years afterwards 'the age of undetermination,'[255] the era of the New York subway graffiti, which were to strike Jean-François Lyotard as paradigms of a whole period, paradigms about powerlessness, about the preference of the obscure over clarity, of blanks over the written text, of lapsus over articulation, an approach which Lyotard was to call 'non-domination.'[256] Ken Norris referred to *Blew Ointment* as a paradoxical and eclectic undertaking endowed with a deeply 'deceptive undifferentiation,'[257] which is yet another way to point to the directionality outlined by both Baudrillard and Lyotard.

The Seventies and the Eighties: From Performances to Theory

What happened during the 1970s and 1980s was symptomatic of the trends which shaped avant-garde poetics in Canada. Nichol displaced his creative energies from the magazine to the performances of the Horsemen; and bissett moved along similar lines. The job of publishing concrete poems was taken over by other little magazines (particularly in the post-1972 period): *Prism*, *Tuatara*, and *Capilano Review* on the West Coast; *Vigilante*, *Elfin Plot*, and *Far Point* on the Prairies; *Ten*, *Connexions*, *Black Moss*, *Evidence*, *Alphabet*, *Quarry*, *Island*,

Is, Exile, Waves, and *Northern Journey* in Ontario; and *Antigonish* in the Maritimes. They all expressed interest in experimental layouts (see Bibliography, 354–9).[258]

The geographical location of these magazines reflects the reception of experimental literature in Canada. Until the late 1970s Toronto and Vancouver were the main creative centres, but this situation underwent notable changes from the mid-1970s into the 1980s, when there emerged both in the Prairies and in anglophone Montreal – heretofore notably silent – an interest in post-modern forms. In the Prairies such activities were distinctly bolstered by the establishment of small publishing houses and by Robert Kroetsch's explorations on both a theoretical and a poetic level. The presence of Douglas Barbour and Stephen Scobie also contributed to a growing awareness of the concept of performance in this particular region.[259] But if one had to make a global judgment on the nature and the impact of experimental publication in Canada during the 1960s, one would have to say that both *Blew Ointment* and *Gronk/Ganglia,* with their flaws and limitations but also their particular editorial and political choices, best reflect these times.

The first practised non-domination and undifferentiation at a time when it was, at least in Canada, most unfashionable to do so. The latter branched out towards European movements and a European experimentalism which was largely ignored both by the mainstream press and the well-established poets. What both publications lacked was a sense of their strategic place within a collectivity, an awareness of what they meant to a specific generation of readers and writers. Yet if one looks, a decade later, at a volume like *Montreal: English Poetry of the Seventies,* a book which echoes somewhat uncannily the experiences of bpNichol and bissett some ten years before, it is easy to see how the reflections of the 1960s were going to impact upon a younger generation in another place. The editors of *Montreal: English Poetry of the Seventies* make it clear that the anglophone culture they grew up in clung rigidly to the values of the past throughout the turbulent 1960s. As Andre Farkas and Ken Norris put it, much of what anglophone Montrealers wrote during those years was 'a pale imitation of Dudek, Layton, and Cohen.'[260]

Changes were slow to emerge, yet the presence of George Bowering as writer-in-residence at Sir George Williams University during 1968–71 also brought a series of readings to the campus which exposed the future Véhicule poets – then students at McGill and Sir George Williams – to the diverse experimentation taking place elsewhere in

Canada and the United States. 'The energies of the current movement were beginning to coalesce,'[261] particularly in the context of Quebec's political reality. With the heightened awareness of language as one of the most powerful historical tools, writers of the new generation were bound to recognize the potential volatility and, as they painfully recognized, 'misuse'[262] of the very language they were working with. The history of the Véhicule poets was one of instability and changes. Ken Norris best recaptured the spirit of this younger generation when he remarked:

> To borrow and modify a Layton metaphor, the English poet in Quebec dances on a tightrope strung between past and future, tradition and innovation, in both poetic and social senses. The present tense is that tightrope, and the dancing upon it is an experience that contains both apprehension and exhilaration. In his essay 'The Insecurity of Art,' Stephen Morrissey asserts that 'the very joy and freedom of art and life is the hidden presence of insecurity.' The English poet in Quebec writes his poetry, lives his life, and makes his aesthetic judgements under the personal and social conditions of that very insecurity.[263]

While their efforts grew out of their experience with the Véhicule Art Gallery during 1972–9 – out of its graphic as well as performance resources – and out of their experience with Véhicule Press during 1976–81, as a group and as individuals they survived the end of their association with both enterprises. Through such magazines as *Cold Mountain Review, The Poetry Magazine, The Montreal Journal of Poetics, Beaux Arts, Broadside Series,* and *Da Vinci,* and through the small publishing houses Véhicule and Maker Press, they established contacts with American magazines and poets (particularly through *Cross-Country,* with which Ken Norris was involved) and with the Québécois 'écrivains de la modernité' (specifically *Cul Q* as a magazine and a publishing house, Claude Beausoleil, and Michel Beaulieu – the latter mostly as a translator into French of contemporary anglophone poetry). The Véhicule poets were unique in several respects. First of all they were the only writers to operate from a multi-media space, at least originally. Secondly they worked on, and elaborated, the concept of performance, taking it one step beyond the oral-poetry stage. Thirdly they compressed within less than a decade the major aesthetic explorations, concretism and post-modernism, which their older counterparts in Toronto and Vancouver had spent twenty years upon.[264]

The marginality of both concretism and post-modern aesthetics in Canada is an issue which easily comes to mind after surveying the productions of *Blew Ointment, Ganglia/Gronk,* and the anglophone Montreal magazines mentioned above. It is an issue which becomes all the more intriguing when one considers, in contrast, the positions of *La Barre du Jour* and *Les Herbes Rouges* during these three decades. While their anglophone counterparts have traditionally been looked upon as radically marginal, *La Barre du Jour* and, to a certain degree, *Les Herbes Rouges* managed not only to steer the literary aesthetics of Quebec but also to address its political fabric, on a number of occasions focusing on historically strategic moments.[265] It might be added that it was not only the capacity to relate literary issues to political ones which set the Canadians and Québécois apart.[266] More significantly it was the reception such texts were given on a broad social spectrum. Raoul Duguay and Nicole Brossard might have been perceived along with others as marginal or avant-garde, yet they were, literally, between 1965 and 1968 on the forefront of cultural activities. The media played an important role in this respect. A comparison of *The Globe and Mail's* and *The Vancouver Sun's* literary reviews with those of *Le Devoir's* highlights the different outlooks of each culture. While in Quebec the press's attitude towards *la nouvelle écriture* did not change noticeably from 1965 to 1985, in Canada it ranged from absolute silence to a political scrutiny bordering upon libel.

The first event to create shock waves in an otherwise serenely indifferent ocean of tranquillity was bpNichol's Governor General's Award (1971) and the interesting political interventions it provoked in the House of Commons.[267] In terms of the reception concrete and post-modern productions were to find in the 1970s, the House of Commons cut a striking and particularly surprising profile. What its interventions marked, with respect to both Nichol and bissett,[268] was a change in the socio-political situation of these writers. They were displaced from a position of obscurity into the kind of journalistic limelight which inevitably accompanies such political encroachments upon literary productions.

Between the late 1960s and the mid-1970s Nichol's and bissett's images changed profoundly: their texts moved from total obscurity into the cockeyed and sometimes ludicrous vantage point of indignant politicians. Such attention did not turn them into household names, nor their books into campus best-sellers, but was nevertheless symptomatic of their displacement on the literary spectrum. In bissett's case, this was purchased at a high cost and probably one that he himself would have done happily without. But these particular occurrences point to a larger situation – in this case to the conflictual meeting ground created by the conservative ethos and aesthetics of some MPS, on the one hand, and texts heretofore ignored by the vast majority of Canadian readers, on the other. Such texts were described in Parliament as the outrageous and pornographic products of the counter-culture. While there is a chronological difference between the attack on Nichol (1971) and that on bissett (1977), as well as a strategic one (the latter was meant to cut off any further funding or publication grants while the first was purely reactive), the terms used in each reveal recurring focuses. Pornography, free-love, radicalism, Marxism, socialism, and the counter-culture appear to be almost inextricably linked in the MPS' language. The convergence of such critical perceptions may bring to mind Yuri Lotman's thoughtful comments on the function of rejection from the social and cultural fabric: 'The elements that a culture rejects from its own description as extra-systematic will be seen to be essential to that culture as the source of its future development.'[269]

But what a careful observer of inter-discursive practices cannot escape noticing here is the convergence between bissett's texts from the early 1960s on and the conceptual horizon demarcated by some Canadian social and political scientists a decade later. The issues raised by bissett's texts concerning linguistic, physical, and social control, political dependency, and economic domination cut across a number of semantic focuses singled out by: (a) American writings of the early 1960s on the counter-culture and on non-commanding, non-structuring forms of communication;[270] and (b) European discourses, particularly those by Foucault, Deleuze, Lyotard, and Derrida, which raised the issues of source, origin, power, and control during the same period of time.

Canadian political and social theory raised – on different registers – and yet with an equal intensity a number of the same questions. Daniel Drache's and Arthur Krocker's reflections on the tradition of dependency theory in the Canadas, on what they term the 'Canadian fate to be both the product of and conditional for external empires,'[271] strongly articulates these concerns. Drache and Krocker address in fact two contexts: the old *and* the new dependency theories when moving from Harold Innis to more recent European interpretations of this concept. From their perspective dependency theory is no longer a purely economic doctrine but an ongoing political reflection on the unequal exchange between centre and margin. As such it recognizes a plurality of factors, ethnic, social, institutional, and cultural in defining the relationship of centre to periphery.

In the same context Susan Crean's and Marcel Rioux's thinking on this problematic opposes two key concepts: heteronomy and autonomy.[272] The first term refers to receiving the laws which govern from another, or being led by forces beyond one's control. 'In such a type of society the different agents of society have aimed at producing a *normal* man, that is one adapted to this kind of society, one who consumes and produces as society dictates.'[273] Crean and Rioux suggest that the great leap which the society of tomorrow has to accomplish will be the passage from the *normal* individual to the *normative*, the latter being one who is capable of accepting and creating norms, of establishing his personality and behaviour on values which he will be able to imagine, produce, as well as welcome.[274] It is the second term, *autonomy*, which bears this idea of non-dependence, non-domination, and the power to decide for oneself. It is a leitmotiv of bissett's writings, a focusing which enhances precisely what the writing subject does not possess, and can only aspire to or yearn for, either from his jail cell or in the grim office of the manpower official who refuses to accept the term *poet* as an employment definition. On a different political level, that of the act of interpretation, Nichol's writings and all of the TRG's raise the same issues. The need to develop a non-dominating exegetical activity, a non-commanding activity, which replenishes the empty cipher is a continuous focus of Nichol's imagination.

The situation of both writers in the wider context of Canadian inter-discursive formations suggests both a position of marginality and a capacity to focus on what precisely is lacking in that culture and constitutes a gap they obsessively go back to in order to comprehend it and possibly displace it: autonomy, not as the craving for an origin or a centre – since it was never there – but as the need for the free assertion of one's individuality, the exercise of one's communal activities, away from the authoritarian structures of an economic/political empire (see Crean/Rioux) or the tyranny of the referent (see Nichol/McCaffery in *Open Letter*, or bissett's 'yu dont need th sentence,' in *What Fuckan Theory*).

What did these convergences augur for the 1970s? Apart from signalling a commonality of concerns they demonstrated the volatility of the concept of marginality, its high degree of variability. Within a decade the borderlines or borderblurs of the literary spectrum were displaced into a singularly less peripheral position and even temporarily – though scandalously in bissett's case – moved into the centre of public attention. While one should not equate such a temporary limelight with a position of centrality for Nichol and bissett, it still remains that their provocative quest for syntactical and grammatical autonomy became less marginalized as time went on and as other writers (the Véhicule poets with their video-performances, Robert Kroetsch, and Daphne Marlatt) developed and asserted the post-modern stance. In this context Lotman's reflections on society's rejection of specific cultural elements and subsequent dependency upon the same elements is particularly relevant. A blind spot may with time become a focus point; a cultural fabric may not only salvage but also concentrate its attention precisely upon those elements which it had previously rejected.

Secondly such convergences also coincided with the highly visible emergence of performances in general and of sound performances in particular into the public sphere. The Horsemen between 1970 and 1975, Owen Sound in the latter part of the decade, and the Véhicule poets produced, performed, and recorded a number of creations which signalled a new era for oral poetry as much as for post-modern art-forms in Canada. It was also the same decade which saw the production in Toronto of the Eleventh International Sound Poetry Festival (14–21 Oct. 1978),[275] and in Vancouver, of the Dada Festival, for which the Western Front Society gathered sound performers. As for anglophone Montreal, it was going to see the blossoming of a new generation of poets.

A number of factors were instrumental in fostering the development of performance art during the 1970s. As has already been mentioned, one factor was the establishment of art galleries conceived not purely as spaces to exhibit pictorial productions but also as loci of activity for poetry performances. Peggy Gale singles out 1970 as a departure point for such activity in Canada and points to A Space Gallery in Toronto as the first centre which consistantly supported non-object art with a special emphasis on video and performance.[276] Subsequently, three dozen such centres sprang up across the country, and, interestingly enough, large institutions, such as the National Gallery in Ottawa, the Art Gallery of Ontario, and the Vancouver Art Gallery, followed suit. But it was the co-operative, artist-run, small-gallery movement, very much a product of the 1970s, which played a key role in the emergence, formulation, and development of the performance art-form. The theoretical background of performative acts has already been dis-cussed. What is of interest here is the place they took in Canada and their function on the artistic spectrum.

Toronto, Vancouver, and Montreal were initially referred to in the critical literature as the main foci, but one witnessed a progressive de-centring of such activities, particularly with the development of artists' galleries in the Prairies.[277] The Intermedia Gallery in Vancouver, which came into being in 1966 (and was in fact defunct by 1970), is emblematic of the rise of a new generation of artists involved in film, painting, poetry, photography, and performance works. From Peggy Gale's viewpoint – and I think she is accurate here – it established the particular interaction between life- and art-style which was to become so characteristic of Vancouver and turned out to be an essential part of the environment bill bissett and the Western Canadian avant-garde emerged from.[278]

Performances being the essence of live-art, they are very much dependent upon an individual artist's communication skills. Performers' personalities play therefore a determining role not only in the strategy of presentation but also in the initial definition of the piece. Gathie Falk, a Vancouver performer who started in the late 1960s, is emblematic of a whole generation. She developed an art-form 'out of homely interests and fantasies, idiosyncrasies refined and elaborated into strategies for public presentation.'[279] As Gale points out, they emerged as 'an embroidery of personality that brought the life/art union into a dialogue taken well beyond its personal or private genesis.'[280] And indeed the fact that Gathie Falk lived in a house filled with strange objects that was a three-dimensional performance piece in itself increased the dramatic quality of her presence.[281]

This same connection between art and life was upheld by the Toronto group General Idea, but from a starkly different viewpoint – one as thoroughly grounded in a specific environment as Falk's, but from which counter-cultural elements, co-operative spirit, and doe-eyed individualism were excluded. Substituted for them were the aggressive, image-building, and simulacra-producing qualities of the post-capitalist era: efficient, glib, mass-audience pleasing, image-conscious, and media-made (the package is the product). Mr Peanut, one of the three characters of General Idea, dressed in a papier-mâché outfit modelled on the Planters advertising anthropomorph, became 'an arrow pointing in an empty landscape, the cultural landscape of the mass media.'[282] As A.A. Bronson also comments, Mr Peanut held a particular magic for *Oui, Esquire, The Village Voice*, and other magazines, not because he had done anything, but because of his existence as 'an available high-definition image.' In fact it seems to have been the emptiness of that image, its lack of content, which produced its desirability. Because it had no connection with any specific event, individual, or viewpoint, it became an open receptacle, 'a mirror on which the media could project anything they wanted.'[283]

Cultural clichés soon became very much an essential component of performance works and gave them a dramatic edge bordering on social or political commentary.[284] In Toronto, General Idea performances operated as reflections, mirrorings, of a certain social class at a certain time (commercial realities, beauty queen contests, the enshrining of art works in museums, the vying for curatorial favours, etc.). In Vancouver performances had a more articulated political edge, following the contours of different societal projects (for example, Pumps in Vancouver, with Kim Tomczak, John Anderson, Rick Hambleton, and John Mitchell during 1975–80, or Video Inn and the productions of the 1979 Vancouver Performance Festival).[285]

One of the increasingly important media which surfaced in performances both in Europe and North America was video. While Gale perceived it in 1981 as characteristic of Toronto, the situation has changed considerably since then with both Vancouver and especially Montreal performance artists (see Tom Konyves' work and the leadership taken by Montreal artists in this area)[286] choosing to use this medium as an intrinsic part of their work. Interestingly enough video was initially a clearly autobiographical and intimate tool operating within linear and discursive structures. Changes slowly emerged in the mid-1970s and video moved from a focus on performer as the sole subject matter to multifaceted personae observed from contrasting viewpoints (see Colin Campbell's and Lisa Steele's work in Toronto).[287] While performance art could never be reduced to video productions, one has still to admit that video introduced new parameters. More than anything else, it provoked a new and much-needed re-evaluation both of television audiences and of this medium's role in society as it took up the possibility of deriving from the hated and despised TV screen 'investigation tools for the deconstruction of language, communication, and information controls.'[288] It was less a result of the availability of different means than an awareness of other norms: commercial, mass-produced, mass-directed. Steele's and Campbell's works were calculated to fascinate through the now familiar structure of daytime television drama, in content, timing, and presentation. It did *not* mean that they were an extension of these forces (media network/post-industrial era strategies,[289]) but simply that they utilized them and forced onto the art world a scrutiny which had long been – and for understandable reasons – censored.

While television in the 1960s had been looked upon by the counter-culture as 'the opium of the masses,' it became with the 1970s performers an ideological 'repoussoir,' an inspirational reservoir. It did not mean that such incursions into television's language and models were to become overpowering, but simply that they had to be counted. In fact, looking at the bi-monthly publication which links all of the parallel art galleries in Canada, one is tempted to conclude that because of their level of interaction and co-operation they signalled the presence of a 'visible lobby for this sort of non-commercial expression.'[290] One should not forget what Chantal Pontbriand said in the late 1970s; namely, that performances could be assimilated to 'interventions' in so much as they transformed physical or social reality.[291] And this is echoed by Alan Sondheim, who suggests that such acts, like others before them, emerge from a complex dialogue between self and society, between self and the specific interests of the art world. While some might be invested in an exploration of a specific aspect of this already existing form, in pushing formalism to its limits, others may want 'to turn inwards, to explore the relationship between self and society, self and history. In short an artist may want to study the relationship between self and world.'[292] As Leila Sujir, a video artist and writer, expresses it in her article on performances in Calgary – quoting, not incidentally, Nicole Brossard – performance artists are important because they reconstitute the past and provide their public with both a collective memory and a vision of the future from a different locus within the mass culture, which, with enormous power, forces homogeneity upon us all. Performance artists allow not only for private, personal, and regional elements to come to the fore, but also for a community's representation of itself and of its uniqueness.[293]

The group performance of poetry, its assertive visibility through the Horsemen, bill bissett, and Owen Sound in the 1970s, while never associated with commercial visibility nevertheless moved these poets away from the bohemian margins of artistic creativity and closer to the mainstream. Group performances, by moving a gestural and collective manifestation upon a stage, fulfilled a different need than that perceived by small presses ten years before. That need could be referred to, if one may borrow Henri Meschonnic's formula, as the capacity to bring together an individual (or a human subject) and sociality (or group awareness). Meschonnic, a French critic and philosopher, focuses his attention on the very same issue which occupied much of the TRG's attention, namely, the Western dualism of sign theory. He interprets the relevancy of much of contemporary oral poetry as precisely a way to challenge this dualism and to convene a different anthropology: one which would salvage, as well as focus on, the historicity of language, and which would be capable of conjuring up the lost cohesion between signifier and signified, between subject and collectivity.[294] While it would be a mistake to equate Meschonnic's programmatic vision with the TRG's, the Horsemen's, or Owen Sound's creativity,[295] still, this French philosopher's evaluation of the 1970s and his view of the following decade provide a relevant perspective on the Canadian experience.

First Meschonnic and these poets share the need to move away from a specific theory of language: from one which is overdetermined by a specific definition of power – scientific, investigative, and political. The domination of structuralist modes of inquiry and of its semiotic inheritors appears to them to have been neglectful of other values, ethical, historical, and anthropological. Secondly both Meschonnic and the Canadian poets emphasize the uniqueness of oral poetry by re-introducing the importance of signification (as opposed to the semiotic dualism of sense and meaning). And thirdly they all stress the importance of bringing to the fore the pulsions of history inherent in language. As Meschonnic puts it: 'L'histoire passe dans le rythme et dépend de lui pour exprimer son énergie.'[296] If there are irreducible differences between the Canadian sound poets' analysis and Meschonnic's, they can be narrowed down to the poets' respective definitions of the sacred, on the one hand, and the anthropological definition of this term, on the other. To the poets, apart from their referring to a specific part of history, the Amerindian's, which they have a strong emotional bond to, the sacred takes on connotations which are overdetermined by specific metaphysical convictions. History to them merges into an atemporal, transcendent dimension which escapes diachronic strictures and operates co-extensively with eternity. As such it can be re-experienced and translated by the Western inhabitants of that space, who thus become the continuators of that tradition. References to it criss-cross the work of bissett,[297] are clearly integrated to his concept of performance practice,[298] and are openly discussed by Nichol.[299]

But 1979 signalled more than the end of a decade. It greeted the finishing point of an era. The 1970s had been the decade of performances, a time dedicated to the joy and energy of their actuality on stage – the 1980s became the time for taking stock, for evaluating those productions and theorizing about their role and significance. The amount of literature produced about the *concept* of performance during the 1980s testifies to this.[300] More than making events actually happen on stage, artists and poets became involved in articulating a conceptual apparatus about them. Theoretical reflections were to dominate the new decade and displace actual productions.

Quebec

'The One Who Opened the Door': Claude Gauvreau

Terms of reference, definitions, and readers' expectations and reception of aesthetic movements do not translate easily from one culture to another. As we have seen, experimental writing theories did not operate in as homogeneous a fashion in Quebec as they did in Canada. What predominated instead was a pluralism which made the critic's task hazardous, if not outright precarious, for as I mentioned above the validity of any strict definition of terms (that of *concretism*, in particular) is conceptually threatened by the terminological explosion which presided over experimental writing in Quebec.

But when one turns from theory to history, it is apparent that the literary historian does not encounter comparable difficulties. The documents are abundant, and though they express a pluralism, they do not present any sequential problems. From the viewpoint of the historian the situation is clear: there was a succession of events during the 1960s which not only indicated a bursting out of definitions as to what the terms *concrete* or *experimental* meant, but also indicated that the different media and definitions used in this process could and would ultimately be fused together. Such indications are tantalizing; they bring specific contradictions to the fore (unity/diversity) as well as provide us with a better articulated picture of the culture they grew out of than do the Canadian experiments of the same time. While developments in Toronto and Vancouver almost exclusively reflected the activities of marginalized groups, their Montreal counterparts during the 1960s were not only well entrenched within their own intellectual culture but were also apt to be the ones who articulated its expectations, goals, and contradictions.

Politics were a key ingredient in this process, so that the literary historian who hopes to grasp the overall situation must take political factors into account. For instance, consider the role played by literary magazines in Quebec during the 1960s. The small 'mag' on the forefront of literary experimentation which published poetry and fiction exclusively was a well-established Canadian institution,[301] one that was indispensable to the development of concrete aesthetics in Canada. This was not the case in Quebec. There the major magazines which printed poetry (*Main Mise, Parti Pris, Hobo-Québec, Cul Q, La Barre du Jour*) did not confine themselves to that task. Political, social, and cultural problems were just as intrinsic a part of their editorial concerns as literary creativity. In the case of *Main Mise* and *Parti Pris*, in fact, they were very much in the forefront of the editors' preoccupations. In *La Barre du Jour* such commitments might have been couched in carefully controlled language, but they were nevertheless intensely present (see, for example, the special issue on Gaston Miron during the aftermath of the October Crisis, and those later in the 1970s on women's writings, 'La Femme et le corps' and 'La Femme et le langage,' to mention only a few). The role played by these magazines and the impact they had on the general reading public are vital to an interpretation of the 1960s. They were the mouthpiece of the Quebec intelligentsia, and they embodied for a while the intellectual directions, as well as contradictions, of successive generations. *Parti Pris*, which best reflected the political passions of the 1960s, did not exclusively confine itself to political theory. Language was very much a part of its political focus. Raoul Duguay, Paul Chamberland, and Gérald Godin, to mention three of the poets who frequently wrote in its pages, were intensely concerned about the power implications of language issues.

In contrast with Vancouver and Toronto of the 1960s, politics and performances dominated the 1960s in Quebec, where they were intensely, as well as intrinsically, bound with one another. While video performances were to follow a similar course as they did in Canada (that is, a slow development in the early 1970s and then a creative explosion as the decade wore on), what characterized the 1960s in Quebec was the exploration of multi-media productions. In the creative effervescence of the mid-1960s in Montreal such manifestations came not only from poets (Raoul Duguay or Claude Péloquin) but also from painters, designers, singers, musicians, and film-makers. In 1964 it was in the context of this intensely cross-breeding intellectual activity that several events ('La Semaine A,' 'Les Trente A')[302] captured the public's attention. Singers such as Robert Charlebois and Pauline Julien, the Montreal artist Serge Lemoyne, as well as poets from *Parti Pris* participated in such events.[303] Throughout this period ephemeral multi-media groups emerged, dissolved, and re-emerged. Les Horlogers du Nouvel Age, Le Zirmate, and L'Infonie were such groups. But their activities did not take place in obscure art galleries or friends' basements. They received mass exposure. Les Horlogers du Nouvel Age performed in Montreal (summer of 1965) in front of audiences of several thousand people; Le Zirmate produced the famous 'infragalaxie event' of Expo 67. Access to a wide audience, to the structures utilized by mass culture, was thus conferred – if only momentarily – to such groups. *Quebec Underground 1962–1972*, edited by Yves Robillard, provides excellent coverage of this period, and because of the rare documents it has managed to unearth succeeds in providing an eventful chronicle of the years both preceding and following Expo 67. The manifesto of the 'Trente A' group, which emphasizes their focus as being the integration of various artistic media into a unified experience (in their terms a 'globalité');[304] the comments of Claude Paradis, a member of the same group, on the importance of producing concrete, classical, and electronic music together in successive moments;[305] as well as Le Zirmate's concepts on the synthesis of painting, corporeal expression, and texts indicate the wide spectrum of aesthetic tensions which characterized this period. Such artistic improvisations were marked by a sense of provocation, defiance, urgency. They were not produced by unassuming and patient individuals who quietly went about their business learning to develop the artistic possibilities of small presses. bpNichol's, bill bissett's, and Judith Copithorne's choices were not exactly theirs.

It is worthwhile to note again the contrast between developments in Quebec and in Canada. bpNichol has stated the case clearly, I believe, not only for himself but for bill bissett, the Horsemen, Steve McCaffery, and Owen Sound: there had never been an avant-garde movement in Canada, in the 1920s, in the 1930s, or in the 1950s. His generation had to find their own precedents, at their own peril.[306] Looking at the situation in Quebec, one can quickly appreciate the difference. At the Théâtre le Gésu in 1970, moments before performing at the now legendary 'Nuit de la poésie,'[307] Claude Gauvreau, one of the early Automatists of the 1950s, was to say to Raoul Duguay: 'At least there will have been someone to open the door for you.'[308]

Duguay had no personal ties with Gauvreau, and 'The Swan,' as one of his biographers was to call him, died in July 1971, a year after the Gésu concert. Moreover, it would appear from Duguay's own account that the bond between them was closer to a rite of passage than a well-defined kinship; indeed, though he admitted that 'The Swan' had had an influence upon his 'far-out period [of] phantasmagoria, mad genius mysticism' (that is, during the mid-1960s),[309] he is justified in describing their trajectories as distinct. Duguay was always concerned with uncovering a cosmogony, levels and structures immanent within nature, the human body, and consciousness,[310] a project wholly alien to Gauvreau's preoccupations. But what is of interest to the literary historian is to rediscover Gauvreau's painful, and at the time mostly unheeded, progress into phonic territory, his links with the Automatist movement in art, and his deep commitment to non-figurativeness,[311] all of which also happen to be concerns of concretism. Keeping in mind these preoccupations helps to begin to interpret those of Gauvreau's texts which contain few identifiable words and basically play on phonemic effects. For example:

Jacques Dulume

Kalumass bossi
buchic
Kalimullac bulic
bari
Kalimok mari mérik
mavrok
Valoche Vali Veuk Vollik Tic
Tollicudinss donss drassic dassigric gassic gossulupe bassig
Ofneuf nif narip niplok de pojik ofton de brak azik sigur
Sisfolla
Fratridrume dagazip sosspoli
Parpidru
Druplonblan
Plaflifla folfeurduim dock de dig dassipip
Possibullé
Possiblère barmuré burmel de bullur curdizuc
Asmoherlé
Sossmochême chumère oeil gré gladi fogré galli de Licice Solli[312]

One should recall Gauvreau's affinities with the concept of automatic writing, his fascination for dada, and his rejection of linear logic, coherence, and reason. His correspondence brings to the fore a determination to overthrow rationality, both as an aesthetic value and a specific social structure. To Paul-Emile Borduas he wrote as early as 1950 about an artist's confrontation: 'The old unused Dadaist hammer came back with full force as well as unexpectedly, with a touch of unprecedented nastiness.'[313] To another friend, whom he defied to lose his mental balance, he declared: 'Why would you find it abhorent to lose your sanity for one moment? All the better to lose it and the devil be damned with it!'[314] Clearly his concept of automatic writing, which subsumed all of his imaginings, his figures of speech, his own mythology, should not be confused with that of the French surrealist movement. For André Breton and Paul Eluard 'psychic automatism' implied a state of cultivated passivity, voluntary indifference, and as total a neutrality as one could manage. On the contrary what Gauvreau was searching for was a direct and active emotion, pure spontaneity, a passionate commotion of the emotive volcano.[315] In other words he pleaded for the rejection of psychic automatism in favour of a surrational one – a description identical to Marinetti's description of automatism.[316] Spontaneity, another recurring dadaist motto, was an obsession of Gauvreau's. The ritualistic killing of birds which once interrupted a routine performance at the Comédie canadienne in 1969, an action which he is said to have inspired,[317] finds an echo in a plea of his: 'One must act with an audacity such that even those who will repress it will have to admit that one inch of freedom was conquered for all.'[318]

The concept of spontaneity and the attitude of the emotional volcano had an influence on Duguay's as well as other performances in the 1960s. The concept of multi-media performance, its weaving of visual, auditive, tactile, and even olfactory elements, is an interpretation of and a tribute to Gauvreau's literary legacy. While the Swan's hermeneutic of a volcano relied totally on the actor/performer, who had the responsibility to enact this emotive concentration and discharge, the performances of L'Infonie or of Le Zirmate diffracted these roles upon different actors and especially different perceptive modes. The volcano on stage – or rather amidst the audience – was not exclusively of human flesh, but also composed of music, of animals (doves played a recurring role in Duguay's menagerie), of slides bombarded on screens, and occasionally rain poured down upon spectators-participants. But the seeds had been sown many years before by a writing often described as seismographic[319] and often perceived as the literary equivalent of Borduas' gestural automatism. Just as the latter refused to give a figurative representation to his fantasies, Gauvreau rejected descriptive and analytic modes. As he puts it himself: 'Language is never descriptive: it is through related images that it aspires to situate affective, emotive, sensual, intellectual states.'[320] But automatism was not Gauvreau's exclusive concern. Fusion, or integration of different artistic modes, was another; in fact, during the late 1940s there were velleities of integration between the arts. The composer Pierre Mercure toyed for a while with the idea of doing an opera with Gauvreau. This collaboration, which was meant to be in the spirit of Schönberg's *Pierrot lunaire*, floundered into inflammatory polemic.[321] Other integrative performances had more successful endings. Mercure, Françoise Sullivan, a choreographer, and Thérèse Renaud, a poet, juxtaposed their compositions.[322] The Automatist circles in the late 1940s were open to such endeavours but did not bring to them the same impulse of defiant humour to integrate disparate elements which artists and poets of the 1960s (Duguay and Péloquin, in particular) later demonstrated. While the Automatists' performances aimed at producing an integrated totality, L'Infonie (Duguay's group) and Le Zirmate (Péloquin's) had no such goal in mind. Their intention was to produce an explosion of noise rather than words, a succession of flashes rather than images. But the very fact that Gauvreau – two decades before them – had conceived of a poetry reading as a bombardment of psychic and sonorous matter – 'poésie libératoire par excellence' – had shown them the way or, more precisely, had allowed them to walk into this territory in order to explore on their own terms.

Besides the flight away from meaning into sonorous matter, other traits of Gauvreau were to be woven into later experimental texts. Eroticism was an important poetic detonator for Gauvreau (see, for instance, his play *Les Oranges sont vertes* and the poem *Etal mixte*).[323] At the time the choice was scandalous, but it was not unique to him. There had been Paul-Marie Lapointe's *Le Vierge incendié* in 1948, which was hardly noticed then but was later perceived as an audacious foray into eroticism. Duguay's *Ruts* (1966) followed this lead, but in a much less tormented mode. And one could add that in the early 1970s, with the *nouvelle écriture*, it was the poetic text itself which became a vast erogenous zone.

Curse words and anglicisms, which recur in some of Gauvreau's work, particularly in *Etal mixte*, became a favourite pattern of defiance of the next generation, from *Parti Pris*, which Paul Chamberland and Raoul Duguay were a part of, to the later emerging counter-culture and the *Cul Q* experimenters, including Denys Vanier, Claude Beausoleil, Yolande Villemaire, Lucien Francoeur, and Patrick Straram, who all excelled at fusing obscenities and English within their texts.

The third key territory opened by Gauvreau was phonic poetry. Although he energetically rejected any association with the lettrists,[324] he was the first to produce pure sound games which had abandoned their semantic ballast. One line from *Etal mixte* –

'thathamanzauskayantes'[325] – has an exemplary value, but one could as easily select a number of poems where, according to Marchand's description, hardly a single recognizable French word can be found. Yet, for all this de facto defiance of semantic decoding, Gauvreau, as a theoretician, never went as far towards the creation of pure sonic matter as the TRG in Toronto or Henri Chopin and Bernard Heidsieck in France. In his view, each signifier had to refer back to a signified outside the poem.[326]

Duguay was to express similar doubts about pure phonic poetry.[327] When one looks back at the performances by Duguay and Péloquin from the mid- to late 1960s, one finds improvisations, but improvisations destined to both scandalize the establishment in various ways (aesthetically, ethically certainly, as well as politically) and to appeal to what they perceived at the time to be a wide public (the Quebec population at large, the masses). Such intentions are not in themselves particularly new. Most literary movements (especially in Western and Eastern Europe) reveal similar propensities. What is interesting in this case is the direct access such artists did have to the 'masses' because of the special situation of Expo 67; and the connections which were made between those artistic manifestations and the political body. Paul Chamberland's personal interpretation, in a 1966 *Parti Pris* article, of Claude Péloquin's experiments is explicit on that score. Such performances, he tells us, even if they only are an individual's quest into the subconscious territory of language ('les dessous du langage'), are necessarily revolutionary.[328]

On first consideration Paul Chamberland's comment seems pretentious and naïve. To experiment with delirium, hallucinations, and forbidden marginal desires hardly strikes one as revolutionary in the mid-1960s. The fact that he establishes a connection between French surrealism and Le Zirmate would seem only to reinforce the reader's scepticism. But it is when he proceeds to differentiate between those experiments of the 1920s (mostly in Paris) and the multi-media productions of the 1960s that one becomes more convinced. Both at the conceptual level (from the vantage point of manifestos and of the body of theoretical texts preceding both surrealism and Le Zirmate) and at an artistic level (from the vantage point of actual performances), it slowly becomes evident that Breton's surrealist performances and multi-media events *were* markedly different.

What makes the difference is not the presence or the absence of political elements. After all, French politics had an important role in the development of surrealism and surrealist writings, and literary manifestos have always had a complex relationship to such factors.[329] But, more to the point, Chamberland helps us understand (a) the fusing of contrasting media, and (b) the affirmation that the private is political, that private selves, the 'subject,' are an intrinsic part of such productions. These are new elements not present in the literary movements of the 1920s and the 1930s. It was not only artistic media (ballet, music) but also quotidian, personal data – until then deemed trivial, banal, or irrelevant – which were interwoven with the history and the politics of Quebec. Such re-evaluations were very much tied to the overall vision of the Quebec counter-culture. As Joël Pourbaix was to put it in *L'Avant-garde culturelle et littéraire des années 70 au Québec:*

> L'appel de l'utopie (et l'appel à l'utopie) se produit à travers l'affirmation d'un je/sujet. Les messages, l'impératif, qui circulent dans les textes restent sous la détermination d'un sujet bien en vue. L'exclusion de la problématique de l'efficacité politique ne tient donc pas seulement au contenu explicite de certains textes, elle a lieu vraiment avec l'ampleur prise dans le texte par le je/sujet, son énonciation, son écriture.[330]

Thus manifestos such as that of the Fusion des Arts group, signed by a collective (see Fig. 72),[331] Raoul Duguay's 'Le stéréo-poème-audio-visuel,'[332] Claude Péloquin's *Le Manifeste infra*,[333] or Patrick Straram's 'Interprétations de la vie quotidienne,'[334] while operating from contrasting and dissimilar angles, all share one common tenet: they suggest the need for artistic manifestations to proceed from pluralistic viewpoints, not to be content with homogeneity, coherence, or logic. All challenge social, political, and semantic hierarchies, and all put forward different means and channels of communication. Péloquin has an unshakeable faith in scientific experimentation (electronic, computerized). Duguay reaches out for spiritual avenues other than traditional Judeo-Christianity while stressing the importance of the physical body.[335] Straram proclaims the need of connecting the personal and the creative, of not allowing them to operate separately.[336]

The Sixties: *Parti Pris*, Multi-Media Performances, Explosion versus Integration, the Mosaic of the Counter-Culture

What is interesting about the 1960s today when one looks at Paul Chamberland's *Parti Pris* writings as well as at the entire artistic spectrum of the period is the contrast, opposition, even contradiction, one detects in these texts and artistic productions between (a) their emphasis on fusion, integration, and the bringing together of heterogeneous elements,[337] and (b) their ideological insistence upon separatism, revolutionary practices, and the bursting out of obsolete political structures.[338]

Inevitably, the dialectical tension between these two main forces raises some questions. On the one hand, the writings of *Parti Pris* are clamouring for an independent Quebec finally set free from the shackles of a federal power increasingly perceived – at least by a large segment of Québécois – as being out of touch with them. But on the other, these same writings are pleading for an integration of artistic media, of instrumental scores, poetic texts, and stage designs (Duguay's Infonie group and its performances would be a case in point here.)[339] Other similarly tantalizing tensions emerge out of the 1960s and become exacerbated during the next decade: that of marginal versus popular forms of culture; of the status of underground art vis-à-vis mass culture.[340] The lengthy preparations for Expo 67 and the groups who worked on this mega-project provided Quebec artists and writers with a unique opportunity, a forum for exchanging ideas, but mainly a mass audience which they normally would not have had access to. Spectators and critics observed and commented upon what was deemed to be a world event. All the groups which preceded, participated in, and followed Expo 67 (Le Nouvel Age, Les Horlogers du Nouvel Age, Le Zirmate, Fusion des Arts, L'Infonie,[341] Luci Associates)[342] stressed the importance of integrating media components; all pleaded for multi-dimensionality, globality.[343]

Two of Duguay's productions, 'Abécédaire Babel' (1970) and 'Bababbelli' (1969) help us focus on this contradiction.[344] The term *Babel* indicates an explosion, an anarchic ungovernableness and diversity, which plunges the world into fragments and prophetically uncoded chaos. Apocalyptic omens are inherently contained within this term. If in biblical terms Babel refers to the second fall – the first happening in the Garden of Eden, as George Steiner reminds us – it was through and because of Babel that humanity was exiled from the assurance of being able to grasp and communicate reality.[345] Yet Duguay's pleading for a fusion of contrasting media indicates a search for unity, totality, harmony. His ambiguous focus on multi-media and a post-Babelian search for a lost tongue beyond 'the prison walls of a scattered and polluted speech, the rubble of the smashed Tower,'[346] indicates the need to have access again to a different dimension, what Claude

Péloquin chose to refer to as a cosmic, psychic beyond,[347] and Steiner 'the inner penetralia of reality.'[348] Certainly performances during these years strived towards that dimension and beyond. Works by Les Horlogers, Le Nouvel Age, and Le Zirmate expressed identical concerns. Chamberland's *Eclats* specifically epitomized this obsession with chaos and his subsequent hope to recover a primeval order beneath the rubble. From *Eclats* one derives the sense that one's survival narrowly depends upon one's capacity to unearth the original idiom enunciated by Kabbalists. But all, Duguay, Péloquin, and Chamberland, suggest that both the beautiful and the ugly, the harmonious and the chaotic, have their place in artistic creation and are begging to be woven together by artists, musicians, and poets. The multi-dimensionality of the work of art is thus a reflection not only of Babel but also of its creators/artists. Its roots are in the human collectivity, in everybody's work:

INFONIE TOTALISANT, TOTALEMENT LE TOUT, TOULTEMPS PARTOUT, AU BOUTT, DANS SA TOTALE TOTALITE, TOTALISANT CELUI QUI CERTAINEMENT, N'IMPORTE QUAND, DANS LA GRANDE CREVASSE DU CANYON CREUX DU NEVADA, CELUI QUI ACCOMPAGNE DE 333, 333, 333, MUSICIENS. LE VOICI, L'ESSENTIEL, L'ETERNEL, LE MACRO-MICRO-BE, LE KIK SUPREME.[349]

The Seventies: The Decade of Feminism, *La Nouvelle Barre du Jour*, *Les Herbes Rouges*, *Stratégie*, and *Chroniques*

What such documents do in essence is to help us discern two of the main contradictions of the 1960s and the 1970s. In the first decade (from 1964 up to 1970) the conflict had to do with political disintegration versus global integration (see, for instance, Raoul Duguay's vision of a 'douce révolution radicale').[350] While the political fabric is about to explode (the October Crisis is only a few years or months away), a certain collective imagination feverishly dreams of harmonious fusion, synthesis. This polarization (of fragmentation versus re-totalization) was carefully analysed two decades later and defined as a form of 'apolitical militantism' which promised revolutionary changes through the transformation of human consciousness.[351] But as a polarization it was not alone. Others were to come to the fore. With the late 1960s came the rise of the counter-culture movement and with it that of different periodicals. Some presented an orientation precisely determined by this new awareness (*Hobo-Québec, Main Mise*), but others offered viewpoints which clearly articulated a radical Marxist approach. *Les Herbes Rouges*, a magazine devoted to the publication of poetry and fiction, emerged out of this period (c. 1978), and soon periodicals devoted to discussions of Marxist-Leninist ideology and to aesthetic and theoretical problems – *Stratégie, Chroniques* – were also to appear.

One contradiction which had surfaced in the late 1960s was to be acutely felt and re-examined in the 1970s. It had to do with mass culture versus the counter-culture, with what Yves Robillard was to refer to in 1973 as underground versus overground.[352] If all agreed that 'la machine capitaliste' was obsolete and representationality had run its course, from Paul Chamberland and Raoul Duguay on the one hand (see *Main Mise* and *Hobo-Québec*) to François Charron on the other (see *Chroniques* and *Stratégie*), there were different conceptions of what the artist's and the writer's responsibilities were in that specific context.[353] How was one to define popular culture, and how did mass culture and the mass media fare in that context? Contradictions surfaced, for instance, on the question of technology and mass-media control. In general writers of the counter-culture movement (and those of *Main Mise* and *Hobo-Québec*, in particular) criticized the bureaucratic and technological apparatus,[354] but in spite of their criticism of the industrial and technological destruction of the ecosystem, for the most part such writers subscribed to a certain mythology of technological progress. Technological innovations can and may free society and encourage a renewal of its resources. Therefore a control of media resources as well as the development of technological skills are encouraged. Jules Duchastel stresses the contradiction which surged up here between 'obsolete economic analyses' to be found in the counter-culture and the dominant discourse which did advocate technological development as a means to move into the post-industrial age.[355] He also suggests some strong links with Marshall McLuhan's theories here and notes that just as McLuhan's global village was not a return to antediluvian tribes but the reconstitution of a tribal environment through electronic media, the counter-culture did not propose a homogeneously unified vision but a multi-dimensional one, a spectrum of collective and individual experiences which do not necessarily and always have a common denominator.[356]

A question which a contemporary observer may feel like posing in the 1980s is whether one vision (the utopian one, 'la posture utopiste' as Joël Pourbaix puts it)[357] preceded the other (the militant Marxist-Leninist position)[358] or whether they unhappily co-existed. I myself am reasonably convinced that the rise of the counter-culture in general preceded by a few years that of the proletarian problematic posed not only by François Charron but also by Madeleine Gagnon, Philippe Haeck, and Patrick Straram. Duchastel, who has carefully followed the developments of the first,[359] notes that the transition period of 1968–70, from the student unrest of 1968[360] to the October Crisis, saw the emergence of a new discourse, under both the impulsion of European student radicalism ('which brings together Marx and Rimbaud: change the world change life')[361] and the American counter-culture, its psychedelic movements and the alternatives it presented at that time. (Theodore Roszak and George Kahl are of course obligatory references, and Duchastel does not fail to comply.)[362]

This second discourse may be located somewhere in the first half of the 1970s, when cultural practices changed, when new modes of action emerged, and when other political practices, more specifically centred upon ecological concerns or on sexual liberation movements, emerged. Such movements both sprang from and differentiated themselves from the counter-culture.[363]

From the viewpoint of the literary historian, Raoul Duguay and Paul Chamberland are the writers who most continuously and coherently contributed to the first wave. Their mystical and metaphysical perspectives on societal transformations as well as Chamberland's critique of familial and sexual norms constitute an impressive and definite body of texts which provide us today with a coherent vision of the literary counter-culture. Their cohesiveness and coherence, however, do not reflect the movement at large, or *Main Mise* in particular, which as I have noted existed within a confluence of contradictions.[364]

What separated them most from the next wave or the writers of *Stratégie* and *Chroniques*? What some have chosen to call 'the politico-philosophical register'[365] markedly separated them. While both advocated the need to liberate societies and individuals from oppressive situations (or states), the counter-culture envisioned such a process from an individual viewpoint ('la révolution c'est dans la tête').[366] It is societies and their organizational patterns which oppress human beings, not the nation state or capitalist structures, and only the liberation of each individual will eventually bring about a collective and cultural liberation. For the counter-culture such a process also necessarily entailed a strong reliance on sexual freedom (away from normative expectations) and the use of drugs (which caste off the shackles of logical and purely empirical reason). While the first claim did not at all conflict with the expectations of the contributors to *Stratégie* and *Chroniques*, the second did not abide well with them. Drugs were perceived and described as one more tool of the repressive state that had to be rejected in order to achieve a true revolution. But the essential difference in vision had to do with their respective perceptions of the individual, on the different perspectives developed about this subject. Individuals for the writers of *Main Mise* operate within an organic complex, that formed by nature, on vegetal, animal, human, and planetary levels. Only a reorganization of human society in harmony with all these other levels can be durable and tangible.[367] Simultaneously a deep mistrust of, as well as contempt for, political revolutions surface among its pages. Political revolutions are obsolete and one dictatorship can only be followed by another.[368] Such an apolitical stance manifests itself in two aspects of *Main Mise*: (a) it does not deal with or consider the economic exploitation of workers any more than the oppression of the Third World (even in the case of Duguay and Chamberland such analyses are somewhat obsolete and belong to their by then distant involvement with *Parti Pris* [1963–68]); (b) what does emerge from this period and is eminently explored by both these writers, as well as by the counter-culture, is a 'cultural internationalism' which advocates the abolition of national and political borders (a substantial transformation from the early 1960s rise of Quebec nationalism). This does not mean that Chamberland champions the federalist cause but that the premises of his discourse operate from different tenets. He was intent to witness the reality of Quebec as an entity of its own, an entity operating in an anthropological context, on a planetary level.[369] Identity, political self-image, and historical expectations cannot be taken away from Quebec, and yet, simultaneously, they exist on a different and heretofore ignored level (by federalists and separatists alike) – that of the planet Earth.

When one turns to *Stratégie* and *Chroniques*, one comes in touch with a totally different vision of history, of literature, and of aesthetic movements. A new generation came of age, conceptually and literarily speaking, in the early 1970s. What these two periodicals did was to deconstruct certain literary expectations and counteract the ideological structures which they carry.[370] As Jacques Pelletier notes it was not only semantic, typographical, and spelling conventions that Charron challenged in the order of poetic discourse when, in the first issue of *Stratégie*, he wrote:

L'entrée

Hummeur par l'axident à ses chevaux j'ouvre
la parenthèse pour te dire quelques lignnnn
quelques mots d'plus: la couverture de la
shop r'gard la belle vache disant que c'était hier

> et troisse et quatre dames tendent à vos arpents
> repris dans un désir chaotique qui vous parle
> d'al seule tache clair d'la pièce si l'bon Dieu
> l'veut: j'entends que l'bon DIEU y parle de l'as
> jolie piquet qu'on déplume et les bras de pâtés
> de suie la véritable montagne s'escalade la crème glac   é
> aborde la question du fonctionnement des menbrs
> liquidée puisqu'j't'aime! et deux tois ptits
> mots, mais il était trop tard
>
> 'ensemble la nuyt comme une femme ouvrir
> ce qui suit, je prononcerai l'étoile la nuy
> pour sans transition la campagne'[371]

But what he did, in a polemical and combative way, was (a) to desacralize poetic discourse through the insertion of economic issues expressed here in joual (a way for Charron to renew the problematic enunciated by *Parti Pris* some ten odd years before), and (b) to attack, in a parodic mode, the bourgeois literary productions which had received recognition from the establishment. His rewriting of Jean-Guy Pilon's 'Rivage' from *Saisons pour la continuelle* (1969) illustrates 'his opposition to any form of mysticism and poetic idealism':[372]

RIVAGE	RAVAGE
Tu es la terre et l'eau	Toé pi la terre pi l'eau
Tu es continuité de la terre	qu'tu continues à m'pogner
Et permanence de l'eau	la permanence du boutte
Le souffle d'or t'irise	qui m'couple le souffle
Né de toi	r'charge moé
Je retourne à toi	avec tout tes pets
Comblé de la vie que je cueille	à toé comblé d'l'odeur que
Dans l'eau où je m'enfonce	j'cueille (tu m'l'enfonces
Chaque vague roule de tes reins	jusqu'aux reins ayoill!)
Me projette sur ton rivage	qu j'te déboites un peu
M'arrache de la terre	la face arrache ta
Et me fait de nouveau m'y briser	couette fa moé la sentir
Mon seul regard m'absorbe	que j't'absorbe par la queue
Dans l'eau des mers	pi qu'ma crème t'peinture
Et de tes yeux que je devine	le cul que j'devine comme
De l'autre côté de la terre	un aliment qu'yentre en action
Car tu es terre et eau	qui tranche net la conversation
Plus haute que toute terre	ôte toé de d'là qu'ma terre
Plus charnelle que toute eau	t'mâche les jos charnels

Charron's textual strategy in this context was to use Pilon's thematic (that of woman/earth/water/stability), a thematic which also was that of a whole generation of poets in the 1950s and early 1960s,[373] but to put it down, to vulgarize it, as Pelletier expresses it (love being here 'une affaire de cul').[374] Pilon's noble text was thus presented by Charron as an obscenity because it hid physical and sexual realities and chose to be idealistic, thus reinforcing bourgeois ideology.[375]

What is relevant to us today as observers of a certain literary history is to see how such political and ideological concerns, which clearly coincided with the rise of small Marxist-Leninist groups in the Quebec of the early to late 1970's,[376] impacted on a whole generation of writers, how a 'littérature de combat' emerged in those years – which have sometimes been compared to the early years of *Parti Pris* and to earlier texts of Paul Chamberland (*L'Afficheur hurle* and *l'Inavouable*, for instance) of Gaston Miron and of Raoul Duguay. It is not only François Charron's works and political writings which one should comment on in this context (though *Interventions politiques* [1974], *Enthousiasme* [1976], and *Propagande* [1977] would probably be the most illustrative) but also Madeleine Gagnon's *Poélitique* and Philippe Haeck's *L'Action restreinte*. What such texts do is to translate for us a certain universe, that of the political militancy and dogmatism of *Stratégie*, which directed its readers towards the only acceptable goal: the Chinese model. Texts were perceived as participants in a glorious battle (for the erection of socialism and a revolutionary party). The Chinese model is evidently presented by Marxist-Leninist militants as the perfect goal. Other elements emerge during this period, including the dominance of the 'we' form (in each of the three authors). One thus expresses one's 'fusion (souhaitée) avec l'avant-garde et le peuple ... il y a volonté d'être autre chose – et plus – qu'un écrivain "compagnon de route": un militant comme et parmi d'autres.'[377]

The middle part of the decade signals another transition: that of the strong affirmation of feminist discourse in Quebec. Madeleine Gagnon published *Pour les femmes et tous les autres* in 1974; Nicole Brossard, *L'Amèr* in 1977. However different their textual and political standpoints may be (the first proceeds from a perspective much indebted to Marxism, the second draws on a lesbian perspective which is mistrustful of ideological allegiances), both give us a feel for much of the contrasting mosaic which feminism will form in Quebec. While *Barre du Jour* (the old and the new versions) seemed to focus on textual politics per se, *Chroniques* opened the area of inquiry to ideological issues. Feminism was not perceived as a form of separatism but contextualized onto an ideological spectrum which comprises several forms of oppression. Most analysts of this period (Jacques Pelletier[378] and Philippe Haeck,[379] to mention only two) tend to summarize it as presenting two different facets, a formalist movement and a political one. While the dividing line is accurately described, it still remains that numerous individuals crossed it both ways. France Théoret, for instance, who was very much on the frontline of the formalist movement in the early 1970s (she signed 'Les Dix Propositions,' for example), also clearly connected textual pulsions and historical ones (*L'Homme qui peignait Staline* would be an excellent illustration of this capacity of hers). On the other hand, most writers change over a decade. François Charron and Madeleine Gagnon provide us with blatant examples of such radical textual modifications. *Chroniques* in the mid-1970s signals a clear transition from the monolithic positions of *Stratégie* to an ideological openness to the merits of other viewpoints (other, that is, than the merits of proletarian revolution or the Chinese model). Jacques Pelletier, with respect to Charron, calls this the conciliatory process. What *Chroniques* welcomes and documents during these years, while keeping Marxist leanings, are positions which describe the emergence of feminism, an interest in psychoanalysis, and a curiosity about social deviance (delinquency and madness in particular) which *Stratégie* never examined. If one considers textual politics as an intrinsic part of literary history, then clearly François Charron's definition of a new dialectic between 'the I and the we,' a dialectic which does not neglect either and thus fuses psychoanalytic pulsions with a sense of history, is not without significance.[380]

The Eighties: The Return to Singularity,
Individualism, Difference

Other similarly significant transitions are that of Nicole Brossard from textual production to feminist consciousness (with *L'Amèr* in 1977) and Madeleine Gagnon's subsequent distancing herself from the politics of texts and exploration of deconstructive practices. The history of literary movements never deals with fixed points and monolithic blocks, but that of the 1970s and 1980s in Quebec is particularly rich in contrasting turnabouts and changes of heart, which explains in part the recurrence of certain terms indicative of those phases. While Philippe Haeck in 1984 could speak about the 'mosaic' of the early 1970s counter-culture,[381] Marcel Bélanger was concluding about the decade of the 1970s that it had 'opened up onto a diversification of experiences, onto a pluralism which signals itself increasingly clearly. As a decade it was characterized by being simultaneously open to the self and to others,'[382] a comment which Suzanne Lamy was to develop in the area she was scrutinizing, that of feminism. She was to summarize the emergence of feminist texts in the same period of time as proceeding 'first from an abundant, passionate excess, then, at the end, from a diffuse light, a muffled, tenacious subversion.'[383] Such a comment strikes me as particularly convincing. There were bursting-out moments of anger in that decade, and certainly *Dieu* by Carole Massé, *Poélitique* by Madeleine Gagnon, and *L'Amèr* by Nicole Brossard were much a part of that explosion. But in the latter part of the decade textual directions preferred a diffuse and deconstructed approach. The text was not about to be circumscribed either by radically ideological imperatives or by purely syntactic or grammatical imperatives, as the early 1970s had attempted to do (see 'Les Dix Propositions'). While theory had triumphed in the 1970s, it seemed to take an ambiguously negotiated leave in the 1980s.

The most striking element of this literary history of Quebec for the last three decades is that it was usually one step ahead of its Canadian counterpart: into performances, while Canada was delineating verbal and aleatory doodles; into theory, while Toronto and Vancouver started discovering the merits of performances; and into deconstructionism when the other culture finally explored the arid territory of the said theory. The other key distinction has to do with the clear interaction between socio-political factors and literary ones. From *Parti Pris*, to the counter-culture, to *Stratégie* and *Chroniques*, and *Les Herbes Rouges*[384] the stakes were obvious. The cultural milieu of the 1970s, Jacques Pelletier tells us, and here he mentions André Beaudet, François Charron, Madeleine Gagnon, and Philippe Haeck (but he could have added Paul Chamberland, Carole Massé, Louise Dupré, Normand de Bellefeuille, and many more), if it was clearly and primarily anchored in the area of literature, never limited itself to it. The Québécois writers re-inscribed their practices within a wider terrain. Such a terrain included socio-economic relations and political pulsions. While such pulsions may be decoded from Canadian texts (and certainly from the reception they were given), they operate more out of a passive/reactive framework on the part of the writers than out of a clearly formulated perspective on their global environment. Once attacked, both bissett and Nichol reacted to the discourse which was attempting to situate and expel them. But with the exception of such moments, they were more involved with developing their own counter-cultural territoriality than providing their readers with an historical reading of their time. One could suggest, alternatively, that the utopian universe of the text was their access to history, thus to change. And I suspect at the end of the 1980s that Québécois writers, in their turn, with and through their deconstructed explorations, may now be going in that direction.

3 The Texts on Their Own: From Isomorphism to Post-Modern Disseminations

Peter Mayer once wryly commented on the difficulty of critically assessing the concrete phenomenon when he suggested that some of it signalled a renewal of art while other parts of it were a mere pastiche of pop.[1] In his view the most important step was to steer a fair course between the pro and contra views, between those who 'reject the movement because of the manifest mediocrity it includes and those who embrace the whole process because of the good.'[2] How does one separate mediocrity from talent? An attentive examination of texts, besides providing readers with an overall grasp of the trends and currents present, should also lead to a nuanced evaluation of the quality of the works in question.

One essential criterion here appears to be the concept of renewal put forth by Mayer. Indeed, what do these texts suggest that we did not know before? In what way do they do it? And is the way in which they are doing it unique, refreshing, and ground-breaking? Obviously, over a twenty-five year period concretism in Canada could not exclusively or even primarily offer momentous breakthroughs. There were failures, lukewarm and mitigated attempts, half-convincing directionalities, as well as precious little gems, humorously and sharply cut off from the mainstream, or tantalizingly determined to veer the latter off-course. Ultimately, impact upon the median (and wider segment of the literary body) could be the most decisive impact of the avant-garde. Pushing the limits, modifying the average, and exerting a bearing upon the larger profile had more far-ranging and deeper effects than the mere production of a few 'lovely' artefacts and tastefully produced objects. This larger impact was being noticeably felt by 1974. The poem's 'look' had changed: in texts that were not remotely connected to concrete experiments typography and semantics had undergone unexpected fusions. The linear and geometrically perpendicular writing of the 1950s and 1960s was rarer. The page was breathing with layouts following less the imperatives of traditional printers than the idiosyncratic needs of a text. Even the writing of narratives (narratives being necessarily more closely connected to prose and fiction) was modified (see the contrast between Nichol's early prose of *Journeying and the Returns* and his later *Martyrology*). Secondly the blurring of generic distinctions was one of the far-reaching effects of avant-garde pulsions within texts. But one should also admit that at times these innovations grew into tics and mannerisms, this being the surest way to stultification and sterility. Forms grow, change, and die. The saving grace of concrete might have been that it did not dwell beyond the 1970s in the purely visual territories it had cut out for itself decades before, but moved onto other, more uncertain ground. The first two phases, isomorphism and constructivism, deal with the initial part of this process; deconstructionism/post-modernism, with the latter.

Any rigid divisions raise problems, all the more so in this case because concrete went on to become polymorphous with the use of multiple media and the facetious rejection of classification, order, and pagination as a clear warning to those who believe in such categories. The following should therefore not be construed as the ultimate charting of the field, but rather as an overall view of the general and interconnected tendencies present in Canada throughout these three decades.

Isomorphism or Expressionism

Writing as synaesthesia, as the connection of all five senses and hence the invocation of all five, to use Peter Mayer's formula again,[3] has long had a firm footing in both Western and non-Western literatures. I pointed out in chapter 1 that Kratylian temptations may be a harking back to writing before the time when the removal of visuality from phonetic symbols gave us an alphabet that was just 'a step away from this aspect of language.'[4] The seventeenth century's closure of this old complicity between language and objects seemingly put an end to the discourse of patterning.[5] But closer to us, Mallarmé's 'Un coup de dés' signalled one of the modern era's sensational returns to this alternately repressed and expressed need.

In the context of the avant-garde Canadian poetics of the mid-1960s it could be said that isomorphism was the most abundantly explored propensity and undeniably also the most facile and the most evident. At one time or other virtually all poets who were in their thirties by the late 1960s and early 1970s had had a hand at doodling various visual-semantic offerings. No one would wish to see an exhaustive list of these various and mercifully brief attempts, but it is necessary to be aware of their widespread currency at the time. *The Cosmic Chef: An Evening of Concrete* (1970), edited by bpNichol, provides the most representative document of the times. While deconstructive inflexions are already present (see, in particular, Nichol's typewriter poem and bissett's contributions), the dominant pattern is explicitly isomorphic (see texts by David UU, Earle Birney, John Robert Colombo, Lionel Kearns, and Barbara Caruso). It exemplifies the intuitive pronouncements already formulated in the Brazilian Pilot Plan: 'In a first moment of concrete poetry pragmatics, isomorphism tends to physiognomy, that is a movement imitating natural appearance.'[6]

Nineteen seventy was Canada's first moment and *The Cosmic Chef: An Evening of Concrete* delineated this first foray. But while isomorphic texts must by definition be composed of linguistic elements (letters, words, sentences, punctuation devices) as well as non-linguistic ones (layout, graphic form, pictorial devices), there are intriguing exceptions to the rule which have managed to exclude verbal elements altogether. David UU's 'Impressions of Africa' (Fig. 3), whose only linguistic component is the title, is one of these. One could object here that rather than fusing word and pictorial shape he is giving us a pictorial, pre-alphabetic rendition of a certain message (or text). The order of this text can be determined by the numbered time-frames, and its semantic thrust by the self-explanatory graphics of each frame. In this culture we encounter abstract skeletons (1), animals depicted on walls of caves (2, 3, 4), as well as magic rituals (11) and various amulets (5, 6, 10). But 'Impressions of Africa' is an extreme case in that it eliminates, for all practical purposes, linguistic components from the picture.

Less extreme but possibly more sophisticated are the two well-known examples of quasi non-verbal concrete by Earle Birney, 'Figure Skater' (Fig. 4) and 'Chat bilingual' (Fig. 5), the latter being one of its author's favourites. The provocative device here is the elusiveness of the letters: practically indecipherable in *Skater*, where the *t* and the *e* have been eliminated; and elaborately stylized in *Chat*, so that the eye must strain to make out the *h*, an *h* whose ambiguity and dualism is aptly reflected in the curved figure of the second design. Amusingly implicit also is the bizarreness of this *h* (which can be read as an *x* in

the first figure and even possibly as a dual and inverted *b* in the second).
This highly facetious cat is as Janus-faced as it is undecodable
(greatness and miseries of the bilingual soul).

Also very rich at the research level are Nichol's 'Captain Poetry'
comics, which struggle with the visual and political realities of letters
as forms by suggesting an isomorphic rendition of linguistic breakdown. The death of the poem was a recurring obsession of the avant-
garde in general, and of dada in particular. The futurists have also left
us long, explosive, raging expositions of this terminal disease. Nichol
experienced similar nihilistic sentiments and left a few laconic
sentences on this matter: 'Please note that the poem is dead';[7] and 'i
killed the poem.'[8] His slow disarticulation of the alphabet in *Captain
Poetry Poems* is worth noting: most frames in this series show a
cumbersome, disintegrated alphabet being hauled away, pushed at or
occasionally stared at by a bespectacled cartoon character called
Captain Poetry. The latter seems keen to expose the death of poetry
and of the words that he struggles to carry out of each frame.
The isomorphic intensity of Fig. 6 is particularly interesting because all three elements (frame, pictorial content, text) are the
letter *A*. The self-deprecating irony here is that language destroying itself still remains language; the death of poetry still brings us
more poetry.

Two categories emerge out of this period. The first is that of
word-tapestries akin to Apollinaire's calligrammes (that is, words are
poured into a shape, be it an umbrella, waterworks, or raindrops, the
semantic message here being: rain is lovely, look at its exquisite
contours). In such cases the reader *must* look outside the immediate
Saussurean limits of the sign (signifier and signified). In such experiments phonemes are inserted into a predetermined graphic shape and
not the other way around. Judith Copithorne produced a number of
these. Her texts are designed with a graphic sophistication and
elegance one is not normally accustomed to in Canada. She had, over
Birney, bissett, and Nichol, the definite advantage of being the graphic
artist working with the tools and materials she is supremely adept at
handling. Her skill with calligraphy and overall design set her 'word-
tapestries' far apart from bissett's. The issues raised by them are
radically different. Bissett sets patterns of textual disintegration and, to
a lesser extent, of visual semantic isomorphism. Copithorne draws a
narrative. The ambiguousness of her texts stems not from their graphic
curves and disseminations, but rather from the elusiveness of their
identity. Are we to interpret them as architectural contours or actual,

identifiable words? Copithorne's signifiers are held in precarious and delicately charged balance. The calligraphics of 'Who you fooling girl?' from *Runes* (Fig. 7) have the uncanny appearance of being calligraphics from another (necessarily unknown) language, drawn not said, penned not enunciated. There are occasional isomorphic temptations (see Fig. 8, also from *Runes*): the chimes mentioned in the latter text could be said to find an isomorphic expression in the soft oscillation of the poem's drawn line. But, for the most part, Copithorne does not strive to achieve such effects; she traces a narrative in space, and more than a transmitter of lexical meaning, each letter is carried across the page as a trace, the aesthetic and graphic energy of a specific mood, of a specific feeling: the balancing and elated movement in Fig. 8; the impulsion of flight in Fig. 7.

The second category is that of works with a more polymorphous structure which make use of linguistic and non-linguistic elements bound to one another with an isomorphic intent. Examples abound, so that one can safely assume that works of this category are the most numerous as well as the most classical instances of concrete both outside and inside Canada. The generic term *collage* is in fact the archetypal category for such experiments. It would, however, be inexact to assume that all collages operate within isomorphic perimeters. A number of them in fact aim at deconstructing their own discourse rather than fusing the various components. The range they delineate is worth examining.

The author who perfected the genre as such in Canada is bill bissett. 'Life cuts thru all plans' from *Th Gossamer Bed-Pan* (Fig. 9) is an early example, and its isomorphism borders on facile representationalism with its collaged scissors doing precisely what the one sentence coldly enunciates. A not-so-oblique tribute to earlier explorations of this genre is paid on the bottom half of the poem and sets it in a certain intertextual field: Tristan Tzara's scissors and the hat into which he randomly threw newspaper cuttings are the intended references here. But more elaborate both in execution and statement are 'th lonliness of literacy' (Fig. 10) and 'a pome in praise of all quebec bombers' (Fig. 11). The first plays with the acrostic device on/one/lon/i and winds up as a wry comment on our so-called urban and sophisticated, yet diffracted, culture which leaves individuals stranded in their respective and alienated private spaces (be they child, man, or woman). In this space inhabited by cars, 'urbanized' trees, and highway lanes, numbers may be interpreted in a literal sense (as the numbers which routinely surge up in any metropolis) as well as in a metaphorical one (numbers are then viewed as money, as material acquisitions). Letters figure prominently, albeit in a way which reflects isolatedness, conditionalism, and incertitude (*eef, ie, if*) as well as the presence of commercialism, ads, and public relations men (see *PR* in bold letters). 'Th lonliness of literacy' is a space filled with letters and numbers yet paradoxically alienating and devoid of a reassuring social fabric. 'A pome in praise of all quebec bombers' brings into conjunction 'dirty concrete' and the jailed Quebec bombers (in a cell which presumably their prison guards order them to keep clean). The fleur de lys (symbol of Quebec nationalism), the exploding and tumbling down signs, and the y's (why) all coalesce to form a statement about a specific political situation as well as about historical occurrences.[9] Collages, in general, whether of an isomorphic or deconstructionist persuasion, were a product of the 1960s, and in Canada bissett was the most prolific producer of them. Collecting his collages in a single volume that covered the 1966–72 period would provide art historians with a telling configuration of the 1960s from both aesthetic and ideological viewpoints.

Earle Birney has produced remarkable collages in this respect. 'Up her can nada' from the 1971 *Rag and Bone Shop* (Fig. 12) has a provocative title, but in spite of its obvious sexual implications the title has its origins in seventeenth-century Spanish explorers' maps. 'Aqui esta nada' was the laconic comment on these maps about the area north of the Great Lakes. The emptiness intimated by *nada* ('nothing') epitomizes early 1960s doubts about a national identity in this country. But in making an expressionist use of a trite historical/sexual pun (the lines of the Laurentian-Ontarian territory as female anatomy), the text reflects Birney's approach to aesthetic effects, an approach which brought him close to the younger generations of concretists. Both the graphic delimitation of the u.s. border as 'northern limits of civil lies' and the crude sexual suggestion implicit in 'up her can nothing / or nada' (that is, she is a gaping hole leading nowhere) do not hesitate to reach out towards americanophobia and misogyny to make their points here.

Expressionism was often a natural choice for poetry in an erotic vein, the playfulness of typography coyly mirroring the frolicsome dalliance of sexual pleasure. 'aint no words for th taste uv yu' from bissett's 1974 *Medicine, My Mouth's on Fire* (Fig. 14) and his 'am/or' from *Awake in th Red Desert* (1968) (Fig. 15) amusingly refer to such possibilities. While such texts have incurred their author a great deal of media wrath and even parliamentary abuse,[10] it is tempting to look at them less from the polemical context they have often been read in and more from an aesthetic angle. How is bissett using isomorphic paradigms here? Is he crudely utilizing a pattern, or does he transform it by pushing it in a different direction? While Fig. 14 does not appear to go beyond the simple playfulness of isomorphic reflection, Fig. 15 attempts in my view to push the limits of this technique into a different territory. As Len Early has pointed out, one part of the poem, 'am,' expresses a fundamental existential loneliness, while 'or' raises the possibility of an alternative.[11] The solution suggested here is the last term, 'amor,' which culminates in the form of an erotic communion sometimes referred to as sixty-nine.[12] Truly bissett still exploits here the traditional representational impulse of isomorphic aesthetics in his visual instantiation of the 'objects' dealt with in the text, here the male and female sexual organs (a phallic shape becomes visible if one inverts the page, while by righting it a female emblem becomes apparent). Yet 'am/or' goes beyond a purely visual game to suggest, albeit still visually and typographically, a different set of issues and a philosophical answer to an existential problem. In doing this bissett tries to push the limits of the isomorphic technique towards the resolution of substantially more serious questions than sheer sexual play.

Yet one has to admit the criticism often levelled at such experiments, sometimes by disenchanted concretists themselves; namely, that once the core artifice, the compositional trick, has been unveiled, there is little more to be said about such texts. While such a reading is reductionist, it is also an accurate depiction of the actual reading experience. Successive perusings of Nichol's 'em ty' poem (Fig. 16) are not likely to provide us with multiple insights. No catch phrase here, but a 'catch twist,' self-consuming and auto-destructible, comparable to a listerner's disarmed pout which greets the sudden illumination of an hitherto incomprehensible pun. Once the illumination is consummated there can be neither repetition nor further exploration. The feat is accomplished and thereby terminated.

Constructivism

The constructivist mode may sometimes present a better concealed and less easily exhaustible pattern, but mostly it strives to open up content possibilities (signified) via the graphic or sonic features of its departure base (signifier). Bissett's 'Waves' from his 1972 *IBM* (Fig. 17) is an interesting instance of constructivist orchestration. It is only the final *s* of the sememe *waves* which creates a series of continuous lines. What is more, the final visual differentiation between all these letters suggests that while their semantic identity is the same (all *are* waves), none resembles the text (there are no two leaves in a forest or two waves in the ocean that are identical to one another). Patterns of regularity and irregularity between lines are similar to those existing between letters: they are all *s*'s, different, repetitive, continuous as well as uneven.

Bissett's frequent and elaborate use of the typewriter was instrumental in allowing him some spectacular feats of constructivist skill. 'bright turning star' (Fig. 18) is illustrative of this process because it manages to create the illusion of circular motion without using the obvious expressionist means (that is, a circular shape) to do this. Instead bissett chose to space his letters in such a way as to form tightly knit kernels which are kinetically designed to create a slow turning motion through a slow left to right reading pattern.

Letting the demands of the medium take the initiative is key to the constructivist process. In giving considerable initiative to the signifier one in fact is allowing physical components and chance occurrences (typewriter, ink, spots, smudges, lapsus, involuntary errors) to partially take over and determine both the outline and the semantic impact of the text. But these factors are not allowed to run wild (as they will be seen to do later during the deconstructionist phase). Still, constructivist inflexions had to allow the medium to work for and by itself, and much of bissett's work tends to choose these directions.

More calculated and less prone to allow for lapsus, for typographical and semantic chance, was bpNichol. Indeed it is significant that he did very little work with collages: run-on lines, graphics, and heterogeneous elements brought together in chance encounters do not figure very high on his list of choices. To those he prefers individual letters and minimal visual-syntactic structures. Letting the medium speak for itself involves here inversions and permutations. See, for instance, 'love/evol' (Fig. 19). The decomposition of the initial linguistic base (four letters / two words – one complete, another, *evol* (*evolution*), incomplete) works along geometrically parallel, perpendicular, and diagonal lines. Visually the text exudes order, control, and symmetry; and grammatically, with its two words, it is equally tight. There are no ruptures or breaking points.

The whole text is contained within these two words. It is revealing here that the linguistic process which gives shape to this utterance does not gloss over a plurality of messages. While isomorphism tends to reduce an utterance to a mere formula, a single code which cannot extend itself into a pluralism of interpretations (compare 'aint no

words for th taste uv yu'), constructivist texts once they have
established a particular utterance are capable of letting it branch out
into substantially different isotopic statements. In the case of 'love/
evol' the first one which comes to mind has to do with a philosophical
and theological reading of the utterance. The linking of evolution and
love reaches out to a wide spectrum of interpretative references (from
Plato to Christian theology if one wishes to limit oneself to Western
master codes, and from the Gnostics to other Eastern and Middle
Eastern spiritual traditions if one refuses to be restricted within
Graeco-Judeo-Christian perimeters). The problematic raised by this
particular utterance is obviously large and opens itself to various
culturally as well as theologically determined interpretations. The
openness of the process which leads to semantic explorations (that is,
the signifier taking us to the signified's field via various interpretative
pathways) contrasts here with the economy of its typographical and
syntactic means. Signifiers are the only material means which are
being put to use here.

'Solitude' (Fig. 20) by Paul Dutton, one of the Horsemen, also
illustrates this particular quality: no props or visual adjuncts here, but
only the letters which form the word *solitude*. Placed in a multitude of
combinations, while spacing between them remains identical throughout, the elements develop like photographer's prints in a dark-room.
All nouns, verbs, and adjectives in the poem are rigorously derived by
subtraction from the original set of letters; nothing is added. The
totality is self-contained, with the kernel term opening a wealth of
signifieds and permutations to the initially sceptical eye of the viewer.
(Compare Fig. 2, 'sem um numero.') Those signifieds operate either as
complete units ('toil' / 'destitute' / 'old' / 'dust' / 'elude' / 'sole' / 'stud' /
'lust' / 'ode' / 'to' / 'dilute') or as unfinished ones ('desult' – calling forth
desultory one can presume – and 'dolus,' impossible for me to
complete let alone identify). With the exception of 'lit' they are all
identifiable within one language. As signifiers they operate along
strictly perpendicular axes, with no element being displaced from its
initial locus except along the perpendicular below it. The visual and
grammatical tightness of the text (one returns to the initial utterance
at the end) does not detract from its semantic questioning and from its
contradictions. If solitude inherently contains 'dust,' 'old,' 'destitute,'
and 'elude,' how are we to integrate 'solid' and 'stud' within this
spectrum of possibilities? Dutton could convincingly challenge a
certain ethic here, that of the stud, of the lonely ranger, who
self-reliant and determined to protect his freedom, but equally and

ambiguously lustful ('lust,' 'lit') as well as 'tied' to this particular choice, is incapable of opting 'out' and therefore destined to live in solitude.

There are questions raised by Dutton's 'Solitude' and Nichol's 'love/evol' which place them on a provocative borderline between constructivist and deconstructionist texts, an area never specifically analysed by concrete theoreticians. Such borderline texts point in the direction of Saussure's anagrams. When the Genevan linguist attempted to decode Latin texts (Saturnian verse as well as Homer's and Virgil's anagrams, for the most part), he was convinced that names were concealed beneath the lines. Begun in 1906 and continued until 1909, his research could not get beyond a level of inconclusive evidence and was never published. His search had been aimed at a latent form and/or content hidden, but nevertheless contained, in the given text.[13] What is interesting is the use to which deconstructionists put this 'inconclusive evidence' or, as Jonathan Culler puts it, the latent patterns which they decoded from these processes:

> Kristeva and others ... have seen in Saussure's work a theory which emphasized the materiality of the text (the signifier as a combination of letters) and expressed the hypothesis of a particular signifying function, which dispenses with the word and the sign as the basic units of meaning ... the text is a space in which letters, contingently arranged in one way can be grouped differently to bring out a variety of latent patterns.[14]

What is opened up here is a field of quasi-unlimited freedom (the only boundaries are the original given letters) as well as an infinite set of possible relations. As Kristeva herself points out one can thus 'draw upon all the languages of past and future' contained in the geno-text.[15] This is a claim which Culler perceives as the myth of the innocence of becoming, the joyful right to produce meaning ad libitum, thus 'securing by the process ... invulnerability to any criticism based on positivistic criteria and levelled ... from the outside.'[16] Such texts are close to deconstructionist operations since their realm of interpretive possibilities can be almost infinitely extended. Latent graphic patterns open up the flow of semantic and typographical possibilities.

But while deconstructed texts were very much a part of a self-conscious exploration by Canadian writers, constructivism never fully developed, nor did it meet the amused fervour which playful isomorphic texts provoked around 1970 among a large number of writers not necessarily committed to concrete aesthetics. In part this may be due to a typographical deficiency among Canadians. If one analyses the most successful constructivist explorations in Europe, one notices that they were almost always the product of extremely sophisticated typographers, writers (particularly in Germany) who were also printers and graphic artists. They were masters of a whole area of skills which were almost unknown among writers in this country. Secondly contructivism was also related to a specific history, to the propaganda experiments of early revolutionary Russia and to media-related communication skills which necessarily took place in a context where the individual (poet/artist) wishes to communicate with a mass audience of listeners and viewers. Such sociological conditions, while very much real in the Soviet Union of the 1920s or even in the Germany of the 1950s and 1960s and Brazil of the 1960s and 1970s, were not present in Canada. Concrete discourse did not address a mass audience, nor did it see itself as potentially capable of doing so.

Could it be then that literary marginality and constructivism are contrary propositions? Robert Zend would disprove that hypothesis in that he succeeded both in exploring the constructivist vein and remaining marginalized. (While he was read and published, his texts were received more by a cult following than by a community.)[17] The sophistication of his craft is a testimony to his extraordinary graphic imagination and to his narrative sense of humour. Letter characters in Zend's poems offer both a complex typographical construction *and* a story. While his 'OAB' poem represents a major document in constructivist narrative,[18] his ditto poems are smaller gems which can be more easily quoted from and examined. Their interest lies both in their constructivist skills (that is, their typographical use of geometric as well as semantic patterns) and in their intuitive and ironic reading of Canadian society during the last two decades (that is, of moments of history embedded in different discourses, and in different individuals also). The focus of the 'me generation' incarnated in Barbara Amiel is also nuanced by the gleeful scrutiny of various political and intellectual figures. His careful constructivist vignettes of, among others, Northrop Frye, Robert Fulford, Glenn Gould, Irving Layton, and Pierre Trudeau, individuals Zend had plenty of opportunities to observe as a film editor and radio producer for the CBC, provide us with a novel angle on each of his subjects as well as a fresh glimpse of society's perception of them (see Figs. 21, 22).

His vignettes occasionally border upon satire (Trudeau = Rude / Pelletier = Pill), but they always do so with the very minimal elements of an individual's name. Subtracting and permutation are the only devices left to the writer here; adding, replacing, or modifying are ruled out. As self-contained units, Zend's ditto poems follow closely the rules of the game. Yet they simultaneously provide us with the amused viewpoint of an attentive observer of social mores, personalities, and idiosyncratic features. The same applies to the many Canadian buildings and institutions upon which Zend has bestowed his gleeful attention (the Canada Council, the Place des Arts, the Poor Alex, Stratford).[19] Irreverence for the trappings of respectability was very much a component of Zend's attentive scrutiny, while simultaneously his gaze had the incisiveness of the outsider's. As a Hungarian writer profoundly mistrustful of the many political and visual labels which had been current in the Europe of the 1940s, he had the capacity to go beneath appearances, to search for the hidden, the particular, the idiosyncratic in each individual. His musings on European complexities do not exonerate North America:

> The label makers of Europe in those years were strongly visual men;
> they selected colours to go with their labels; thus the German nazis
> wore brown shirts, the Italian Fascists black shirts, the Hungarian
> nazis green shirts, the colour of the Communists was red, the Jews were
> identified by yellow. Europe in the 30's was very much like the
> Rubic cube in the 80's ... Getting rid of the labels so fashionable in
> Europe was not the least reason why I left my country in 1956. But
> the free world did not deliver me from evil labels.[20]

Looking for the hidden aside was also what John Robert Colombo meant when he noted that such texts could not be read like ordinary poems, that they had to be scanned like radar or TV tubes.[21] But the 'work process' which Colombo imputes here to the reader does not detract from a sense of playfulness, and this is where constructivist Zend joins ranks again with other Canadian writers inherently more familiar with isomorphic techniques or deconstructed practices.

The Deconstructivist Mode: The Pull towards Post-Modernism

> The greater this freedom of choice, the greater is the uncertainty
> that the message actually selected is a particular one. Thus greater
> freedom of choice, greater uncertainty and greater information all go
> hand in hand.

> Warren Weaver, quoted by Louis Essary in *Precisely* 5, no. 3 (1979), 95

La clef est définitivement perdue. Là est la différence entre le plaisir cryptogrammatique simple (toute la catégorie de la trouvaille, où l'opération se solde toujours par un résidu positif) et l'irradiation symbolique du poème ... si le poème renvoie à quelque chose, c'est toujours à rien.

Jean Baudrillard, *L'Echange symbolique et la mort*, 302–3

To construct and to deconstruct: while both impulses underlie the concrete experience, the latter appears to be the prime motivating impulse of post-modernism. Very much present at the end of the First World War in dada, it made a spectacular come-back in the imagination of the late 1970s. Post-modern developments point – as Jean Baudrillard has shown – to the implosion of the signified, a spiralling motion wrenching itself free from the semantic constraints of the constructivist/structuralist order. In a sense nothing could seem more removed from the transparency of isomorphism than disseminated texts. While threatening the very possibility of a fusion between sound and sense, they also present a philosophical antithesis to Kratylian yearnings. And yet there is a deceptive terrain upon which the two occasionally meet; for example, that of bpNichol's 'Allegories' and *Captain Poetry Poems*. Looking back at Fig. 6, when Poetry (the captain) exposes the death of words and of their components (the alphabet) it is easy to see how one could equally look at this as not only the isomorphic 'mise en scène' of a specific utterance (namely, language is being destroyed), but as the process itself, the ineluctable and methodical demise of all representation. If deconstruction involves both the setting of the stage *and* the dismantling of it, then all of the 'Allegories' and *Captain Poetry Poems* go beyond the mere isomorphic articulation of a code, beyond a key structure waiting to be unlocked. One could argue that the 'Allegories' of *Love: A Book of Remembrances* (see Figs. 23, 24, 25), rather than announcing the code which is going to be processed in various directions ('The poem is dead,' says Captain Poetry), operate in a much more ambiguous, de-centred manner. All the textual elements physically present are engaged in a self-destructive process. While they comprise the basic components of a cartoon, they are also involved in a self-dissemination experiment: frame, characters, and text in bubbles are setting as well as dismantling the stage. In the same manner, *ABC, the Aleph Beth Book* uses letters as the resilient and bizarre components of an old and unknown order, here to endure but not to be decoded. If we look at Fig.

26, we will concede that it could be a *W*, or possibly an *M*, or even three *U*'s, while Fig. 27 practically escapes the possibility of any deciphering. *ABC* and *Captain Poetry Poems* suggest that there are survivors in this linguistic deluge and that however damaged, or crippled, they may be, they still are ineluctably there, as signs for the eye to see even though their signatum is neither self-evident nor within reach.

To attempt a classification of deconstructed texts smacks of the absurd. But to throw some light on this complex matter one could suggest different directionalities here, which do not cover the whole ground but give the reader a sense of the range of possibilities at hand. There are *effaced* texts, scripts which the eye strains and necessarily fails to decipher. Gerry Gilbert's 'INTO' from *Is* (see Fig. 28) is a case in point. No aggrandizement can salvage Gerry Gilbert's piece. It only brings to the fore the utter semantic disconnectedness of the deceptively ordered remnants we are being offered. Bissett's untitled piece from *Th Jinx Ship* (Fig. 29) explores the stylistic and philosophical possibilities of such barely decipherable, damaged texts. Yet disintegration here does not happen on the same stark allegorical levels as in Nichol's 'Allegories,' nor does it uphold the same rigour of stylization.[22] In bissett's work the dots, smudges, punctuation lines and dismembered sentences play a different game. They do not prophesize the death of the text as Captain Poetry does, nor even turn it into Gilbert's visual chaos, they merely mutilate it. One detects here the effects of what Jean-François Lyotard calls 'le sceau d'un manque,'[23] the imprint of a lack, the trace left upon the subject by this withdrawal, this slow denial, the signifier moving away, refusing itself, not opposing or destroying itself, but simply wandering off: a libidinal power similar to that of John Cage's, which does not oppose or criticize but 'goes around and infiltrates discourse [contourne et infiltre le discours].'[24] Such texts implicitly point back to the attitude of non-domination, non-power, developed by Freud when he elaborated modes of psychoanalytic approach.[25] One searches here for that which is not heard, that which creates opacity, silence: the obscure detail (not manifest meaning), the lapsus (not that which is elegant), the blank, the inky mess. Self-effacement and cumulative defacing are processes which occur over and over in bissett's work. It is tempting to suggest that no one else in Canada worked so hard at such methodical deconstructing processes. The scaffolding and squashing of one-sentence narratives, the lines repetitively and inexorably piled upon one another, is a standard bissett feature (see Fig. 30). This method can be pushed to the point that the accumulative weight of sheer letters, compressed one upon another, forms a simple aggregated mass of graphics (see Fig. 31).

Another more complex and ambiguous approach is that of *dissimulated* texts. To some degree these exhibit longings for a hidden code, a buried structure, to be unearthed for all to see after much patient archeological searching. Karl Young's *Should Sun Forever Shine* (see Fig. 32) takes us into such territories. The author assures us that his work is based upon fragments of early Latin writing, an allusion here to Saussurean efforts to find a decoding procedure in his anagrams. The process is made all the more ambiguous by the succession of perfectly identifiable words and non-signifying phonemes. The elusive sequence is essential for building up an effect of intense puzzlement in the reader. One proceeds from clearly enunciated sentences (albeit often humorously ominous) – 'The murderers say / with hands and hair / and tightly bind the wound /'[26] – to letter-columns which resist identification. The eye and the mind strive to reconstruct the ambiguous ruins, knowing all along that what they see is counterfeited and dissembled. Nevertheless they grope for a coherent sequence hidden beneath the masks, the disruptions, the successive searings into the narrative. This process, one of retracing, reordering, and reconstructing a narrative, resists the deconstructed strategy explicitly at work in the text, turning the reader into a logotherapist, a logotect.

A third mode is that of the *exploded* text, multi-composite, made up of disparate and even mismatched elements. An important number of bissett's collages as well as those of the Véhicule poets (to be found in magazines such as *Da Vinci, Maker,* or in Tom Konyves' *Poetry in Performance*) abundantly demonstrate such preferences. John McAuley's work in *Hazardous Renaissance* (1978) manifests this reluctancy to represent, this same rejection of expressionist modes. The results are diffident, difficult, and tantalizingly undecodable. It is possible that arriving on the scene as late as the Véhicule poets did (late 1970s), they developed a sense that isomorphism and expressionism had reached a point of exhaustion, to borrow John Barth's turn of phrase. As discourses they were no longer viable.

Collage and video poems were ideal vehicles for exploding Kratylian temptations, even though not nearly all collages and video poems can be said to proceed from them. In fact, as has been seen earlier, collages as an art-form may operate along isomorphic or constructivist strategies, especially those political collages which explicitly pit themselves against a certain order (in bissett's case, the military power of the United States, nuclear build-up, middle-class economic, social, and sexual expectations, consumers' foibles, and a certain pervasive Canadian docility at this end of the century's morass). Such are not the texts which concern us here. Not that explosions are devoid of any political thrust, but the latter term must be redefined. Deconstruction could not avoid the concept of power. By dismantling the order of sentences, writers are necessarily undoing a specific order, a particular perceptual system. Lyotard has focused on this problem, albeit in a disillusioned fashion, when he commented that 'there is more revolutionary potential in American pop art – even if that is not a lot – than in the discourse of the communist party.'[27] Lyotard's vantage point is the 1880–1920 period, in which he sees deconstructionist effects contagiously spreading to most art-forms. In his view the artist's task becomes not so much that of constructing new forms or even good forms as deconstructing old ones. In music, for instance, the old scale was discarded and dodecaphony introduced. In painting cubism ushered in a radical rupturing away from mimetic forms. What the artist rejects in all these instances is the sacredness of art, a dimension which would turn it into a surrogate religion by bringing on a participation in 'un même sous-sol de sens ... un même sacré,'[28] a shared geological level of significance. Graphic space, typography, and the signifier become the revolutionary values introduced by Mallarmé's 'Un coup de dés,' and critical activity moves away from the 'social signified,' in Lyotard's terms. Baudrillard confirms as well as develops this generalized dissemination. Social structures reveal the same anagrammatic dispersion as the literary signifier: 'Car le secret d'une parole sociale, d'une révolution c'est bien aussi cette dispersion anagrammatique de l'instance du pouvoir, cette volatilisation rigou-reuse de l'instance sociale "transcendante."'[29]

But just as Saussure failed to establish the key-word, the latent sememe-theme, in unearthing the disarticulated and hidden crypto-gram, all that emerges out of this quest is 'its dissemination, dismemberment, deconstruction.'[30] And here Baudrillard undermines Starobinski's subtle structuralist search precisely because it falls – in spite of itself – into the trap of the generating formula 'whose scattered presence in the text would be another version of [the key-word] but whose presence you could and should always identify.'[31] Reading would then be reduced to an identifying process, and uncovering this key is but the unveiling of a formula which exhausts and depletes meaning. The intensity of a radical revolutionary impulse lies in admitting this total loss. The formula does not exist, the key is

definitely lost. Here lies the difference between a purely cryptogram-
matic pleasure – wherein the finding procures pleasure – and the
symbolic irradiation of the poem. One finally admits that God is not
the hidden subject of the utterance, nor poets the subjects of the
enunciation. 'C'est le langage lui qui prend la parole pour s'y perdre ...
le texte poétique est l'exemple enfin réalisé de la réabsorption sans
résidu, sans trace, d'un atome de signifiant ... le poétique est devenu le
lieu de notre ambivalence vis à vis du langage, de notre pulsion de mort
vis à vis du langage, de la puissance propre à l'extermination du code.'[32]

The need to escape from the order of even a fragmentary meaning, to
destroy the possibility of ever grasping a reassuring and signifying
finality is never as explicit as in the six texts performed in London by
bpNichol and Steve McCaffery and subsequently published in *In
England Now That Spring* (see Figs. 33, 34). Not that these texts
deconstruct meaning any more, or less, than bissett's letter-tapestries,
but they bring to the fore the activities of oral poetry and performances
in the 1970s.[33] During that decade the trajectories which phonic poetry
and video performances determined for themselves were geared
towards ephemerality. Initially their documents were as impermanent
and fugitive as the concept of dissemination: basically they dispersed
themselves in space. It was not until the mid-1970s that actual
recordings or prints survived the experience of performance.[34] The six
London texts, half-way between numbers and letters – sometimes
both – and sometimes choosing to be erratic tracings which merge into
meaningless glyphs, direct us precisely towards the fugitive drifts
referred to by Lyotard and Baudrillard. Texts speak, give voice to
different impulsions, argue them out, expatiate upon them. They also
fold in and double over, refuse transparency, clarity. They interpose
between themselves and the eye complex twists which create opacity
and oppose to the reader a barrage of arduous, often unresolvable tasks.

Isomorphism and deconstructionism, the two directionalities chosen by concretists in Canada, are as diametrically opposed as possible.
There is an uncanny antinomy between the polarities which have
underlain the discourse of concretists from the beginning. Nonetheless, deconstructionism took over and progressively dominated the
field in the mid-1970s, before becoming the dominant discourse of
post-modernist practice. The progressive emphasis of theory – in
particular by French deconstructionist thought – might have been a
significant factor in this course of events, but it could not have been an
absolutely determining one.

Textual disruptions destabilized literature and/or discourse a long time before being philosophically theorized about. The dadaist experience is an almost emblematic case in point here. The very ambiguity of the concretists' textual positions in Canada, their perpetual oscillation between fusion and disruption, must have been obliquely present in Nichol's mind when he noted that bill bissett was a conservative, a traditionalist operating within the demands of a radical return to the roots of language, to the foundations of language.[35] Nowhere better than in his 'Allegories' does Nichol himself illustrate this particular point.

In questioning and torturing the primary components of our Western linguistic script he forces us to scrutinize the opposition/tension which underlies the politics of concretism. It should be noted that the first phase, the isomorphic longing for primeval unity, was the almost-too-facile fad of the 1960s. Practically all poets of bissett's and Nichol's generation had a hand at it. There was a definite ludic element about it. It was perceived as a playful game that could be briefly and facetiously performed, a sort of typographical and semantic acrobatics in which graphic artists may not have wanted to become involved because of the obviousness of its technique, but which tempted writers for a brief while since, after all, verbal/visual doodles and mischievous icons had been noticeably absent from the Canadian literary scene. What Nichol refers to as an anamnesis and a necessary regurgitation is a significant phenomenon, not only in his own individual development but also in that of a whole generation.[36] Texts had to be brought back into the field, and what may have looked to some like a ludicrous hankering after the 1920s and the 1930s was also a taking stock, a belated awareness that needed to be achieved before other textual politics could be raised. Yet this analysis has a disturbing and dangerous linear component about it, in that it proposes to look at creative and imaginary acts as if they were disposed on a horizontal line: critics, readers, and audiences would thus only discover them by going backward or forward. As Nichol put it in 1985: 'There is not one tradition ... that supplants another, but there are streams that co-exist.'[37]

But the development of post-modernism has placed us, both as a society and as producers of imaginary constructs, in a wholly different terrain. The post-modern imagination rejects linearity. Links within a large contextual ensemble – whether it includes dadaism, futurism, constructivism, or other isms – do not operate along straight horizontal lines and genealogical structures. Intersections, palimpsest, and blanks would be more appropriate descriptive tools.

Two Canadian writers appear to me to be essential to a perception of the post-modern stance in this culture. In contrast to bissett and Nichol they did not come to such experimentation through concretism but followed a different growth process. The isomorphic or constructivist explorations of the 1960s did not function as motivating factors for their creativity. Both Daphne Marlatt and Robert Kroetsch, though in different ways, were to explore post-modern perspectives during the 1970s and the 1980s and to address a number of issues from novel angles. They both shared an awareness that the British and American forms which had for the past 150 years been operating as systems fostering our intellectual security – as well as insecurity – in fact confronted a universe at odds with them. Both raised the question of origins, the dream of origins, that of cosmologies which may or may not be located.[38] For instance, one notices immediately in Kroetsch's work how he seems led towards those metaphors that best express unformed, preconscious experience.[39] As a writer Kroestch constantly comes back to the chaos of origins (or the dream of origins) or those cosmologies which cannot – thank heaven – be located, and this is what makes his world 'prefixual'; incapable of finding satisfaction with words, he insists upon prefixing them with new beginnings: the *un*named, the *de*-created, the *de*-mythologized.[40] Kroetsch himself in *Labyrinths of Voice* recognizes his two-sided stance about tradition versus deconstruction when, after quoting Boris Tomaschevsky – 'The writer constantly tries to solve the problem of artistic tradition, which in literary experience is like the encumbrance of an ancestral heirloom' – he quickly adds: 'The writer constantly tries to solve the problem of artistic tradition ... [but] I guess I don't like to solve the problem.'[41] As a borderman caught between extremes, Kroetsch confronts the problem of tradition versus innovation, and Robert Lecker points out that the lesson to be drawn from this fundamental tension is not which side wins out in the end, but rather what strategies this writer uses as a borderman desperate *both* to invert models, parody history, and scorn convention and search for 'his father, his father's father, and other fathers too. Cervantes, Chaucer, Conrad, Dante, Faulkner ...'[42]

Kroetsch's interest in French literary theory, particularly Julia Kristeva's and Roland Barthes' work, comes as no accident into the total picture of his work, both the fiction and the poetry. While fiction lies – to a degree – beyond the confines which I set out in this book, examining a bit more closely the developments of *both* and their relevance to deconstructive approaches might help situate the problematic of post-modernism. It has been persuasively shown how Kroetsch's fiction (*But We Are Exiles, The Words of My Roaring, The Studhorse Man, Gone Indian, Badlands, What the Crow Said*) defies a centred system, how it characteristically pulls two ways at once by de-creating, de-mythologizing, and hiding while simultaneously creating, re-mythologizing, and un-hiding. With his most recent fiction, *Alibi* (1983), another element comes to the fore, embodying the aesthetics of Roland Barthes' *The Pleasure of the Text* ('The text is a fetish object and this fetish desires me'):[43] 'An alibi implies a cover-up, dressing/undressing, untelling and telling. The Barthesian seductive interplay of this fiction lies in its intermittence in this staging of an appearance-as-disappearance. The garment used here is language: Kroetsch here will hint, will slowly undress the text, will reveal glimpses of this body, but he will not reveal all, will not satisfy our desire, simply because desire satisfied is desire negated.'[44] One critic took the author to task precisely for failing to reveal, to fulfil, to undress possibly.[45] And it is true that on a certain level Kroetsch plays with our desire to see the whole conundrum offered to us – that of a journal destroyed and then recreated and re-edited – resolved, reconstructed into closure. But, as Lecker patiently demonstrates, 'within Kroetsch's Con/Text such a resolution would destroy the act that has engaged us; the performance remains erotic only so long as something remains covered up.'[46] While *Alibi* is a story about the creation of alibis, it still remains that the reader is never allowed to reach a form of synthesis, that the parts of the text can never be conclusively made to fit together. To use Barthes' image of the spider dissolving in the constructive secretions of its web, the author's unmaking here can only provide us with a text that 'dissolves as it is formed.'[47]

Such a 'grammar of delay'[48] equally underlies Kroetsch's poetry, particularly his approach to the long poem. His equating the act of long-poem writing (and reading) with the act of making love gravitates/hinges around a certain definition of delay. For him, delay in both these acts is simultaneously technique and content. By resisting narrative progression lovers/poets resist closure, orgasm, death. Writing a long poem is an erotic gesture which postpones fulfilment, delays the reader's ultimate response. In his critical essay on the form of the long poem Kroetsch focuses on this basic tension, not only in his own long poems but in Canadian long poems in general, and what he isolates as the core contradiction is 'the temptation of the documentary,' on the one hand, with its wealth of facts, its verification and closure, and 'skepticism about history,' on the other (with its attendant mistrust of facts, verification, and closure). As tension it produces 'a kind of madness in the recording, a pressure towards madness and against it; photographs, collages, analyses, protests of accuracy and source, after-words.[49]

This yearning for coherence amidst disjunction is very much part of the strategy underlying *The Ledger* (1975). By definition a ledger reminds us of the inscribing of credits/debits, balancing figures, but here it is also 'a book of final entry' because it describes the author's inward journey to record his past, his grandfather's and his family's story. Thus *The Ledger* 'calls up ancestral voices while recording its own attempt to speak,'[50] its author's attempt to find his voice, his style, and as such it captures this unstable dialogue between interpretation and fact, between fiction and reality. *Seed Catalogue* (1977) (see Fig. 35) similarly overlaps facts (a specific monotonous horticultural list) with poetic musings (on the absence of western philosophers, royalty, and bottle openers). *Seed Catalogue* simultaneously explores a need to break with tradition, to break away from Western enclosure (its Sartres and Heideggers), to 'undo, erase, unform,' as Lecker puts it,[51] and an obsession with evoking names and places (the Seine, Rhine, Danube, Thames) that seem as irrelevant to the speaker in a Prairie town as seem the scabios and schizantas which 'transpire' through the typography of the poem to the reader anxious to move on with the story. *Seed Catalogue*, as do Kroetsch's other long poems, his essay 'For Play and Entrance: The Contemporary Canadian Long Poem,' and his fiction, confronts us with a traditional desire – that of giving form through writing to the unformed, scattered, and unretrieved memories of a Prairie town – but also breaks form through delay, parataxis, erasure, and superimposition. As a strategy of the lost and found and lost, it strives 'to recognize and explore our distrust of system, of grid, of monisms, of cosmologies perhaps, certainly of inherited story,' yet at the same time 'it attempts to create a world that has some unity.'[52] While Kroetsch reminds us in 'For Play and Entrance' that there can be no joined story,[53] he 'wants that joined story as much as he resists it.'[54]

If along with disseminated practices the attempt to ground narrative in history was what best characterized post-modernism, no one was better aware of this than Daphne Marlatt. While the process which was to see her through the 1960s and the 1970s was markedly different from that of the young concretists and while she had more affinities with Tish and Black Mountain than any of the avant-gardists who explored the concretist dream,[55] she had defined by the late 1970s a textual territory which was subtly but inescapably delineating post-modernism in Canada.

Her intuitive exploration of the brooding remnants of collective memory brought her to try to retrace her own, her mother's, and her family's vagaries across three continents as well as that of a Japanese fishermen's community.[56] The family narrative and her mother's tongue are first searched for in *How Hug a Stone* (1982); the fishermen's community in *Steveston* (1974). Both explorations, the personal and the communal, are also pursued in *Touch to My Tongue* (1984), where they leap into still another territory, that of women's tongue and women's bodies. Such feminist concerns are what best connect Quebec's literature of the last fifteen years with that of Canada's. But while the first emerged out of a community of women, the voices of Daphne Marlatt or Lola Lemire Tostevin appear to be relatively isolated. But reference to Quebec women writers is explicitly made by Marlatt, who appears to draw energy from it:

> Julia Kristeva says: 'If it is true every national language has its own dream language and unconscious, then each of the sexes – a division so much more archaic and fundamental than the one into languages – would have its own unconscious wherein the biological and social program of the species would be ciphered in confrontation with language, exposed to its influence, but independent from it' (*Desire in Language*, 241). i link this with the call so many feminist writers in Quebec have issued for a language that returns us to the body, a woman's body and the largely unverbalized, presyntactic, postlexical field it knows. postlexical in that, as Mary Daly shows, with intelligence (that gathering hand) certain weeds (dandelion sparks) seed themselves back to original and originally-related meaning. this is a field where words mutually attract each other, fused by connection, enthused (inspired) into variation (puns, word play, rime at all levels), fertile in proliferation (offspring, rooting back to *al-*, seed syllable to grow, and leafing forward into *alma*, nourishing, a woman's given name, soul, inhabitant).[57]

The relationship of women to language is sketched in lines which contrast the old proprietorship of the other culture with the sense of complicity, of openness to lexical explosions and rule-breaking, of the new one:

> she leaps for joy, shoving out the walls of taboo and propriety, kicking syntax, discovering life in old roots.

> inhabitant of language, not master, not even mistress, this new woman
> writer (Alma, say) in having is had, is held by it, what she is given to
> say. in giving it away is given herself, on that double edge where she has
> always lived, between the already spoken and the unspeakable, sense
> and non-sense. only now she writes it, risking nonsense, chaotic
> language leafings, unspeakable breaches of usage, intuitive leaps.
> inside language (48)

Critics have often commented – specifically in the context of
post-modern aesthetics and the Canadian long poem –that the feeling
of being disenfranchised by language and left unaccounted for in
history, already present in the early years of Canadian literature, came
to find its most intense articulations in later years.[58] Marlatt's intense
feeling for specifically articulating the unaccounted for, the inarticulated, comes to the fore in *Touch to My Tongue*:

> language thus speaking (i.e., inhabited) relates us, 'takes us back' to
> where we are, as it relates us to the world in a living body of verbal
> relations. articulation: seeing the connections (and the thighbone,
> and the hipbone, etc.). putting the living body of language together
> means putting the world together, the world we live in: an act of
> composition, an act of birthing, us, uttered and outered there in it. (49)

Marlatt's natural and unself-conscious discarding of the specificities
of literary genre is also 'a resolving of the dilemmas of modernism.'[59]
How Hug a Stone is part travelogue, part narrative of the mother's lost
story, of the daughter's reminisced childhood tongue; what was
familiar is now relic: 'sweetshop, pillarbox. clipped monosyllables
with a distinctive pitch pattern. remnants of old English, even moth,
snake, stone. word henge to plot us in the current flow. without
narrative how can we see where we have been? or, unable to leave it
altogether, where we came from.'[60]
In the same vein *Touch to My Tongue* is part musings on linguistic
theory, part meditation on Mary Daly's post-lexical fields and Julia
Kristeva's *Desire in Language*, part celebration of the lover's body and
tongue. As a post-modern stance it reaches not only for an erotics of
language that unites both self and other but, more to the point, for a
'writing that unites both our external and internal selves,'[61] a concern
which Marlatt articulated very early on. Her interview with George
Bowering is explicit on that point:

> Language is leafing out, it's everything that is growing that is or-
> ganisms, that is body. It's a body. I love that phrase, the body of lan-
> guage. And I'm trying to realize its full sensory nature as much as
> possible. We live in the world. That's my basic assumption. I don't
> want to get out of this world. I want to learn everything I can about
> what it is to live in this world, to be mortal, which I take to be in the
> body. And language, you know, generates itself & it dies, but it's all
> there in the body, & that's why I love the music.[62]

But to go back to her abiding tension with history; it would be mistaken to suggest that it stands as the simple relationship of biography
to writing. History for Marlatt is also stories, and 'stories can kill,' so
that history may also be simply 'the shell we exude for a place to live
in? all wrapped up.'[63]

Thus history in *Steveston* is specifically a geographical locus, the
physicality of the Fraser River and the community which ekes out a
meagre existence at its mouth just as 'words do at the mouth of the
body.'[64] And it is this physicality which determines the writing of a
past and present chronicle, not the observer's tentative objectivity nor
the historian's gaze, but the attempted fusion of observer and object.
Language is a body substance and so is *Steveston*, its underwater
weeds, the burnt stilts of its houses, its marshlands, and the wooden
cutting boards where women behead the fish. This doubleness of
perception, of the historian as discoverer and explorer, but also as
dweller, was best articulated in her interview with Bowering:

> Put yourself inside the head of a bird as he's flying down a channel of
> water. Okay. Now the image would be what you see if you are outside
> on the bank looking up at him. That's not what I'm interested in. I'm
> interested in getting you inside his head in flight. And everything's
> moving. There is still no reference point because he's in flight, you're
> in flight. Who ever's reading.[65]

Steveston is not the lyric discourse of a writer observing the strange
and obsolete ways of a fishermen's community. When it attempts to
ground the narrative in history (their stories), it does not do so as a
documentary which accepts the convention of the represented speaker,
but rather, 'through its incorporation of other texts, other perspectives, other voices, [it] ... moves to drown out the singular represented
subject in a chorus of voices.'[66] Smaro Kamboureli sees in the

development of this form the emergence of a dialogic discourse in the Bakhtinian sense of the word.[67] She stresses the polyphonic nature of this form and reminds us of Bakhtin's perception of it as a text 'constructed like mosaics out of the texts of others.'[68] Even though Kamboureli's main focus here is Eli Mandel's *Out of Place*, her remark may be taken in a broader sense. Marlatt's *What Matters: Writing 1968–1970* and *Touch to My Tongue* specifically bring Hélène Cixous' words to a critic's mind: 'A female text is never-ending, it goes on and at a certain point the book ends but the writing continues ... a female textual body is always without end. It is aimless, endless and pointless ['sans but et sans bout'], it never concludes ... what happens is an infinite circulation of desire from one body to another.'[69] And Godard concludes that 'through the collective weaving of a matricial fiction ... and this ubiquity of fictional production the feminist writer inundates (and so exhausts) the male writer with an "amniotic flow of words." '[70] Such a flow she contrasts with the metaphor which has conventionally regulated textual production, 'that of the phallus/pen which marks the uterus/page informing the female as it deforms her.'[71] Thus such writing not only uncovers female language but also exorcises a certain perception of reality. As Marlatt puts it succinctly: 'It is / my mime / against the grain.'[72]

Lola Lemire Tostevin, in the Afterword to her *Gynotext* (1983), circumscribes a common territory for herself when she notes that

> phenotext [is] the familiar language of communication, the formula of linguistic analysis, while genotext operates at a level which does not necessarily reflect normal structures but generates elements of language in process ... A sprouting which develops as a seed instead of sentence. It is against this double background that *Gynotext* was conceived. At the ridge where becoming of subject is affirmed and developed through process.[73]

Both Tostevin's *Gynotext* and *Color of Her Speech* (1982) generate such processes. The duality of her reflexes is compounded also by that of her linguistic origins; French and English oscillate in the writing pulsions of Tostevin, so that pheno- and geno-text also intersect with two contrasted cultural idioms. The oscillation becomes reversal becomes oscillation as the last three lines of '4 words French 1 word English' in *Color of Her Speech* reveal: the lullaby is also by a lie (farewell to and simultaneously close to a lie).[74] The demultiplications are infinite and point in Tostevin to a fine ear for disseminated feminist practices.

Typography/Layout/Spelling/Syntax/Metrics

The other essential question which confronts the critic is that of the systemic changes which concretism and post-modernism worked upon texts. What was their nature, their function, their impact? Typographical and calligraphic aesthetics were most striking in the 1960s, but also the least durable. They corresponded to the Kratylian phase of the experience, and while they inserted into texts typefaces hitherto unknown to literature, the experiment was as short-lived as Judith Copithorne's tastefully designed books. The only typefaces that were to survive the next two decades and make decisive inroads into the deconstructionist phase were bissett's grim typewriter letter-types. These never changed and became his essential trademark.

The multifarious nature of Canadian concrete typography, its uninhibited mixture of hand-scrawled characters, Gothic letters, light effects,[75] and typing-over techniques, is a trademark of Canadian writers. The diversity of the means used – while devoid of the craftsmanship and exacting elegance of more professional concretists like the British Edwin Morgan and Ian Hamilton Finlay or Brazilian poets Haroldo de Campos and Decio Pignatari – was also a significant characteristic of Canadian poets. Subsequent developments indicate that both the imperfections and the diversification of the typographical means used set the course of textual politics in the direction of deconstructionism. What might have looked at the time to be an amateurish playfulness and a refusal to commit oneself to 'clean concrete' turned out to be choices of a more complex nature as well as the progressive privileging of dissemination instincts over isomorphic perfectionism.

Some changes were to have more lasting effect on the broader literary spectrum. Such was the case for layouts, which after the 1960s were never quite the same in Canadian poetics. The awareness of space as a graphic and signifying agent was to become a permanent addition. A random comparison of layouts prior to 1964 and after 1980 is revealing in this respect. Even writers who had never or seldom experimented with concrete techniques had by 1980 abandoned regular margins and straight-lined verse. One could suggest here that projective verse and Black Mountain poetry had already opened the field widely to such an airing of the line, but the point is that the graphic alignment of print on the page, while never going back to the visual antics of concrete, retained from it a flexibility and a suppleness that registered the moods of the poem in a manner which was experimented with long after projective verse and isomorphism had disappeared from the field.

It is a truism to affirm that poetry necessarily breaks strict grammatical rules of semantic usage and word order, yet in this instance they were once again the most seriously challenged areas. If one looks at the texts of only four Canadian concretists (Judith Copithorne, Earle Birney, bpNichol, and bill bissett), one finds that their defiance of these specific categories varies greatly. Copithorne is the most conventional of the four, and her only serious syntactical provocation is in the reading order of her texts, which may be read clockwise, counterclockwise, from centre to periphery, left to right, top to bottom. The alternatives are as numerous as the number of subsequent sequences, so that in fact one does not have here a set text but a range of possible texts depending upon the eye's whim. But her syntactical structures are simultaneously respectful of accepted patterns. Absent here are the gaps, omissions, and breaks so common to concrete.

An examination of Birney's syntax provides similar pointers. Since visual arrangements and verbal layouts were his forte, the next logical step for him was to experiment, as did Copithorne, with different reading orders. Version no. 2 of 'Like an Eddy' (Fig. 36; cf. Fig. 13) illustrates this technique, and in fact the attractiveness of the text stems from the eye's resistance to going from right to left in order to extract sense out of it. Syntactical continuity is equally threatened in 'On the Night Jet' (Fig. 41); but this is the product of a simple optical illusion for, in fact, a careful reading of the spaced-out letters amply demonstrates Birney's faithfulness to traditional syntax. Clearly grammatical disruptions did not press any demands upon him.

An examination of Nichol's texts yields more tantalizing results. For instance, consider 'Clover' (Fig. 37), a poem divided in three parts. Throughout most of 'Clover' lexically identifiable words are absent, and we are left with single letters and groupings of vowels and consonants spread in irregular stanzaic shapes, defying not only syntax but also semantics.[76] Recognizable groupings form clauses, but these lack verbs, prepositions, and even subjects. Series of subordinate clauses are not connected to a main clause, and time prepositions do not introduce anything, but are left hanging in midair: 'when when when in heaven and hell.'[77]

Discontinuity and omissions are favourite tactics of Nichol in the area of syntax. A careful examination of The Martyrology, which is the most emblematic testimony of his whole writing career, confirms this assertion. See Figs. 38 and 39 from Book v, which examines vital and textual drives operating through various phonological break-downs ('He(a)ven / ologies / mologies / rep/tition / s en s'e's sence') These sound/sense variations are also cyclothymic breathings. But no single clause has a departure point and/or an ending, and it is just as difficult to point out which clause is missing as to determine where one started from. Sentences (and here the term might be more appropriate than *clauses*) are a transcribed but inarticulated libidinal flow. At the other end of the spectrum Nichol almost deprives the reader of the act of reading. The 'Allegories' (tormented letters) or the uncertain letter scribblings transmuted into numbers ('Mushy Peas') are illustrative of such self-conscious excesses (see Figs. 33, 34).

Bissett's work is the most ambiguous of all on the level of syntax and grammar. His programmatic statements about the radicalness of his challenges have been more than brutal. Both his collages (see *Sunday Work!* and *Lost Angel Mining Company*) as well as his scaled-down stanzas sometimes need to be turned at a ninety degree angle to be deciphered. These variable reading patterns frequently give us several texts instead of one: the reader chooses, and the combinations are his creation (see Fig. 40, from *What Fuckan Theory*). The large white spaces which separate printed matter into graphic figures may give the optical illusion that the text is syntactically discontinuous, but, remarkably enough, it is not. Very few elements are missing here. Occasionally an indefinite article or an auxiliary seem to have been deleted, but each of the potential texts is relatively sound from the viewpoint of grammar. Consider, for example, the opening lines from Fig. 40:

> its a saving i poemd 13 on one page
> i
> like
> bing
> a poem
> i fell
> like
> a
> poem today hony

The only affront to correct syntax here is the transformation of the noun *poem* into a verb. Whereas Nichol omitted key words in his clauses and gave only the fragments of a whole we shall never see, bissett offers us a series of possible texts, several alternate poems.

Obviously many of them have gaps too, but seldom at the structural-grammatical level. When he does cut an element out of his sentence, it is a letter (in Fig. 40, in the middle of the page, the *e* of 'b cause' and the *e* of 'xpect' are missing).

Bissett himself had a revolutionary vision of syntax and a peculiarly anarchistic concept of words as units keen on defending their freedom from any authority (grouping, rule, reference) whatsoever: 'words can also be non-directory, non commanding, non structuring, non-picturing ... away from the conscious death-sentence.'[78] His syntax illustrates these principles to some degree. The layout of his collages –particularly those from *Th Jinx Ship nd Othur Trips* – not only puts sentence structure to a hard test but also destroys it.

In other texts, such as *Living with th Vishyun* or *Medicine, My Mouth's on Fire*, the grammatical structures offer so many combinations that they become comparable to geometrical variables. The absence of punctuation (see Fig. 40) allows for a variety of structures, depending on the reading order. Absent from his work are the gaps, blanks, and omissions used widely by Nichol. Absent also are the nonsensical words inserted into the text to disrupt it. The only occasion when bissett uses onomatopoeias and conglomerates of syllables is when he mounts them into a geometrical figure and juxtaposes them with the rest of the text (see Fig. 30).

If one places Birney, Nichol, bissett, and Copithorne on a scale that measures their ability (or their need) to challenge conventional syntax, Copithorne and Birney appear to be the least audacious. Next comes bissett, whose reading order and orthography go definitely against the grain of convention. But Nichol is the most serious challenger because he not only breaks grammatical rules (by choosing words which make no sense and inserting them into sentences which are bound to be absurd) but because he also ignores semantic imperatives.

Spelling is another area which warrants some examination. Not all four challenged basic spelling rules. In fact, Birney and Copithorne were extremely docile in this area. Birney occasionally practised humorous phonetic spelling in non-concrete poems and prose works.[79] As for Nichol, his spelling is remarkably conservative compared with other aspects of his writing (such as syntax, logic, and semantics). Phonetic spelling, a technique which not only concretists but also Tish and Black Mountain poets before them had practised extensively, is to be found only occasionally in Nichol's poems. When he does use it, it is with onomatopoeias and lexically unidentifiable words.[80] All others are spelled according to dictionary specifications.

Bissett likes to break rules of orthography, and his spelling idiosyncrasies will be understood only by a well-trained bissett reader. Phonetic spelling is one of his outstanding trademarks. No Canadian poet spells the way he does, and yet it is possible to become so accustomed to his code that no transposition or effort is involved. *You* invariably becomes *yu*; most terminal endings in *le*, such as *single*, become *ul* (*singul*); *ought* is transcribed as *ot*; *thought* and *brought* as *thot* and *brot*. All past participles are contracted into *d*'s, such as *sd* for *said* or *movd* for *moved*. Long diphthongs such as the [i:] of *beautiful* are recorded as *beeutiful*. Phonetic representation is obviously what bissett is striving for. Most vowels, consonants, and diphthongs which are spelled in a way very different from their actual pronunciation find in bissett's text a different graphic representation and usually one which is close to their sound identity. One should also recognize the relative consistency of his writing.[81] Defective verbs such as *could* and *should* are invariably spelled *cud* and *shud*; present participle endings usually become *in* (*turnin*, *greetin*). He advocates and practises a return to the carefully recorded script of a sound track in his books from 1966 on. *What Fuckan Theory* best represents bissett's ideas on these issues. For him, breaking the chains of oppression meant breaking traditional spelling rules. But he created new rules for his readers, rules which are ultimately closer to a phonetic reading of English than to texts respectful of orthographic rules.

Be it a rhythm or a form, what characterizes metre in English is a certain type of stress recurrence, a specific association of strong-stressed and weaker-stressed syllables.[82] The disruptions and modifications introduced in the field of metrics are comparable to those which affected the area of syntax. Since by definition visual concrete poems are written for the eye's perception, they set out to explore the laws of sight and optics and their relationship to our semantic universe. Metrical elements remain therefore somewhat secondary to visual ones. Does this mean these became obsolete during the isomorphic and constructivist phase of the movement?

In most of Birney's poem-drawings metrical patterns are non-existent. In a number of cases, this is due to the quasi disappearance of linguistic elements. In 'Chat bilingual' (Fig. 5), 'Figure Skater' (Fig. 4), or both versions of 'Like an Eddy' (Figs. 13 and 36) the only language materials are the title. In other poems, where the visual arrangement of words has been given obvious priority, such as 'On the Night Jet' (Fig. 41) or 'There Are Delicacies' (Fig. 42), metrical patterns can be studied only in close relation to layout techniques.

Consider, for instance, 'On the Night Jet' (Fig. 41). Here the simple order of succession of each of the poem's components – and therefore its rhythm – is completely dependent on the reading order adopted by the reader. A simple visual law is that the eye tends to read first what it can immediately decipher, then slowly interprets the other letter-puzzles. The necessarily halting deciphering of the poem has several effects upon its metrics. First, it gives the poem a variety of metrical patterns; second, whatever pattern is determined by chance or by the eye alone is unsustained and interrupted – a free-flowing reading being exactly what this type of layout sets out to destroy. Where there is no multiplicity of reading orders, the halting effect is retained through the visual complexity of the word arrangement. One question that comes to mind is whether this halting quality, the brokenness of the metrics, can resist the effects of time and habit. A third and fourth reading of 'There Are Delicacies' indubitably reduces the hesitancy of its rhythmical patterns. The metrics of the poem are not a fixed quantity, but are dependent on previous perceptions of the text – the only constant being precisely their changeability. One could even reach the point (after n readings) when hardly any visual effort is involved and the metrical pattern becomes what it would have been had the lines been set in a straight, horizontal, left-to-right order.

Typographical characters have as much impact upon metrical patterns as layouts. Revealing in this respect is Birney's 'Campus Theatre Steps' (Fig. 43), which uses five different kinds of typefaces. The modifications introduced into the overall rhythm of this poem are linked to the size, spacing, and aesthetic of these typefaces. The trembling print of 'the Griffins are' expresses excitement, rising expectations, and therefore a change or a rise in the tone of voice. On the contrary, the utilitarian print used for last week's movie title 'The Miracle Worker' imposes a certain evenness on the reading, a rhythmic uneventfulness. The italics of 'the international hit' break the regularity of the straight typeface and consequently affect the continuity of its metrics.

Do the typefaces Nichol uses affect his metrics in the same way? Consider several examples: the 'Allegories' from *Love: A Book of Remembrances*; the phonetic, onomatopoeic pieces from *Love*; the visual poems from *Still Water*; the comics from *Captain Poetry Poems*; and the typographical feats from *ABC, the Aleph Beth Book*. One common denominator emerges: there are no multiple reading orders here. The elements are organized in such a way as to allow for only one metrical arrangement. The order is given or set and cannot be modified.

Metrics in 'Clover' (see Fig. 37)[83] present both traditional and avant-garde elements. The fact that there is only one metrical pattern is certainly traditional: we are being given a specific structure and there are limits to the alterations we can make to it. The fact, however, that a good portion of the poem is composed of letters instead of words, unconnected clauses instead of sentences, and onomatopoeias instead of recognizable idioms demonstrates a propensity for avant-garde forms. The white spaces set between the letters which begin the poem are clearly indicative of a specific rhythm. The author does not want us to read these letters as a continuum but as separate units. In this instance, the text and its layout operate as the visual indicators in a musical score. The white spacing which follows the m of line two shows that the reader's voice should give line two as much time value as line one. Since there is only one letter in line two – as opposed to three in line one – it is logical to assume that the blank stands for a pause. The length of the pause is determined in each line by the size of the spacing left between two units. It is equally clear that the spacing between lines varies from single to triple. This also is an indication of the tempo and rhythmic structure scored by the author. It is evident that lines paired closely together function virtually as stanzas, while isolated letter units operate within a wider time structure. The score becomes more complex in the third stanza, as the spacing and therefore the rhythm becomes more and more discontinuous and unexpected.   ·

If the typography of Nichol's poems has a major effect upon their metrics, it plays a similar role in Birney's, though with the difference that here we are dealing with much more rigid forms, since both the eye and the ear are given less freedom. Yet Nichol and Birney share specific patterns. For instance, Birney's shape poems are comparable to Nichol's allegories – both have reduced linguistic matter and therefore metrics to an absolute minimum. 'Allegory no. 26' (Fig. 25) and 'Allegory no. 3' (Fig. 24), for example, reach the point of no return where words and metrics have been obliterated. From this viewpoint they are very close to Birney's 'Figure Skater' (Fig. 4).

However interested she was in the visual aspects of the poem, Copithorne seldom went to such extremes as Birney and Nichol. Though the most talented and proficient in terms of the graphic aspects of poetry, she never obliterated the linguistic component to the extent the other two did. With Birney she shares one important feature: a wide range of metrical patterns dependent upon an equally wide variety of reading orders. Whereas Nichol wrote in recognizable lines – occasionally grouped in stanzaic patterns – Birney and Copithorne drew their words and arranged them as visual objects, Copithorne by turning them into arabesques or pure graphics, Birney by splitting them into letters and dispersing them on the page. They preferred this approach to the line and the stanza – as used by Nichol – which must have seemed to them to be false, rigid, and predetermined moulds. Because all Copithorne's words are drawn and all her letters endowed with an intensely idiosyncratic style, the reading of her poems is initially a deciphering experience. It would be inaccurate to suggest that clearly defined rhythmic patterns emerge out of her texts. Her metrics are consciously undetermined, so that the reader, the individual eye, is left to map out a variety of rhythmical patterns, depending upon the associations made between different words. In this sense she is non-commanding, non-assuming, non-hierarchical. Still, one striking recurring feature of her metrics is the repeated use of the terminal ending of the present participles. Copithorne is the only Canadian concretist to make a systematic utilization of the diphthong [in], a peculiarity which gives a unique character to her lines since one inevitably associates this sound pattern with her poetry.[84]

In terms of metrics, bissett was possibly the most original of the four. He shared Nichol's taste for onomatopoeias and nonsense syllables but pursued this interest consistently by building up his onomatopoeias into mantric patterns. Bissett's 'yu cum' (Fig. 30) is an instance of such variations on given vowels (u and um), but there are many more in So th Story I to and Liberating Skies.

One should not forget that bissett showed a great deal of bravura about shaking the traditional line and its left-to-right norms. He consistently rejected stanzaic patterns. His metrics therefore depend upon the order the eye chooses. Another favourite device of his was the dada phonic variations on one word – the forms of this word varying constantly: nominal, adverbial, participial, etc. An instance of this technique is shown in Fig. 45, where we observe the metrical values of a given root (please) through many of its derivatives (pleasing, pleased, pleasant). The tonal key in this case is the root (pli:s), the metrical device the exploration of the rhythmic qualities of all derivatives.

More than any other Canadian concretist his metrics were broken, halted, interrupted (either by graphics inserted between two words or by black blocks which deliberately smudge the text). He moved into this area with a destructive urge which pushed him on to eliminate numerous grammatical, syntactical, and semantic units from his poems. The final outcomes of such radical moves are often the debris of a forever unknown text. Metrically speaking it gives us semantically disconnected pieces. Whereas it is always possible to put the pieces together again in Birney's poems – the reading process thus becoming a reorganizing, integrative experience – with bissett it is impossible. It seems as if the text is playing against us, preventing us from finding our rhythmic patterns. In Fig. 46, for instance, the remnants of a text are so hopelessly muddled that no recurring rhythm can be found. We are left with an uncontrollable debris of metrics.

Conclusion

The politics and poetics of concrete in particular and of post-modernism in general have been under attack from a variety of sources. The questions raised about both and the challenges which put the latter to task are of two kinds. The first proceeds from a formalistic perspective and suggests that the concept of a *breakthrough*, dear to avant-garde aesthetics, is fraught with dangerous assumptions.[85] The second concerns itself with ideological issues and suggests that any pretense at changing the sign system does not in any way imply that one is modifying the political system. If anything, such delusions play into the hands of the political powers in place. Emblematic in this respect are the changes (from initial approval to ultimate disillusionment) in Herbert Marcuse's positions between the 1960s and the 1970s. His initial statements on non-objective art, abstract painting, and twelve-tone composition appear – in a first phase – to coincide with European perceptions of the breakthrough determined by such forms:

> These are not merely new modes of perception re-orienting and in-tensifying the old ones, rather they dissolve the very structure of per-ception in order to make room ... for what? ... the senses must learn not to see things anymore in the medium of that law and order which has formed them: the bad functionalism which organizes our sensi-bility must be smashed.[86]

Part of the whole problematic hinges around this 'for what?' interrogation of Marcuse in 1969. His programmatic intentionality here is clear and runs against the grain of Roland Barthes' and Susan Sontag's arguments for an art which is self-sufficient and self-justifying, and against the use of language for means beyond itself.[87] For Marcuse it is essential to bring release from the rationality of the established system, but equally important to change the latter.

His disillusionment with vanguard art did not take long to appear. In 1972 his *Counter-Revolution and Revolt* refers to post-modern disruptions as symptoms rather than criticisms of one-dimensional society.[88] This disillusionment was shared by many others who had initially and simplistically seen in the rise of the counter-culture a radical cure of the ills of capitalist consumer culture. In fact, the proliferation of what they now called 'new industries for the profitable dissemination of ... alienation and liberation' was to them but a hypocritically disguised and stylized powerlessness redefined as sexual potency (an obvious barb at Barthes et al. here) which only mirrored the old system it purported to despise. As Jay Martin disparagingly put it, 'Both are permissive, media-oriented, pleasure-oriented, a-historical.'[89]

With the late 1970s there appeared another breed of theoreticians who bypassed the problems set by the opponents of post-modernism (Graff et al.) in a subtle, politically elusive, *and* provocative way: Jean-François Lyotard in France, and the contributors to *L-A-N-G-U-A-G-E* in the United States, to name only a few. These writers depict politics and writing as linked in complex ways, as leading to certain kinds of hegemonies, to 'policies over the body,' over communities, as Bruce Andrews puts it.[90] Thus, to challenge present modes of discourse is also to interrogate the political institutions and apparatus of a formal democracy, to use Andrews' terms again. This questioning goes far beyond a naïve disruption of signifiers (signifiers are not the political system – the state is)[91] and suggests instead diffuse, ubiquitous, deconstructive processes. Writing does not need to satisfy itself with pulverizing relations and discharging excess. It can also charge material with possibilities of meaning, create relations rather than just demolish them, and thus reach and act on the world. Such suggestions are not a plea for backtracking into naturalism or social realism, but rather an effort to accept the interlacing of realms of experience and to open the closed circuit of the sign. To undermine the great master discourses of Western culture has been the task which feminist poetics in this culture has most clearly undertaken. I have shown how writers such as Daphne Marlatt and Lola Lemire Tostevin have scrutinized such possibilities and have skilfully placed us in front of their paradoxes. Such an opening or such an interlacing is also at the core of the experiments of the Horsemen, Owen Sound, and a number of late 1970s performers. As a release of energies, phonic poetry provides a personal and therapeutic function as well as a collective one.[92] The ludic and playful patterns developed by dada during the First World

War period were not lost on subsequent generations of phonic poets. Aleatory elements in particular and their subsequent facetiousness in general were important pointers never lost on the Canadian sound groups.

The therapeutic function of sound, however, was a different matter. It was not clearly put forward in the international concrete movement, just as it had not been articulated during the dadaist years (either at the Cabaret Voltaire or in later Berlin, Paris, and New York developments). Some critics will be quick to interpret this phenomenon as part of the social fabric of the late 1960s and early 1970s, when therapy in group-encounter sessions was a frequent predisposition of Western society. The fact that this particular function did not survive beyond those times would force one to concede that such an assumption has some validity. Nevertheless, two other related factors should be highlighted here: that such sessions slowly turned into 'performances' as the decade grew on; and that these performances (video or others), with their deconstructionist values, were one of the most outstanding phenomena of the late 1970s and early 1980s. They were only obliquely related to concretism in that they dealt from the beginning with a number of elements concretists were basically unfamiliar with: stage, props, decors, costumes. The Véhicule poets who emerged out of the 1970s are a pivotal group of artists in this respect. Having started out with concrete experimentations, they moved on to sound performances, then to video ones (particularly Tom Konyves), and subtly integrated themselves into a core of aesthetic concerns akin to concretism but already at some distance from it.

Looking at the textual developments of these three decades several points come to the fore. There was from the early 1960s on a sense of polarity in Canadian concrete. This polarity was a tension between order, on the one hand (that is, Kratylian faithfulness to what was perceived as order), and chaos (that is, destruction of the representation of old political and word orders), on the other. The link with dada has often been pointed out, and indeed it is obvious on different levels. Linguistically, politically, and metaphysically concretism – as dadaism half a century earlier – presented different alternatives.[93] The pull towards post-modernism which manifested itself in this culture from the mid-1970s on and became increasingly evident with the emergence of performance art presented a different set of possibilities. Antinomies gave way to more generalized, more diffuse deconstructive practices. Feminist writings – both Marlatt and Tostevin are significantly present here as well as male writers in sympathy with the dissemination of old practices (Kroetsch's and bissett's texts should be mentioned specifically) – modified this polarity. The question was not whether one should represent or explode reality, but rather how to watch it implode and observe the process. The polemical intents of the late 1960s and early 1970s (*What Fuckan Theory*/TRG manifestos) have given way to the disseminated practices of the 1980s. Robert Kroetsch and Daphne Marlatt in this decade are not rewriting another history; they are giving us possible stories. bpNichol is not offering us a room with a view on the death of language or Captain Poetry's musings, but a poem which goes on and on, saints which muse on and on, because there is no finish line, no end, no beginning, just an infinite spiral which goes on and on.

THE TEXTS ON THEIR OWN (QUEBEC)

From Calligraphics to 'la nouvelle écriture'

Standing Outside Time: Paul-Marie Lapointe's *Ecritures*

While it is true that there are few concrete texts in the strict definition of the term to be found in Quebec culture, there have been derivations from and forays away from concrete. One writer, however, produced a volume that fits almost too perfectly the concrete expectations of the late 1960s, except that his book came out in 1980, went by unnoticed, and – however well-established its author – did not create the progressive ripples of interest usually provoked by such texts. It came too late, at a time when the *nouvelle écriture* had considerably altered readers' expectations. When *Ecritures*' isomorphic and constructivist texts came out, such practices were too removed from *La Nouvelle Barre du Jour*'s and *Les Herbes Rouges*' contemporary interests to find an echo in Montreal literary circles. In more than one sense it was unfair to Paul-Marie Lapointe's personal trajectory (from his 1948 *Le Vierge incendié*, one of the first surrealist poetic works produced in this country, up to these 1980 texts), which should have alerted readers and critics to the significance of the successive poetic stages thus retraced by this author. It is true that there are elements of anachronism in *Ecritures*; true also that this book retraces all of the successive stages international concrete went through, from the isomorphic mid-1950s, to the later constructivist elaborations of the late 1950s, to the final semiotic explosions of the early 1960s in Brazil, with the strange qualification that it all happened in 1980 and came from a writer who, in spite of his early affinities with surrealism and automatic writing, had never even distantly associated with the concrete movement or the *nouvelle écriture.*

To a degree *Ecritures* stands outside immediate Québécois history, outside its collective and contemporary pulsions, and if it has any intertextual links these are clearly outside North America. While it can be very easily connected to an international context (mostly European and Brazilian), it stands aloof from the discourse of *la modernité* which was the dominant practice of the times. And yet while its aloofness is convincing one cannot help retracing in its pages deconstructionist instincts which have not been detected by critics or observers. Indeed constructivism largely dominates the text as well as a few witty attempts at isomorphism, but there also are other pulsions present in this book which stand on a precarious line between constructivism and deconstruction. Consider, for instance, 'Arbres' (Fig 47). In some ways such a text operates in a constructivist vein: it decomposes various components and regroups them in random phonemic clusters. Such regroupings both distract us from, as well as bring us back to, the core word (barbare/berbere/barbe brr/ear/bar). But what slowly emerges here is the presence of several idioms, emerging in and out of French sounds, so that a native language (French in this case) opens up and takes us towards other known (English) or un-known, undecodable ones. The laws of random association allow us to come into contact with such idioms. Such multilingual explorations are akin to Nichol's gropings in *The Martyrology.* Like his they betray an archaeological sense of language (that is, our idiom, the house we dwell in, changes constantly in and through time) as well as a cosmopolitan one: this idiom of ours is not the only one on the planet; it intersects and interconnects with others (for example, the 'ear' of Lapointe's 'Arbres,' which merges in with 'barbare' and 'berbere').

Lapointe's formidable aloofness might be more apparent than real. Seen from a larger context, his work was far from set apart from the poetic discourse of the 1980s, even though few critics commented on it and fewer writers referred to it.

Calligraphics and Performance Scores:
Raoul Duguay's *Le Manifeste de l'infonie* and *Lapokalipsô*

It might be tempting to see Duguay's two volumes as works closer to musical/dramatic scores than to texts for the eye alone. While the Horsemen seldom published their scores,[94] Duguay saw his as care-fully annotated descriptions of the tonal, rhythmic, and structural features of his work. He even referred to *Lapokalipsô* as 'une partition poétique ... une suite de suites en contrepoint.'[95] The 'Concerto en si b dur pour 33 machines à écrire' (Fig. 48) is another score for a more facetious exercise of Duguay's (incidentally it was actually performed by thirty-three typewriters and aroused quite an outrage at the time).

Apparent discontinuity in Duguay's texts masks a tight structural organization.[96] The lines of Le Manifeste de l'infonie are numbered from 1 to 333 (a kabbalistically significant number). Lapokalipsô is also composed of 333 pages as well as of a set of series which interconnect and finally converge towards a single point: the letter O, the poetic analogue of totality, beginning and end, the omega point.[97]

This sense of self-containment recurs throughout the apparent multifariousness and whimsical diversity of these texts. Can one speak of isomorphism here? Not in the strict, narrow sense of the word (sound/sense, sense/shape), but from a broader perspective the multi-directionality of the texts is isomorphic with some features of the surrounding society (Babel / The Fall / a utopian yearning for unity again). The crazy inventory, the ragtag of sonic/cultural/verbal directions given by Duguay in 'Hosanna Osaka O' (Fig. 49), mirrors contemporary confusion. Yet it also ineluctably aspires to order. The letter o closes most poems in Le Manifeste de l'infonie and this one is no exception, taking us from Hydro Quebec to chewing gum via rising tides. Note in the middle of the poem that 'O Est à la Fois un Désordre Total et un Ordre Total.'

Duguay's pyramids (see Fig. 50) function within the same broadly defined isomorphic perimeters. The initial reaction to them might waver between irritation (why squeeze on the same line chant/prière/parole/machine/télévision/plan?) and mirth (the conjunction of homme/animal/végétal/minéral/mû does force ludicrous acrobatics onto the reader's mind). There are obvious binary oppositions in this text; for instance, orient/plein/amour versus occident/vide/faim. Such oppositions have an obvious political connotation, but there also are very simplistic ones (oui/non, univers/cellule, ordre/désordre) which neither reveal any ideological bent nor attempt to engage the reader in unravelling processes.

Interestingly enough Fig. 50 is not systematically symmetrical. Words are not necessarily paired off either in terms of their metrical feet or in terms of semantics (that is, words are not necessarily paired off according to oppositional semantic vectors). Yet for all its apparent absurdity this pyramid is curiously related to very tightly structured metaphysical concepts, including the Egyptian perception of eternity (pyramids being used in maintaining matter in a specific, determined state). Apart from the first line (the symbol of all unity ô), all others are divided by a blank space in the middle. The total number of letters on each side of this space is the same (except for line 33 with 27 letters on one side, 28 on the other: but it is the last line and could the end of the world be as symmetrically balanced as its beginning?). The predetermined nature of the layout, its rigidity as a form, points to picture-making more than to concrete poetry. There is nevertheless a tempting isomorphic suggestion in the poem's strategy (based upon the tensions between semantic disorder and graphic order). The 'sacredness' of the form (the pyramid) cannot hide the fact that we are faced here with absurd word-series, disconnected fragments, lined up in succession with one another. The fact that absurdity is contained within order and not outside of it indicates a tangible and possibly divinely controlled order, one which carefully maintains and protects a given form. In more than one way this text could be said to be non-deconstructionist, pro-centre, and pro-metaphysics of presence (the ô being the presence).

This ô, or yearned-for unity, calls back to mind the Palongwahoya myth often mentioned by Nichol and frequently used by bissett. But the mythology of the centre of Duguay's texts does not relate to native Indian myths but rather to Western occult sciences. At that particular time in history (late 1960s, early 1970s) the North American counter-culture had opened its doors to both Eastern mysticism (Buddhism/Hinduism) and Western occultism (astrology, Tarot). The insertion of texts directly derived from such traditions was frequent in those days. Duguay – and to a degree Chamberland – were both extremely susceptible to these referential fields. It was not rare, for instance, to find in current magazines text-announcements celebrating the coming of a specific astrological configuration and doing so in an elaborately calligraphed fashion (see 'La Naissance d'Ora' [Fig. 51]).

While such pulsions are very much akin to Nichol's (*The Martyrology*), they are in direct contrast with the simultaneous developments of *la nouvelle écriture*. In the context of what I called earlier the 'multi-dimensional period,' that of the political and social upheavals of the 1960s, a time when global challenges were the order of the day, it is curious to observe the two diametrically opposed expectations of that period: explosiveness (on political, sexual, social, and artistic levels); and globality, totality, fusion. There also are clear indications that such a psychedelic culture contained a utopian vision as well as the certitude that the whole fabric of human existence could and would be changed.

Beneath the humorous cumulative effect of Duguay's totalizing concepts the reader is being made to perceive the sum total, the aggregate whole, of a certain project (see Fig. 52, from *Le Manifeste de l'infonie*). This fusing of jocosity and momentous totality is present throughout Duguay's scores of that period. In fact, both books' titles, *Le Manifeste de l'infonie* and *Lapokalipsô*, are seminal indications of later development. The first parodies the manifesto as form and yet aspires to be a total sound, the totality of sound 'totalisant, toultemps dans tout.' The latter announces an apocalypse (and what could be by definition more comprehensive?) as well as a dance, a festive celebration, a calypso.

The calligraphics of Duguay are worth close consideration, partly because they are an inherent part of the various scores examined above, and partly because in numerous cases their form and layout are deceptively similar to those of medieval illuminated texts. For example, 'O vie' (Fig. 53) could easily be seen as reminiscent of some of Copithorne's calligraphics, except that in this case one does not notice even a vestigial effort to integrate form and sense. This poem appears to be an 'adorned' version of a conventionally printed text, the original version having been improved by – and essentially framed with – a variety of embellishing graphic decorations. But this is an instance when the calligraphic effect is deceptive, when, in fact, it covers up for the functionality of a musical score. Upon closer examination Fig. 53 reveals different shades of calligraphy which indicate distinct phonic emphases for each sound. Such a diamond-shaped text could at first be taken for a picture-poem, but a more attentive decoding reveals its complex functioning as a phonemic score to be sung or chanted. A graphically different but functionally similar device is to be noted in 'L'Apocalypse' (Fig. 54). A different weight of typeface is used here to signal emphasis as well as intimate a warning of apocalyptic catastrophes unless capitalism modifies its ways. The primary characteristic of such a text is comparable to the preceding one. Both are scripts to be performed, produced on stage, rather than poems to be read in the silence of one's mind.

Illuminated texts such as 'Puissent' (Fig. 52) and 'O vie' (Fig. 53) remind us that their medieval antecedents had specific functions, mainly religious and ecclesiastical; and, in fact, the semantic pointers operative throughout *Le Manifeste de l'infonie* belong to a similar field: devotional, exhortative, and structured as entreaties to the divinity (use of the exhortative subjunctive, prophetic imperatives, etc.). The calligraphed section of the book stands as an illuminated

Book of Prayers; the other half, as a facetious carnival of the various aesthetic and social codes which constituted the fabric of the 1960s. See in the latter respect 'Cuisine micromacrobiotique infoniaque,' 'Calendrier des éphémerides infoniaques,' and 'Vibration-percussion yin-yang' (Figs. 55–7). Their relevance as concrete materials is more than dubious. But their pertinence to the experimentalism of that decade in North America does not need to be proved. The inversion of registers, genres, styles, and codes is particularly related to the *carnavalesque*, a code explicitly formative and determining of the 1960s in Quebec.[98] Duguay gives to this reversal a strong public connotation:

> J'utilise ... les anomalies du langage – recto tono, bégaiement, zézaie-
> ment, chuintement, nasonnement, grassayement – dans le but de
> mettre en relief certaines dimensions du langage oral ou pour établir
> des contrastes entre la langue populaire et la langue littéraire. Ou alors,
> je transforme les paroles des chansons ou arias, des 'westerns,' du
> chant religieux, de la chanson folklorique, militaire ou populaire. Par
> exemple, j'écris des paroles religieuses sur un air de 'western.' etc. ...
> j'inverse les valeurs pour les mettre mieux en lumière, pour provoquer
> une conscience plus aiguë de la diversité des expressions, des degrés
> de conscience, et des différences vitales qui existent entre les diverses
> couches sociales. De la morale, quoi ... Tout est à dire ...[99]

Collages as Forms: Constructed and Deconstructed

Political articulation was of paramount importance in the poetic texts of the period 1965–72, and it is interesting to see how collages at that time dealt with these concerns. One notices two opposite tendencies in the same form. One is integrative, the other deconstructionist. Yet both operate in an isomorphic way by reflecting certain world states, specific ontological data. The ideological politics of the first are more articulated than those of the latter, which presents the dissemination of certain expectations and by definition avoids resolutions or purpose-ful determinations: textual and ontological realities are purposefully kept in a state of chaos. 'Here they are – their very being is political' could be the latter's motto.

'Vers le grand changement' by Paul Chamberland (Fig. 58) illustrates the integrative approach very eloquently. Published in 1974 in the counter-culture periodical of those years *Main Mise*, it manipulates two historical levels in an explicitly charged ideological fashion. The two periods brought into close contact and under scrutiny are ancient Egypt and Watergate America. Jacques Pirenne's quotation brings to the fore a certain political context interwoven with social malaise, violence, and economic crisis. The French historian's excerpt is graphically parallel to the photographs of the First Lady and President Nixon, but it sparks off a semantic nexus about and across a Memphis-Washington axis. The question and answer clauses 'qui êtes-vous? – je suis la mère de l'espèce humaine et je suis son enfant' operate within similar perimeters.

In ancient Egypt the divinity was both male and female/ mother/ child. Here in the contemporary United States Pat Nixon is the First Lady (Our Lady), and her husband the leader and quintessence – at least in Chamberland's terms – of that culture. The dual nature of the Egyptian divinity thus finds an unstable counterpart in the presidential couple. This collage produces meaning (a meaning incidentally tied to a specific political period and not necessarily understandable to a post-Watergate reader) by integrating heterogeneous elements. Under the guise of presenting us with chaotic conjunctions it in fact fabricates a unified, global meaning, and if there is rupture, in this case it is directed towards the emergence of a new order, here not linear but centripetal, moving from an outwardly bizarre discontinuity towards the dense focus of a meaning-producing logic: the United States are chaotic, troubled, and seminally so is the whole of mankind.

Other collages found in the pages of *Main Mise*, *Hobo-Québec*, and *Cul Q* bear upon political concerns in a substantially different way. History and politics, whether of ancient Egypt or the contemporary United States, do not necessarily come into the field. Rather one witnesses sexual and semantic disseminations. The breakdown of sentences is accompanied with desultory erotic photographs, fragments of diaries never to be recovered in their entirety. Mainly, and this to a much larger degree than in Chamberland's writing, the quotation-collage as a form is ushered in. Contemporary philosophers and theoreticians, Brecht, Mao, Deleuze, are high on the list of the quoted, but there are also quotations from other Quebec writers: Denys Vanier quotes Paul Chamberland and Patrick Straram; the latter inserts excerpts by Denys Vanier and Lucien Francoeur; Francoeur uses Vanier and Chamberland; Nicole Brossard is virtually quoted by everyone everywhere. There is a dizzying and incestuous merry-go-round of quotes going on in the collage-montages of the period. Chamberland had – as early as 1972 – used a large number of epigrams and excerpts from rock and pop musicians: Jim Morrison, the Beatles, Janice Joplin. But with the next generation this practice becomes a generalized endogamy.

Collages abound in magazines of the early and middle part of the 1970s. As the decade wore on they slowly left the way for other experimentations to replace them. (*Rockeurs sanctifiés*, by Lucien Francoeur, a book of collages which won its author the 1983 Prix Emile Nelligan cuts an odd figure in this context. By the time it came out it had the quaint contours of a relic that was making use of a form which had then become obsolete.) Chamberland had helped set in motion an interest in this form. Yet his work is very much the product of a specific approach, the integration of *apparently* heterogeneous elements into either an oblique or an explicit political statement. Madeleine Gagnon in *Poélitique* (1975) proceeds from similar departure points, with the exception that she tends not to use newspaper cuttings, but rather political speeches (Mayakovsky, Mao, political pamphlets from strike-organizing committes; see Fig. 59). Also her own text is more frequently integrated within collaged quotes (either vertically or horizontally laid out). Chamberland is either more economical with his own words or more inclined to disseminate excerpts randomly rather than on horizontal/vertical axes. The respective final results – while demonstrating a similar focus upon social justice and political freedom – are widely dissimilar. Gagnon's work has an inimitable didactic ring in *Poélitique*. Chamberland's procedures are regressive, elusive, ambiguous. He quotes less from theoreticians and political prophets than from obscure, historically unconnected sources. The 'fait divers' is the main staple of such texts. The sheer weight of them, their convergence upon the page and their slowly decodable signifying processes, have a more subtle and hence more effective ideological strategy than Gagnon's montages of the same period.

Politics as such tend to ease out of the field in the mid-1970s. With Lucien Francoeur, Josée Yvon, Denys Vanier, and Patrick Straram collages undergo serious redefinitions. As forms, they become less of an historical statement and more of an individual, subjective deconstruction of acceptable sexual and social expectations. The use of quotidian pulsions, of trite, everyday details concerning the speaking 'I' and that 'I' only, might disorient readers accustomed to the inner coherence and montaged consistency of Chamberland's and Gagnon's works.[100]

All of Straram's work in *Hobo-Québec* between 1971 and 1975 or in *Les Herbes Rouges*[101] acts as a seminal indicator of such desultory and random choices. What he says of Denys Vanier's work would equally apply to his own or to Josée Yvon's: 'The text/terrorism of Denys

Vanier is a deconstruction of the whole socio-cultural edifice upon which the dominant capitalist class is resting.'[102] An excerpt from 'Transpercées,' a series of collages by Josée Yvon and Denys Vanier (Fig. 60), gives an idea of the various disseminated codes operating here. The text is 'framed' by two political statements: on top, by a curious tautology from *Le Journal de Montréal*; at the bottom, by Hitler's picture/caricature accompanied with a cliché which as a commentary about this particular historical character has a ring of incongruity about it. The generalized disintegration spelled out in the intermediate text deals with (1) the pervasive use of drugs; (2) human incapacity to understand death, to enjoy food, sex, and aesthetic desires; (3) the diffuse presence of religion and escapist mysticism which are being used as last resorts. The last word before the final explosion – the radical rejection of all last-ditch solutions ('on ne veut plus de critères') – is 'il ne peut plus s'agir que d'un show'; that is, game playing and the inversion of old values are the only possible answers for a text sandwiched between the absurdities of history. The long yearned-for explosion ('enfin que tout explose') can be read as a semantic dispersion upon the page as much as a call for an actual apocalyptic ending. Paradoxical elements not only frame the story but also disrupt its tragic connotations either through further debonair clichés ('d'abord qu'on est propre dans sa cuisine!') or through the use of quotidian, apparently irrelevant details (the ping-pong game). As a self-destructive construct, 'Transpercées' is neither particularly original nor rich in suggestive/contradictory detail. But it reflects a time of a surfeit of disseminative pulsions keen on tearing poetic discourse apart. As such it deserves an attentive scrutiny. One should also add that a vast number of its contemporary equivalents would reveal similar processes.

'La nouvelle écriture' and Its Three Mainstreams:
The Energy of Female Writing; From Focusing on the Signifier
to Rewriting History

Destroying linear expectations and continuity does not necessarily mean that one is deconstructing a text. Deconstruction implies not only a breaking down of textual constituents, an explosion, a dispersion over the page, but also a dissemination of meanings which then turn into undeterminable, unstable, shifting quantities. Paul Chamberland's collages (and I am thinking here specifically of his work in *Le Prince de Sexamour* [1976], though all of his writings after *Eclats de la pierre noire d'où rejaillit ma vie* [1971] would reinforce this particular conviction) do not present unstable meanings. While they function as a montage of different texts (newspaper cuttings and excerpts from various other sources), they also offer a continuity of argument, a logic, a coherence in ideological development, which distances them from the disseminated processes explored by a younger generation of poets. Sense is arrived at through contrasted and impressionistic touches, but it is definitely constructed and unified after the reading has been completed. There are no widely opened variations upon and interpretations of such a text; its functions are spelled out, its signifying modes articulated, and all converge towards a final term: *utopie*. All of Chamberland's subsequent work goes in that direction.

Claude Beausoleil's first collages in 1974 with *Journal mobile* and those he published in *Cul Q* around the same period reinforce this sense of a generational gap between writers. Their signifying processes undergo rampant dilapidations (see, for instance, 'Fiction théorique' and 'Etes-vous marxiste?' [Figs. 61, 62]). Ideological pulsions are not absent from them but may operate as well in a desultory, undermining fashion. The only priority (if this can be defined as ideology) is to prevent the surfacing of a readable text. Unreadableness is the order of the day.

Nicole Brossard and Mallarmé's Shawl

I mentioned in chapter 2 the theoretical energy and questioning which emerged around Nicole Brossard and *La Barre du Jour* in the mid-1960s. Indeed, if one wishes to examine what Philippe Haeck called (with a sense of humour and a flippancy somewhat uncommon among his contemporaries) 'Mallarmé's shawl,' Nicole Brossard's texts are extremely relevant to the whole inquiry. They also constitute a key to the awakening of feminist consciousness in Quebec in the mid-1970s.

Much has been written about her and much has been said about her commitment to feminism in general and to women's writings in particular. She is a writer who evolved considerably over the years, and critical statements about her work need to be articulated around specific periods. From 1965 to 1975 she became one of the determining leaders of what was called – erroneously according to André Roy – formalism.[103] She appears 'to view texts as production, as process, literary experience as a laboratory of discourse, of the speaking subject, and the writing practice as an heterogeneous experience which emphasizes the importance of the signifier.'[104]

It still remains that the texts from this first period – *Mordre en sa chair* (1966), *L'Echo bouge beau* (1968), *Suite logique* (1970), *Le Centre blanc* (1970), *Mécanique jongleuse* (1974) – are curled upon themselves, tantalizingly self-referential, prone to play with interlocking sets of mirroring devices, a feat comparable to what André Roy finally calls the 'miroir aux alouettes,' a decoy, a lure to trap birds or here the reader's associations, words, thoughts, and subconscious moves. Brossard herself once referred to the act of writing as 'un jeu de miroirs déformant le texte et la vision.'[105] Words engineer another reality beyond the real when they are strong and powerful ('les mots qui engendrent au delà du réel qui rayonnent si fort et si puissament');[106] they reject the order of traditional discourse; they break syntax, grammaticality; they affirm a writing which sets out to be 'délictueux' (criminal), corrosive, with an inoperative grammar for those who plan to think the present as if it were the past.[107] Transgression becomes the keynote of Brossard's texts during this period, on all levels, that of logic, consistency, grammar, genders, syntactical order: 'un grammaire ayant pour règle: la masculin l'emporte sur le féminin doit être transgressée, susciter manoeuvres de fond, de lames de plaisir. ... d'humour (ce petit e muet féminin qu'on ajoute à la forme du féminin).'[108]

But displacing is not the only necessity; other imperatives, apparently contradictory ones, emerge in Brossard's writings. She started by referring to women's texts as writings condemned to confinement, to be closed in upon themselves as women are enclosed within their homes, pushed outside history's boundaries or let in only by accident, by mistake.[109] But then what initially appeared to be a disadvantage became a tool, a means to transform the very nature of creativity. Women's texts and those which have emerged out of the *modernité* turn about and around, practise excess, madness, vertigo, emptiness,[110] tactics needed to gain a supplement at the end, not of the line, but of the whirling motion. Hence her fascination, her searching, for blanks, holes, in the text, for empty pockets where imaginations can insert themselves, sneak through, and create. *Le Centre blanc* is in and by itself an epitome for this search: 'White for me is ecstasy in the text ... Nirvana, dying within to experience a rebirth from one's own energy. It is very much related to the mystic approach of the great Eastern and Western mystics ... Also to my interest for biological retraction, biofeedback.'[111] It would be redundant to spell out the many instances where such preferences were explicated. Let us say that most of *La Barre du Jour*'s writers have practised this use of blanks, spacings between words, which often obliterate the linearity of sense and force the reader to insert, substitute, add, imagine.

Sometimes the blank becomes a bar, more or less elongated, which functions as the narrator's self-censorship. (See, for instance, Louise Dupré's 'Les Désordres du privé.')[112]

The year 1977 was to mark a decisive turning point in Brossard's development as a writer. As Louise Forsyth put it: subverting language and deconstructing codes simply turned out not to be enough for her.[113] With L'Amèr (1977) she enunciated women's millenarian prisons and determined to spell out the traps, the shackles, the handcuffs which have ensnared them. Such a commitment could not convincingly operate without historical/referential pointers. Auto-referentiality, for all its operative energy, became a hindrance in this specific context.

Later texts, Amantes (1980), Le Sens apparent (1983), Journal intime (1984), to name only a few, epitomize this unresolved oscillation between a-semy on the one hand and determined semic pointers on the other. A commitment to feminism does not preclude or exclude the ambiguity of sense and its systematic deconstruction. But it nonetheless hampers the undetermined moves of a signifier. Any ideological commitment will of necessity control – albeit in varying degrees – the vagaries of its signifier through the structural impulses of its signified (and its referential field is never remote from these processes).

The ambiguities of Brossard's texts after 1977 reflect all of the above. She was not alone in this respect either. The whole Barre du Jour generation depended on meaning about as much as it undermined it.[114] While never delineating its edges, nor appearing to wish to do so, it turned about and contradicted this latter urge. L'Amèr is only an emblematic instance of these contradictory impulses. It functions simultaneously as a deconstructive process, a polysemy, and an a-semy (that is, both as a pluralization of meanings and as a rejection of all meanings).[115] The process here stands also as a reflection of the mother (Mer/a-mer/La mer: mother/non-mother/bitter/sea).[116] As term and persona, she is both nameless and present, both mute and explicitly determined to impose here inflexion upon history. The unresolvable ambiguity of sense presented by the title is central to the ambivalence of the mother: both to be killed and to become; both to disappear as a belly ('j'ai tué le ventre')[117] and to become a woman who puts an end to male written history in order to operate from her own locus of desire.[118] One of her strategies here appears to be the capturing of symbolic production (that is, the changing of a political system, a certain socio-historical hierarchy) as well as the undermining of the field of discourse (that is, one moves away from old, well-centred structures and turns to perturbing, unsettling, narrative modes; one chooses elliptical rather than centrifugal or straight lines of discourse).[119] In her first period (1966–75) Brossard's works struggled to reveal as little as possible or to be self-effaced,[120] as if language were always threatened by its own outbursts, its uncontrollable semantic outgrowths; she strove towards a white centre, to the solitude of what France Théoret would call an 'a-theological text.'[121] This was the time when undecidability predominated, when Brossard's main focus, in Normand de Bellefeuille's words, was to sabotage the subject, discourse, and representation as well as tragedy, metaphysics, and morals.[122] But after L'Amèr and 'e muet mutant' nothing could be the same again.

Published in 1975, 'e muet mutant' (see Fig. 63) in its opening lines immediately focuses on the return of the subject: 'une écriture qui n'efface pas son origine, qui au contraire la tente et la creuse.'[123] Note here that the return of subjectivity does not preclude semantic multiplicity. The verb tente can be interpreted in various ways: to tempt, attract, give pleasure, but also to open up, set up, pitch as in pitch a tent.

As a text which confronts both the system's censorship and women's self-censorship, 'e muet mutant' is bent on addressing the whole issue of transgression. Women's writing breaks rules of grammar, of propriety, of history – yet Brossard also skilfully confronts one of the Kristevian principles of the 1970s (see Révolution du langage poétique), namely that the male writers' transgressions of the nineteenth and twentieth centuries are relevant to women's present search: 'Notre parcours de recherche est autre que celui de Mallarmé, Rimbaud, Bataille, Blanchot. Nos clés d'informations n'ouvrent plus sur les mêmes désirs et anticipations.'[124] Also the feminine text 'doit couper les ponts d'avec la symbolique qui immobilise la pensée féminine.'[125] 'e muet mutant' concretized the efforts of a whole generation of women. It did so by rejecting the great master discourses of the past, from Cartesian logic to avant-garde transgressions, but also by reintroducing a history and a metaphysics which had been previously evacuated from the field (see Bertrand, et al., 'Les Dix Propositions').

Pierre Nepveu has a fine grasp of Brossard's transition from one period (pre-1975) to the other and of the various continuities which bind them. He phrases it by saying that she displaced the whole question of energy towards the subject, as if she had found again an energy which could not be reduced to the old categories of production, labour, history.[126] The implication here is the construction of a new eco-system (in Gregory Bateson's acceptation of this term) in which energy is not viewed in terms of reserve, conservation, and expense, but as that which circulates, relates, and synthesizes,[127] a choice which Nepveu sees as more and more evident in her later work: *Le Sens apparent* and *Amantes*. There is a spiritual dimension here (Nepveu calls it 'religieuse') raised by this question of energy, a dimension which has its new modes of representation, its new ways of being thought about, which Nepveu alludes to quickly but which in those years (1982–3) was central to the emerging divisiveness among the formulators of the *nouvelle écriture*: the split between the materialists and the others, between the enemies of representation and those who could not see how it could be eliminated.

André Beaudet more clearly zeroed in on the whole issue when he suggested that by refusing 'to represent,' or to set up a certain reality on stage, the writers of *la modernité* in effect had evacuated the whole theatre, spectators, set designers, and extras included.[128] But if in the early 1970s they decried the trap of representation, of writing as mirror, as reflection, and appealed to the reader's capacity to view writing as production, as material output, fabricated, created, not derived or inherited,[129] later Carole Massé, François Charron, Madeleine Gagnon, France Théoret, and André Beaudet himself looked upon the act of writing as the exploratory ground of the subject. The subject was both writing subject and reading subject: *writer* and *reader*.

Women's writings of this whole period (from 1975 on), as well as those which came out of both *La Nouvelle Barre du Jour* and *Les Herbes Rouges*, explored avenues opened by the subconscious writing 'I.' Such texts abound in lapsus, punning, and labial derivations which escape rational control. Words run the way colours run off a fabric. There are trembling motions between words, pulsations between different frequencies. France Théoret's *Bloody Mary* is replete with such examples: 'Des passes, je me fais la passe, je suis ma propre maison de passe.'[130] The very title of the book reflects this instinctive, almost irresistible, drive towards punning. Mary is simultaneously the Virgin, shepherdless, kingless, a monument to the glory of the Son, a drink, to be consumed rapidly, swallowed, downed, and literally blood, menstrual and surgical.[131]

Referential ambiguities, the bursting out of single referentials, are constantly and skilfully used by Nicole Brossard and Madeleine Gagnon. One should not forget that to Brossard reference is 'a mécanique piégée' (a trapped/trapping automaton).[132] Consequently one is never certain of one's ground; the terrain shifts underfoot and refuses solid assurances. Is one dealing with a mask or a werewolf ('soulever le *loup*),[133] with a drug closet or Plato's pharmakon (hence Derrida's)?[134] To Gagnon, if all words are but digressions, this means that a writer digresses the course of the radical 'gram' as in grammatical/grammes (weight)/paragrammes (measure)/programme in *Antre* (see Fig. 65). It is more than just quotidian pulsions, ordinary conversations/monologues, and desultory disconnected thoughts making their way into the text; it is the vast subconscious which is seared open, let through, let out, made free: history, which is re-traced, reconstituted, to be read and rewritten in turn by others. Hence the frequent use of different typefaces which reflect the different voices speaking in the same text, from the same persona.

Inaugurated by Théoret and Gagnon, this revealing of the many threads in a many-coloured coat was carried on throughout the whole decade. *Poélitique* fuses this technique with different layouts, bent on breaking the linearity and horizontality of texts (namely, the poem/poster); *Bloody Mary* combines stark, bold uppercase typefaces with ordinary ones. Carole Massé's *Dieu* (see Fig. 64) amalgamates italics and standard print: the first are quotes, the sources of which are only to be identified in an appendix at the end of the book (they include Madame de Lafayette, Laure Conan, Anna Freud, Sophocles, Marie de L'Incarnation, among others). The first quote in italics is from Lenin, the second from John Lennon, but only a quick reference to the appendix will provide us with this information, if we care to know. *Dieu* operates in an interestingly deconstructed mode. The text itself gives us the initial impression that italicized inserts are part of the textual flow. Apart from the typographical difference, nothing separates them from the body of the text (no footnotes, no initials). Yet, in a sense, they *are* set apart since a perusal of the appendix does reveal their actual authorial source, though never their textual location. Massé plays on two separate registers at once: an instinctual, libidinal level, that of the textual flow; and a calculating, attentive, investigative one, that of the learned subject curious to retrace sources. Typography – initially a seemingly innocent device – reaches out for complex effects and affects here.

But *Dieu* deserves an attentive scrutiny because it also addresses in a novel and provocative way the complex history of God the Father, of all fathers, of any father in women's lives. Hence it challenges meaning and law, and does so by the signifier's derision through puns, labial derivations, and homonymic digressions on the *m* sound, for instance (incidentally the initial of the author's last name), or even on the author's name:

> une fille entre deux arbres retourne la tête vers moi vers vous séparée par la clôture de l'Homme lisant l'Histoire qu'il a écrite d'elles d'ici nous nous écrivons maintenant sans nous nier elle et moi moi et lui lui et elle massée mâchée mâchurée macérée maillée mangée matricée mamelonnée mimée médusée mouillée morcelée mémoire miroir moi[135]

Dieu operates as a dizzying constellation of subterranean memories about fictive and historical bound women and of fragmentary quotes by other women, and men also. Their thoughts are fused with the mutterings of a visionary, a woman who wanders through history and all stations of the cross. But each station of the cross is a scansion of her own long journey. She is alternatively subject and object of her discourse, its main agent, its magistral inscriber, who scrutinizes several centuries, and also its medical patient, specimen, woman in labour, actress. She writes and is being written; she is a collection of fragments, made up of broken moments, of broken fictions. The text suggests that it is not totalities but broken up pieces which can adequately translate the flux of reality: 'Tout est impossible, les fragments seuls sont dicibles et irréprésentables au tableau de l'ombre et de la lumière.'[136] Only misrepresentations can represent, just as the end of *Dieu* makes a semblance of providing us with a totality by giving us the last third of the alphabet, except that this alphabet encounters various scabrous variations or accidents – 'Et Filia et Speculum Sancti Atchou!' – and that its last term, 'Zero,' proposes a free fall, a jump into the void. 'Il ne reste rien,' concludes the author in her closing line.

Such radical implosion is not easily duplicated. But there are other ways to disseminate a text, and other writers have followed less totalizing impulses. Nicole Bédard and France Mongeau (see 'L'Oscillée'[137] and 'Croquis d'un texte en suspens' [Fig. 66]) offer us texts parallel with one another. The eye may or may not follow them in continuity. But such texts are not purely 'two-stream layouts.' Simultaneously they are texts which are full of holes, of tears and cuts, unmendable, puzzling in their authentic fragility; they are manuscripts which can never be restored to their primeval intactness, so that we are left with the fragments, the rubble jumble of their long spaces, long silences. Such disseminations are also well illustrated by

Hughes Corriveau's 'La Troisième Figure' (Figs. 67, 68), in which a voice is being ruptured by irregular deletions. More than long silences, 'La Troisième Figure' gives us an imperfect recording, a flawed document wherein the sophistication of the voice cannot hide its technical and physical wounds. It is the exhausted voice of a certain decline, a prefiguration (ten years before) of Denys Arcand's *Decline of the American Empire*. The social fabric, the dreams, the sexual pulsions of a whole generation are worn out, beaten, decadent, yet there remains an anxious desire to articulate their downfall, their disappearance, in a flow of words.

A juxtaposition of most women's texts and men's texts (especially writers from *La Nouvelle Barre du Jour*) brings to the fore a number of substantial differences. Deconstruction and disseminations took on different inflexions. With the first group textual politics were inextricably linked to sexual ones, while with the latter the extent and depth of that connection were necessarily less polemical and at times ambiguously elusive. It still remains that writers of the male persuasion (and I am thinking here more specifically of individuals such as André Roy and François Charron) implicitly adhered to the instinctive choices of female writings (lapsus/puns/disconnections/derivations). It was almost as if the contagious, irrepressible need to be 'feminine' or to be feminist had cut across the whole area of poetic discourse.

Philippe Haeck, Madeleine Gagnon, and Brecht's Cigar

The works that Haeck refers to as 'Brecht's cigar' cover an area broader than this lapidary formula might lead one to believe. They include texts by Patrick Straram (*Irish Coffees au no name bar* [1972]) and by Madeleine Gagnon (*Pour les femmes et tous les autres* [1974]) which I have previously examined as being illustrative of what the concept of collage could do (either an expressionist ideological statement or the deconstruction of the very concept of statement). Haeck's *Tout va bien* (1974) and his essays from *L'Action restreinte de la littérature* (1975), in particular 'Pour un enseignement réaliste de la littérature,' which collages excerpts from Brecht's 'On Realism,' are very much part of this creative and political inquiry. All of François Charron's earlier texts which enunciated a political commitment to Marxism-Leninism — *Pirouette par hasard poésie* (1975), *Projet d'écriture pour l'été 1976* (1973), and *Interventions politiques* (1974) — also explore these textual commitments. All these texts practise the politics of collage in a tantalizing way. Excerpts from revolutionary Chinese texts constellate *Interventions* and occasionally turn it into a crude political pamphlet.[138] But beyond the rough edges of ostentatious provocativeness it is curious to see the insertion of other multi-dimensional texts: theoretical reflections on class and language (43); on language and creativity (24, 34); quotations from Canadian labour history (5); outright exhortations to join the ideological struggle; and finally, posters ('affiches' in the French texts) which combine all three impulsions (see Fig. 69). One cannot speak of the text as a whole precisely because there is no whole and the deconstruction of a certain state of things is too much in evidence to allow for a coherent regrouping of the pieces. Also, as Gaétan Brulotte suggests, such works operate from two strategically opposed viewpoints. On the one hand they function as conflictual spaces, battlegrounds; they insult a certain enemy – in this case capitalism – and dream of eliminating it. But, on the other, as discourses of hatred, they reveal themselves as *symplectic* (a term used by Barthes); that is, such discourses are also integrative: they set out to destroy the other, but do so by possessing it, by seizing upon its difference and absorbing it.[139]

As time went by, the antagonisms tangibly present between Mallarmé's shawl and Brecht's cigar eased. In 1975 Haeck could write: 'A formalist is the one who has nothing to say which is why he borrows the old or new forms he likes: the formalist fabricates literature, he embroiders for the sake of a few cultivated readers. A realist writer has something to say, knowledge he wants to put to some use, at the disposal of the readers for whom he is writing.'[140] Less than five years later, such a stand was nuanced to the extent that its author could view both pulsions as essentially capable of being merged with one another.

Brecht's cigar does not necessarily burn Mallarmé's shawl; nor does the latter have to extinguish Brecht's cigar. If indeed there are conflicts between the supporters of formalism and those who uphold history as a reference point, still it can be possible to integrate within one's writing both the sense of the sacred (the power of writing), and history (the effects of writing). And Haeck adds that after all Mallarmé and Brecht are on the same side, against cautious and ignorant academicism, against the present state of the world. Their words are filled with our gasps.[141]

The Undeterminable and the Return of the Subject

La nouvelle écriture, which grew out of the mid-1970s, was to reflect this unceasing oscillation between the Derrida effect (homonymic practice, peacock ludism, the game of differences)[142] and a recognition of the ambiguities of history, of the will to rewrite it, or even to start writing it. Women's writings of the post-1975 period (Madeleine Gagnon's, Carole Massé's, Nicole Brossard's, France Théoret's) and that of a number of men writers (André Roy, Philippe Haeck, François Charron, André Beaudet, Normand de Bellefeuille, and certainly Claude Beausoleil in *Une certaine fin de siècle*) set out to do just that.

The hesitancy to expurgate, to keep history out of the text, or to vacate the theatre – as Beaudet had put it – was noticeable, not only in women's writings but also among men who had previously favoured the paths of formalism over ideological commitment. This come-back of the referential field (or of the actors' conflicting memories of it), of the writer's subjectivity (and concomitantly of the reader's), was all the more striking for having been fiercely spurned a decade before. It is particularly noticeable among the formalists of the preceding decade (Nicole Brossard in *Journal intime* [1983], Claude Beausoleil in *Une certaine fin de siècle* [1983], Louise Dupré in *La Peau familière* [1983]), but also significant among those who had privileged political values over personal pulsions (François Charron would be the most emblematic example among those). Common to all is a refusal to determine, to define the text. The theoretical obsessions of the 1970s were followed by the passion for the indeterminate, for the inclusion of all possibilities: news items, erotica, silence, half-hearted confessions, tenuous banalities of small gestures suddenly made significantly heavy with layers of heretofore unsuspected meanings. Louise Dupré's novel *La Peau familière* operates here as an almost too emblematic example: a woman sets the table while the 1982 news of the Israeli invasion of Lebanon becomes an hallucinatory rumour.[143] Such a text, as others of the post-1980 period, functions or dysfunctions in a certain manner: words and syntagmas unfold within a certain history, a certain contemporary praxis, yet they cannot and will not be dogmatic (note the distance here from early *Herbes Rouges* writings). Rather, they present themselves as a disseminated chronicle left to us by an evasive scribe whose tablets are alternately decipherable, illegible, half-erased, or broken in a thousand pieces. Maybe it is Madeleine Gagnon in *La Lettre infinie* (1984) who translates best the mood and the pulsions of the *nouvelle écriture* after Mallarmé's shawl and Brecht's cigar have strangely joined one another:

> There cannot be a letter, or a text, which finds once and for all its ultimate revelation. Everything is to be started over again.
>
> In order to write I escaped the constraints of codes. I speak to you and I must be evasive to you, open to all interpretations.

Each word becomes a vanishing point over all other smooth and undifferentiated words.[144]

New writing in the 1980s both rests upon and crushes a multiplicity of meanings, which are more than a sheer accumulation, a thick strata of sense, and which unfold as a game, as a playful activity, a balancing performance between opposites and potentialities.

Charron's paintings (see Figs. 70, 71) proceed from the same premises: scribblings, traces, or undecipherable messages? Still they oblige us to face the reality of non-text, a non-painting, from which we can unearth (palimpsests ...) or upon which we can superimpose. Choices are infinite, unlimited. Semantic limits or 'garde-fou' have vanished. Since there cannot be last words but by necessity only imperfect ones which carry the uncertainties of post-modernist disseminations in Quebec, one could ask Claude Levesque to leave us such a trace about this period:

> Cet espace disséminé du livre – qui est aussi bien l'espace même du
> langage et du monde – se constitue comme un système épars, discon-
> tinu, de relations spatiales et temporelles non linéaires, comportant
> des strates et des niveaux hétérogènes, se séparant et se retrouvant
> selon un temps et une logique que Freud, entre autres, nous a aidés à
> comprendre. La coque du mot se trouve passablement malmenée entre
> les vagues coupantes du langage: en vérité, le mot comme unité –
> l'unité-mot – n'y résiste pas. Le mouvement de l'espacement agit sur le
> mot, le desserre, le dé-limite, l'étage, l'ouvre à d'autres mots, à d'autres
> phrases, l'anagrammatise, l'inscrit dans des ensembles instables, non
> plus des termes (identiques) mais ce mouvement qui les écarte d'eux-
> mêmes et les rend étrangers à eux-mêmes. Les pirouettes incessantes
> du signifiant, le glissement sans fin de 'tournures,' de métaphores,
> de métaphores de métaphores qui ne laissent place à aucun propre,
> à acune vérité nue, emportent dans leur déferlement, toute fixité,
> toute limite, toute marge calculable, toute frontière infranchissable. La
> violence du langage emporte tout sur son passage, lui qui n'est que
> passage, ne se posant qu'en changement de lieu. Elle emporte l'homme,
> l'homme comme unité, totalité originelle, comme conscience de soi
> et du monde. Ainsi le langage qui exige de jouer son jeu sans l'homme,
> perpétue un double sens irréductible, 'une alternative dont les ter-
> mes se recouvrent dans une ambiguïté qui les rend identiques en les
> rendant opposés.'[145]

The preceding chapters have taken us from the terrible longing for representation which concretism exemplified to the systematic dismantling of its very possibility. We have seen that it was not only a revolution in the concept of representation which ushered in postmodernism – modernism after all had in its time raised numerous questions about it (see Adorno, Brecht, Benjamin, et al.)[146] – but undecidability, the oscillation between absence and presence or, to paraphrase Derrida, the refusal to pin down and fix a specific signified to a given signifier. It was the rejection of logocentrism, this specific and most Western philosophy extending from Plato to Saussure and Freud, which demarcated post-modernism from all preceding avant-gardes. We have seen that this rejection, or rather this turning away – and at times even this deconstruction – of the master discourses of the past has itself encountered a severe critique, from individuals such as Jean Baudrillard, who has cautioned his post-modernist contemporaries about the imperialism of the signifier and its overall devouring practices. But Baudrillard's sense of alarm should not be mistaken for an ethical exhortation or moral dissuasion. There is no exhortatory intent here; rather, the cynical attentiveness of the cultural critic, the lacerating irony of the observer of the political economy of signs.

Similarly one cannot, unless one is ready to risk overall simplifications, pretend that *la modernité* and post-modernism are not very much related to one another by bonds other than diachrony. It is not only their succession in time which constitutes their kinship, but their obsessive relationship to the impossibilities of representation. We have seen how Kratylian instincts have overdetermined Western imagination from Plato's times until today. We have also seen how both modernism and *la modernité* dealt with those pulsions: alternately satisfying and rejecting them (concretism versus dadaism). Post-modernism in a sense displaced the whole issue and refused such binary polarities. Perpetually sliding signifiers – an effect of the post-modern condition – do not raise the possibility or impossibility of representation. Such an opposition is simply not relevant to deconstruction; the search for or rejection of a representational founding has ceased to be operative.

The different paths which concretism and post-modernism followed in the dual cultures of Canada and Quebec demonstrated, I believe, different perceptions of both an aesthetic and, at an ideological level, nostalgia for centres, fathers, and order. While English Canadian writers, even in their post-modern moments – and I am thinking here specifically of bill bissett and bpNichol – could not help hankering back for a centre, a focus, Quebec writers far more happily and freely deconstructed the linguistic universe which they surrounded themselves with. André Roy's famous invocation 'je ne crois plus, quelle joie' best exemplifies this trust in a de-centred universe. It is true that such an assurance was nuanced towards the early 1980s by a sense that the public had been evacuated from the theatre, that an absolute and total indifference to the concept of representation had indeed alienated an important part of the community and that by expurgating history from the text one was also eliminating one's listener. History, its return, but not on the terms of representational logic, might be what best embodies the post-modern moment in our two cultures. André Beaudet sounded the alarm on a theoretical level, but Canadian writers such as Robert Kroetsch and Daphne Marlatt, and Québécois artists and poets such as François Charron, Carole Massé, Claude Beausoleil, and Louise Dupré, signalled a substantial and collective move away from the formalist and arid land of La Barre du Jour in the preceding decade. But this time in their history was not a reflection of past events, a re-enactment, a re-production. More subtly it was a re-emergence of what the eye could trace in its flawed, imperfect, unsatisfactory manner. It was necessarily subjective, decentred, inaccurate, but as a simulacrum conscious of its limitations, possibly more revealing and richer than official history itself.

And this in itself is what distances all the avant-garde (old or new, from concretism to la modernité through futurism and constructivism) from post-modernism. History is on our threshold and it is made of many stories, hers and yours. Its threads will be woven together, by many hands, in a multi-layered process. No unitary voice speaks from its components, but the many voices and the many whispers which have long been silenced and now emerge to question the very possibility of totality and finality. Theirs is an open, in-process history: scribes at work, scribes who listen and share their voices.

Conclusion

It is tempting to look upon concretism in general, and more particularly in Canada and Quebec, as a complex resurgence of the Kratylian controversy. And it is equally convincing to perceive its two main developments, isomorphism and constructivism, as contemporary developments of aletheia (the unveiling) and homoiosis (adequation/correspondence) respectively.[1] The break between these first two phases and deconstructionism is total, absolute, and for all practical purposes irreversible. One could not conceive of a more radical opposition between two forms as well as between two kinds of ontologies. The reversal seems almost simplistic both in its intent and in its effects. To move from the yearning for a lost presence, for a quasi-perfect adequation, to the affirmation of a de-centred system, deprived of truth, origin, nostalgia, and guilt, and open to interpretation,[2] is an almost too symmetrical reversal not to raise questions. It is as if one system had to produce its opposite, its dichotomized 'other,' in order to prove its existence. The difference between the perfect coincidence described by Fenollosa[3] and much sought after by concretists and the anagrammatic dispersion outlined by Baudrillard[4] is no less than one system standing the other on its head. Such a move or such a need went beyond the confines of the literary imagination, and I have shown how it followed patterns suggested by linguistics, logic, macro-societal structures in general, and the realities of the political economy.

What is peculiarly noteworthy about the Canadian and Québécois experiences of such a reversal are the substantial differences one notes between the Canadian reaction to deconstructionism and the Québécois' perception of similar dissemination instincts. If Canadians need a centre, the Québécois' reflexes and needs are the opposite. Freeing oneself from the great patriarchal night, as François Charron puts it, is the only continuous reference point. And it is quite telling if one puts this back into an historical context – that of Duplessis' Grande Noirceur, of 'Refus Global,' of the subsequent rise of nationalism in the 1960s, and the rebelliousness it aroused amidst Charron's contemporaries. Otherwise there are no fixed points: moving lines and shifting dots rather. There are many ways to free oneself, to free words, to turn hierarchical structures upside down, askew, and around, which is what both forms of post-modern texts in Quebec – Mallarmé's shawl and Brecht's cigar – committed themselves to.

Yet Canadian and Québécois writers shared an essential, albeit ambiguous, vanishing point throughout these three decades. From the seriously playful concretists of the 1960s, through the occasionally tongue-in-cheek theoreticians of the 1970s, up to the demanding deconstructionists of the 1980s, all shared what Robert Kroetsch once called 'the narratives of a discontent with a history that lied to us, violated us, erased us even.'[5] Women's writings during the last two decades have confirmed as well as enriched such an analysis of our two literatures. Daphne Marlatt, Lola Lemire Tostevin, Madeleine Gagnon, Nicole Brossard, and France Théoret are not alone on the territory of post-modern feminist aesthetics.

Which of these experiments will stand the test of time, which will survive the next two decades? Twenty-five years is too brief a span of time to allow us an even partial objectivity about them. But some intuitions can be gleaned from the field, and some deductions are bound to emerge.

As an area, poetics are bound to be constantly moving, changing. The radical move from one end of the spectrum (concretism) to the other (deconstructionism) is a clear testimony to this. But what is even more remarkable is the subtle shift such poetics have effected on the perception of the literary spectrum as a whole. What seemed outrageous and even obscene at one time (recall the reactions against bpNichol in 1970 and bill bissett in 1978) ultimately found its way into a mild collective acceptance. In Quebec this phenomenon was to be taken one step further. The provocations of the 1970s ('Les Dix Propositions,' for instance) became the mainstream by the mid-1980s, and one could easily point out that *La Nouvelle Barre du Jour* and *Les Herbes Rouges* have – by 1988 – become the de-facto poetic establishment. If collaging, chanting, and calligraphing were of dubious taste in 1968, if Nicole Brossard's texts could be frowned upon in 1969,[6] by 1988 the systematic deconstruction of texts – one's own and others' – had become a common practice in Quebec. What does this augur for the near future? The parallel as well as substantially different developments to be found in the two cultures suggest that sudden reversals and radical discontinuities are the only predictable occurrences that one may prepare oneself for. Turnabout and volte-face are the order of the day.

While not all of these writers would identify with bpNichol's and Raoul Duguay's visions of their personal and metaphysical directions, Nichol's words about a possible way to live one's own history, and one's responsibilities vis-à-vis that history, are worth remembering:

> Raoul Duguay and me chanting late evening,
> 'we are each other's echoes'
> Keeping the shadow away
> we set the axis in motion father
> holy sound to bring death's bird down[7]

silencio silencio silencio
silencio silencio silencio
silencio   silencio
silencio silencio silencio
silencio silencio silencio

1   Eugen Gomringer, 'silencio,'
    from Mary Ellen Solt, *Concrete Poetry: A World View*
    (Bloomington: Indiana University Press 1969), 91

```
sem um numero
      um numero
         numero
            zero
             um
              o
                nu
                 mero
                  numero
                   um numero
                    um sem numero
```

2   Augusto de Campos, 'Sem um numero,'
    from Mary Ellen Solt, *Concrete Poetry: A World View*
    (Bloomington: Indiana University Press 1969), 95

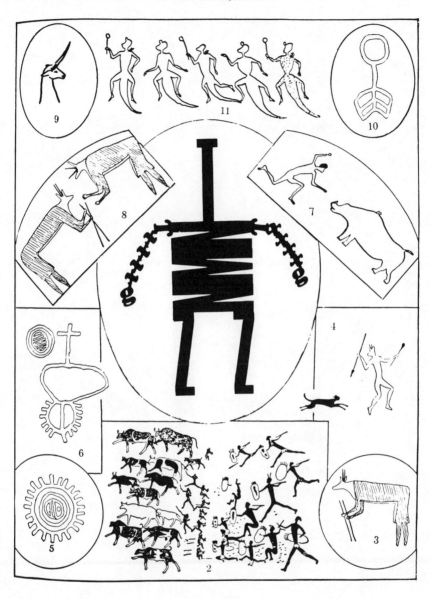

3   David UU, 'Impressions of Africa,'
     from *Capilano Review* 1, no. 1 (Spring 1972), 49

4   Earle Birney, 'Figure Skater,' from *What's So Big about Green?*
     (Toronto: McClelland and Stewart 1973), n. pag.

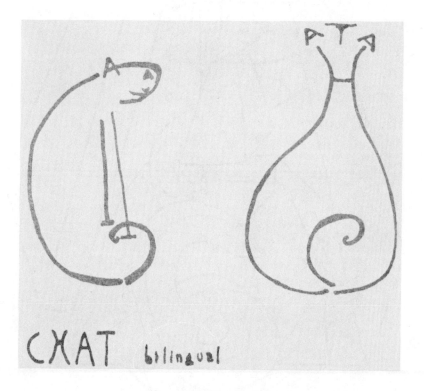

5   Earle Birney, 'Chat bilingual,' from *What's So Big about Green?*
     (Toronto: McClelland and Stewart 1973), n. pag.

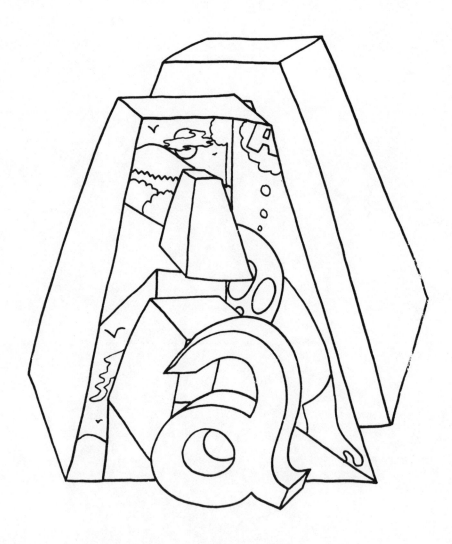

6   bpNichol, 'Captain Poetry Poem,'
from *Blew Ointment Magazine*, Aug. 1970, n. pag.

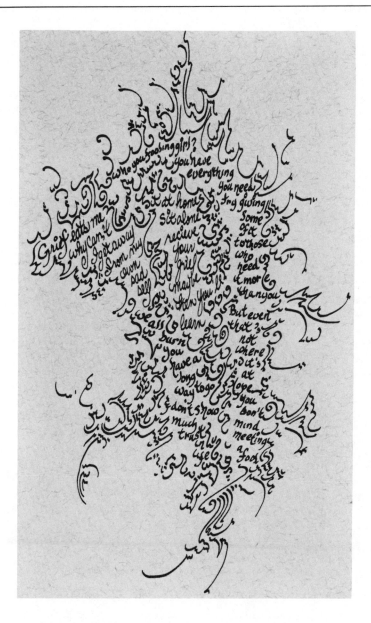

7   Judith Copithorne, 'Who you fooling girl?' from *Runes*
      (Toronto: Coach House Press 1970), n. pag.

8   Judith Copithorne, 'Untitled,' from *Runes*
      (Toronto: Coach House Press 1970), n. pag.

9   bill bissett, 'Life cuts thru all plans,' from *Th Gossamer Bed-Pan*
     (Vancouver: Blew Ointment Press 1967), n. pag.

th lonliness of literacy

10   bill bissett, 'th lonliness of literacy,' from *Selected Poems*
      (Vancouver: Talonbooks 1980), 91

11 bill bissett, 'a pome in praise of all quebec bombers,'
from *Selected Poems* (Vancouver: Talonbooks 1980), 116

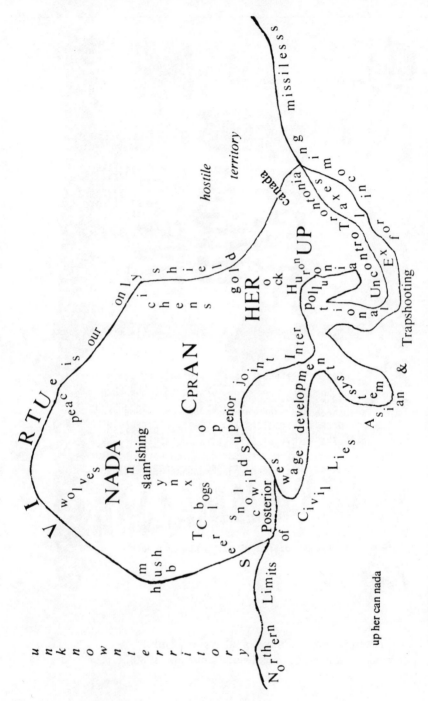

12   Earle Birney, 'Up her can nada,' from *Rag and Bone Shop* (Toronto: McClelland and Stewart 1971), n. pag.

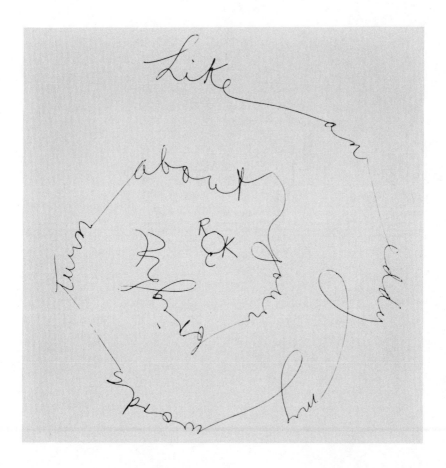

13   Earle Birney, 'Like an Eddy' [version no. 1],
from *Pnomes, Jukollages and Other Stunzas*
(Toronto: Ganglia Press 1969), n. pag.

```
ʎnɟ ʌn ǝʇsɐʇ ɥʇ ɹoɟ spɹoʍ ou ʇuᴉɐ
aint no words for th taste uv yu
ʎnɟ ʌn ǝʇsɐʇ ɥʇ ɹoɟ spɹoʍ ou ʇuᴉɐ
aint no words for th taste uv yu
ʎnɟ ʌn ǝʇsɐʇ ɥʇ ɹoɟ spɹoʍ ou ʇuᴉɐ
aint no words for th taste uv yu
ʎnɟ ʌn ǝʇsɐʇ ɥʇ ɹoɟ spɹoʍ ou ʇuᴉɐ
aint no words for th taste uv yu
ʎnɟ ʌn ǝʇsɐʇ ɥʇ ɹoɟ spɹoʍ ou ʇuᴉɐ
aint no words for th taste uv yu
ʎnɟ ʌn ǝʇsɐʇ ɥʇ ɹoɟ spɹoʍ ou ʇuᴉɐ
aint no words for th taste uv yu
ʎnɟ ʌn ǝʇsɐʇ ɥʇ ɹoɟ spɹoʍ ou ʇuᴉɐ
aint no words for th taste uv yu
ʎnɟ ʌn ǝʇsɐʇ ɥʇ ɹoɟ spɹoʍ ou ʇuᴉɐ
aint no words for th taste uv yu
ʎnɟ ʌn ǝʇsɐʇ ɥʇ ɹoɟ spɹoʍ ou ʇuᴉɐ
aint no words for th taste uv yu
ʎnɟ ʌn ǝʇsɐʇ ɥʇ ɹoɟ spɹoʍ ou ʇuᴉɐ
aint no words for th taste uv yu
ʎnɟ ʌn ǝʇsɐʇ ɥʇ ɹoɟ spɹoʍ ou ʇuᴉɐ
```

14   bill bissett, 'aint no words for th taste uv yu,'
     from *Medicine, My Mouth's on Fire*
     (Ottawa: Oberon Press 1974), n. pag.

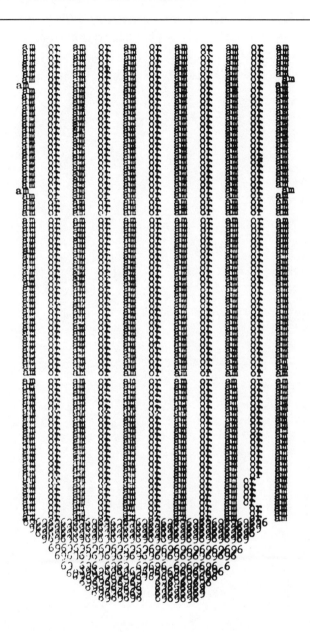

15   bill bissett, 'am/or,' from *Awake in th Red Desert*
      (Vancouver: Talonbooks 1968), 23

em ty

16   bpNichol, 'em ty,' from *Still Water*
(Vancouver: Talonbooks 1970), n. pag.

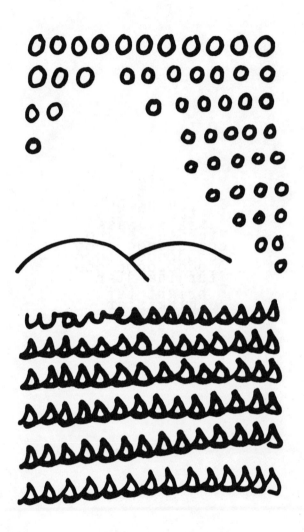

17 bill bissett, 'Waves,' from *IBM*
(Vancouver: Blew Ointment Press 1972), n. pag.

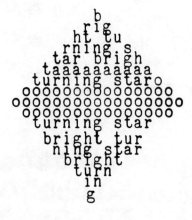

18   bill bissett, 'bright turning star,' from *Pass th Food, Release th Spirit*
      (Vancouver: Blew Ointment Press 1973), n. pag.

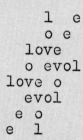

Blues

19 bpNichol, 'love/evol,' from *Konfessions of an Elizabethan Fan Dancer* (Toronto: Weed Flower Press 1973), n. pag.

```
solitudesolitudesolitudesolitude
     t    o i      l
        des    u    l t
        des  t      itu     t   e
    li    s   t
          e   tude
          d   i    l u    t   e
    l      o    s   t
        t      i de
    lit
    o i      l
    so
          d  ol  u   s
solitudesolitudesolitudesolitude
        t     i   e      d
    soli  d
          e  l ude
    s  tud    i    o
          d     u   s   t
    ol   d
    sol    e
    s  tud
       l   u   s   t
    o   u      t
    o    de
        t    o
solitudesolitudesolitudesolitude
```

20   Paul Dutton, 'Solitude,' from *Horse d'oeuvres: Four Horsemen*
     (Toronto: General Publishing 1975), 39

```
N O R T H R O P   F R Y E            J O H N   R O B E R T   C O L O M B O
   O                                                         C
n     T h              e             o                         l
      T     o p                                    e  '    c   l
                                            r            t          o
                                       r
```

```
C A N A D A   C O U N C I L           P I E R R E       B E R T O N
     N            o                   P     e   r              t
C a n                                 F          e       e r
      D       o
```

```
B A R B A R A   A M I E L             G L E N N   G O U L D   ( I )
                M    e                    L            o u   d
                M    e
                M    e
```

```
            S T R A T F O R D   ( I )
                 R      o
                   a        d
                     T   o
                   A     r
                     t
```

21   Robert Zend,
     'Northrop Frye,' 'John Robert Colombo,' 'Canada Council,' 'Pierre Berton,'
     'Barbara Amiel,' 'Glenn Gould (i),' 'Stratford (i),' from *Beyond Labels*
     (Toronto: Hounslow Press 1982), 87, 89, 91, 93, 95, 96, 108

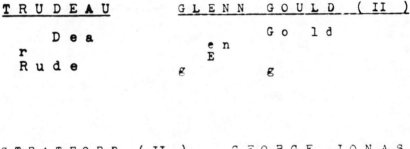

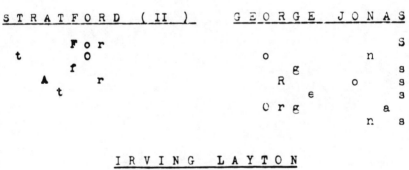

22   Robert Zend,
      'Pelletier,' 'Molière,' 'Trudeau,' 'Glenn Gould (II),' 'Stratford (II),'
      'George Jonas,' 'Irving Layton,' from *Beyond Labels*
      (Toronto: Hounslow Press 1982), 96, 98, 99, 101, 104, 108, 111

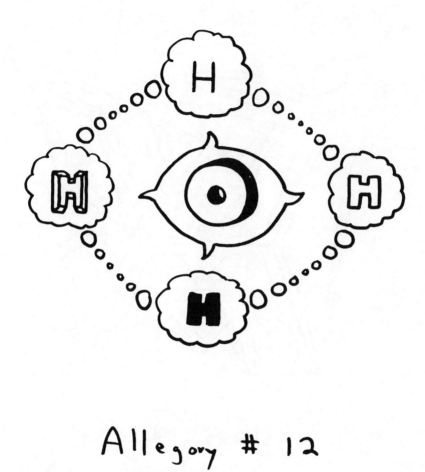

Allegory # 12

23   bpNichol, 'Allegory no. 12,' from *Love: A Book of Remembrances* (Vancouver: Talonbooks 1974), n. pag.

Allegory #3

24   bpNichol, 'Allegory no. 3,' from *Love: A Book of Remembrances*
      (Vancouver: Talonbooks 1974), n. pag.

Allegory # 26

25　bpNichol, 'Allegory no. 26,' from *Love: A Book of Remembrances* (Vancouver: Talonbooks 1974), n. pag.

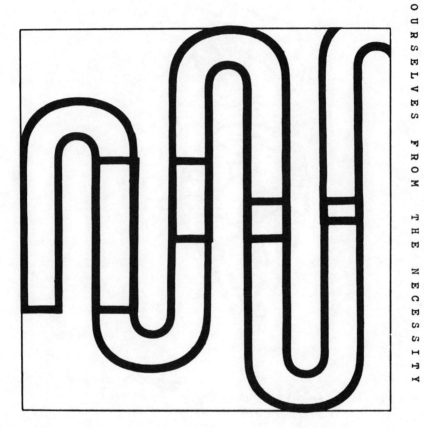

OURSELVES FROM THE NECESSITY

26   bpNichol, 'Untitled,' from *ABC, the Aleph Beth Book*
      (Ottawa: Oberon Press 1971), n. pag.

OF PLACING BOUNDARIES

27 bpNichol, 'Untitled,' from *ABC, the Aleph Beth Book*
(Ottawa: Oberon Press 1971), n. pag.

28   Gerry Gilbert, 'INTO,' from *Is*, no. 6 (Spring 1969), n. pag.

29 bill bissett, 'Untitled,' from *Th Jinx Ship nd Othur Trips* (Vancouver: Very Stone House 1966), n. pag.

purpul red yellow opn th
green fingrs streeming

from th treez   our tongues

inside each othr
suck out th meal

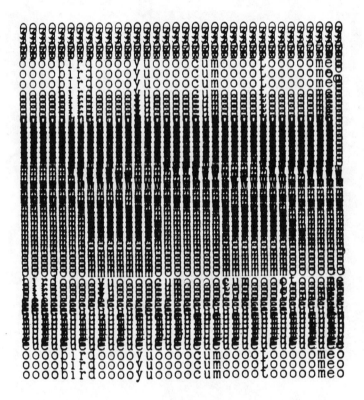

30   bill bissett, 'yu cum,' from *Liberating Skies*
     (Vancouver: Blew Ointment Press 1970), n. pag.

31   bill bissett, 'Untitled,' from *Medicine, My Mouth's on Fire*
      (Ottawa: Oberon Press 1974), n. pag.

RANIUSAUCTIO
NEERTOTHENEW
LYSETTLEDGOD
STHESENATORS
ONTHEROLLBEW
ARELESSTHING
SBECOMETOOCE
RTAINTHERIVE
RRETURNEVENI
NGSTAREMBRAC
ETHEJOYTHEGO
DSGIVETAKEIT

32   Karl Young, 'Raniusauctio,' from *Should Sun Forever Shine* (Toronto: Underwhich Editions 1980), n. pag.

33   Steve McCaffery and bpNichol, 'Mushy Peas,'
     from *In England Now That Spring* (Toronto: Aya Press 1979), n. pag.

34   Steve McCaffery and bpNichol, 'Mushy Peas'
      [continued], from *In England Now That Spring*
      (Toronto: Aya Press 1979), n. pag.

4.

It arrived in winter, the seed catalogue, on a January
day. It came into town on the afternoon train.

Mary Hauck, when she came west from Bruce County, Ontario,
arrived in town on a January day. She brought along
her hope chest.

She was cooking in the Heisler Hotel. The Heisler Hotel
burned down on the night of June 21, 1919. Everything
in between: lost. Everything: an absence

of satin sheets
of embroidered pillow cases
of tea towels and English china
of silver serving spoons.

How do you grow a prairie town?

The gopher was the model.
Stand up straight:
telephone|poles
grain elevators
church steeples.
Vanish, suddenly: the
gopher was the model.

How do you grow a past|
to live in

the absence of silkworms
the absence of clay and wattles (whatever the hell
                they are)
the absence of Lord Nelson
the absence of kings and queens
the absence of a bottle opener, and me with a vicious
                attack of the 26-ounce flu
the absence of both Sartre and Heidegger
the absence of pyramids
the absence of lions

35   Robert Kroetsch, 'Untitled,' from *Seed Catalogue*
     (Winnipeg: Turnstone Press 1977), 23

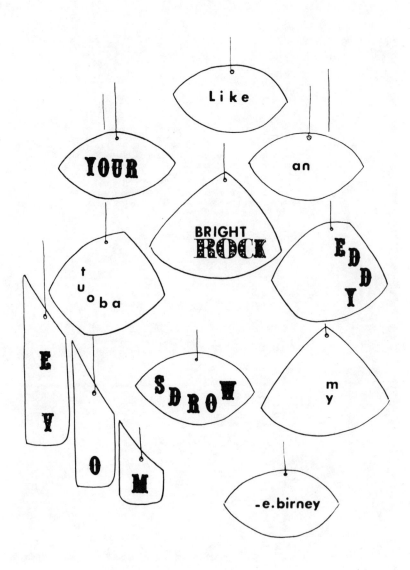

36   Earle Birney, 'Like an Eddy' [version no. 2],
      from *Pnomes, Jukollages and Other Stunzas*
      (Toronto: Ganglia Press 1969), n. pag.

```
c  m  n  o  able
sky
        a white that is white
t t t
u  l  o  r  b
green s o
blue but able
able to be able
b  c  d  e
f i r a l m x

a  b  a  b
be able to be
c or w or
unable to be a
be b be h be
a or v or
blue green white
green green blue white
white blue white blue
green green green green

next to o
a t or e
d f the cloud the
w or sky or
m  r  f  h  i  j

l  o  l  o  l  m  n  o
the w suspended
the l removed
everything becomes itself

d t s r t
j l v q m n a f
s h c i z t z k g
```

37   bpNichol, 'Clover' [excerpt], from *Love: A Book of Remembrances*
(Vancouver: Talonbooks 1974), n. pag.

there are dreams that portend
signs that foretell
i am for telling all i see
because it seems you asked it of me

journal entry: august 26 77
'i drive the martyrology daily
retracing lines i have already written'

driving east on 60 thru Algonquin Park
mid-October 77
Lake of Two Rivers
clouds divide the earth & sky

first snow clumped upon the trees & phone lines
dark greens & red of needles rotting
white spreads thru the trees
over the rock outcroppings
the face of nature is the face of place
not as particular but a general term

i watch the clouds turn
barely cling together in the grey sky
Hidden Intersection where the mind meets the mind
right turn left
there is no polarity if you drive straight ahead
up then into a place called heaven

this drive
drives on the physical plane
part of a general tension or persuasion
'there's too much play in that line'
by which is meant 'slack'
an s lack
absence of a feminizing fact or two

push towards H *e(a)ven*
shown in my life/writing

2
do become
1
note

38   bpNichol, excerpt from *The Martyrology: Book v*
(Toronto: Coach House Press 1982), n. pag.

          jotting in a larger work — x
is tense is
tially shall he
this or that
posited as 'free'
will he
do drive drown
THE SUPREMES
being only themselves til
a superstar emerges

ologies
          caus martyr
mologies
          the head's a spin
'he's seeing stars'
minute movies or
the thimble theatre we dub 'life'
silent screens in darkened rooms
like a 'low-life' or a low mood
fragment of a cyclothymic brooding

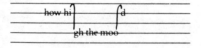

you can sense the rep
          the tition
s sense
          s en s 'e's sence
'typing error responsible for suspicion'
'botch-a-you you botch-a-me'
ba be
     bi
          bo
               bu by
'ba ba loo'
just a variation on
initial initial me

viz:

39   bpNichol, excerpt from *The Martyrology: Book v*
(Toronto: Coach House Press 1982), n. pag.

```
              its a saving i poemd I3 on one page
          i                                    it
        like                                 does
        bing                              o package pink
        a poem                            black lirpin
        i fell                                    cocks
        like                                            nd
             a                         ooooooooooze lushious
        poem today hony                cunts
          its a legal                            blonde
     signs           document          iull  be
     looks             if she          again
     lazy              but it                you
     to               like hees  too             as a
        this          this far  no        what i meant was
     walk                        its back          i feel as nakid
        what           crumbul          its       poets
         does he say                     it              modul
             about  sin o                on                o
                christ i was  a          cud          bill   i ull
                choir boy                else          reed it
                they xpect               what          no
                     until i             puts              did this
                  say                    bandage       yellow
             aufwiedersehh               boris            trip
                  what a                        karloff
                he sd where                       a beeutifull
                     is he                        fuck
                  in         doyu       painting
                  no         poetry              do yu want sum
                     in      more        questions i shud ya no
                         deathless       i wish i askd peopul more
                           ifeel         in sum new brunswick
                           poemd         college
                           byus          josephs
                     that seven years in saint
                     i thot it was a good idea b cause
                        of th way  he  drives  she might
                     abort
                          this is th way she can play on
                          a  singul string  it also
                          hums
                              when yu finally get in  there
                          its a womans face
                                     axus nd crabbly
                                     he sd
                                     yu play
                                          with
                     dreams inside  yellow curtains do
                     yu think yu cud halp us lift th man
                     in four  sum of it  rubs off
                                          nothing
                                 like this before did
                                 i i ul get yu for
                                          this
                                 if it takes
```

40   bill bissett, 'its a saving i poemd,' from *What Fuckan Theory*
      (Toronto: Gronk Press 1971), n. pag.

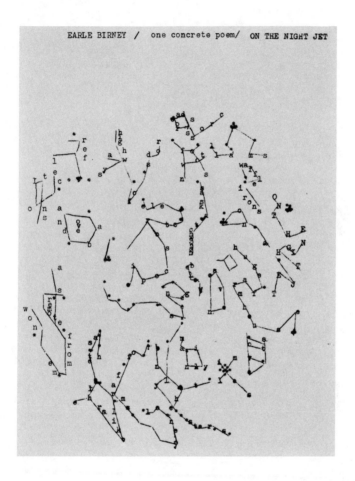

41   Earle Birney, 'On the Night Jet,' from *Elfin Plot*, no. 10
     (Winter 1971), n. pag.

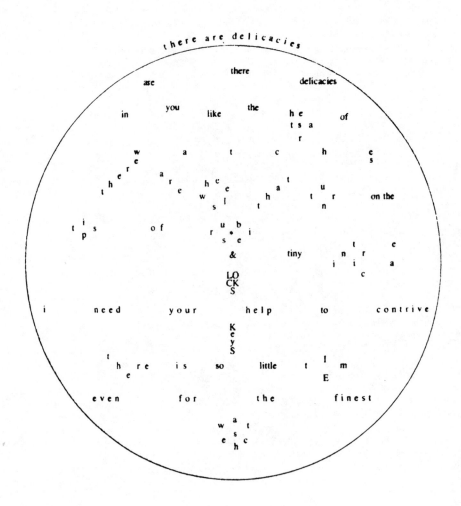

42   Earle Birney, 'There Are Delicacies,' from *What's So Big about Green?* (Toronto: McClelland and Stewart 1973), n. pag.

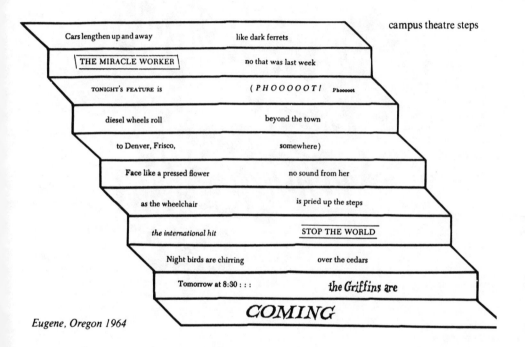

campus theatre steps

Cars lengthen up and away   like dark ferrets

THE MIRACLE WORKER   no that was last week

TONIGHT'S FEATURE is   (P H O O O O O T !   Phooooot

diesel wheels roll   beyond the town

to Denver, Frisco,   somewhere)

Face like a pressed flower   no sound from her

as the wheelchair   is pried up the steps

the international hit   STOP THE WORLD

Night birds are chirring   over the cedars

Tomorrow at 8:30 : : :   the Griffins are

COMING

Eugene, Oregon 1964

43   Earle Birney, 'Campus Theatre Steps,' from *Rag and Bone Shop*
(Toronto: McClelland and Stewart 1971), n. pag.

This is a first edition
of two hundred copies
designed by
Judith Copithorne
February   1969

44   Judith Copithorne, 'Riddle Song,' from *Release*
(Vancouver: Baux-xi Gallery 1969), n. pag.

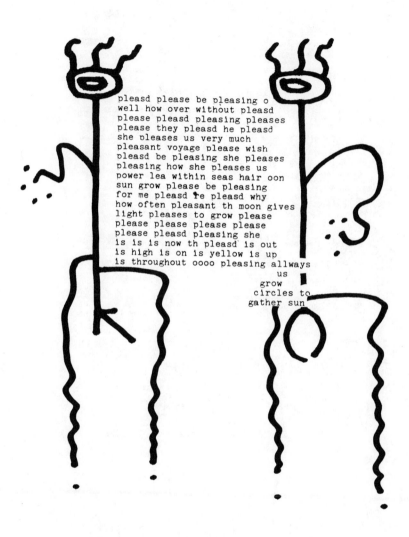

```
pleasd please be pleasing o
well how over without pleasd
please pleasd pleasing pleases
please they pleasd he pleasd
she pleases us very much
pleasant voyage please wish
pleasd be pleasing she pleases
pleasing how she pleases us
power lea within seas hair oon
sun grow please be pleasing
for me pleasd te pleasd why
how often pleasant th moon gives
light pleases to grow please
please please please please
please pleasd pleasing she
is is is now th pleasd is out
is high is on is yellow is up
is throughout oooo pleasing allways
                us
              grow
            circles to
          gather sun
```

45   bill bissett, 'pleasd please be pleasing o,'
      from *Th Jinx Ship nd Othur Trips*
      (Vancouver: Very Stone House 1966), n. pag.

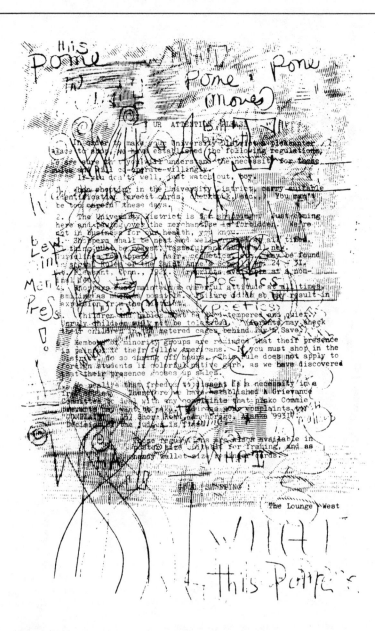

46   bill bissett, 'Untitled,' from *What Poetiks*
(Vancouver: Blew Ointment Press 1976), n. pag.

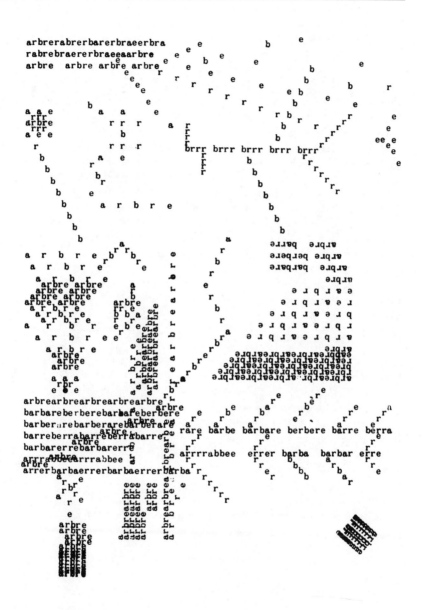

47   Paul-Marie Lapointe, 'Arbres,' from *Ecritures*
(Montréal: L'Obsidienne 1980), n. pag.

Concerto en si b dur · pour 33 machines à écrire

(40)	1.	2 ç 3 . 4 ? 5	â : 7 + 8 $\frac{1}{4}$ 9 $\frac{3}{4}$ 0
(46)	2.	) q(w' e& r t%	y$ u/ i'' op ''$\frac{1}{2}$ /
(44)	3.	=$ a %s d&f 'g(	)hj $\frac{3}{4}$k$\frac{1}{2}$ 1+; : àâ
(50)	4.	z ?x cç vb ?n m:,	+.$\frac{1}{4}$é $\frac{3}{4}$é). (. 'm&
(56)	5.	n b% v$v/c ''x''z/	à$;%1 k&k' j(h)
(60)	6.	g$\frac{3}{4}$f$\frac{1}{4}$d +s: aâ = ?$\frac{1}{4}$p	c9çiu ? yât :r+c$\frac{1}{4}$
(66)	7.	w$\frac{3}{4}$q)-(0)'9&8 7	%6$5/4'' 3 ''2/4$5
(63)	8.	%6 7&8' 9(0)-$\frac{3}{4}$q$\frac{1}{4}$	w+e:rât ? u:yçiço
(69)	9.	p ?$\frac{1}{2}$â = :a +s$\frac{1}{4}$d$\frac{3}{4}$f)	g(h'j&k 1%;$à /
(72)	10.	z''x ''c/v$ b%n m&	,'.(é) é$\frac{1}{4}$.$\frac{1}{4}$,+ m:
(76)	11.	nô ? vcçxz aâs:d	+f$\frac{1}{4}$g$\frac{3}{4}$ h)j(k '1&;
(88)	12.	à% = $ $\frac{1}{2}$/o'' i''u/	y$t% r ew 'q(2)
(92)	13.	3$\frac{3}{4}$4 $\frac{1}{4}$5+ 6:7 â8 ?	9oç ç09 ?8â 7:6
(100)	14.	+ 5$\frac{1}{4}$ 4$\frac{3}{4}$ 3) 2(q'	w& e r% t$ y/ u
(104)	15.	'' i '' o / $\frac{1}{2}$ $	= % à ; & 1 ' k
(116)	16.	(j) h $\frac{3}{4}$	g $\frac{1}{4}$ f + d
(120)	17.	....	ô ....
(126)	18.	S â à Z ç	X ç C V ?
(132)	19.	b â N : m + ,	$\frac{1}{4}$. $\frac{3}{4}$ é) é (. '
(138)	20.	& M N% B$ V/ C''	X'' Z/ $;% L- K
(144)	21.	&j' H(g)F$\frac{3}{4}$ d$\frac{1}{4}$S	+a: = $\frac{1}{2}$?PO çIç
(152)	22.	u :Y ?T âR:E +W$\frac{1}{4}$Q	$\frac{3}{4}$-)0 (9'8 &7 6 %
(160)	23.	5$4/ 2''3''4 /5$6%	7 8&9 '0(-) q$\frac{3}{4}$W$\frac{1}{4}$
(168)	24.	E+ R:TâY ? UIçOP$\frac{1}{2}$	? = A:S + D$\frac{1}{4}$F$\frac{3}{4}$G)H
(176)	25.	(j'K&k L%;$à/z	(X''c/V$ v%B n& M
(184)	26.	(,(.)é$\frac{3}{4}$.$\frac{1}{4}$.+,:Mâ	N ?BVçCXZ âà:;+L$\frac{1}{4}$
(192)	27.	k$\frac{3}{4}$J)h(G f&D s%A	$ = /$\frac{1}{2}$''p'' 0 /i$U%
(200)	28.	T&R'W (Q) 0$\frac{3}{4}$9$\frac{1}{4}$8+	7:6â5 ? 4.3 ç22ç.
(208)	29.	4 ?5â 6:7+8 $\frac{1}{4}$9$\frac{3}{4}$0)	q(W'e &R t% Y$j/
(230)	30.	I''O P''$\frac{1}{2}$/ = $A %S D	&F'G (H)J$\frac{3}{4}$K$\frac{1}{4}$ L+;
(233)	31.	:à â z ?X cçV b ?N	âm: ,+. $\frac{1}{4}$é$\frac{3}{4}$ é).
(266)	32.	(,' M& N B% V/	C'' X'' Z/ à$;% L
(333)	33.	— k & K ' j	(H) g $\frac{3}{4}$ F $\frac{1}{4}$ d + S

(la parenthèse contient la vitesse métronomique)
(Une bonne secrétaire doit répéter toutes les phrases)
(à toutes les vitesses à l'endroit et à l'envers)

48 Raoul Duguay, 'Concerto en si b dur pour 33 machines à écrire,'
from *Lapokalipsô* (Montréal: Editions du Jour 1971), 319

HOSANNA OSAKA O

Notes ou Eparpillements ou Images Jaillies au Cours de l'Audition
D'une Oeuvre de Retlaw Uaerduob,Composée pour Accompagner le Docu
Mentaire de l'Hydro-Québec à l'Exposition Universelle d'Osaka '70
Toute l'Oeuvre Est Fondée sur la Seconde.La Noire Vaut Une Second
E.L'Interprète,Tous des Infoniaques,Doit Calculer Mentalement ce,
Qui se Passe.Chaque Musicien Est à la Fois Commandé et Libéré par
La Forme,ainsi que Tout Homme dans la Prison Ouverte du Monde Act
Uel.Il Doit Placer son ou ses Son(s) Sur, A Côté,Au-Dessus,Au-Des
Sous,A Gauche,à Droite,en Avant,en Arrière,au Centre et en Dessou
R du Dessur de l'Espace-Temps qui Lui Est Réservé (Sporadiquement
Par Intermittence) à l'Intérieur de la Grande Structure Unifiée.O
L'Oeuvre Est un Grand Crescendo dont Chaque Musicien Echafaude le
Pinacle jusqu'au Lever du Soleil.Car Tout Commence Vraiment Là Où
La Lumière S'Allume à l'Horizon de l'Homme.Le Do Concert Est Fin
O Cinglante Cymbale de l'Ange Annonciateur.O OM Universel Continu
De l'Alléluiaque Allégresse d'Etre Homme.O Etirement Elastique de
L'Onde Sonore.O Commencefin de l'Arrachement Final des Timbales,O
Marées Montantes du Grand Flux Suprême.O Que Tout Tourne Autour e
T Sur le Do Royal Qui Tombe Sur la Première Lettre de l'Alphabet
La Finale Est Ainsi Construite que l'Espace S'Ouvre et Progresse,
Vers le Grand Serrement de l'Unité Sonore Amplifiée.Ainsi Se Lève
Le Soleil Qui Aspire l'Hymne de la Matière,Qu'Il Alimente et Fleu
Rit et Enchante Toultemps.A 872:Espace-Son Total.L'Image Sonore d
U Film Rend Témoignage à l'Infinie Floraison de l'Esprit.L'Infon
Ie,Ici comme Ailleurs,Est au Bouttt'Toultemps.La Structure de l'E
Difice Sonore Est à la Fois Précise,Claire,Solide comme le Roc et
Floue,Vaporeuse,Flottante comme les Nuées.Une Quantité Innombrabl
E de Choix Est Proposée aux Infoniaques.De Telle Sorte que Hosann
Na Osaka OOO Est à la Fois un Désordre Total et un Ordre Total.O,
Envergure de l'Espace MicroMacroScopiqueOptique.Tout En Même Temps
O Grain de l'Onde.O Montagne de Métaux Vulcanisés à l'Or.O CanCan
Des Souvenirs Rappelés O Entente Grandissante des Peuples.O Rasse
Mblement de Tous les Hommes dans le Grand Fleuve Vertical aux 333
Echelles Rythmiques.O Discontinuité du Continu.O Mobile Statique.
O Grappes de Clartés Soudaines.O Gouttes Cristallisées des Cordes
Pincées.O Atomes des Harmoniques Etendus dans le Vaste Chant du O
O Rosace de Vibrations Intérieures.O Gerbe de Silence,Spirale à O
Tous les Instruments Sont Privilégiés.Accélérés Succédanés.Dépar
Ts Brusques.Arrêts Stoppiques.La Civilisation.O Vitesse.Image Mon
Tée par Jacques Gagné.Aimée Danis Réalise.Tape Ampex no 13 99 39.
Cocorico.Coucou.Train Evaporé.Foule.Partie de Baseball.Foire.Term
Inus.Toulmonde Embarque.Rill du Mangeur de Gomme Balloune.Collage
Suspense Inoui.Plénitude des Silences.Allez Passez les Poules.Inv
Ention de Signes et Dessins Infoniaques.Partition Picturale.Tout,
Appel A sa Réponse.Toute Réponse Appelle la Paix.Le Train du Ciel
S'En Vient.Michel,le Technicien du Son Apprend à Diriger son Cerv
Eau Amplifié.O Dents de la Matière.O Turbulence Totale du Silence
Plein comme un Oeuf.O Roulement Soutenu de la Vague.O Liberté d'O

49   Raoul Duguay, 'Hosanna Osaka O,' from *Le Manifeste de l'infonie*
(Montréal: Editions du Jour 1970), 74

ARBRE GENEALOGIQUE DE TOULMONDE

```
                                 ô
                                a a
                              ma  t a
                             oui  non
                            tout  rien
                           fleur  ortie
                          oiseau  vipère
                          univers  cellule
                       ordre  un  désordre
                        astérisme  nébuleuse
                    atome  pain  beurre  feu
                    air    liberté  eau  esclave
                 soleil   champ  ville   ruelle
                 planète    terre  globe   lunaire
                 lumière   jardin  ombre  asphalte
              arbre  joie   jour  nuit  pleur  peur
              maison  table  blé  chambre  province
            pays  pierre  temps  espace  poussières
            orient  plein  amour  occident  vide  faim
             sourire   caresse  toi  lui  crainte  travail
            bonheur  printemps  on  eux  muscles  fer  pied
         main  sein  femme  bonté  sexê  bras  femme  roche
         cœur   essence  soif  foi  corps  existence.  prison
         lûmière  feuille  été  jus  automne  plastique  béton
         montagne   cheval   sentiers  vallée  automobile  ciment
         œuf  éclosion  santé  maman  bombe  explosion  sang  bobo
       musique  étoile  neige  sapin  cri  sommeil  crépuscule  loi
      couleur  rythme  papillon  jeu  ver  gris  vitesse  stop  meute
     danse  vague  océan  rivage  sel  accident  visage  écume  coulée
    chant  prière  parole  livre  sol  machine  radio  télévision  plan
   dessin  ligne  courbe  volume  pas  building  argent  électricité  go
  fruit  légume  lait  miel  céréales  hot  dog  hamburger  steak  patates
enfant  femme  beauté  paix: HOMMME  HOMMME  animal  végétal  minéral  mû
```

50   Raoul Duguay, 'Arbre généalogique de toulmonde,' from *Lapokalipsô*
     (Montréal: Editions du Jour 1971), 14

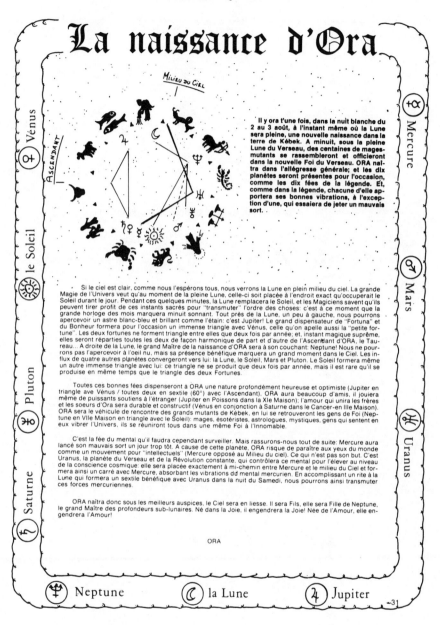

51   Raoul Duguay, 'La Naissance d'Ora' [excerpt],
      from *Main Mise*, no. 31 (juillet 1974), 31

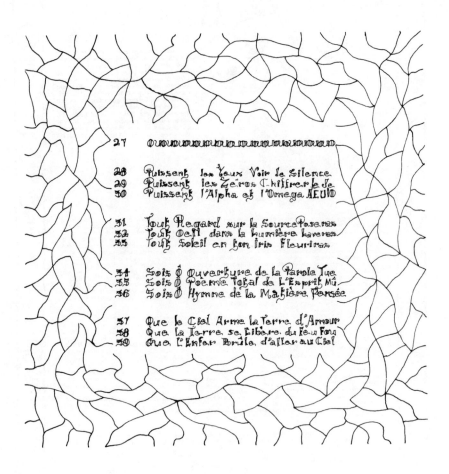

52   Raoul Duguay, 'Puissent,' from *Le Manifeste de l'infonie*
(Montréal: Editions du Jour 1970), [36]

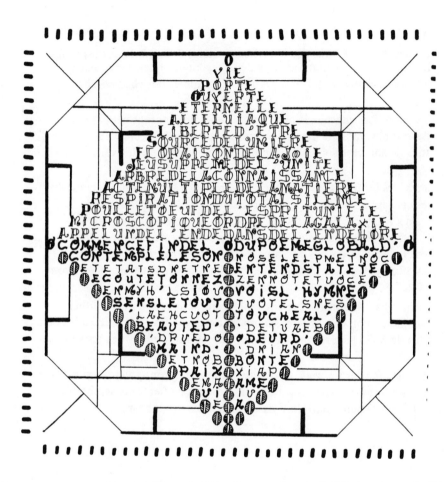

53 Raoul Duguay, 'O vie,' from *Le Manifeste de l'infonie*
(Montréal: Editions du Jour 1970), [8]

L'APOCALYPSE

B.3.
les décapités **cochons** des blanches capitales **danseront** dans les sangs
les capitalistes s'**épilant** le cul y dénicheront des **queues** d'oiseaux
les singes **signeront** les belliqueuses biographies des **chauves** chefs

les banquiers **engraissés** aux bouses des vaches auront **peur** des bourses
debout devant leurs **glaces** les femmes **avaleront** des peaux de serpents
sous de sombres **soleils** les ruminants ne paîtront pas les verts **signes**

à travers les **froidures** des vents se vitrifieront les **yeux** des fauves
les carnassiers **pères** dépèceront les fesses de leurs fécales **filles**
les nécrophages **fils** feront des confitures avec les **croqués** vautours
les criards **cochonnets** craindront les pustuleux **pis** des taries truies
les cholériques **coches** chieront leurs **groins** grugeront leurs étrons
les affolées **femmes** frémiront devant les affamés **cochons** qui crieront

bientôt ils s'**abaisseront** se **rassembleront** pour redevenir zoolithes
comme de non comestibles **champignons** les villes **endormiront** les bêtes
plus de **3333** générations de jeunes **attendront** le réveil des ammodytes

dans les mortes **natures** jusqu'aux **pôles** ramperont poissons et oiseaux
les taxidermistes donneront des **pas** pour empailler leurs **semblables**
la publique **place** pullulera de quadrupèdes se **claquant** fort le corps

54   Raoul Duguay, 'L'Apocalypse,' from *Lapokalipsô*
(Montréal: Editions du Jour 1971), 263

CUISINE MICROMACROBIOTIQUE INFONIAQUE

1. *Le Menu de Madame par Elocin Sproc* :
. a) Riz   Nituké:Ri-Hi-Hi-Chouchalotte.Faire   revenir   dans   l'huile,
d'olive des lanières de choux et quelques échalottes coupées asse
z grossièrement.laisser mijoter sur feu doux.Servez-vous du riz n
aturel,déjà cuit.faites échauffer dans un peu d'eau.après évapora
tion de l'eau ajoutez quelques noisettes de lécithine (beurre vég
étal) et du sel de mer.(Cette Récette Est Conseilleillée aux Hourloks
. b) Vermicelle Ogura:Orobinerouse:faites bouillir des azukis (pe
tits haricots rouges) jusqu'à ce qu'ils soient tendres puis salez
les.mélangez-les à du vermicelle cuit (pâte aux œufs) et faites-
les chauffer dans une casserole.versez le tout dans un moule, lais
sez refroidir.ôtez du moule et coupez en tranches.peut être servi
chaud par temps froid.selon le goût vous pourriez ajouter la noix
de muscade,ajouter persil,quelques gouttes de tamari et hachis fa
it d'une ou deux échalottes sautées à l'huile.(Bon pour les Yeux.
. c) Tarte de légumes-Croûte-Cuite-Croutch! Préparation pâte:fari
ne,huile de sésame, sel, l'eau, pétrir, abaisser. faire revenir dans u
n peu d'huile carottes-oignon-poireau et faites cuire à l'eau.gar
nissez un plat avec de la pâte que vous remplirez de légumes.déla
yez de la farine d'arrowroat dans un peu d'eau froide et faire cu
ire dans le jus de nituké.versez cette sauce sur la garniture au,
lieu de la couvrir de pâte.cuisez au four.(Délice pour les Prikis

2. *Cinq des 333 récettes au Menu Oshawa in Excelsis Deo d'Eerdna.*
a) La Soupe Pizzicato à l'Aquarium Symphonique:Panets.Carottes.
Navets.Céleris   parfumés   de   Romarin,d'Estragon,de   Laurier,fleuris,
d'Algues Marines et Vermicelle de rizés.(Bien Flacoter Avant Mmm.
b) Le Concerto pour Saveurs Estivales:Piqué de noires Olives,na
nti de cerfeuillées Endives et drapé de sauce Miso,du Boulgour.(O
le Chant de Grâces Est de Mise Avant de Sentir le Gazouillement O
c) La Rosace Hihihihyok de Jlakapoplik la Schlout : Accompagné d
e Chou-fleur persillé,Kacha encadré d'Oignons émincis et dorez au
Gruyère.(Le Fumet de ce Plat Plane Longtemps dans vos Oreilles Si
d) Le Relevé de Papilles aux Odeurs Chantantes : Millet thymisé,
parsemé d'Azukis.(Recommandé aux Ouistitis en Remplacement des Fè
ves au Lard Salé;Bon pour la Libération des Ballons Stomachaux O.
e) Le Dessert de la Schloupinette : Sous une poudrerie de Noix B
résiliennes,de la compote de pommes aux Raisins Corinthiens.(Il S
uffit de Laper le Son de cette Dégustation Paradisiaque pour Rire

3. *Trois des 333,333,333 Récettes des Infoniaques à la Crêpe Douce*
a) Crêpe au Blé Miracle Qui Enfante la Paix dans l'Estomac Bleu
b) Crêpe à la Verge d'Or Gantée d'une Gerbe de Thym Chantant O.
c) Crêpe au Sarrazin de Séraphin Richement Couverte de Neige Or

55   Raoul Duguay, 'Cuisine micromacrobiotique infoniaque,'
       from *Le Manifeste de l'infonie* (Montréal: Editions du Jour 1970), 111(b)

INFONEURLIEU
HORLOGE ESPACE-TRIANGLE-TEMPS DE L'INFONIE
CALENDRIER DES EPHEMERIDES INFONIAQUES

A. FORMES(S) TRIANGLES (S) INFONIAQUES :
— *Dimension des3cadrages physiques :*
   a) largeurs : 3' X 3' X 3' mille milles
   b) épaisseurs : 11' X 11' X 11' mille milles
   c) longueurs : 33' X 33' X 33' mille milles
— *Dimensions des 33 aiguilles ostensibles :*
   a) longueurs : 3' X 33" X 333'
   b) épaisseurs : 3' X 11" X 33'
   c) largeurs : 3' X 3" X 3'
— *Dimensions des 333 couleurs visibles :*
   a) épaisseurs : 33v X 3' X 333"
   b) longueurs : 11v X 33' X 3"
   c) largeurs : 3v X 333' X 33"

B. SIGNAUX-SIGNES-SYMBOLES :
— *Rythmes des temps.temps-espace.espace:de du des:3,333 :*
   a) temps des 333 micro-points vivants de la Grande Respiration-Seconde ;
   b) temps du 33 secondes au micro-point près,de la Minute Bougeante ;
   c) espace de 3 minutes qui marchent vers le Lieu de l'Heure ;
— *Rythmes des temps.passe-temps.espace:du de des: 33,333 :*
   a) temps du 33 heures construisant l'Echaufaudage de la Journée ;
   b) espace de 33 journées lumineuses dans les Champs de la Semaine ;
   c) passe-temps des 33 semaines roulantes de la Grande Vague du Mois.
— *Rythmes des temps.pense-temps.espace:des du de : 333,333 :*
   a) pense-temps de 3 mois printemps-été-automne de l'Année ;
   b) temps du 33 années qui s'amassent dans le Trésor du Siècle ;
   c) espace des 333 siècles soutenant le Temple du Millénaire Pacifique.

C. MESURE(S) ORDRE(S) LIEU :
— *Mouvements des 333,333,333 stéréophoniques œils infoniaques :*
   a) 3 points se rassemblant dans la Droite ;
   b) 11 droites allant de tous bords tous côtés vers la Courbe ;
   c) 33 courbes passant par le Centre-Gauche de la Droite.
— *Mouvements des 33,333,333,333,333,333 stéréovisuelles oreilles lousses :*
   a) 333 droites qui paralysent la Sucée du Pouce Courbé ;
   b) 333 courbes qui parsèment le Chemin du Pied Plat ;
   c) 333 points qui pullulent dans la Fleur de la Verge en Pointe.
— *Mouvements des 333,333,333,333,333,333,333,333,333 stéréo-Endedans :*
   a) 33 courbes se dessinant dans les Eaux du Pays ;
   b) 11 droites s'érigeant dans les Colonnes de Feu de la Terre ;
   c) 3 macro-points accueillant le Souffle dans l'Air du Cosmos Vivant.
     L'OEIL EST LE MICROSCOPE-STETHOSCOPE-TELESCOPE DU TOUT TOULTE
     L'OREILLE EST LE MICROPHONE-STETHOSCOPE-AMPLIFICATEUR DU TOUT 1
LA TETE EST LE CHRONOMETRE-STETHOSCOPE-MESURE DU TOUT TOTALEMENT 1

56   Raoul Duguay, 'Calendrier des ephémérides infoniaques,'
from *Le Manifeste de l'infonie* (Montréal: Editions du Jour 1970), 105

PAIN-BEURRE
POEME-MUSIQUE
SILENCE-   SON
VIBRATION-PERCUSSION
YIN   YANG

57 Raoul Duguay, 'Vibration-percussion yin-yang,'
from *Le Manifeste de l'infonie* (Montréal: Editions du Jour 1970), 82

58   Paul Chamberland, 'Vers le grand changement,'
     from *Main Mise*, oct. 1974, 21

Ils diront sûrement ça n'est pas de la poésie. Ça n'est pas beau. C'est vulgaire. Puis c'est plein d'angli-cismes assonnants. Si au moins ça discordait aux termes de l'automatisme. Ils diront ces sur-moi du système poétique MERDE.

Et puis ça ne se compte plus c'est par
centaines et milliers qu'il faudrait
les nommer Gypsum, Firestone,
Shellcast, Copermine, Ayers, Carter White Lead,
Van Heusen, Canadian Steel, Enseignants,
Infirmières, postiers, Perkins, Etudiants,

"Maintenant, on commence à comprendre ce qui se passe chez d'autres
travailleurs. Avant, quand on enten-
dait parler de grèves à la radio et à la
télévision, on disait 'pas encore une
grève' ou y sont-y fatiquants avec
leurs grèves? Aujourd'hui on discute
ensemble des problèmes d'usines, des
luttes menées par d'autres travailleurs.
Quand il y a une grève à une place, on
s'en parle et on se sent solidaires des
travailleurs en lutte... On comprend
aussi que des boss qui exploitent des
travailleurs, y en a pas juste à Perkins,
mais dans les autres usines. On sait
aussi que c'est toujours pour faire plus
de profits possible que les boss nous
exploitent. Tu sais, on est parti de
loin..."

Foyer des Hauteurs, Pavillon Saint-Dominique
SEVEN UP à Québec magasin Pollack
Abattoirs de Victoriaville COFIS
Great Lakes à Berthier à Saint-Denis
Les patriotes Matelas Suprême à St-Narcisse
Employés municipaux d'Alma employés de
bureaux à Gatineau Fournier Steel

59 Madeleine Gagnon, 'Et puis ça ne se compte plus,' from *Poélitique* (Montréal: Les Herbes Rouges 1975), n. pag.

les ivrognes au front petté, les junkies trébuchent en plein milieu du trafic, les
négresses étendues sur le trottoir.
plus rien. nous avalons chacun chez soi notre psychose anxio-dépressive.

la normalité a été inventée par des étouffés-garrottés-psychiatres-neurologues-
analystes-psychanalystes. les crackpots les plus dangereux :
notions de valeurs, de standing.
elle est à une bonne hauteur la taverne.
on ne connaîtra jamais rien même à l'autopsie des corps.
la nourriture ne goûte plus, on n'a plus soif, la lecture fatigue, le cul endort :

on se dirige vers le refuge du mysticisme.
des carabines sans munition
aujourd'hui comme tous les autres jours, juste une petite routine.
les groupies du rock and roll devenues les groupies des guru.
enfin que tout explose !
on ne veut plus de critères
enfin que tout explose
ils sont tous morts en criant l'impossible et nous voyons bien que le Programme, la tragédie, la comédie continue . . .
d'abord qu'on est propre dans sa cuisine !

Comme à Parthenais (sept. 74), j'ai joué et gagné une partie.de ping-pong a-
vec Cotroni, aujourd'hui, avec Josée, j'avale la décharge du monde au motel
Jenny Rock, il ne peut plus s'agir que d'un show de combat, d'agression.

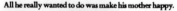

All he really wanted to do was make his mother happy.

60   Denys Vanier and Josée Yvon, 'Transpercées' [excerpt],
      from *Hobo-Québec*, nos. 21–2 (jan.–fév. 1975), 9

fiction théorique

&&&&&&&&&&&&&&&&&&&&&&&&&
&&&&&&&&&&&&&&&&&&&&&&&&&
&&&&&&&&&&&&&&&&&&&&&&&&&
&&&&&&&&&&&&&&&&&&&&&&&&&
&&&&&&&&&&&&&&&&&&&&&&&&&
&&&&&&&&&&&&&&&&&&&&&&&&&
&&&&&&&&&&&&&&&&&&&&&&&&&
&&&&&&&&&&&&&&&&&&&&&&&&&
&&&&&&&&&&&&&&&&&&&&&&&&&
&&&&&&&&&&&&&&&&&&&&&&&&&
&&&&&&&&&&&&&&&&&&&&&&&&&
&&&&&&&&&&&&&&&&&&&&&&&&&
&&&&&&&&&&&&&&&&&&&&&&&&&
&&&&&&&&&&&&&&&&&&&&&&&&&
&&&&&&&&&&&&&&&&&&&&&&&&&
&&&&&&&&&&&&&&&&&&&&&&&&&
&&&&&&&&&&&&&&&&&&&&&&&&&
&&&&&&&&&&&&&&&&&&&&&&&&&
&&&&&&&&&&&&&&&&&&&&&&&&&
&&&&&&&&&&&&&&&&&&&&&&&&&
&&&&&&&&&&&&&&&&&&&&&&&&&
&&&&&&&&&&&&&&&&&&&&&&&&&
&&&&&&&&&&&&&&&&&&&&&&&&&
&&&&&&&&&&&&&&&&&&&&&&&&&

(25 & X 25 &)

61   Claude Beausoleil, 'Fiction théorique,' from *Avatars du trait*
(Montréal: L'Aurore 1974), n. pag.

êtes-vous marxiste?

"les arithmétiques transfinies
et les mathématiques sanguinaires"
Salvador Dali

$$$$$$$$$$$$$$$$$$$$$$$$
$$$$$$$$$$$$$$$$$$$$$$$$
$$$$$$$$$$$$$$$$$$$$$$$$
$$$$$$$$$$$$$$$$$$$$$$$$
$$$$$$$$$$$$$$$$$$$$$$$$
$$$$$$$$$$$$$$$$$$$$$$$$
$$$$$$$$$$$$$$$$$$$$$$$$
$$$$$$$$$$$$$$$$$$$$$$$$
$$$$$$$$$$$$$$$$$$$$$$$$
$$$$$$$$$$$$$$$$$$$$$$$$

(20 $ X 10 $)

62   Claude Beausoleil, 'Etes-vous marxiste?' from *Avatars du trait*
(Montréal: L'Aurore 1974), n. pag.

La parole de la femme est sans conséquence, avons-nous dit, puisque entre autres raisons, elle ne s'insère pas dans l'histoire (elle est sans pouvoir décisionnel). Mais il n'en va pas de même pour ce qu'elle écrit et publie. D'abord parce que son geste devient public, qu'il passe par des voies hiérarchiques, un jugement culturel; le filtre qu'affronte toute personne qui décide de porter sur la place publique une forme (le produit d'une pensée qui s'arque et qui prend élan du plaisir des mots) quelconque. D'abord parce que son geste est inscrit, concret: le livre. Il entre dans des lieux intimes et publics (librairies, bibliothèques, établissements d'enseignement, etc.). Il entre dans l'histoire. Il participe à la mémoire collective.

La femme qui écrit passe donc enfin dans l'histoire (ne pas confondre avec à l'histoire). Elle devient sujet. Elle propose. *Impose son sujet* — souvent celui de sa parole censurée. Elle transgresse le discours masculin dans la mesure où elle cesse de se transgresser, dans la mesure où elle s'élargit du verbe et ne lui court plus après. Le sens de sa transgression est déjà joué irrémédiablement dans le fait que c'est elle qui s'offre, qui organise, qui décide quand ça s'arrête, quand ça continue. Elle ne peut avoir que des complices (qui jouent le même rôle qu'elle (lire / écrire)). Point de rôle différencié.

Son propos, même quand il reproduit les avatars liés a la condition de la parole censurée, s'exerce toujours dans le sens de l'exploration, de la découverte. Toute écriture (si médiocre qu'elle puisse être) est une affirmation de soi et, en ce sens, c'est le lieu par excellence ou la femme y trouve une autonomie.

Manifestement l'écriture de la femme en est une qui doit s'imposer doublement au regard. S'exposer comme un corps de femme sexagénaire. S'exposer pour ce qu'il est et non pour la représentation que les autres s'en font. Le texte féminin doit faire casser (cesser) le plus grand nombre de peurs, de tabous, d'intimidations. Pas une seconde s'écrire dans la distraction et l'habitude. Il doit couper les ponts d'avec la symbolique qui immobilise la pensée féminine. Par quels méandres? Par quelles techniques?

63 Nicole Brossard, '*e* muet mutant' [excerpt],
from *La Barre du Jour*, no. 50 (hiver 1975), 10–27

un peuple en retard de
l'inconscient opératoire du sujet un sujet en retard
de la conscience productive du peuple   à la croisée les origines d'une révolution manquée à refou-
ler l'une et l'autre part de la question de son adve-
nir entre conscience et inconscient   qui ne prévoit
l'oeil en perte de sa vision totale et les marges du
jeu pose sa voyance politique en voyeurisme tyran-
nique   à la croisée les origines d'une révolution
marquée *dans la parfaite connaissance de la culture
créée au cours du développement de l'humanité*
le Parti en retard de la révolte spontanée des masses
les masses en retard des pulsions agressives des sujets les sujets en retard de leurs enfances désirantes
les enfants en retard de leur matrice immémoriale
jouissive Dieu au bout pour boucher l'échappée où
ça parle sans nous   pour colmater la brèche où se
dérobe la totalité d'un dire et d'un faire   venger
le commencement et perdre les dents venger l'en-
fance et perdre la dépense venger la coïncidence et
perdre la résonance l'instance de dire et d'écrire
    je dis il était écrit *God is a concept by which we
measure our pain*   comment perdre Dieu? ce rapport aveugle à nous-mêmes Tout déjà perdu cons-
truire chaque parcelle de conscience et de connaissance   alors elle doit écrire sur ces prostituées qui
se soumettaient au contrôle administratif et sani-
taire que l'on appelait les filles soumises car nous
avons toutes été des filles soumises montures doci-
les instruments maniables élèves dont le devoir
était de ne jamais déroger aux leçons du maître
chaque jour ce vieux maître nous relevait la jupe
écartait de l'index et du pouce des lèvres doulou-
reuses « je conçois que l'oeuvre d'art doive exprimer la profondeur de l'Homme à l'élite donnée... »
ses derniers mots s'enfouissaient dans les tissus et
organes repoussés refoulés écrasés   ses disciples à
la porte écoutaient et prenaient note de la théorie
glapissante qui montait de ces gouffres prodigieux
d'abstraction de spéculation pure nous étions toutes grosses de nos maîtres et notre progéniture était
monstrueuse   nous rencontrions aussi des hommes sans utérus gros de leurs maîtres on avait dé-
veloppé chez eux d'autres organes aux mêmes fins
et c'est ainsi que s'inscrit l'histoire de l'enseignement

64   Carole Massé, 'Untitled,' from *Dieu*
(Montréal: Les Herbes Rouges 1979), 44

paragrammes mouvance du texte grammes scripturaux grammes bougeants vibre de fictions programmes grammes de sucre grammes de sexe c'est l'infini des codes linguistiques psychiques l'infini des dés hasart mallarmé mozart cixous stockhausen haeck straram grammes pour grammaire apprentissages tisser les trames réglées du début à la fin contraintes transgressions ou pour mouvance désir tendresse et toute la mode et la modernité ensemble pour orgasmes n'avoir plus rien au programme ni angoisse ni colère ni guerre ni passion ni tendresse et pour seul désir que ce mouvement lointain et précis qui défriche et déchiffre les inscriptions de graphes et d'amours laissées
cela qui prenait un son pour un autre un mot pour un autre un objet un visage tout un corps quitté avec l'image dedans pour un autre gravée
les yeux de roche mimaient cette farce à leur rythme d'antre les morts

65   Madeleine Gagnon,
'paragrammes mouvance du texte grammes scripturaux,'
from 'Antre,' in *Autographie 1: fictions* (Montréal: VLB 1982), 210

dans une pose rouge
inutile
posée la par magie
pour des mains de
passants
soif d'un rythme
contre un lettrage
jamais les mêmes qui
reviennent
oubliée elle
et son vieux sourire
rouge
la pluie de la ville
s'y perd
et on repasse
doucement
comme attire
soudain
par un espace de
lettres
vide d'elle
où nos mains
rouges impressions
d'une seconde
contre la pluie
de la même ville
et c'est mon corps
immobile près d'elle
de son ombre
souvenir d'une
affiche
publicité rouge
contre la ville
d'un lettrage mouillé

j'écris l'affiche— celle d'Un autre
corps plus mince— plus beau—
suivre ses pas dans la ville—
comme d'un hasard, la nuit—
seule témoin— les mots se cher-
chent aux bords de ses doigts—
gant de satin noir— imprévu sur
sa peau blanche— je les trouve et
les note— des mots plus longs—
plus durs que les miens— comme
pour leur dire— le temps de
retourner la tête— et perdre son
visage— comme dans un rêve—
celui qui reviendra sans doute—
seule— mais trop tard, trop tard
pour savoir— pour la voir me
regarder— restent ses mots, pour
mes doigts épuisés— ses mots à
elle qu'il me faut lui voler— qui
viennent d'elle, d'avant elle—
cette fraction de seconde— la
même— comme une obsession—
affiche d'un moment, tombée
dans la pluie— je l'ai cherchée
longtemps— dans la ville— qui
se rit de moi—

devant ce bar à
regarder —
à surveiller derrière
dans un verre sans
alcool
en attendant la fin
d'une autre cigarette
entre ses longs
doigts
gant noir en satin
sur sa joue
elle
mince de son corps
s'étire
indolore à la pose
d'un sourire qui se
Boude
face au même va et
vient
d'un pas
et elle sans bouger
par le reflet de son
ombre
à écouter sa voix
que l'autre fait
entendre
ce va et vient d'un
pas
fatigué
les lèvres qui
s'entr'ouvrent
vers le satin d'un
gant
noir
sur ma joue

l'avoir suivie longtemps— mar-
chant derrière elle— pour la sur-
prendre plus loin?— l'avoir suivie
partout à travers la ville— hostile
à mon corps, la nuit— et difficile
à reconnaître— elle— mes pas
sont morts, perdus d'eux-
mêmes— d'avoir mal marché—
mal cherché et d'avoir pleuré
aussi— mais la suivre encore—
son ombre blanche— et si
froide— qui me frôle sans savoir— parfois comme un souvenir— les mêmes mots entremêlés
aux mêmes pas— simplement de
l'avoir aperçue— elle, à peine
vue— sans visage— il n'y a plus
qu'elle et moi— appuyées ici
deux presque seules de nos
corps— elle, et moi— elle qui ne
me voit pas— je, qui ne la
regarde plus— comme oubliée—
brusquement attirée par une fraction de seconde— dans ce bar sans
doute— et ce satin sur sa peau, si
noir—

66   France Mongeau, 'Croquis d'un texte en suspens' [excerpt], *La Nouvelle Barre du Jour*, no. 114 (mai 1982), 28–9

dans   l'instant   même
de   m'entendre   dire
j'ai retourné   le   bref
tracé   ici   devant
toujours   pour   voir
toujours   ici ou bien
serré   ou   bien tracé
la ligne   qui   m'allait
comme un galbe   parfait
tracé   et mouvementé
comme   il   se   devait
sans   doute   en
t'approchant   près
tout   près   à te toucher
presque   tant   distante
si   longtemps
qu'entre   nos   retours
aléatoires   la   tête
tournée   vers   lui
il   fallait   créer   des

67   Hughes Corriveau, 'la Troisième Figure' [excerpt],
      from *La Nouvelle Barre du Jour*, no. 64 (jan. 1978), 13

liens   tiers   en
nos   fils   complexes
de   l'un   à   l'une
à   l'autre   enfin
ne   sachant   plus
défiler   nos   emprises
multiples   en   nos
muettes   tensions
clos   et   muets
en   nos   fermetures
en nos murs   journaliers
en nos places immédiates
chacun en nos   coins
isocèles   formant   ici
figures et nos rhétoriques
ne sachant pas très bien
le   discours et la lettre
où courir   le texte
le mot   lui-même
en sa clôture de bouche
à bouche   transmis
en nos   langues rejointes
et   mouillées pour l'autre
lien   conçu   en   nos
peaux perçues   en   sa
percale   place

68   Hughes Corriveau, 'La Trosième Figure' [continued],
La Nouvelle Barre du Jour, no. 64 (jan. 1978), 14

ni regret ni respect une chose pas négliger
pratique / théorie / pratique mouvement
perpétuel établir un programme partir de la base
constamment évaluer l'intervention comment
pourquoi militer se donner une ligne juste claire
on se retrouve ensemble parmi les gens d'accord
j'insiste deux mots seulement « organisation de
masse » pas de après demain le temps ne se perd
pas faire progresser le phénomène / la montée /
même à contre-courant / ne jamais désespérer
traverser ponts villes torrents vas-y demi-baissé
bondis!

69   François Charron, 'Untitled,' from *Interventions politiques*
(Montréal: L'Aurore 1974), 62

70   François Charron, *Exprimer sa pensée*, 1979,
     gouache and pastel on paper, 54″ × 72″

71   François Charron, *Crucifixion*, 1982,
     mixed media on paper, 20″ × 26″

1. Il faut cesser de considérer la sculpture, la peinture, le cinéma, la musique et la littérature, comme des formes autonomes de langage artistique et suivre pas à pas l'évolution stylistique qui les enferme dans une histoire des formes, Il faut cesser de se referer à l'histoire de l'art, car l'art est aliénant pour les gens et pour les artistes en premier lieu: l'art est une mystification.

2. Aux artistes, nous recommandons donc de s'intégrer directement aux domaines suivants: (a) architecture, urbanisme, design (b) loisirs (c) information. Les démarches strictement formelles sont intéressantes mais doivent être intégrées dans des projets socialement fonctionnels. L'histoire de l'oeuvre qu'on ne peut juger qu'en se référant à ses critères internes est terminée. On ne peut juger d'une conception plastique, d'un morceau de musique ou d'un film etc... sans se référer aux catégories sociales que sont les trois domaines plus haut cités. C'est là et non dans l'art qu'il y a révolution à instaurer.

3. Affirmer que l'art est mort implique une position de principe qui repose sur l'idée suivante: l'efficacité sociale de l'art est un mythe. L'oeuvre d'art est un objet de consommation comme n'importe quel autre, un objet de culture intégré à la mécanique générale de la culture et qui est incapable de la remettre en question. Décréter la mort de l'art implique que l'on prend position contre le statut privilégié de l'artiste et contre la notion d'art garante de la liberté d'expression des citoyens, avec tout ce que cette notion retient de "sacré", d'éternel et de non "basement matériel". L'artiste n'est pas plus spécialement créateur que tout autre catégorie de gens de la société.

4. Livres, films, peintures etc... sont des objets de communications, c'est-à-dire des objets plus ou moins efficaces selon tels ou tels milieux et occasions. Ils n'ont dans le combat révolutionnaire pas plus d'importance que n'importe quels autrés types d'activités correspondant à tels ou tels types de militants.

5. L'expression individuelle en tant qu'expression de la façon dont un individu voit le monde, est cependant capitale. D'autant plus qu'elle incitera le plus grand nombre de gens à communiquer entre eux et à être de plus en plus libres. De ce fait, il existera toujours des personnes qui proposeront à leurs contemporains des expériences inédites. Mais il n'est pas dit que ces personnes soient de celles qu'on appelle actuellement artistes ou vedettes.

Mai 1969.

72   Manifesto of the Fusion des Arts group,
     from *Quebec Underground 1962–1972*, ed. Yves Robillard
     (Montréal: Médiart 1973), I, 282–3

Notes

INTRODUCTION

1 On the whole issue of avant-garde theory Peter Burger's *Theory of the Avant Garde*, trans. Michael Shaw (Minneapolis: University of Minnesota Press 1974) as well as Charles Russell's *The Avant-Garde Today* (Chicago: University of Illinois Press 1982) would constitute important reference points. Reference should also be made to John Barth, who was among the first to use the term *post-modernism*. See, in particular, 'The Literature of Exhaustion,' *The Atlantic* 220, no. 2 (1967), 29–34, and 'The Literature of Replenishment: Postmodernist Fiction,' *The Atlantic* 245, no. 1 (1980), 65–71. On the breaking point between avant-garde and post-modern aesthetics Guy Scarpetta's masterly *Eloge de l'impureté* (Paris: Grasset 1985) would probably be the most significant contribution.
2 Scarpetta, *Eloge de l'impureté*, 14
3 See Jean-François Lyotard, 'Réponse à la question; qu'est-ce que le postmoderne?' *Critique* 419 (1982) 357–67, and his *La Condition postmoderne* (Paris: Minuit 1979).
4 Jonathan Culler, *The Pursuit of Signs* (London: Routledge and Kegan Paul 1981), 5
5 See Jean Baudrillard, *The Mirror of Production* (St Louis: Telos Press 1975); Lyotard, *La Condition postmoderne*; and Timothy Reiss, *The Discourse of Modernism* (Baltimore: Johns Hopkins University Press 1986).
6 I do not use this word with any disparaging intention here but with the respect I owe to those who in working with language do not proceed from absolutes but with the tentativeness and temptations of a researcher.
7 See Fred Jameson, *The Prison-House of Language* (Princeton: Princeton University Press 1972).

8 For Derrida see *La Grammatologie* (Paris: Minuit 1967) and *La Dis-sémination* (Paris: Le Seuil 1972). For Baudrillard see *The Mirror of Production* ('The sign no longer designates anything, the code becomes the instance of absolute reference' [127]) and *Pour une critique de l'économie politique du signe* (Paris: Gallimard 1972) ('Le monde est l'effet du signe et le signe est devenu circulaire' [62]). For Lyotard see *Dérive à partir de Marx et de Freud* (Paris: Union Générale d'Editeurs 1973), especially his comments on dodecaphony and deconstructionism: 'The arts do not fulfil any religious function anymore and do not let us participate in meaning' (219).

9 Quoted in Umberto Eco, *Theory of Semiotics* (Bloomington: Indiana University Press 1979), 14

10 See Umberto Eco's own ambiguity about Saussurean postulates: 'Saussure did not define the signified any too clearly leaving it half way between a mental image, a concept and a psychological reality: but he did clearly stress the fact that the signified is something that has to do with the mental activity of anybody receiving a signifier ... provided that he did not share a Platonic interpretation of the term idea ... The sign is implicitly regarded as a communication device taking place between two human beings intentionally aiming to communicate or to express something' (*Theory of Semiotics*, 15).

11 Compare Saussure's later distinction between paradigmatic and syntagmatic planes, these being defined as purely combinatory systems removed from any constraints other than internal and structural.

12 See Jameson's parallels between Husserlian phenomenology and Saussurean linguistics, *The Prison-House of Language*, 106.

13 See Anne-Marie Pelletier's comments on Frege in *Fonctions poétiques* (Paris: Klincksieck 1977), 14–16.

14 See Paul Ricoeur's discussion of the two-fold rise of semantics and semiotics in *The Rule of Metaphor* (Toronto: University of Toronto Press 1977), 74.

15 I.A. Richards, *The Philosophy of Rhetoric* (Oxford: Oxford University Press 1936), 40

16 Monroe Beardsley, *Aesthetics* (New York: Harcourt, Brace and World 1958), 115

17 Ricoeur, *The Rule of Metaphor*, 134

18 The works to which the reader should be referred in this respect are J. Dubois et al., eds. *Rhétorique générale* (Paris: Larousse 1970) and A.J. Greimas, *Sémantique structurale* (Paris: Larousse 1966). Ricoeur's comments on the research pursued by the latter and especially on the shift from word to sense (Greimas, 30–55) are explicit: 'It becomes

more difficult to see where a bond is possible between the semiotics of the word and the semantics of a sentence. The locus of exchange between predication and naming becomes obscured' (*The Rule of Metaphor*, 136).

19 From 1969 on, *semiotics* has been the preferred term. For a more detailed account of philosophical and methodological differences between the two terms, see Eco, *Theory of Semiotics*, 30.

20 The list is very long and the charge 'semiotic imperialism' has often been levelled at this methodological approach. Semiotics aims at encompassing far more than the traditional territory of hermeneutics; it covers an immense field, ranging from zoosemiotics and medical semiotics to psychoanalysis, and from musical codes and formalized languages to unwritten languages and secret codes.

21 Paul Ricoeur, *Interpretation Theory: Discourse and the Surplus of Meaning* (Fort Worth, Texas: Texas Christian University Press 1976), 9

22 Ibid.

23 Shoshana Felman, *Literary Speech Acts*, trans. Catherine Porter (Ithaca: Cornell University Press 1983), 75

24 The impact of this conception of the code and of the signifier was acutely felt in the realm of political and anthropological thought. A three-step process was reduced to one of its terms, and the homology of the sphere of commodity with that of competitive capitalism was achieved. See Baudrillard, *The Mirror of Production*, 122–9.

25 Douglas Greenlee proposes to dismiss the distinction between sign and representamen; in his view, both terms are used interchangeably by Peirce. See his *Peirce's Concept of Sign* (The Hague: Mouton 1973), 46.

26 Greenlee notes that Peirce's position was not always so unflinchingly clear. Concerning the three alternatives open to the sign (surrogative/referential/interpretive), he suggests that while Peirce always dismissed the first, he retained an interest in the second. Only towards the end of his life did he choose the third. See Greenlee, 5.

27 Peirce quoted in Eco, *Theory of Semiotics*, 69

28 Ibid. 66

29 Peirce's lack of absolute assurance about this issue, already pointed out by Greenlee (46), is justified by this critic on the grounds of a disparity of opinions present in the American logician's writings but never accurately acknowledged by him. Greenlee refers to these positions as (1) hypostatic and (2) factorial. But the important fact here, and the only one which truly concerns us, is that ultimately Peirce rejected the object of reference as inessential (Greenlee, 110) and from his tri-

partite division of signs (icons, indices, symbols) concluded that all signs were symbols (Greenlee, 135).

30 On this 'fetishization of capitalism' see Baudrillard, *Pour une critique de l'économie politique du signe*, 100–7. While he originally centres most of his discussion upon the realm of political economy, he subsequently opens it to other areas in the arts and humanities.

31 Baudrillard, *Pour une critique de l'économie politique du signe*, 185 (translation mine)

32 Julia Kristeva, *Révolution du langage poétique* (Paris: Le Seuil 1974), 29 (translation mine)

33 See Stéphane Mallarmé, 'Mystères dans les lettres,' in *Oeuvres complètes* (Paris: Gallimard 1945), 382–7, and *Un coup de dés jamais n'abolira le hasard / A throw of dice will never abolish chance*, trans. Daisy Aldan (New York: Tiber Press 1956), n. pag.

34 The text Kristeva refers to here is 'Les mots anglais' (Mallarmé, *Oeuvres complètes*, 919): 'Sound and sense skilfully fitted to each other, this is the double clue which guides the philologist' (*Révolution*, 236 [translation mine]). The term *pulsion* recurs frequently in her writings of this period and articulates her psychoanalytic concerns within literary discourse. See 'Sémiotique et symbolique' in *Révolution*, 17–100, and particularly here references to Freud's *Essais de Psychanalyse*, Mélanie Klein's *La Psychanalyse des enfants*, and Jacques Lacan's *Ecrits* (27, 47). Kristeva also reminds us that linguists such as Emile Benveniste and Ivan Fonagy stress the role of subjectivity and speaking subjects within the enunciation process (*Révolution*, 19–38).

35 The manifesto proclaimed in 1912 was signed by D. Burluk, A. Kruchyonykh, V. Mayakovsky, and V. Klebnikov. See Szymon Bojko, *New Graphics in Revolutionary Russia* (London: Lund Humphries 1972), 39.

36 Kristeva, *Révolution du langage poétique*, 50–69

37 *The Surrealist Revolution* 1, no. 1 (1931), 17

38 See Hans Richter's comments in *Dada, Art, Anti-Art* (New York: McGraw-Hill 1965), 30.

39 Ibid.

40 See Isidore Isou, 'La Fin des dadaistes falsificateurs de la culture et de la critique universitaire obscurantiste,' *Revue Ô*, no. C (June 1965), 10–21, and Maurice Lemaître, *Le Lettrisme devant Dada et les nécrophages de Dada* (Paris: Centre de créativité 1967).

41 See Paul Zumthor, *Langue, texte, énigme* (Paris: Le Seuil 1975), particularly 'Jonglerie et langage,' 36–54.

42 E.E. Cummings, whose poetic output both preceded and overlapped the

concrete movement, never associated with it. Mary Ellen Solt and
the Brazilian concrete theoreticians look upon his work as the foundation stone of concretism. See Mary Ellen Solt, *Concrete Poetry: A
World View* (Bloomington: Indiana University Press 1969), 47, and
Augusto de Campos et al., eds., *Teoria da Poesia Concreta* (São Paulo:
Livraria das Ciudades 1975), 153. All his stylistic innovations were
used by concretists: word-dismemberments, permutations, and rhetorical capitalization and punctuation, not to mention his expressionist
emphasis on white spaces and space in general. While he never discussed the isomorphic relationship of meaning and typography, he
practised it extensively. For a more detailed study of Cummings'
typography and lay-out see Rudolph von Abele's 'Only to Grow:
Change in the Poetry of e e Cummings,' PMLA 70 (Dec. 1955),
913–33, and Barry A. Mark, *e e Cummings* (Boston: Twayne Press
1964).

43 See William Carlos Williams, *Selected Essays* (New York: Random
House 1954), 42. To Williams the writing of a poem commenced
with words handled with care but also as *objects* arranged in the hope
that they would produce ideas. Interesting in this context is Williams' ire against Kenneth Rexroth, who had failed – in his view – to
grasp the importance of the Joycean rupture between words and ideas
and of the concept of verbalism purloined by Gertrude Stein: 'To Rexroth words have absolute meanings synonymous with the context of
ideas which he accepts ... Dangerous grounds' ('In Praise of Marriage,'
Quarterly Review of Literature 4, no. 2 [1944], 147).

44 Charles Olson, *Projective Verse* (New York: Totem Press 1959), 10

45 See Ihab Hassan, *Para-criticisms* (Urbana: University of Illinois Press
1975); and Lyotard, *Dérive à partir de Marx et de Freud*, and *La
Condition postmoderne*.

46 Baudrillard, *Pour une critique de l'économie politique du signe*, 164–8

CHAPTER 1 THEORETICAL BACKGROUND OF A CRISIS

1 He did so in a magazine called *Art concret*. See further references to
this event in George Rickey, *Constructivism: Origins and Evolution*
(New York: G. Braziller 1967), 40.

2 Hans Arp, *On My Way* (New York: Wittenborn and Schultz 1948),
73

3 Solt, *Concrete Poetry: A World View*, 11

4 Pierre Schaeffer, *La Musique concrète* (Paris: Presses Universitaires de
France 1967), 10

5 Ibid. 16. Schaeffer borrowed this graph from Albert Richard's 1949 article published in *Polyphonie*.

6 Ernest Fenollosa, *The Chinese Written Character as a Medium for Poetry*, ed. Ezra Pound (1936; rpt. San Francisco: City Lights 1963), 15 (italics mine)

7 See Jacques Derrida, *Of Grammatology*, trans. G.C. Spivak (Baltimore: Johns Hopkins University Press 1976), 76: 'All the philosophical projects of a universal script ... invoked by Descartes, outlined by Father Kircher, Wilkes, Leibniz, etc., encouraged seeing in the recently discovered Chinese script a model of the philosophical language thus removed from history.' See also Madeleine David's important monograph on the general history of writing, *Les Dieux et le destin en Babylonie* (Paris: PUF 1949), and James G. Février's *L'Histoire de l'écriture* (Paris: Payot 1959).

8 See Michel Foucault, *The Order of Things* (London: Tavistock Publications 1970). According to Foucault, as late as the sixteenth century artificial signs owed their effectiveness to their mimetic relationship with natural signs. From the seventeenth century on that trend was reversed.

9 E.A. Llorach stresses that while none of these kinds of writings can be found in an unadulterated state, these divisions are indicative of systematic and slow changing processes from ideographics to phonographics. See A. Martinet, *Le Langage* (Paris: Gallimard 1968).

10 See Jean Piaget, *Le Structuralisme* (Paris: Presses Universitaires de France 1968), 97.

11 William Warburton, *The Divine Legation of Moses* (London 1738), translated into French as *Essai sur les hiéroglyphes des Egyptiens* (Paris 1744). See Book IV, sections 2–6. Warburton established three distinct stages, from 'language action' to 'metaphorical language' and finally the present 'abstract language.' See Tzvetan Todorov, 'Introduction à la symbolique,' *Poétique* 3 (1972), 299 for further comments on this issue.

12 Ibid. See also Gérard Genette, *Mimologiques* (Paris: Le Seuil 1975), and chap. 3 ('Of Grammatology as a Positive Science') in Derrida, *Of Grammatology*, 74–93.

13 The Brazilians paid special tribute to both. See 'Plano Piloto,' in de Campos et al., eds., *Teoria da Poesia Concreta*, 156–8, which gives a twentieth-century turn to the old Chinese prejudice.

14 Oyvind Fahlstrom did not publish his statement in book form but simply circulated it on mimeographed sheets. It was translated into English by Mary Ellen Solt in 1969 and deserves to be studied closely

because it prefigures – even if somewhat sketchily – theories which others were to elaborate upon. See 'Manifesto for Concrete Poetry,' in Solt, *Concrete Poetry: A World View*, 75–8.

15 Fahlstrom occasionally slipped on this terrain. Remarkably inconsistent with the rest of his theories, for instance, is his concession that words may be accepted as symbols (see Solt, *Concrete Poetry*, 79). But symbol of what? Should this term be used in its Peircian acceptation, in which case Fahlstrom is consistent with himself, or in its more generally accepted use – that is, symbol of something? Both possibilities coexist here and Fahlstrom does not clarify this ambiguity.

16 Solt, *Concrete Poetry: A World View*, 77

17 Solt is convincing when she suggests that he had no direct impact upon Eugen Gomringer's early writings since no one in Latin America or Europe in the late 1950s was aware of his existence.

18 See Zumthor, *Langue, texte, énigme*, 43, 46, 50–4. Medieval literature as a whole is depicted here as a gloss demanding a re-creation, and enigma becomes a genre. Kernel words are viewed by Zumthor as a 'formule géneratrice.'

19 Solt, *Concrete Poetry: A World View*, 78

20 For concrete developments in this area see Solt, *Concrete Poetry: A World View*, 75–82.

21 In fact, with the exception of Claus Bremmer, the members of the Darmstadt Circle were not German. Emmett Williams was American, Diter Ross Icelandic, Daniel Spoerri Romanian. But Darmstadt provided them with the cosmopolitan richness and the graphic resources to pull their skills together and produce the first international anthology, *Konkrete poesie international*, ed. Claus Bremmer and Daniel Spoerri (Stuttgart: Hansjorg Mayer 1957).

22 Max Bense, 'Konkrete poesie,' *Rot*, no. 21 (1965), 15–21. Translated by I. Montjoye Sinor in Solt, *Concrete Poetry: A World View*, 74

23 See Max Bense, *Einführung in die Information Theoretische Aesthetics* (Reinbeck bei Hamburg: Rowohlt 1969), 22–3, 41, and his *Zeichen und Design* (Baden-Baden: Hyis Verlag 1971), 30–1.

24 See Bense's statements as early as 1957 in Bremmer and Spoerri, eds., *Konkrete poesie international*, 19–27, 32–51, and also his 'Konkrete poesie' (1965).

25 See Eugen Gomringer, 'The First Years of Concrete Poetry,' trans. Stephen Bann, *Forum* 4 (15 April 1967), 7.

26 For this phrase, and the subsequent two quoted phrases, see Eugen Gomringer, 'From Line to Constellation,' *Image*, Nov.–Dec. 1964, 10–21.

27 Gomringer makes no reference to the medieval *jongleries*, which certainly demanded a high degree of the reader's involvement if any sense was to be made of a text. See Zumthor, *Langue, texte, énigme*, 43–6.

28 See Roland Barthes, *Le Plaisir du texte* (Paris: Le Seuil 1973), and Kristeva, *Révolution du langage poétique*, especially 613.

29 See Franz Mon, 'On the Poetry of Surface,' trans. I. Montjoye Sinor and Mary Ellen Solt, in Solt, *Concrete Poetry: A World View*, 19–20; and excerpts from Max Bense, in Bremmer and Spoerri, eds., *Konkrete poesie international*, 19–27, 32–51. Words for Bense are not used as carriers of meaning but as material elements of construction. See also his 'Konkrete poesie.'

30 See 'Plano Piloto para Poesia Concreta' in de Campos et al., eds., *Teoria da Poesia Concreta*, 154–6.

31 There was a double irony in this choice of name. First the Brazilians knew that literary experts would have a hard time explaining the term. Secondly it referred to the Pound-Fenollosa tradition (imagistic/ideogrammatic) and merged it within concretist aesthetics. See Pound's Canto no. 20: 'Noigandres, eh, *noigandres*, / Now what the DEFFIL can that mean!' See also Solt, *Concrete Poetry: A World View*, 12.

32 On this whole question see Gérard Genette's extensive compilation of the Kratylian heritage in *Mimologiques*, as well as my discussion of this problem below (see pp. 28–34).

33 For this and the terms immediately following see de Campos et al., eds., *Teoria da Poesia Concreta*, 155.

34 'There will never be a sign without the simultaneous presence of these two functives' (*Prolegomena to a Theory of Language* [Madison: University of Wisconsin Press 1963], 48).

35 Ibid. 60

36 He does so in the following passages: 'We shall always find that there is a relation between a correlation of expression and a correlation of content. If such a relation is not present, that is precisely the reason for deciding that ... there are two different variants of the same sign' (ibid. 68); 'Content line and expression line are partitioned according to a common principle' (ibid. 70); and 'We understand nothing of the structure of language if we do not constantly take into first consideration the interplay between two planes' (ibid. 75).

37 Ibid. 112 (italics mine)

38 See Eco, *Theory of Semiotics*, 191.

39 Ibid.

40 Charles Morris himself states: 'An iconic sign is similar in some re-
    spects to what it denotes. Iconicity is thus a matter of degree' (*Signs,
    Language and Behaviour* [New York: Prentice Hall 1946], 72). And C.S.
    Peirce, more subtly: a sign is an icon when it 'may represent its
    object mainly by its similarity' (*Collected Papers*, vol. II [Cambridge:
    Harvard University Press 1932], 157).
41 Eco, *Theory of Semiotics*, 201
42 Ibid. 100
43 See the 'wordless poem' or semiotic poem devised by Décio Pignatari
    and Luiz Pinto ('Nova linguagem, nova poesia,' *Invencao* 3, no. 4
    [1964], 82–3).
44 See Derrida, *Of Grammatology*, 78–9.
45 Hjemskv, *Prolegomena*, 52–4. See also Eco's more complete analysis of
    the colour spectrum and the perception of its wavelengths in various
    cultures, in *Theory of Semiotics*, 76–81.
46 See comments on Claude Bremond in Eco, *Theory of Semiotics*, 145.
    See also Greimas, *Sémantique structurale*.
47 Pierre Garnier, *Spatialisme et poésie concrète* (Paris: Gallimard 1968), 11
48 Pierre Garnier, 'Deuxième Manifeste pour une poésie visuelle,' *Les
    Lettres*, 8th ser., no. 30 (avril 1963), 16, 17
49 Umberto Eco, *Opera aperta* (Milano: Bompiani 1962), translated as
    L'Oeuvre ouverte (Paris: Le Seuil 1965)
50 Grammatical disruptions in and by themselves are not a particularly
    new phenomenon in poetry. One could easily demonstrate that
    'making strange' is indeed the most salient and recurring feature of the
    poetic text. See Gérard Genette, *Figures II* (Paris: Le Seuil 1969),
    123–53, and Jan Mukarovsky, *Structure, Sign and Function*, trans. John
    Burbank and Peter Steiner (New Haven: Yale University Press 1977),
    56.
51 Garnier, 'Deuxième Manifeste pour une poésie visuelle,' 23
52 Pierre Garnier, 'Manifeste pour une poésie nouvelle, visuelle et phon-
    ique,' *Les Lettres*, 8th ser., no. 29 (1963), 2
53 'signifiant' in French. See Solt's translation of his manifesto 'Why I Am
    the Author of Sound and Free Poetry,' in *Concrete Poetry: A World
    View*, 82.
54 Ibid. 83
55 Paul Claudel, *Oeuvres en prose* (Paris: Gallimard 1965), 98
56 See Gérard Genette, 'Avatars du cratylisme,' *Poétique* 3 (1972), 367–94,
    as well as his *Mimologiques*.
57 Roland Barthes, 'Proust et les noms,' in *To Honour Roman Jakobson*
    (The Hague: Mouton Press 1967). See 154–8 especially.

58 Socrates says: 'Kratylus is right in saying that things have names by nature and that not every man is an artificer of names, but only he who looks to the name which each thing by nature has and is able to express the true form of things in letters and syllables' (*The Dialogues of Plato*, trans. B. Jowett [New York: Random House 1937], 180–1).

59 Genette comments on what he feels was the implicit Socratic rejection of a Golden Age wherein language would have been perfect and then subsequently betrayed by history. See *Mimologiques*, 11–37.

60 '... par des touches y répondant en coloris ou en allure, lesquelles existent dans l'instrument de la voix, parmi les langages, et quelquefois chez un' (Mallarmé, quoted in Genette, *Mimologiques*, 36).

61 Genette establishes a clear division between what he terms primary Kratylism and secondary Kratylism. See *Mimologiques*, 36–9.

62 Genette suggests the term *divorce* (*Mimologiques*, 39).

63 The use of the term *syllables* at a time when writing could not have been involved should not be misconstrued here. Socrates was referring to 'articulated sounds,' the guarantee for the phonematicity of a sound being in ancient Greek its reference to a letter. See Genette, *Mimologiques*, 29.

64 Victor Goldschmidt argues that in fact this symbolism is not unique to Plato (*Essai sur le Cratyle* [Paris: Champion 1940], 151). Democritus and Hippias would also have attempted an examination of each isolated letter. To which Genette replies that both were Hermogenes' followers.

65 On the problems raised by this term – absent from 'Kratylus' – and on the errors of the so-called Socratic etymologies, see *Mimologiques*, 18–19.

66 'Kratylus,' in Jowett, trans., *The Dialogues of Plato*, 94–200

67 Ibid. 213–15

68 On direct motivation see reference to Denys d'Halicarnasse, *Mimologiques*, 39–40.

69 On the rich tradition of hermeneutic etymology see Zumthor, *Langue, texte, énigme*, 144–58. Also see John Wallis' 'Soni Rerum Indices' and 'De Etymologia' in *Grammatica Lingua Anglicanae* (Oxford 1673), 148–64.

70 See Fahlstrom, in Solt, *Concrete Poetry: A World View*, 75–8.

71 See Genette, *Mimologiques*, 42–7.

72 'Hinc ad ipsarum inter se rerum similitudinem processisse licentiam nominandi' (ibid. 43).

73 Genette points out how the metonymic relation picks up from the metaphorical one when the latter does not seem sufficient to ensure the analogical relation between several signifieds (ibid. 44).

74 The exception here is interesting and will recur in other writings by different authors. See Derrida on the 'Chinese prejudice,' in *Of Grammatology*, 76.

75 Gottfried Wilhelm Leibniz, *New Essays* (Cambridge: Cambridge University Press 1981), 283. Leibniz adds: 'There is something natural in the origins of words, something that reveals a relationship between things and the sounds and motions of the vocal organs' (ibid.).

76 Aspirations to a perfect and logical language are not new. See Genette's comments on Father Mersenne's treatise on Universal Harmony, in *Mimologiques*, 69.

77 On graphic mimesis see quotations from the following works in Genette, *Mimologiques*, 71–83: Franciscus Mercurius, *Alphabeti Vere Naturalis Hebraici Brevissima Delineatio* (Sulzbaci 1657), Johann Wachter, *Glossarium Germanicum* (1736), and Rowland Jones, *Hieroglyphic* (1768).

78 On phonic mimesis see Mercurius, *Alphebeti Vere Naturalis Hebraici Brevissima Delineatio*.

79 Leibniz is careful to introduce a distinction between divine language, clearly arbitrary 'ab instituto divo,' and Adam's language, definitely motivated. The whole question of Adamic language was abundantly commented upon by Jacob Boehme, who saw in it a universal code and the expression of truth. See Wolfgang Kayser, 'La Doctrine du langage naturel chez Jacob Boehme, *Poétique* 3 (1972), 337–65.

80 Court de Gebelin was aware of Charles de Brosses' system and basically defines writing as painting. The alphabet *must* become an ideogram, and its smallest particles, phonemes, must become ideophones. He developed a hieroglyphic alphabet which attempted to establish a link between ideographic values and phonic symbols. See the third volume of his encyclopaedia *L'Histoire naturelle de la parole* (Paris 1776).

81 In the area of graphic mimesis de Brosses, in his *Traité de la formation mécanique des langues* (Paris 1765), equates truth with conformity of words to things. See also Court de Gebelin's *Le Monde primitif* (Paris 1776), which stresses the necessary relationship between words and ideas, ideas and objects. Since writing is heretofore defined as painting, the language of origin would necessarily be mimetic, as would the sum total of the elements present in all languages.

82 In de Brosses (*Traité de la formation mécanique des langues*), this deficiency signals an unfortunate deviation from primordial roots. See Genette, *Mimologiques*, 85–117.

83 Genette, *Mimologiques*, 149

84 The term is Genette's. See *Mimologiques*, 199–200.

85 Ibid. 241

86 Ibid. 239

87 See Stéphane Mallarmé, 'Petite Philologie à l'usage des classes et du monde, les mots anglais,' in *Oeuvres complètes*, 881–1053.

88 Genette points out that Mallarmé's position on the imperfections of the lexicon is identical to Socrates', for whom the '*r* sound has harsh connotations and in whose eyes the word *sklerotes* ('harshness') *should have been* closer to *skrerotes*' (Genette, *Mimologiques*, 272 [translation mine]).

89 Ibid. 280 (translation mine)

90 See Genette's reference to Malherbe's parallelism between the two: prose cancels itself out within its function, while poetry 'se récupère automatiquement' (*Mimologiques* 289).

91 See Paul Claudel, 'The Religion of Letters,' in *The East I Know* (New Haven: Yale University Press 1914), 42–8, and also his 'Positions et propositions,' in *Oeuvres en prose*, 1–10.

92 For Jean-François Champollion, in his *Traité sur l'écriture démotique* (1824) and his *Précis du système hiéroglyphique des anciens égyptiens* (1827), demonstrated that hieroglyphics were partially based on a phonetic system and not exclusively on an iconic one.

93 Claudel, *Oeuvres en prose*, 86. There are exceptions in which Claudel views the spatial symmetry of the word as important. See his comments on *arbre* ('tree'), for instance (ibid. 101).

94 Genette, *Mimologiques*, 345 (translation mine). The difference here with constructivism, dadaism, lettrism, and concretism, in which linguistic matter is self-determined only, is evident.

95 On the correspondence Ponge sketched between the density of things and semantic weight see Marcel Spada, *Francis Ponge* (Paris: Seghers 1974), 60.

96 See 'Signe, singe,' in Genette, *Mimologiques*, 351–75.

97 'Economimesis' was originally published in S. Agacinski et al., *Mimésis des articulations* (Paris: Flammarion 1975), 55–93, and in English translation, in *Diacritics* 11, no. 2 (1981), 3–25.

98 Jacques Derrida, *Dissemination*, trans. Barbara Johnson (Chicago: University of Chicago Press 1982), 193

99 Ibid.

100 Jacques Derrida, *Writing and Difference*, trans. Alan Bass (Chicago: University of Chicago Press 1978), 275

101 See Derrida, *Of Grammatology*, 34.

102 Timothy Reiss persuasively decomposes the two characteristics of

analytico-referential discourse. This discourse, which develops mainly in the course of the seventeenth century, is defined by (a) its process of analysis whereby the fundamental structures of language are identified with those of thought (hence the attempt to discover in a general grammar the universals of the thinking process) and by (b) its concern for referentiality: the main assumption here being that thought and language are separate and that language is nothing more than the medium of expression for a thought capable of seizing representations of the real. See Reiss, *The Discourse of Modernism*, chaps. 5 and 6. See also his 'Peirce and Frege in the Matter of Truth,' *Canadian Journal of Research in Semiotics* 4, no. 2 (Winter 1976), 7.

103 Jonathan Culler, *On Deconstruction* (London: Routledge and Kegan Paul 1983), 186

104 See Paul de Man's comments on the nostalgic mystique of origins in *Blindness and Insight* (New York: Oxford University Press 1971), 235–7. Christopher Norris' insightful comments about de Man's perceptions suggest that while de Man is not arguing that there once existed a state of linguistic innocence and grace, the rhetoric of his essay often carries such suggestions 'if only by way of contesting the positivist assumptions of a critic like Richards.' See Christopher Norris, 'Some Versions of Rhetoric: Empson and de Man,' *Genre* 17, nos. 1–2 (Spring–Summer 1984), 208.

105 See Christopher Norris, *Deconstruction: Theory and Practice* (London: Methuen 1982), 2, and Culler, *On Deconstruction*, 12.

106 Frank Lentricchia, *After the New Criticism* (Chicago: University of Chicago Press 1980), 159

107 See Jacques Derrida, 'Signature, Event, Context,' in *Margins of Philosophy*, trans. Alan Bass (Chicago: University of Chicago Press 1982), 307–30. See also Norris' discussion in 'Some Versions of Rhetoric.'

108 Norris, 'Some Versions of Rhetoric,' 192. Reference here is to Hartman's *Saving the Text* (Baltimore: Johns Hopkins University Press 1981).

109 Ibid. 196. Here Norris refers to Paul de Man's *Allegories of Reading* (New Haven: Yale University Press 1979).

110 In his article see his suggestions about 'the limited plausibility' of a perception of deconstruction which would put it down as an updated version of New Critical dogma (191, 213).

111 See Jameson, *The Prison-House of Language*, 29–33. See also Christopher Norris, *The Deconstructive Turn* (London: Methuen 1984), 3.

112 J. Hillis Miller, 'Stevens' Rock and Criticism as Cure (Part II),' *Georgia Review* 30 (1976), 336

113 Hartman, *Saving the Text*, 61
114 Ronald Schleifer and Robert Con Davis, 'Introduction: The Ends of Deconstruction,' *Genre* 17, nos. 1–2 (Spring–Summer 1984), 6
115 See Derrida's references to Heidegger's 'The Origin of the Work of Art,' quoted in Culler, *On Deconstruction*, 142.
116 Derrida, *Writing and Difference*, 292–3
117 Norris, 'Some Versions of Rhetoric,' 194
118 Ibid.
119 de Man, *Allegories of Reading*, 12
120 Barbara Johnson, *The Critical Difference* (Baltimore: Johns Hopkins University Press 1980), 40
121 Culler, *On Deconstruction*, 150
122 Derrida, 'Economimesis,' *Diacritics* 11, no. 2 (1981), 3. The original French text reads: 'Mais il ne suffit pas de faire le tri ou de mesurer des longueurs. Pliées à un nouveau système les grandes séquences se déplacent, changent de sens ou de fonction' (in Agacinski et al., *Mimesis des articulations*, 57).
123 Jacques Derrida, 'The Conflict of Faculties,' as quoted in Culler, *On Deconstruction*, 156
124 Michael Ryan argues that Derrida and Marx deploy similar strategies in their critique of idealism, naturalism, and positivism. He contrasts these with Lenin's theory and practice, which he describes as founded on a logocentric paradigm that equates meaning with vanguard-party rule by eliminating play, specifically the play of difference which constitutes the essence of revolutionary activity. See *Marxism and Deconstruction* (Baltimore: Johns Hopkins University Press 1982), xiv.
125 See: Gerald Graff, *Literature against Itself: Literary Ideas in Modern Society* (Chicago: University of Chicago Press 1979); Edward Said, 'Reflections on Recent American Left Criticism,' in *The Idea of Textuality: Strategies of Reading in Contemporary American Criticism* (Bloomington: Indiana University Press 1982); and Terry Eagleton, *Walter Benjamin or Towards a Revolutionary Criticism* (London: NLB 1982).
126 Gayatri Spivak and Michael Ryan argue that Derrida's bourgeois followers have ignored the radical and Marxist implications of his project. See Spivak, 'Revolutions That as Yet Have No Model: Derrida's *Limited Inc.*,' *Diacritics* 10, no. 4 (Winter 1980), 29–49. Spivak's participation in the Cérisy seminar dedicated to 'la politique' and 'le politique' in the work of Derrida would also be relevant to the present discussion. She argued that the challenge facing deconstruction was to incorporate the concerns of Marx into its methodology and analy-

sis. See her 'Il faut s'y prendre en s'en prenant à elles,' in *Les Fins de l'homme: à partir du travail de Jacques Derrida,* ed. Philippe Lacoue-Labarthe and Jean-Luc Nancy (Paris: Galilée 1981), 505–15.

127 See Lentricchia, *After the New Criticism,* 186.

128 Barbara Foley, 'The Politics of Deconstruction,' *Genre* 17, nos. 1–2 (Spring–Summer 1984), 113–34

129 Ibid. 128

130 See Jacques Derrida, *Positions* (Chicago: University of Chicago Press 1981), 62–7. See also his critique of Western power structures vis-à-vis the rest of the world in 'White Mythology' and in 'The Ends of Man,' which examines the correspondence between the West's linguistic violence and its other forms of violence (political/economic/ethnological/military). Both are published in his *Margins of Philosophy,* trans. Alan Bass (Chicago: University of Chicago Press 1982).

131 *Margins of Philosophy,* 213

132 See Culler's discussion of Freudian deconstruction (including Freud's own dismantling of this hierarchy) in *On Deconstruction,* 160–70.

133 Robert Con Davis, 'Psychoanalysis and Deconstruction,' *Genre* 17, nos. 1–2 (Spring–Summer 1984), 139

134 See Miller, 'Stevens' Rock and Criticism as Cure,' 331.

135 In Miller's estimation, himself and most of the Yale deconstructionists, including Barbara Johnson and Paul de Man, as well as Jacques Derrida and Sarah Kofman, fit this category of writers who wrestle with the aporia of language itself. On the other hand and with a certain qualification ('to some degree'), he views Gérard Genette, A.J. Greimas, Roland Barthes, and Tzvetan Todorov as belonging to the other category. See 'Stevens' Rock and Criticism as Cure,' 336.

136 Shoshana Felman, *Le Scandale du corps parlant* (Paris: Seuil 1980), 105 (translation mine)

137 Davis, 'Psychoanalysis and Deconstruction,' 146

138 See Felman's reflection on irony as the crucial feature constitutive of literature lacking in psychoanalytic theory and theory as such. Irony in her view drags authority into a scene it cannot master and fundamentally deconstructs the fantasy of authority. See Shoshana Felman, 'Turning the Screw of Interpretation,' *Yale French Studies,* nos. 55–6 (1977), 94–207. See also her treatment of the ambiguous overlap of Lacanian irony/authority in 'La Méprise et sa chance,' *L'Arc,* no. 58 (1974), 40–8.

139 See Jane Gallop, 'Psychoanalysis and Feminism in France,' in *The Future of Difference,* ed. Hester Eisentstein and Alice Jardine (New York: Barnard Women's College Center 1980), 106–21.

140 Ibid. See also Hester Eisenstein and Alice Jardine's Introduction to *The Future of Difference*, xv–xxvii.

141 Gallop, 'Psychoanalysis and Feminism in France,' 109

142 Ibid. 110

143 Johnson, *The Critical Difference*, 4

144 See Jean Baker Miller on using the very psychological qualities evoked by the oppression of women as a means of increasing women's strength in *Towards a New Psychology of Women* (Boston: Beacon Press 1976).

145 Eisenstein and Jardine, Introd., *The Future of Difference*, xxiv

146 Quoted in Elaine Marks, 'Women and Literature in France,' *Signs: Journal of Women in Culture and Society* 3, no. 4 (Summer 1978), 841

147 See Donna Stanton, 'Language and Revolution: The Franco-American Dis-connection,' in Eisenstein and Jardine, eds., *The Future of Difference*, 73–87, to which a large part of this section is indebted.

148 Another interesting deconstructive move in this area which would deserve closer scrutiny if the restrictions of space and time were not so imperative has come from another French critic, Sarah Kofman, whose work has had substantial impact upon both literary criticism and feminist theory. In *L'Enigme de la femme: la femme dans les textes de Freud* (Paris: Galilée 1980) she shows how Freudian theory, which clearly privileges man and defines woman as an incomplete man, deconstructs itself and how its own assumptions are exposed and undermined by forces within the text which a re-reading can bring out. An archi- or proto-woman is concealed in Freudian theory and thus only covertly identifies the primacy of the feminine. See also Culler, *On Deconstruction*, 169–74.

149 Luce Irigaray, *Speculum de l'autre femme* (Paris: Minuit 1974). On Freud see 'La Tache aveugle d'un vieux rêve de symmétrie,' 9–162; and on Plato and the myth of the cave (metaphor for the womb), 'L'ὑστέρα de Platon,' 301–457.

150 The most obvious texts in this respect are *Révolution du langage poétique* and *Polylogue* (Paris: Seuil 1977). They are key to an understanding of her discussion of the interactions between the semiotic and the symbolic as well as to her theory of language. I should also refer the reader to a number of texts which discuss Kristeva's theories and in some cases challenge her conclusions. See: Toril Moi, 'Sexual/Textual Politics,' in *The Politics of Theory*, ed. Francis Barker (Colchester: University of Essex Press 1983), 1–14; Philip Lewis, 'Revolutionary Semiotics,' *Diacritics* 4, no. 3 (Fall 1974), 28–32; and A. White, 'L'Eclatement du sujet: The Theoretical Work of Julia Kristeva,'

University of Birmingham Center for Contemporary Studies, stencilled occasional paper, Birmingham 1977.

151 See Julia Kristeva, 'Poésie et négativité,' in *Sémiotikè* (Paris: Seuil 1969), 246–77. To Kristeva the revolutionary subject, whether masculine or feminine, is a subject which is able to let the *jouissance* of the semiotic motility disrupt the strict symbolic order. While it never takes over, it still translates itself in textual terms as negativity, a negativity that masks the death drive which to her is the most fundamental semiotic pulsion.

152 See Julia Kristeva, 'Féminité et écriture,' in *Revue des Sciences Humaines* 168: 177–84.

153 See Gayatri Spivak, 'French Feminism in an International Frame,' *Yale French Studies*, no. 62 (1981), 174.

154 Hélène Cixous, 'The Laughter of the Medusa,' trans. Keith Cohen and Paula Cohen, *Signs* 1, no. 4 (Summer 1976), 879–80

155 This last geographical distinction is not entirely accurate. Madeleine Gagnon participated in *La Venue à l'écriture* (Paris: 10/18 1977), and Nicole Brossard, while published in Quebec, also had a substantial number of her works produced by Flammarion.

156 See Moi, 'Sexual/Textual Politics.'

157 See Josette Féral, 'The Powers of Difference,' in Eisenstein and Jardine, eds., *The Future of Difference*, 88–94.

158 See Kristeva, *Polylogue*, 519. See also her 'Woman's Time,' *Signs* 7, no. 1 (1981), 13–35, where she envisions a feminist struggle as a three-tiered process:
(1) Women demand equal access to the symbolic order. Liberal feminism, equality.
(2) Women reject the male symbolic order in the name of difference. Radical feminism. Feminity extolled.
(3) Kristeva's own position: women reject the dichotomy feminine versus masculine, which she describes as metaphysical. The very notion of identity is hereby challenged. See especially 'Woman's Time,' 33–4.

159 *Polylogue*, 519 (translation mine). Kristeva continues: 'A female praxis can only be negative, in opposition to what exists, in order to say that "it is *not* that" that "it is still not that." I mean by "female" what cannot be represented, what cannot be said, what remains outside of labelling and ideologies.'

160 From their viewpoint such choices run the risk of turning women into helpless marginals.

161 For a strongly articulated contrast between the Anglo-American approach and the French one see Moi, 'Sexual/Textual Politics'; Chris-

tiane Makward, 'To Be or Not to Be ... a Feminist Speaker,' in Eisenstein and Jardine, eds., *The Future of Difference*, 96–105; and Alice
Jardine, *Gynesis* (Ithaca: Cornell University Press 1985), in which she
describes the distinctions between the French and Anglo-American
modes of criticism as remaining 'in the mid 80's extremely tenacious.
While the sex of the author, images of women and gender stereotypes continue to be the touchstone of feminist criticism in the States,
in France such a bedrock of feminist critical inquiry has been dis-
lodged not to say dismantled' (56). See also Maggie Humm, 'Feminist
Literary Criticism in America and England,' in *Women's Writing*,
ed. Moira Monteith (Brighton: Harvester 1986), 90–116, who gives a
provocative recapitulation of the respective contribution of English
and American critics in this area. She contrasts the 'first wave of American critics (mainly Showalter, Spacks, Moers, Howe) with the second
one, more open to Deconstructionist and psychoanalytic moves'
(97–8). Humm compares these recent American shifts with British
feminist critical developments clearly centred on ideological and cultural issues, Althusser and Marxism (and occasionally radical psy-
chiatry) being reference points which in her view are preferred in Great
Britain to Lacan and Derrida. She analyses how in Great Britain
criticism becomes an ethnographic, rather than a literary, setting up
of questions about culture and the creation of alternatives. British
feminist critics, according to Humm, would demonstrate the notion of
meaning as an ideological force but would tend to refuse aesthetic
value judgments: the politics of a text being thus described as a function of its context.

162 Makward, 'To Be or Not to Be ... a Feminist Speaker,' 99
163 Quoted in ibid. 96
164 Ibid.
165 Ibid. 100. On this question of the association feminity/silence see Julia
  Kristeva, 'Questions à Julia Kristeva,' *Revue des Sciences Humaines*,
  no. 169 (déc. 1977), 500, who depicts it as both obscurantist and alienating. See also Hélène Cixous: 'silence is the traditional confinement,
  a trap where the future will be lost' (*Les Cahiers du Grif*, no. 7 [juin
  1975], n. pag.).
166 In this sense all of Irigaray's writings should be mentioned as making
  an irreplaceable contribution to the deconstruction of the 'white
  fathers' (in this case Freud and Lacan).
167 On Jardine's quasi equation between 'modernité' and 'post-modernism'
  see *Gynesis*, 14. See also her commentary on the implication of 'the
  feminist critic's relationship to men's writings, women's writings, the

canon, the academy ... problems [which] become even more complex
when the focus of one's energy is modernity or, more precisely, contemporary thought reflecting on the post-modern gesture' (ibid. 55–6).

168 Concerning the impact of Nietzschean and Heideggerian philosophies
on the concept of the speaking subject, see Jardine, *Gynesis*, 58. See
also Michel Foucault, 'What Is an Author?' in *Textual Strategies*, ed.
Josué Harari (London: Methuen 1981), 141–60.

169 *Gynesis*, 61

170 In *Gynesis* Jardine comments: 'Irigaray and Kristeva are uniquely concerned with analyzing the male tradition; from Freud to the philosophers of the avant-garde Hélène Cixous' focus is on the male poets
(Genet and Hölderlin, Kafka, Kleist, Shakespeare) and on male theoreticians (Derrida, Heidegger, Kierkegaard, Lacan, Nietzsche)' (62). On
the male theoreticians Jardine reminds us that 'Lacan has much advice
for women analysts but only focuses on one woman writer, M. Duras.'
Derrida only makes an oblique exception in 'Violence and Metaphysics,'
and Deleuze and Guattari refer to Virginia Woolf as 'having incor-
porated "becoming woman" in her texts but not to the same extent
as Henry James, D.H. Lawrence or Henry Miller' (61–2).

171 'To the obsolescence of the master narrative device of legitimation
corresponds notably the crisis of metaphysical philosophy and that
of the institution of the university which depends upon it. The narrative function loses its foundations, the great hero, the great perils, the
great quests, and the great goal' (Lyotard, *La Condition postmoderne*,
7–8, as translated by Alice Jardine, in *Gynesis*, 65).

172 Jardine, *Gynesis*, 16

173 Cixous, 'The Laughter of the Medusa,' 879

174 Baudrillard's and Lyotard's texts would be obvious references here.

175 See George Steiner's reflections on this continuous search in *After
Babel* (London: Oxford University Press 1975), especially 58–64.

176 See Jean Baudrillard, *L'Echange symbolique et la mort* (Paris: Gallimard 1976), 316–19, on the radical destruction of the sign among the
Tel Quel writers and their subversion of linguistics through poetics.

177 André Roy, '9 septembre,' *Chroniques*, nos. 29–32 (automne 1977–
hiver 1978), 315–16 (translation mine)

178 See Books II and IV of bpNichol's *The Martyrology*, and also chapter 4 of
Brian Henderson's excellent PHD dissertation, 'Radical Poetics,' York
University 1982.

179 See Derrida, *Of Grammatology*, 75.

180 Charron's 'grande nuit patriarcale' is also, although by no means exclusively so, a reference to Duplessis' time, to the 'Grande Noirceur'

documented by another generation of writers. See Gérard Bessette, *Le Libraire* (Paris: René Juillard 1960), and Roland Giguère, *L'Age de la parole: poèmes 1949–1960* (Montréal: L'Hexagone 1965), in particular his 'La Main du bourreau finit toujours par pourrir,' a poem written in 1951. See also Paul Emile Borduas' 1948 manifesto 'Refus Global,' in George Vincenthier, *Histoire des idées au Québec* (Montréal: VLB 1983), 209–15. On a later feminist use of these terms see Nicole Brossard's reference to 'La Grande Noirceur du dedans des ventres des femmes' in 'L'Avenir de la littérature québécoise,' *Etudes françaises* 13, nos. 3–4 (oct. 1977), 389.

CHAPTER 2 HOW THEORY SUGGESTS NEW ROLES

1 *Open Letter* became Nichol's and McCaffery's forum from 1972 on. See Nichol's comments on this in 'A Contributed Editorial,' *Open Letter*, 3rd ser., nos. 8–9 (Fall 1978), 5–7.
2 bill bissett, *Stardust* (Vancouver: Blew Ointment Press 1975), title page
3 bill bissett, *Pass th Food, Release th Spirit* (Vancouver: Blew Ointment Press 1973), n. pag.
4 *Medicine, My Mouth's on Fire* (Ottawa: Oberon Press 1974), n. pag.
5 *Ice* (Vancouver: Writers' Forum 1974), n. pag.
6 Even though it does include these elements too: 'yu cin put lettrs on top uv lettrs / milly uns uv tiny bubbuls endlessly / pool uv lettrs yu cin swim in' (*Pass th Food*, n. pag.).
7 bill bissett, *What Fuckan Theory* (Toronto: Gronk Press 1971), n. pag.
8 Ibid.
9 'but i aint defining / deifyin or generalizin / just frget all th rules / suspend it' (*What Fuckan Theory*, n. pag.)
10 *What Fuckan Theory*, n. pag.
11 Ibid.
12 *Pass th Food*, n. pag.
13 Ibid.
14 Jerome Rothenberg is an American sound poet who does research on the mouth and on native Indian chanting.
15 Which is exactly what bissett did with Blew Ointment Press. He printed typewritten material without using typesetting.
16 *What Fuckan Theory*, n. pag.
17 The TRG is composed of bpNichol and Steve McCaffery. Their singularly creative association produced over ten years of theoretical writings.

18 See Steve McCaffery, 'Tenderizing Buttons,' *Open Letter*, 2nd ser., no. 6 (Fall 1973), 93–103.

19 See comments about these semiotic poets in Steve McCaffery, ed., 'The Politics of the Referent,' *Open Letter*, 3rd ser., no. 7 (Summer 1977), 60–107. See also *Open Letter*, 5th ser., no. 1 (Winter 1982), which reproduces a *L-A-N-G-U-A-G-E* issue. For further comment on these American poets and their place in their own literary spectrum, see Lee Bartlett, 'What Is Language Poetry?' *Critical Inquiry* 12, no. 4 (Summer 1986), 741–53. Bartlett specifically mentions McCaffery. See p. 751.

20 See 'Manifesto II,' which reports the loss of Manifesto I, in *Open Letter*, 2nd ser., no. 4 (Spring 1973), 75.

21 Ibid.

22 'TRG Report 2: Narrative (Part 5) – "Manifesto as Interlude,"' *Open Letter*, 2nd ser., no. 9 (Fall 1974), 73. Hereafter referred to as 'Manifesto as Interlude.'

23 See bpNichol's comments on the avant-garde and the Canadian collective memory in 'Interview/bpNichol,' *Capilano Review*, nos. 8–9 (Fall 1975–Spring 1976), 333. Hereafter referred to as *Capilano* interview.

24 'Manifesto as Interlude,' 73–4

25 They are quick to assert that one is not dealing with a 'movement' here, but rather with an interconnectedness of concerns that embraces Saussure, the Russian Formalists, Barthes, Lacan, and Derrida. See McCaffery, ed., 'The Politics of the Referent,' 61.

26 They mention an abundant documentation on this particular matter, from George Herbert to Apollinaire through contemporary concretists. See 'TRG Research Report 2: Narrative Part 1,' *Open Letter*, 2nd ser., no. 6 (Fall 1973), 117.

27 See my reference to the lettrists in the Introduction, p. 14, as well as Solt, *Concrete Poetry: A World View*, 19, 32.

28 Starting from the 1970 excerpt from McCaffery's *Transitions to the Beast*, up to the 1980 *Open Letter* issues.

29 'TRG Report 2 (Narrative, Part 5): The Search for Nonnarrative Prose, Part 2,' *Open Letter*, 3rd ser., no. 2 (Spring 1975), 52. Hereafter referred to as 'The Search for Nonnarrative Prose, Part 2.'

30 The use of the term is the TRG's, ibid. 54.

31 McCaffery, ed., 'The Politics of the Referent,' 64–5

32 Ibid. 64

33 Derrida, 'Structure, Sign and Play in the Discourse of the Human Sciences,' in *Writing and Difference*, 281

34 Ibid.
35 Steve McCaffery, 'Absent-Pre-Sences,' *Open Letter*, 3rd ser., no. 9 (Fall 1978), 130
36 Compare Roland Barthes in *The Pleasure of the Text*: 'First the text liquidates all metalanguage, whereby it is a text: no voice (Science, Cause, Institution) is *behind* what it is saying. Next, the text destroys ... its sociological reference ... Lastly, the text can, if it wants, attack the canonical structure of language itself ... lexicon ... syntax ... It is a matter of effecting ... a new philosophic state of the language-substance ... outside origin and outside communication' (as quoted by McCaffery, in 'Absent-Pre-Sences,' 131).
37 'TRG Report 2: Narrative (Part 3) – "Charting the Obvious," ' *Open Letter*, 3rd ser., no. 9 (Fall 1978), 67. Hereafter referred to as 'Charting the Obvious.'
38 Jackson MacLow, 'Language-Centered,' *Open Letter*, 5th ser., no. 1 (Winter 1982), 26
39 Ibid.
40 See the definition of this term in *The Shorter Oxford English Dictionary* (1973): 'the art of divination by means of lines and figures.'
41 Quoted from Wittgenstein (no precise reference given) in McCaffery, ed., 'The Politics of the Referent,' 64
42 Steve McCaffery, 'Notes on Trope, Text, and Perception,' *Open Letter*, 3rd ser., no. 3 (Fall 1975), 40. Hereafter referred to as 'Notes on Trope.'
43 Ibid.
44 Ibid.
45 Compare the manifesto from the 'Groupe d'Etudes Théoriques,' in *La Presse*, 14 April 1970, 4.
46 See the reference to the native Indian myth of Palongwahoya, in *Capilano* interview, 325.
47 'Charting the Obvious,' 67
48 'Manifesto as Interlude,' 78
49 Ibid.
50 Ibid. 79
51 For example, *verse* comes from the Indo-European *wert*, 'to turn,' which also produces the Latin *versus*, 'to turn a furrow.' By analogy the written line becomes a furrow (ibid. 79). With *page* from the Latin *pagina*, one goes back to a trellis: a column of writing (ibid. 81–2).
52 'Notes on Trope,' 53
53 For an examination of other terms, such as syntax, page, content, verse, and rhetorical figures (metonymy, metaphor, pun), see 'Notes on Trope.'

54 Obviously the texts examined are not exactly *Superman* comics, but avant-garde cartoons by Art Spiegelman, Will Eisner, Philip Druillet, and Victor Morosco. Excerpts are included in 'The Search for Nonnarrative Prose, Part 2,' which examines cartoons' linguistic dynamics. Most of the cartoons mentioned present radical frame alterations.

55 Ibid. 54

56 Concerning this need to go back to older meanings and other historical contexts, see the parallel which is made between the comics' exoskeletal drive and the scholastic tradition which indexes the core text back to another text, that is, a macrosyntactic structure (ibid. 52).

57 Ibid. The didactic intent and the ethical implications cannot be missed here.

58 Ibid. 54, 55

59 'Notes on Trope,' 50

60 Ibid.

61 Ibid.

62 Steve McCaffery, *Transitions to the Beast* (Toronto: Ganglia 1970), n. pag.

63 For more documentation on this issue see Decio Pignatari's and Luiz Pinto's comments on the semiotic poem, 'Nova linguagem, nova poesia,' *Invenção* 3, no. 4 (1964), 82–3. See also Solt's partial translations of these documents in *Concrete Poetry: A World View*, 14–16.

64 The Four Horsemen was a sound poetry group founded in 1970 and originally composed of Rafael Barreto-Rivera, Paul Dutton, Steve McCaffery, and bpNichol. Subsequently bpNichol withdrew from the group and the Four Horsemen became the Horsemen. Owen Sound, a group involved in the same therapeutic community as the Horsemen, came into existence in 1975. The members of Owen Sound are Michael Dean, David Penhale, Steve Smith, and Richard Truhlar.

65 'Charting the Obvious,' 64

66 The dadaists certainly made ample references to it, particularly Hugo Ball, Tristan Tzara, and Karl Schwitters.

67 Paul Dutton, 'Open Journal: Milwaukee,' *Open Letter*, 3rd ser., no. 8 (Spring 1978), 44–51

68 Steve McCaffery, 'Discussion, Genesis, Continuity,' in *Sound Poetry: A Catalogue*, ed. Steve McCaffery and bpNichol (Toronto: Underwhich Editions 1979), 32–3. McCaffery does not quote any source for this French term.

69 Ibid. 33

70 Antonin Artaud, as quoted in Jacques Derrida, 'The Theater of Cruelty and the Closure of Representation,' in *Writing and Difference*, 238

71 Ibid. 241, 240

72 Ibid. 240. Artaud's words as quoted by Derrida seem quite appropriate to describe the Horsemen's perspectives on language.

73 Ibid. 242–3

74 'I propose to bring back into the theater this elementary magic idea, taken up by modern psychoanalysis' (ibid. 242).

75 McCaffery, 'Discussion, Genesis, Continuity,' 32

76 References to this research are to be found in *Open Letter*, 2nd ser., no. 9 (Fall 1974), 70–7, and 3rd ser., no. 4 (Spring 1976), 61–74.

77 McCaffery, 'Discussion, Genesis, Continuity,' 33

78 Letter received from Steve McCaffery, 28 Feb. 1980

79 See Murray Schafer, 'The Theater of Confluence,' *Open Letter*, 4th ser., nos. 4–5 (Fall 1979), 30–47.

80 See Sean O'Huigin, *Poe Tree* (Windsor: Black Moss 1978) and *The Ink, the Pencils and the Looking Back* (Toronto: Coach House Press 1978).

81 Conversation with the poet, 28 May 1979

82 For more documents on Murray Schafer see the whole of *Open Letter*, 4th ser., nos. 4–5 (Fall 1979), which is dedicated to him by McCaffery and Nichol. It also includes a complete bibliography of his work.

83 'Loving,' *Open Letter*, 4th ser., nos. 4–5 (Fall 1979), 49

84 Ibid.

85 'Loving' received its premier on the French CBC-TV network in 1966; it was produced by Pierre Mercure. In 1978 the New Music Concerts in Toronto gave it its first complete production in a semi-staged version directed by George Luscombe.

86 See in particular '/ ʔ/ככ,' *Exile* 4, nos. 3–4 (1977), 167–240.

87 Bernard Heidsieck, 'Sound Poetry How?' *Open Letter*, 5th ser., no. 1 (Winter 1982), 101

88 bpNichol, *The Martyrology: Books I and II* (Toronto: Coach House Press 1972) and *The Martyrology: Books III and IV* (Toronto Coach House Press 1976). As these volumes are not paginated, I can specify the location of references only by Book numbers, which are given in the text.

89 See Dutton, 'Open Journal: Milwaukee,' 48, and McCaffery, 'Discussion, Genesis, Continuity,' 32–3.

90 See Derrida, 'La Pharmacie de Platon,' in *La Dissémination*, 90–5. On Derrida and Nichol see also Roy Miki's powerful analysis *Tracing the Paths: Reading/Writing 'The Martyrology'* (Vancouver: Talonbooks 1988), 95–117.

91 In a chapter on the vagaries of indexing (from the viewpoint of a con-

temporary art researcher) Bruce Barber reminds us that 'happenings,' 'body art,' and performances have been classified separately in the *Art Index*. '*Performance* Art' appears for the first time in 1972–3 (vol. 21) with six listings and at this point is split from 'Body Art.' In the 1973–4 *Index* (vol. 22) one notices for the first time '*Performance* and Video Art.' See Bruce Barber, 'Indexing: Conditionalism and Its Heretical Equivalents,' in *Performance by Artists*, ed. A.A. Bronson and Peggy Gale (Toronto: Art Metropole 1979), 183–204.

92 See Chantal Pontbriand, ed., *Performance* (Montréal: Parachute Editions 1981). Its subtitle, 'Multidisciplinary Aspects of Performance/ Postmodernism,' specifically underlines the connection between the two. A number of contributors address this issue in their articles. See Bruce Barber, 'The Function of Performance in Postmodern Culture: A Critique,' 32–7; Douglas Crimp, 'The Photographic Activity in Postmodernism,' 70–6; Ivanka Stoianova, 'De quelques aspects multidisciplinaires des performances artistiques dans les conditions postmodernes,' 118–26; and Craig Owens, 'The Allegorical Impulse: Towards a Theory of Postmodernism,' 37–42. See also the important *Performance in Postmodern Culture*, ed. Michel Benamou and Charles Caramello (Milwaukee: Coda Press 1977), especially Richard Palmer, 'Towards a Postmodern Hermeneutics of Performance,' 19–32; Campbell Tatham, 'Mythotherapy and Postmodern Fictions: Magic Is Afoot,' 132–58; Ihab Hassan, 'Prometheus as Performer: Towards a Posthumanist Culture?' 201–20; and Charles Caramello, 'On Styles of Postmodern Writing,' 221–34.

93 Rose Lee Goldberg, 'Performance: A Hidden History or the Avant, Avant Garde,' in Bronson and Gale, eds., *Performance by Artists*, 170.

94 Guy Scarpetta chooses the second option: 'La fonction-performance (sous sa forme integrée) n'est pas récente: elle est présente dans le théâtre médiéval (Mystères, Carnaval) ... tout ce qui compte le plus n'est pas le texte ... mais le jeu physique, l'irruption des singularités, des jongleries, des *événements*. Il reste des traces de cela dans la Commedia dell'Arte, et parfois, dans le cinéma burlesque, notamment chez les Marx Brothers. La performance ... renoue donc avec une longueur d'onde très ancienne ... On commence donc à entrevoir ceci; que le théâtre classique n'est au fond qu'une parenthèse, historiquement datable. Le corps, dans ... la performance cesse d'être uniquement un signe, l'acte cesse d'être uniquement un exécutant; c'est lui qu'on aime, pas ce qu'il représente' ('Erotique de la performance,' in Pontbriand, ed., *Performance*, 140).

95 See her introduction to *Performance*, where she uses the expression 'une histoire à rebours' (6).

96 Thierry de Duve, 'La Performance hic & nunc,' in Pontbriand, ed., *Performance*, 20 (translation mine)

97 Birgit Pelzer, 'La Performance ou l'intégrale des équivoques,' in Pontbriand, ed., *Performance*, 28 (translation mine)

98 Daniel Charles, 'Le Timbre, la voix, le temps,' in Pontbriand, ed., *Performance*, 111. Daniel quotes Lyotard's *La Condition postmoderne* here.

99 Jean-François Lyotard, 'The Unconscious as *mise-en-scène*,' in Benamou and Caramello, eds., *Performance in Postmodern Culture*, 88

100 See Maria Gloria Bicocchi and Fulvio Salvadori, 'Performances and Communication,' in Bronson and Gale, eds., *Performance by Artists*, 206: 'Alone on stage an actor physically transforms an abstract scheme, the script into a consumable object for the public.'

101 Palmer, 'Towards a Postmodern Hermeneutics of Performance,' 20

102 de Duve, 'La Performance hic & nunc,' 20 (translation mine)

103 See Philip Monk's analysis of the viewer's role as based upon such infelicities, in 'Coming to Speech: The Role of the Viewer in Performance,' in Pontbriand, ed., *Performance*, 148.

104 On this whole question of performances as 'acts deprived of guarantee' see Felman, *Le Scandale du corps parlant*.

105 Pelzer, 'La Performance,' 31

106 Barber, 'The Function of Performance in Postmodern Culture,' 36

107 Peter Frank, 'Auto-Art: Self-Indulgent and How!' *Art News*, Sept. 1976, 43–9

108 Barber, 'The Function of Performance in Postmodern Culture,' 36

109 See specifically Pontbriand, Introd., *Performance*, 7.

110 'It makes sense to live only for the moment, to fix our eyes on our own private performance, to become connoisseurs of our own decadence, to cultivate transcendental self-attention' (James Hougan, quoted in C. Lasch, *The Culture of Narcissism* [New York: Norton 1978], 4).

111 Emile Benveniste, *Problèmes de linguistique générale* (Paris: Gallimard 1977), I, 237–50

112 Owens, 'The Allegorical Impulse,' 40

113 Ibid. 40, note 12

114 Ibid. 37

115 Owens quotes Barthes' statement 'The sign itself must be shaken' (*Image, Music, Text* [New York: Hill and Wang 1977], 167).

116 See Régis Durand, 'Les Limites de la théâtralité,' in Pontbriand, ed., *Performance*, 48–54, and Lasch, *The Culture of Narcissism*.

117 See René Payant, 'Le Choc du présent,' in Pontbraind, ed., *Perfor-mance*, 127–37.

118 Ibid. 136 (translation mine)

119 See Palmer, 'Towards a Postmodern Hermeneutics of Performance,' 20 on Austin's and John Searle's reactions to such tendencies.

120 Ibid. 20

121 See Palmer's mention of Jean Gebser's *Ursprung und Gegenwart* on the rise of perspective as the key to modernity, ibid. 22.

122 Ibid. 31

123 See Jerome Rothenberg, 'New Models, New Visions: Some Notes to-wards a Poetics of Performance,' in Benamou and Caramello, eds., *Performance in Postmodern Culture*, 11–18.

124 Ibid. 15

125 'Modern literalism' and the 'naturalizing' of visionary reality are, from Palmer's viewpoint, very much the expression of the modern age. The post-modern alternative is anchored upon a much different ground: a reclamation of the premodern hermeneutics of allegorical and eso-teric forms of interpretation, such as the Kabbala, as well as a different 'placing' of thought forms. And here Palmer quotes the famous Heid-eggerian text on the way to language: 'To think is to enter into a dia-logue, to find one's way patiently to the place of that about which one speaks' (Palmer, 'Towards a Postmodern Hermeneutics of Perfor-mance,' 30).

126 See Jean-François Lyotard, *Des Dispositifs pulsionnels* (Paris: Minuit 1974), 95.

127 See Monk, 148.

128 Palmer, 'Towards a Postmodern Hermeneutics of Performance,' 30

129 See Palmer's comments on special sections of *Life* magazine, *Mac-lean's*, and of CBC *Morning Side*, ibid.

130 Pelzer, 'La Performance,' 30

131 Chantal Pontbriand, 'The Question in Performance,' *Open Letter*, 5th ser., nos. 5–6 (Summer–Fall 1983), 21

132 Owens, 'The Allegorical Impulse,' 40

133 Durand, 50

134 Peggy Gale, 'History Lesson,' in Pontbriand, ed., *Performance*, 97

135 Pontbriand, Introd., *Performance*, 7

136 Thierry de Duve, 'Minimal Art Revisited: A Plea for a New Genre of Theater,' *Open Letter*, 5th ser., nos. 5–6 (Summer–Fall 1983), 234

137 Ibid.

138 de Duve, 'La Performance hic & nunc,' 22

139 Ibid. De Duve refers here to Benjamin's essay 'L'Oeuvre d'art à l'ère de

sa reproductibilité technique' (1931), which defines aura as 'die eon-malige Erscheinung einer Ferne, so nah sie sein mag.'

140 Ibid. 26 (translation mine)

141 Ibid. 25–8

142 Durand, 52

143 Ibid. This whole section is very much indebted to Durand's article on performance and theatricality.

144 Ibid. Durand quotes *Artaud*, ed. Philippe Sollers et al. (Paris: Union Générale d'Editeurs 1973).

145 See Lyotard, *Des Dispositifs pulsionnels*, 95.

146 Durand, 51

147 Ibid.

148 See Durand, 52–3 (translation mine).

149 Felman, *Le Scandale du corps parlant*, 152

150 Durand, 54

151 Bicocchi and Salvadori, 'Performances and Communication,' 206

152 Renée Baert, 'La Vidéo au Canada: en quête d'une identité,' in *Vidéo*, ed. René Payant (Montréal: Artexte 1986), 42

153 Cécile Cloutier, 'La Nouvelle Poésie,' *Liberté* 9, no. 4 (juillet–août 1967), 118–27

154 Clément Moisan, *L'Age de la littérature canadienne* (Montréal: L'Hexagone 1969), 157. Moisan is referring here to Claude Péloquin's *Manifeste infra* (Montréal: L'Hexagone 1967).

155 Raoul Duguay, 'Le Stéréo-poème-audio-visuel,' *Culture Vivante*, no. 12 (12 fév. 1969), 35

156 See Solt, *Concrete Poetry: A World View*, 34

157 Moisan, 157

158 Claude Péloquin, 'Manifeste infra,' in *Oeuvres complètes: le premier tiers* (Montréal: Beauchemin 1976), 83

159 'Prendre les mots pour des choses, des éléments ... les triturer, les entrechoquer ... faire danser' (*Le Temps des poètes* [Montréal: HMH 1969], 196–7).

160 Raoul Duguay, 'Or Art (Poésie) total du cri au chant au,' *Quoi* 1, no. 2 (printemps–été 1967), 11. The capitalization is Duguay's. See Charles Olson, *Projective Verse* (New York: Totem Press 1959) for a similar expression of the materiality of language.

161 Mikel Dufresne quoted by Duguay, in 'Or Art (Poésie) total du cri au chant au,' 12

162 Ibid.

163 Ibid.

164 Ibid. 15

165 Ibid. 13
166 Ibid. 14
167 Ibid. 15
168 Ibid. 14
169 Luc Racine, 'La Parole et le chant,' *Quoi* 1, no. 2 (printemps–été 1967), 18
170 Duguay, 'Le Stéréo-poème-audio-visual,' 35–42
171 Ibid. 36
172 Ibid. 37
173 Coincidences between his formulations, the Horsemen's, and Owen Sound's are explicit. See McCaffery and Nichol, eds., *Sound Poetry: A Catalogue.*
174 See bissett, *What Fuckan Theory*, or Garnier, 'Deuxième Manifeste pour une poésie visuelle,' 16–17.
175 Raoul Duguay, 'La Transe et la Gression,' *La Barre du Jour*, Automne 1973, 48. The capitalization is Duguay's.
176 Ibid. 55
177 See his interview with Jean-Pierre Tadros, 'Tendances et orientations de la nouvelle littérature,' *Culture Vivante*, no. 5 (1962), 60, 62, and with Richard Giguère in 'Poetry Is Yrteop,' *Ellipse*, no. 17 (1975), 80–97. See also 'Questionnaire Mainmise,' *Main Mise*, no. 51 (sept. 1975), 17–27.
178 'Poetry Is Yrteop,' 87
179 Raoul Duguay, *Le Manifeste de l'infonie* (Montréal: Editions du Jour 1970), 88
180 Ibid. 92–5
181 Ibid. 91
182 Raoul Duguay, 'Interview' [interview with Raoul Duguay by bpNichol], *Open Letter*, 2nd ser., no. 6 (Fall 1973), 65–73
183 Raoul Duguay, 'The Invisible Child: An Interview with Raoul Duguay by Caroline Bayard,' *Only Paper To-day* 3, no. 1 (Sept.–Oct. 1975), 2
184 Duguay, 'Or Art (Poésie) total du cri au chant au,' 11
185 Duguay, 'The Invisible Child,' 2
186 Caroline Bayard and Jack David, *Out-Posts/Avant-Postes* (Erin, Ont.: Press Porcépic 1978), 22
187 Ibid. 23
188 Duguay had many theoretical differences with the collective which founded *La Barre du Jour* (Nicole Brossard, Marcel St-Pierre, Roger Soublière, Jean Stafford). He decided to break away from it and create his own magazine, *Quoi*, in 1967. (He was followed by Luc Racine and Michel Beaulieu.) *Quoi* was short-lived and did not survive beyond the first two issues.

189 'Les Dix Propositions,' *La Presse*, 4 April 1970, 34, cols. 5–8.
190 France Théoret, 'L'Implicite et l'explicite de la nouvelle écriture,' *La Nouvelle Barre du Jour*, nos. 90–1 (mai 1980) [Colloque sur la nouvelle écriture], 169
191 'Les Dix Propositions,' 34. Note here the closeness of this text's concern and terminology with the TRG's.
192 Ibid.
193 Claude Bertrand, 'Introduction à l'histoire de la rupture' (suite I), *La Barre du Jour*, juin–juillet 1968, 63–71; suite II, *Le Barre du Jour*, oct.–déc. 1968, 47–52
194 François Charron and Roger des Roches, 'Notes sur une pratique,' *La Barre du Jour*, no. 29 (été 1971), 4, 6
195 Madeleine Gagnon and Denise Boucher, *Retailles* (Montréal: Editions L'Etincelle 1977), 9
196 Ibid. 97
197 Ibid. 85, 88
198 France Théoret comments: 'La nouvelle écriture fonctionne dans l'immédiateté des textes seconds' ('L'Implicite et l'explicite de la nouvelle écriture,' 165).
199 Nicole Brossard, *L'Amèr ou le chapitre effrité* (Montréal: Quinze 1977), 15. Subsequent references to this work appear in the text.
200 See Madeleine Gagnon, 'Pour les femmes et tous les autres,' in *Autographie I: Fictions* (Montréal: VLB 1982), 75, 76, 85, and also 'Poélitique,' ibid. 101.
201 'Tout le vocabulaire d'une certaine modernité depuis une dizaine d'années (texte, sexe, plaisir, pulsion, production, structure) a voulu et parfois cru faire reculer cette angoisse d'être au monde et cette incapacité à pouvoir contenir, expliquer ... le cours des existences et des évènements. Faire de la jouissance une logique aura été la nouvelle rédemption de la littérature' (François Charron, Préface, *Feu* [Montréal: Les Herbes Rouges 1981], 3).
202 Normand de Bellefeuille, 'La Gageure du lisible,' *La Nouvelle Barre du Jour*, nos. 90–1 (mai 1980), 148
203 Ibid.
204 Normand de Bellefeuille, 'Le Caca et le lisible,' *Les Herbes Rouges*, no. 38 (août 1976), 1–27
205 de Bellefeuille, 'La Gageure du lisible,' 149
206 In contemporary terms Rina Lasnier might best exemplify these values.
207 See François Charron, 'L'Ecriture commence par un rêve,' *La Nouvelle Barre du Jour*, nos. 90–1 (mai 1980), 24.
208 Ibid. 27
209 Francine Saillant, 'D'Ecrire ça,' *La Nouvelle Barre du Jour*, nos. 90–1

(mai 1980), 132. This is very close to McCaffery's comments on collages and montages in 'Notes on Trope,' 50. It also seems that Saillant is describing bissett's practices with such techniques.

210 François Charron, 'Notes sur l'expérience de la peinture,' *Les Herbes Rouges*, nos. 75–6 (nov. 1979), 40–1

211 Claude Beausoleil, 'Reliefs d'arsenal: une écriture d'avant-garde,' *Cul Q*, nos. 4–5 (été–automne 1974), 88

212 Charron, 'L'Ecriture commence par un rêve,' 26

213 Ibid.

214 Paul-Marie Lapointe, 'Ecriture-Poésie 1977,' *La Barre du Jour*, no. 58 (sept. 1977), 37–8

215 Charron, 'L'Ecriture commence par un rêve,' 25, 22

216 Charron, 'Notes sur l'expérience de la peinture,' 18

217 Compare *The Martyrology*: 'How can I live who cannot be without you ... only the skies empty my tears / hell i could fill the space with moaning / oh you are gone & i am left / lonely father / i am lonely father / father i am lonely' ('Friends as Footnotes,' Book II)

218 Charron, 'Notes sur l'expérience de la peinture,' 52

219 The texts which come most readily to mind are of course the American L-A-N-G-U-A-G-E issues so often in *Open Letter* as well as the anthology *L-A-N-G-U-A-G-E Book*, ed. Bruce Andrews and Charles Bernstein (Carbondale, Illinois, 1983). What has been referred to as the 'so-called language school' (see Bartlett, 'What Is Language Poetry?'), including such poets as Michael Palmer, Ron Silliman, Michael Davidson, Lyn Helginian, and Jackson MacLow, practises a self-awareness that 'calls forth language and subjects it to an examination of its mediatory function. For these poets the critical activity of deconstruction, of investigating a text as an endless play of sub-texts is a means of poetic creation' (Stephen Fredman, *Poet's Prose: The Crisis in American Verse* [Cambridge: Cambridge University Press 1983], 134–5).

220 Paul Chamberland, 'Entrevue Hobo-Québec,' *Hobo-Québec*, no. 2 (fév. 1972), 8

221 Paul Chamberland, 'Manifeste des enfants libres du Québec,' *Hobo-Québec*, no. 2 (fév. 1972), 8, 9

222 Saillant, 131

223 Bayard and David, *Out-Posts*, 97. The reference to the alchemist's work intersects here also with Marguerite Yourcenar's novel *L'Oeuvre au noir* (Paris: Gallimard 1968), which recounts precisely such a history and such tormented processes.

224 Ibid.

225 Paul Chamberland, *Le Recommencement du monde* (Longueuil: Editions Le Préambule 1983), 109

226 Nicole Brossard, 'L'Epreuve ou les preuves de la modernité,' *La Nouvelle Barre du Jour*, nos. 90–1 (mai 1980), 61

227 Claude Beausoleil and André Roy, 'Pour une théorie fictive,' *Cul Q*, nos. 4–5 (été–automne 1974), 46–9

228 See the poem 'Aint no words for th taste uv yu,' in *Medicine, My Mouth's on Fire*, n. pag.

229 McCaffery perceptively intuited the potential of bissett's libidinal strategy. See Steve McCaffery, 'Bill Bissett: A Writing outside Writing,' *Open Letter*, 3rd ser., no. 9 (Fall 1978), 7–23.

230 Nicole Brossard, 'Mais voici venir la fiction ou l'épreuve au féminin,' *La Nouvelle Barre du Jour*, nos. 90–1 (mai 1980), 67

231 Claude Beausoleil suggests a new spelling, 'polytique,' in 'Hypothèses,' *Dérives*, no. 8 (1977), 19, 21, which carries with it implications of multiplicity, polyvalence, diversity.

232 Saillant, 135, 131

233 Paul Chamberland: 'Je me trouve dans une situation de post-Marxiste' (in Bayard and David, *Out-Posts*, 101). See also Raoul Duguay's planetary perceptions of the sacred in 'La Naissance d'Ora,' *Main Mise*, no. 3 (juillet 1974), 31–9.

234 Most notably from François Charron. His 1983 exhibition 'Crucifixions' caused divisions, dismissals, and controversy in the *Spirale* magazine. See: André Beaudet, 'Dialogue avec l'invisible,' *Spirale*, no. 34 (mai 1983), 14; Bertrand Bergeron, Marcel Labine, and Jacques Samson, 'Quand l'oraison déborde,' *Spirale*, no. 35 (juin 1983), 3; and André Beaudet, 'Noli me tangere,' *Spirale*, no. 36 (sept. 1983), 15.

235 Roger Seamon, 'Open City: Vancouver 1968,' *Far Point* 1, no. 1 (Fall–Winter 1968), 48–59

236 See Frank Davey, 'The Present Scene,' *Delta*, no. 19 (Oct. 1961), 1–2.

237 Charles Olson, *Projective Verse* (Brooklyn: Totem Press 1959), 9

238 Charles Olson, 'Projective Verse II,' in *The Poetics of the New American Poetry*, ed. Donald M. Allen and Warren Tallman (New York: Grove Press 1973), 147

239 James Reid, 'Editorial,' *Tish*, no. 4 (Dec. 1964), 1

240 Garnier, 'Manifeste pour une poésie nouvelle,' 3

241 William S. Choy, 'Space and Its Relation to Poetry,' *Delta*, no. 19 (Oct. 1961), 21–2: 'There has been a needless neglect of space in the writing and enjoyment of poetry ... The Tao of the printed word, it seems to me, has been criminally ignored.'

242 bpNichol, 'The Typogeography of bill bissett,' in bill bissett, *We Sleep inside Each Other All* (Toronto: Ganglia Press 1966), n. pag.

243 For specific data on Black Mountain see Martin Duberman, *Black*

Mountain: An Exploration in Community (New York: E.P. Dutton 1972).

244 See Ken Norris' detailed discussion of *Tish* and its impact on Canadian modernism in *The Little Magazine in Canada 1925–1980* (Toronto: ECW 1984), 97–131.

245 Frank Davey, Introd., *The Writing Life*, ed. C.H. Gervais (Coatsworth, Ont.: Black Moss Press 1976), 19

246 Warren Tallman, 'Wonder Merchants: Modernist Poetry in Vancouver during the 1960's,' in Gervais, ed., *The Writing Life*, 52.

247 Warren Tallman, 'Poet in Progress: Notes on Frank Davey,' *Canadian Literature*, no. 24 (Spring 1965), 24–5

248 Frank Davey, 'Introducing *Tish*,' in Gervais, ed., *The Writing Life*, 150

249 *West Coast Seen* (1969), an anthology dedicated to the American-born projective theoretician Warren Tallman, still included Judith Copithorne and bill bissett. Similarly a number of poems included in this volume could have easily been published in *Blew Ointment* magazine. Scissions, word breaks, and typographically rupturing patterns recur frequently in it. If anything the anthology unintentionally emphasizes the formal closeness of objectivists and concretists.

250 See *Capilano* interview, 333; Bayard and David, *Out-Posts*, 18–21; and Ken Norris, 'An Interview with bpNichol,' *Essays on Canadian Writing*, no. 12 (Fall 1978), 247.

251 Norris, *The Little Magazine in Canada 1925–1980*, 144–5

252 bill bissett, Letter to Ken Norris, 27 Nov. 1979, ibid. 143

253 See Stephen Scobie 'Vingt ans de poésie concrète,' *Ellipse*, no. 17 (1975), 180–8.

254 Ibid. 183. See in particular Scobie's comment 'Les débuts de la poésie concrète sont tout aussi embrouillés, accidentés et fortuits que dans les autres pays.'

255 Baudrillard, *L'Echange symbolique et la mort*, 18

256 Lyotard, *Dérive à partir de Marx et de Freud*, 272

257 Ken Norris, 'The Role of the Little Magazine in the Development of Modernism and Post-Modernism in Canadian Poetry,' diss., McGill University 1980, 262

258 If the two key pioneers were *Blew Ointment* and *Gronk/Ganglia*, one cannot discard the avant-garde focus put forward by *Elfin Plot* as early as 1969, the occasional curiosity showed by James Reaney in *Alphabet* (especially his 1971 special concrete issue), as well as the openness demonstrated by *Is* or *Tuatara* in the early 1970s.

259 But Stephen Scobie was to move away from the Prairies to Victoria in the early 1980s, thus curtailing the number of performances he was to give with Douglas Barbour.

260 Andre Farkas and Ken Norris, eds., *Montreal: English Poetry of the Seventies* (Montreal: Véhicule Press 1978), xi. Their overall assessment is that although Irving Layton and Leonard Cohen developed a Jewish romantic lyricism and Louis Dudek's rationalist constructions provided an Apollonian counterpart to their Dionysian creativity, no vital movement evolved out of the Montreal of the 1960s. While 'Al Purdy, Milton Acorn, David Solway and Seymour Mayne produced significant work, the movement as a whole failed' (p. x). In their terms 'it had nothing new to offer in terms of poetics and poetic techniques' (ibid).

261 Ibid. xi

262 Ibid.

263 Ken Norris and Peter Van Toorn, eds., *The Insecurity of Art: Essays on Poetics* (Montreal: Véhicule Press 1982), 8

264 Ken Norris provides an excellent critical summary of the Véhicule generation and its specific singling out of the post-modernist stance for the group, a choice which incidentally meets with some resistance from Stephen Morrissey and Andre Farkas. See Ken Norris, *Talking Poetries* (Montreal: Maker Press 1980), n. pag.

265 See, in particular, the 1971 issue on Gaston Miron and the October crisis in *La Barre du Jour*.

266 bill bissett addressed such political issues as well as related them to textual politics. But until a political fracas broke out concerning the support of his work by the Canada Council (see below, note 268), he was largely ignored by an important part of the reading public.

267 The publication of *The True Eventual Story of Billy the Kid* (1970) aroused a certain number of questions. The Honourable T. McCutcheon (PC) asked: 'In view of the recent Canada Council grant based on the writing of a treatise relating the life of Billy the Kid, can the parliamentary secretary say if this is a change of direction from subsidizing Marxism to markmanship with short guns? (*Hansard*, 10 June 1971, 6554–7). See also *Hansard*, 29 June 1971, 7458. Other members of Parliament expressed their indignation on the latter occasion: *pornographic, trashy,* and *obscene* were some of the epithets used by MPs to refer to Nichol's book. For further documentation on these events see Jack David's biography of Nichol facetiously titled 'A Published Autopopography,' in *Essays on Canadian Writing*, no. 1 (Winter 1974), 39–46. On Nichol's treatment of the historical, or rather mythical, figure of Billy the Kid, or his post-modern treatment of a myth (which Michael Ondaatje in his *The Collected Works of Billy the Kid* was to handle quite differently), see Stephen Scobie's perceptive

'Two Authors in Search of a Character,' *Canadian Literature*, no. 54
(Autumn 1972), 37–55.

268 The brunt of parliamentary attacks against bissett came from Robert
Wenman (PC, Fraser Valley West), who called for a review of the
Canada Council's mandate and accountability by tabling eight of bissett's poems which he referred to as pornographic poetry. John Fraser
(PC, Vancouver South) supported Wenman's view and suggested that
taxpayers' dollars should not be used to support such 'garbage' (see
The Globe and Mail, 3 Dec. 1977). It is worth noting here that both
members side-stepped the issue of censorship and insisted rather on
fuzzy arguments such as 'common sense judgement says that taxpayers' dollars not be used to support such work' (ibid.). Such questions in Parliament had been preceded by several years of continuous
attacks on radio station CJOR by Ed Murphy, a Vancouver broadcaster.
Murphy documented his complaints in 1977 in a booklet entitled *A
Legacy of Spending*, in which poems by bissett were reproduced to
emphasize his point. Wenman attempted to table this booklet in parliamentary committee (see Eleonor Wachtel's lengthy examination of
the whole affair in 'Why bb into cc Won't Go,' *Books in Canada*, June–
July 1979, 3–6). The press did not jump on Wenman's bandwagon;
see, for instance, *The Vancouver Sun* editorial of 6 Dec. 1977 'Life
Imitates Smut': 'If one really wants examples from Bissett's poetry
to boggle the standards, there are more obvious candidates than the
eroticisms which we admit are present. His spelling for instance
now there's real subversion for you ... In the meantime Wenman and
others looking for the real stuff should try those magazine stands on
Granville Street that Mayor Jack Volrich has been complaining about.'
The Montreal Star (3 Dec. 1977) printed the Canada Council's defen-
sive response to these attacks and also quoted bissett's own response.
But the most thorough rejoinder was 'He Is a Poet, a Painter, a Publisher, a Pacifist and He Talks to Alan Twigg,' printed in *The Georgia
Straight*, 2–9 June 1978, 11–15. Talonbooks (bissett's publisher) and
an impressive number of Canadian writers were to counter-attack by
taking a full-page ad in *The Vancouver Sun* (22 Sept. 1978; see also
Allan Fotheringham's reaction in the next day's edition of the same
paper) and by threatening to file a libel suit. *The Vancouver Sun*'s
writers appear to have been bitterly divided on the whole issue. Doug
Collins maintained that bissett's poetry was garbage and that the ad
placed in his own paper was only 'a plea from a mutual admiration
society for continued state aid for Canada Council welfare bums'
(*The Vancouver Sun*, 27 Sept. 1978). On the other hand Christopher

Dafoe documented the other side's reaction and gave personal support to bissett (see *The Vancouver Sun*, 29 Sept. 1978 and 4 Oct. 1978). See also 'Canada Council Replies,' *The Vancouver Sun*, 30 June 1979; and, on Margaret Atwood's support for the benefit held at UBC for bissett, Allan Fotheringham, 'The Neanderthals, Ms Atwood,' *The Vancouver Sun*, 19 July 1979. Finally, concerning the announcement of the 1980 Canada Council grant to bissett, see *The Vancouver Sun*, 25 April 1980.

269 Yuri Lotman quoted by Ann Shukman in 'The Dialectics of Change: Culture, Code and the Individual,' in *Semiotics and Dialectics*, ed. Peter Zima (The Hague: Mouton Press 1981), 315. Shukman discusses Lotman's first major attempt at a theory of semiotic change delineated in his 1974 monograph *The Dynamic Model of a Semiotic System*.

270 Herbert Marcuse's political writings would best focus on such issues, to which one should add Theodore Roszak, *The Making of the Counter-Culture* (New York: Doubleday 1968), and Patrick Conover, *The Alternate Culture and Contemporary Communes* (Monticello: Illinois Council of Planning Librarians 1976).

271 Daniel Drache and Arthur Krocker, 'The Labyrinth of Dependency,' *Canadian Journal of Political and Social Theory / Revue canadienne de théorie politique et sociale* 7, no. 3 (Fall/automne 1983), 6. Drache and Krocker give numerous references concerning what they define as the development in Canada of a comprehensive, eloquent, and internally coherent discourse on dependency. While they refer the reader to Kari Levitt's pioneering study *Silent Surrender: The Multinational Corporation in Canada*, they also suggest that dependency theory should be 'written in a new key,' that the capital/labour nexus might not have been 'the principal theatre of conflict in the Canadian mode of development and that the situation calls for an historically nuanced interpretation of the sources of Canadian dependency' (ibid. 20).

272 See Susan Crean and Marcel Rioux, 'Overcoming Dependency: A Plea for Two Nations,' *Canadian Journal of Political and Social Theory / Revue canadienne de théorie politique et sociale* 7, no. 3 (Fall/automne 1983), 50–81. This is an English translation of the last chapter of Susan Crean and Marcel Rioux, *Deux Pays pour vivre: un plaidoyer* (Montréal: HMH 1980), 89–112.

273 Ibid. 54

274 See K. Goldstein's opposition between normal/normative in *Le Rapport de la commission d'enquête sur l'enseignement des arts*, vol. 1 (L'Editeur officiel du Québec 1969), 38. Quoted in Crean and Rioux, 'Overcoming Dependency,' 55

275 This was a major event which brought to Toronto sound performers from both North America and Europe. See McCaffery and Nichol, eds., *Sound Poetry: A Catalogue.*

276 Peggy Gale, 'History Lesson,' in Pontbriand, ed., *Performance,* 93–110

277 See the whole issue of *Parallélogramme: Contemporary Canadian Art News / l'actualité de l'art au Canada* 12, no. 2 (Dec. 1986–Jan. 1987).

278 Gale, 'History Lesson,' 94

279 Ibid.

280 Ibid.

281 'She kept her dead parakeet in her freezer and friends would give her other small corpses to keep it company' (ibid.).

282 A.A. Bronson, 'The Rise and Fall of the Peanut Party,' *Arts Canada,* March/April 1977, 72

283 Ibid. 96

284 For example: the period of 'sponge dancing,' a comment on the water-ballet tradition by Glen Lewis; the 'leopard skin' phase, a metaphor for glamour and libido enacted by Eric Metcalfe and Kate Craig (see Gale, 96); and Mr Peanut's running for mayor in the Vancouver civic election of 1974, in which he received over 1000 votes.

285 See *Parachute,* no. 20 (Fall 1980), 4–17 for documentation on these artists.

286 See Payant, ed., *Vidéo,* which documents both historically and critically the developments of video in nine different countries. It includes eighteen texts delivered during the Video 84 Conference held in Montreal (Oct. 1984) and is particularly illuminating about the development of video installations in Montreal and Toronto.

287 Gale, 'History Lesson,' 97

288 Ibid.

289 See Tom Sherman's 'Envisioner,' where he narrates the viewing/reading habits of modern man (ibid. 92).

290 Ibid. 93

291 Bronson and Gale, eds., *Performance by Artists,* 9

292 Alan Sondheim, *Individuals, Post-Movement Art in America* (New York: Dulton & Co. 1977), vii–viii

293 See Leila Sujir, 'Comment remplacer la mémoire perdue et comment nous représenter,' *Parallélogramme* 12, no. 2 (déc. 1986–jan. 1987), 32–9. She quotes Nicole Brossard's 'Tender Skin My Mind' from *In the Feminine,* ed. Ann Dybrikowski (Edmonton: Longspoon Press 1985), 180.

294 See Henri Meschonnic, *Les Etats de la poétique* (Paris: PUF 1985).

295 Particularly on the whole issue of 'anthropology,' where their perceptions of what is markedly human are different.

296 Meschonnic, *Les Etats de la poétique*, 51. A closer examination of
Meschonnic's reflections upon this problematic and of Nichol's
might be warranted here. To begin with the latter, we have: 'Return to
the dichotomy, the seeming paradox at the root of language ... we
have already seen that the real multilevelled life of language denies the
social actuality of surface' ('Lunwage: A Domesday Book,' n. pag.,
bpNichol Collection, Simon Fraser University, Vancouver). And also: 'I
have just said that language (and ... by language I mean a whole
system of verbal speech communication irregardless of its outward
form) assumed the power of a cosmic force, words have long had a
cosmic significance' (untitled and undated, but placed in the period
1969–70 in the bpNichol Collection, Simon Fraser University).
Turning now to Meschonnic's comments on oral poetry: 'What is involved here is a focusing on and hinging together of the dissociative
forces at work between the individual (the subject) and the collectivity
(or sociality)' (*Les Etats de la poétique*, 52, translation mine); 'The
question of rhythm is essential to/for the theory of language. If one
maintains this concept of rhythm on the level of the sign, of the
dualism from meaning, rhythm will remain a sub-category. What one
must do is join, fuse together, the two disjuncted elements. Marriage
is only accomplished when an expressivity embedded in meaning has
found in rhythm the imitation of meaning' (ibid. 99); 'The static
model of dualism cannot comprehend poetry because it has nothing to
do with history, with life – the orality which is so much a contemporary preoccupation relativizes dualistic anthroplogy and linguistics'
(ibid. 104). There is, however, a major difference between Meschonnic's
concept of the sacred and Nichol's; in fact, they part ways on their
perception of this term. Meschonnic points to it as 'antagonistic to
history. The sacred is the mortal enemy of the radically historical' (ibid.
53). Nichol's viewpoint on the same question must be by now quite
familiar to the reader.

297 See 'i wanta a rattul,' in *Th High Green Hill* (Vancouver: Blew Ointment 1972), n. pag. See also Len Early's reflections on bissett's at-
traction to shamanistic rituals in 'Bill Bissett: Poetics, Politics and
Vision,' *Essays on Canadian Writing*, no. 5 (Fall 1976), 23–4.

298 bissett in performance wears traditional Amerindian dress and re-enacts
ethnological Amerindian chanting and dancing.

299 The most explicit reference is to be found in the *Capilano* interview.

300 See bibliographical information on performance theory in notes 92–6 above.
301 See Norris, *The Little Magazine in Canada 1925–1980*
302 'Les Trente A' was supposed to last thirty days but fell apart much earlier due to lack of funds.
303 On the *Parti Pris* poets and 'La Semaine A' see Yves Robillard, ed., *Quebec Underground 1962–1972* (Montréal: Médiart 1973), I, 119. On Serge Lemoyne's concepts on multi-media events see *La Patrie*, 12 March 1964.
304 See Robillard, ed., *Quebec Underground*, I, 135 for a photocopy of this document. See also Fig. 72.
305 Ibid. 136
306 *Capilano* interview, 333
307 Such events can only be appreciated when placed in their socio-political context. From the late 1950s mass poetry readings were part of a social, communal ritual endowed with partly shamanistic, partly political, properties. This probably reflected the curious conjunction of the rise of the counter-cultural movement, on the one hand, and the exacerbated nationalist passions of the time, on the other. It may be worthwhile noting that this powerful chemistry had all but dissipated by the latter part of the 1960s. As was noted by Robert Levesque (*Le Devoir*, 11 Nov. 1981), if the 1970 'Nuit de la poésie' was a triumph its 1980 counterpart at the UQAM was an abysmal failure.
308 See Duguay, 'Poetry Is Yrteop,' 80–1: 'Au moins il y aura eu quelqu'un pour t'ouvrir la porte.'
309 Janou St-Denis, *Gauvreau, le Cygne* (Montréal: Editions du Noroît 1978), 84 (translation mine)
310 See Bayard and David, *Out-Posts*, 17.
311 See Jacques Marchand, *Claude Gauvreau: poète et mythocrate* (Montréal: VLB 1979), 342, where Gauvreau describes Roland Giguère as an imaginative figurative artist, namely a surrealist, Gaston Miron as an expressionist figurative, and himself as an imaginative non-figurative artist.
312 Claude Gauvreau, *Oeuvres créatrices complètes* (Montréal: Parti Pris 1977), 250
313 Marchand, *Claude Gauvreau*, 58 (translation mine)
314 Ibid. 61
315 Ibid. 187
316 Ibid. 153
317 For Gauvreau's own account of this peculiar event see his '15 Février 1969,' *Liberté* 2, no. 1 (jan.–fév. 1969), 95–7.

318 Marchand, *Claude Gauvreau*, 187
319 Ibid. 199
320 Ibid.
321 See *Le Petit journal*, 20 Nov. 1949, 35; 17 Nov. 1949, 56; 11 Dec. 1949, 48; and 18 Dec. 1949, 65.
322 See Marchand, *Claude Gauvreau*, 204 for references to 'Dualité,' performed 3 April 1948, and 'Les Deux arts' performed 8 and 9 May 1949.
323 The play was written between 1958 and 1970, and the poem between 1950 and 1951. Both are collected in *Oeuvres créatrices complètes*.
324 This issue comes up over and over both among critics and throughout Gauvreau's correspondence. Alain Bosquet views him as a lettrist unrelated to lettrism (*Poésie du Québec* [Paris: Seghers 1968], 118); Marcel Bélanger describes his style as 'instinctive Lettrism' ('La Lettre contre l'esprit ou quelques points de repère sur la poésie de Claude Gauvreau,' *Etudes littéraires* 3 [déc. 1972], 488); and Raoul Duguay does not hesitate to apply that epithet to him ('Poetry Is Yrteop,' 81). Gauvreau himself kept his distance from Isou's school, which he felt was only a school of 'abstract art' (see Marchand, *Claude Gauvreau*, 231).
325 Gauvreau, *Oeuvres créatrices complètes*, 228
326 See Claude Gauvreau, Letter to Jean Isidore Cleuffeu, 13 April 1950, in Marchand, *Claude Gauvreau*, 13–16.
327 See Duguay, 'The Invisible Child.'
328 Paul Chamberland, 'Entretien avec Claude Péloquin,' *Parti Pris* 3, no. 9 (avril 1966), 38–45
329 See Pascal Ory and Jean-François Sirinelli, *Les Intellectuels en France, de l'affaire Dreyfus à nos jours* (Paris: Armand Colin 1986), 77–114.
330 Joël Pourbaix, 'Paul Chamberland: la posture utopiste,' in Jacques Pelletier, ed., *L'Avant-garde culturelle et littéraire des années 70 au Québec* (Montréal: Université du Québec à Montréal 1986), 93
331 Fusion des Arts as a group had a four-year span (1965–9). On the history of the groups see Robillard, ed., *Quebec Underground*, I, 179–83. The manifesto of Fig. 72 was published in May 1969 when the group was dissolved.
332 See above, note 155.
333 Claude Péloquin, *Manifeste infra* (Montréal: L'Hexagone 1967)
334 Patrick Straram, 'Interprétations de la vie quotidienne,' *Parti Pris* 3, no. 6 (jan. 1966), 52–7, and 3, no. 8 (mars 1966), 67–71
335 'Parce que ce qu'il faut régler d'abord, c'est le corps' (Raoul Duguay quoted in Robillard, ed., *Quebec Underground*, I, 421).

336 Quotations from one of his texts in *Parti Pris* might illuminate this
particular point: 'Je n'aime d'oeuvre qu'intégralement personnalisée
et ce surtout dans l'énoncé de rapports avec d'autres, oeuvres et hommes' (*Parti Pris* 3, no. 8 [mars 1966], 69). And again: 'Il en va pour
moi de l'écriture comme de l'existence, je ne conçois l'une et l'autre
qu'intégrales, vécues "au coeur" de toutes les mises en question qui
leur sont inhérentes avant que de les communiquer, pour communiquer – c'est-à-dire vivre et l'écrire plus intensément, pour plus inciter à
d'identiques intégralités, lesquelles seules font la vie vivable' (ibid. 68).

337 See, for instance, the manifesto of the Fusion des Arts group (Fig. 72).

338 For the ideological directions of the independence movement in the
mid-1960s see Jean Marc Piotte, *Un parti pris politique* (Montréal:
VLB 1979); Pierre Maheu, *Un parti pris révolutionnaire* (Montréal: Parti
Pris 1983); Gilles Bourque and Gilles Dostaler, *Socialisme et indépendance* (Montréal: Boréal Express 1980); and Gilles Dostaler, 'Québec politique,' *Parti Pris* 5, nos. 8–9 (été 1968), 8, which is an early
statement on the whole problematic. See also Paul Chamberland, *Un
parti pris anthropologique* (Montréal: Parti Pris 1983), which col-
lects many of his articles from the *Parti Pris* magazine.

339 Several texts outline these integrative pulsions. One can start one's
research on this subject with documents pertaining to the Fusion des
Arts group (see Fig. 72, and the introduction to the 'Cahiers de Fusion'
written in 1969 and reprinted in Robillard, ed., *Quebec Underground*, I, 179–83). See also the paper titled 'Synthèse des arts,' written
by Yves Robillard and presented to Leslie Brown, general commis-
sioner of the Canadian pavillion at Expo 67 (ibid. 185–7); and François
Soucy's 'Notes d'atelier' on the concept of *synthèse des arts* (ibid.
188–91). Duguay's thoughts on both media integration and the political
responsibility of artists who 'must work for the liberation of human
beings and challenge the existing order as well as accept being challenged in turn' can be found in his paper 'Approche d'une définition
du rôle efficace de l'artiste dans la société québécoise' (ibid. 324–7
[translation mine]).

340 Yves Robillard, some years later, was to meditate on such concerns; see
'Underground versus Overground: s'il y a lieu, ou bien y rester en
l'occurrence,' in Robillard, ed., *Quebec Underground*, II, 106–9. See
also Jean-Pierre Roy's reflections on this question in his paper 'Pour
une problématique formaliste de l'art populaire' (ibid. 329–36).

341 For more information on this whole period see Robillard, ed., *Quebec
Underground*, I, 119–50.

342 On Luci Associates, which followed Expo 67, see the review by Doris

Giller, 'Light Show Is Yule Tide in Multiple Media Version,' *Montreal Star*, 20 Nov. 1968, reprinted in Robillard, ed., *Quebec Underground*, I, 44.

343 See Raoul Duguay's 'Spectacle Global,' in Robillard, ed., *Quebec Underground*, I, 413–32.

344 See Robillard, ed., *Quebec Underground*, I, 414–16.

345 Whatever innumerable speculations have been entertained as to the nature of Adam's tongue (Hebrew, Chaldean, or an original speech severed into seventy-two shards as Brahmin, Celtic, and north African mythologies suggest), they all concur that a primary and fundamental idiom has been irretrievably lost. See Steiner, *After Babel*, 59.

346 These are Steiner's words, but they are uncannily reminiscent of Duguay's during these years (1967–74).

347 For Péloquin, see Robillard, ed., *Quebec Underground*, I, 147.

348 Steiner, *After Babel*, 60

349 Duguay, *Le Manifeste de l'infonie*, 29

350 L'Infonie, both as a show and a text, best captured that vision. See Jean Basile's reading of the first in Robillard, ed., *Quebec Underground*, I, 425–6, and also Alain Pontault, 'Reprise de Babababellll,' *Montréal Matin*, 10 March 1969, 28.

351 Jules Duchastel, 'La Contre-Culture: l'exemple de *Main Mise*,' in Pelletier, ed., *L'Avant-garde culturelle et littéraire des années 70 au Québec*, 79

352 See above, note 340.

353 The most important texts one could refer the reader to on this subject, apart from the literature to be found in *Main Mise* and *Hobo-Québec* by Raoul Duguay and Paul Chamberland or in *Stratégie* and *Chroniques* by François Charron, would be Paul Chamberland's *Le Courage de la poésie* (Montréal: Les Herbes Rouges 1981), *Un parti pris anthropologique* (Montréal: Parti Pris 1983), and *Terre souveraine* (Montréal: L'Hexagone 1980). Raoul Duguay in his 1968 paper 'Approche d'une définition du rôle efficace de l'artiste dans la société québécoise' (in Robillard, ed., *Quebec Underground*, I, 412–26) is also explicit about political aesthetical concerns. His *Ellipse* and *Out-Posts* interviews throw some light on his perceptions of politics versus artistic creation and on his clear determination to choose a utopian viewpoint over Marxism. The political orientations of François Charron may be gleaned from the following: his interview in *Chroniques* 1, no. 3 (mars 1975), 8–25; 'Comment ça s'écrit,' *Chroniques* 1, no. 2 (fév. 1975), 8–11; 'Quelle Révolution,' *Chroniques*, no. 22 (oct. 1976), 56–65; 'Deux modèles d'assaut,' *Stratégie* 3, no. 4 (hiver 1973), 7. Books such as *Littérature/obscénités* (Montréal: Edi-

tions Danielle Laliberté 1973) and *Propagande* (Montréal: Les
Herbes Rouges 1977) as well as *Interventions politiques* (Montréal: L'Aurore 1974) will also provide the reader with relevant information.

354 See Duchastel, 'La Contre-Culture: l'exemple de *Main Mise,*' 74: 'Such
a critique is one of the favourite arias of the counter-culture tenors'
(translation mine).

355 See Guy Sarrazin and Luc Racine, *Pour changer la vie* (Montréal: Editions du Jour 1973).

356 He quotes George Kahl's perceptions on this new culture and on *Main
Mise*'s obvious yet fully accepted contradictions ('La Contre-
Culture: l'exemple de *Main Mise,*' 71).

357 See Joël Pourbaix, 'Paul Chamberland: la posture utopiste,' in Pelletier,
ed., *L'Avant-garde culturelle et littéraire des années 70 au Québec,*
83–92.

358 See Jacques Pelletier's perceptive reading of François Charron's trajectory in Pelletier, ed., *L'Avant-garde culturelle et littéraire des années 70 au Quebec,* 99–118.

359 The following articles by Jules Duchastel document this period and
its social phenomena: '*Main Mise*: la nouvelle culture en
dehors de la lutte des classes?' *Chroniques,* nos. 18–19 (juin-juillet
1976), 38–58; 'La Contre-Culture: une idéologie de l'a-politisme,'
in *La Transformation du pouvoir au Québec,* ed. Jacques Godbout
et al. (Montréal: Albert St-Martin 1980), 253–64; 'Culture et contre-
culture: idéologie et contre-idéologie,' in *Idéologies au Canada
français 1940–1976,* ed. Fernand Dumont et al. (Québec: PUL
1981), 173–216; 'Milieux culturels: culture et transformation sociale,'
in *Cultures populaires et sociétés contemporaines,* ed. Gilles Pronovost (Québec: PUQ 1982), 141–54.

360 Duchastel notes the occupation of CEGEPs during the fall of 1968, a sort
of continuation of May 1968 in Europe, as being significant in this
context. See Duchastel, 'La Contre-Culture: l'exemple de *Main Mise,*'
62.

361 Ibid.

362 See his bibliography, ibid. 80–1.

363 Ibid. 80. Duchastel adds that in this early part of the decade the movement lost in intensity what it gained in exposure and diffusiveness.

364 Duchastel is here again an attentive observer of this periodical's contradictions. On the logical conflict between practical communal experiences and this review's quasi-theological perspective, see 'La Contre-
Culture: l'exemple de *Main Mise,*' 66. On economic contradictions
affecting the area of political structure see pp. 68–70. On the puzzling

and uncertain oscillation between technology and theology, and on the rejection of rationalist postulates on the one hand and the fascination with scientific 'progress' and intersidereal adventures on the other, see p. 75. The last word should be George Kahl's when he suggests that the counter-culture was not a homogeneous system but a collection of experiences (p. 71).

365 Ibid. 66

366 Ibid. 67

367 Ibid. 69

368 Ibid. 69

369 See *Un parti pris anthropologique* and *Terre souveraine.*

370 See Jacques Pelletier's examination of François Charron's work in the context of this generation, in 'L'Itinéraire de François Charron: des lendemains qui chantent au temps des incertitudes,' in Pelletier, ed., *L'Avant-garde culturelle et littéraire des années 70 au Québec,* 100.

371 François Charron, 'L'entrée,' *Stratégie* 1, no. 1 (hiver 1972), 65

372 See note prefaced to 'Deux modèles d'assaut,' *Stratégie* 3, no. 4 (hiver 1973), 7.

373 In this context 'les poètes de l'Hexagone' are the obvious target of Charron's polemical questioning.

374 Pelletier, 'L'Itinéraire de François Charron,' 102

375 See Charron's own comments about the 'idealists,' in *Stratégie* 3, no. 4 (hiver 1973), 7.

376 See Pierre Milot's abundant documentation on these movements: 'Généalogie du discours et des pratiques marxistes-léninistes' in Pelletier, ed., *L'Avant-garde culturelle et littéraire des années 70 au Québec,* 17–42.

377 Pelletier, 'L'Itinéraire de François Charron,' 106

378 Jacques Pelletier, Introd., *L'Avant-garde culturelle et littéraire des années 70 au Québec,* 14

379 See his 'châle de Mallarmé, cigare de Brecht' metaphors as well as the double vision he imputes to the Quebec avant-garde and to any other: 'Avant-garde movements are divided in two: on the one hand formalist pleasure, literary rituals (Baudelaire, Flaubert, Mallarmé) and concern about metaphysical notions, death before all; on the other history, listening to voices (Woolf, Duras) and masses (Michelet, Brecht)' (*Naissances: de l'écriture québécoise* [Montréal: VLB 1979], 318 [translation mine]). Haeck strongly wishes for a resolution of this dialectical opposition but leaves it at an optimistic as well as hypothetical level.

380 François Charron's comment on this new dialectic interplay takes

place in the context of his review of Philippe Haeck's *Nattes*, which came out in 1975 at the Herbes Rouges. See Charron, 'Comment ça s'écrit,' *Chroniques* 1, no. 2 (fév. 1975), 8–11.

381 Philippe Haeck, 'La Mosaique contre-culturelle,' in *La Table d'écriture: poétique et modernité* (Montréal: VLB 1984), 80

382 Marcel Bélanger, 'Ouverture et liberté,' *Le Devoir*, 21 Nov. 1981, 10 (translation mine)

383 Suzanne Lamy, 'L'Emergence du féminin,' *Le Devoir*, 11 Nov. 1981, 13 (translation mine). The whole 'Culture et Société' section of this issue deals with Quebec literature in the 1980s.

384 Les Herbes Rouges functioned simultaneously as a periodical and a publishing house: each book published was also an issue of the periodical. As an intellectual and creative focus Les Herbes Rouges' texts are essential to an understanding of the 1970s and 1980s. See Richard Giguère and André Marquis, 'Les Herbes Rouges 1968–1988: persister et se maintenir' [entrevue avec Normand de Bellefeuille, Carole Massé, André Roy, France Théoret], *Lettres Québécoises*, no. 51 (automne 1988), 10–17.

CHAPTER 3 THE TEXTS ON THEIR OWN

1 Peter Mayer, 'The Concrete Phenomenon,' *Journal of Typographical Research* 2: 383

2 Ibid. 389

3 Ibid. 387

4 David Seaman, 'Early French Visual Poetry,' *Precisely* 5, no. 3 (1979), 23

5 See Reiss, *The Discourse of Modernism*, chapter 1.

6 Quoted in Solt, *Concrete Poetry: A World View*, 13

7 bpNichol, *Captain Poetry Poems* (Vancouver: Blew Ointment Press 1970), chapter 8 [n. pag.]

8 bpNichol, *Nights on Prose Mountain* (Toronto: Ganglia Press 1969), n. pag.

9 This piece was originally published in *The Cosmic Chef*, ed. bpNichol (Ottawa: Oberon Press 1970), n. pag.

10 See chapter 2, pp. 112–13.

11 Early, 'Bill Bissett: Poetics, Politics and Vision,' 7

12 Ibid. 8

13 Jean Starobinski, *The Anagrams of Ferdinand de Saussure* (New Haven: Yale University Press 1979).

14 Jonathan Culler, *Structuralist Poetics* (London: Routledge and Kegan Paul 1975), 249

15 Julia Kristeva, 'Sémanalyse et production du sens,' in *Essais de sémiotique poétique* (Paris: Larousse 1971), 229
16 Culler, *Structuralist Poetics*, 251
17 See Robert Fulford's comment on the back cover of *OAB I* (Toronto: Exile Editions 1983): 'He was a close relative to the scholarly loner of Borges' labyrinthine library.'
18 See Robert Zend *OAB I* and *OAB II* (Toronto: Exile Editions 1985).
19 All the ditto poems are to be found in *Beyond Labels* (Toronto: Hounslow Press 1982), 87–112.
20 *Beyond Labels*, 4–5
21 See 'Introducing Dittos,' in *Beyond Labels*, 86.
22 The antinomy 'clean/dirty' has always held a certain fascination for concretists. See, for instance, bissett's 'a pome in praise of all quebec bombers' (Fig. 11), which states, 'Keep yr cell clen/dirty, dirty concrete.'
23 Lyotard, *Dérive à partir de Marx et de Freud*, 13
24 Ibid. 17
25 See 'Leçon d'inpouvoir,' ibid. 271–5.
26 Karl Young, *Should Sun Forever Shine* (Toronto: Underwhich Editions 1980), n. pag.
27 Lyotard, *Dérive à partir de Marx et de Freud*, 247 (translation mine)
28 Ibid. 220
29 Baudrillard, *L'Echange symbolique et la mort*, 299
30 Ibid. 301 (translation mine)
31 Ibid. (translation mine)
32 Ibid. 305
33 Canadada, Owen Sound, Tom Konyves' performances on video, and Douglas Barbour's and Stephen Scobie's oral performances enter this category.
34 Tom Konyves' video work, available from the author, the *Canadada* LP, and bissett's record in *Medicine, My Mouth's on Fire* would be exceptions to the rule. Also available upon request are the recordings from the Toronto Festival of Concrete.
35 See bpNichol, Preface, *We Sleep inside Each Other All*, by bill bissett (Toronto: Island Press 1966), n. pag.
36 *Capilano* interview, 333
37 bpNichol and Steve McCaffery, 'Discussion,' *Open Letter*, 6th ser., nos. 2–3 (Summer–Fall 1985) [Longliners issue], 292
38 Relevant references by Kroetsch on this problematic can be found in Robert Kroetsch, 'Beyond Nationalism: A Prologue,' *Open Letter*, 5th ser., no. 4 (Spring 1983), 83–9. See also Dennis Cooley and Robert Enright, 'Uncovering Our Dream World: An Interview with Robert

Kroetsch,' *Arts Manitoba* 1, no. 1 (Jan.–Feb. 1977), 34. On Marlatt's questions about origins, primary reference texts should be *How Hug a Stone* (Winnipeg: Turnstone Press 1982) and *Touch to My Tongue* (Edmonton: Longspoon Press 1984). Secondary references about Kroetsch's post-modern stance can be found in Louis K. MacKendrick, 'Robert Kroetsch and the Modern Canadian Novel of Exhaustion,' *Essays on Canadian Writing*, no. 11 (Summer 1978), 10–27. See also Robert Lecker, 'Bordering On: Robert Kroetsch's Aesthetic,' *Journal of Canadian Studies* 17, no. 3 (Fall 1982), 124–33; and P.L. Surette, 'The Fabula Fiction of Robert Kroetsch,' *Canadian Literature*, no. 77 (Summer 1978), 6–19. Secondary references about Marlatt's affinities with the post-modern stance can be found in: Donna Bennett, 'Their Own Tongue,' *Canadian Literature*, no. 107 (1985), 152–5; Travis Lane, 'Self-conscious Art,' *The Fiddlehead*, no. 142 (1984), 96–107, especially p. 97; and Chris Hall, 'Two Poems of Place: Williams' *Paterson* and Marlatt's *Steveston*,' *The Canadian Review of American Studies*, no. 15 (1984), 141–57. On her perceived affinities with phenomenology, see: Frank Davey, *From There to Here* (Erin, Ont.: Press Porcépic 1974), 194–5; Fred Wah's Introduction to her *Selected Writing: Net Work* (Vancouver: Talonbooks 1980) 7–21, especially p. 16; and Robert Lecker, 'Daphne Marlatt's Poetry,' *Canadian Literature*, no. 76 (1978), 56–67, especially p. 61.

39 See Robert Lecker's perceptive study *Robert Kroetsch by Robert Kroetsch* (Boston: Twayne 1986), 19.

40 MacKendrick, 'Robert Kroetsch and the Modern Canadian Novel of Exhaustion,' 17.

41 Shirley Neuman and Robert Wilson, *Labyrinths of Voice: Conversations with Robert Kroetsch* (Edmonton: NeWest 1982), 4

42 Lecker, *Robert Kroetsch by Robert Kroetsch*, 21

43 Roland Barthes, *Roland Barthes*, trans. Richard Miller (New York: Hill and Wang 1977), 27

44 Lecker, *Robert Kroetsch by Robert Kroetsch*, 110

45 See Alberto Manguel's review of *Alibi*: 'The story makes no sense, the characters never build up, the story is interfered with, clues are hidden and never revealed' ('No Excuses,' *Books in Canada*, Oct. 1983, 22). See Lecker's comments on this, *Robert Kroetsch by Robert Kroetsch*, 107–8

46 Lecker, *Robert Kroetsch by Robert Kroetsch*, 109

47 Ibid. 122

48 Robert Kroetsch, 'For Play and Entrance: The Contemporary Canadian Long Poem,' *Open Letter*, 5th ser., no. 4 (Spring 1983), 91

49 Ibid. 93
50 Lecker, *Robert Kroetsch by Robert Kroetsch*, 135
51 Ibid. 141
52 Ibid. 143
53 Kroetsch, 'For Play and Entrance,' 93
54 Lecker, *Robert Kroetsch by Robert Kroetsch*, 143
55 On Marlatt's link with Black Mountain, with the simultaneity of ex-
    perience as was well as feminist theory *avant la lettre* [sic], see Barbara
    Godard, 'Epi(pro)logue,' *Open Letter*, 6th ser., nos. 2–3 (Summer–Fall
    1985) [Longliners issue]: 'Marlatt's search for wholeness is part of
    her Black Mountain inheritance, her attempt to break out of the subject
    position by using her proprioceptive eye to explore a field of forces'
    (328).
56 See Eva Marie Kröller, 'Canadian Identity and the Long Poem,' *CRNLE
    Reviews Journal*, no. 1 (1986), 33–6, especially p. 35.
57 Daphne Marlatt, *Touch to My Tongue* (Edmonton: Longspoon Press
    1984), 48. Subsequent references to this work appear in the text.
58 See Bennett, 'Their Own Tongue.' Here the author is commenting on
    Robert Kroetsch's and Dennis Lee's work as well as Daphne
    Marlatt's.
59 Ibid. 153
60 Daphne Marlatt, *How Hug a Stone* (Winnipeg: Turnstone Press 1982), 19
61 Bennett, 'Their Own Tongue,' 155
62 Daphne Marlatt, 'Given This Body: An Interview with Daphne Mar-
    latt,' in 'Three Vancouver Writers: Interviews by George Bowering,'
    Open Letter, 4th ser., no. 3 (Spring 1979), 60
63 Marlatt, *How Hug a Stone*, 51
64 Roy Miki, 'The Cosmology of the Long Poem,' *Open Letter*, 6th ser.,
    nos. 2–3 (Summer–Fall 1985), 76
65 Marlatt, 'Given This Body,' 79
66 Godard, 'Epi(pro)logue,' 315. Godard's remarks here are directed to the
    documentary long poem in the Canadian tradition.
67 Smaro Kamboureli, 'Locality as Writing: A Preface to the Preface of
    Out of Place,' *Open Letter*, 6th ser., nos. 2–3 (Summer–Fall 1985)
    [Longliners issue], 267–77
68 Mikhail Bakhtin, *The Dialogic Imagination*, ed. Michael Holquist
    (Austin: University of Texas 1981), 68–9
69 Hélène Cixous, 'Textes de l'imprévisible: Grâce à,' *Les Nouvelles Lit-
    téraires*, 26 May 1976, 56 (translation mine).
70 Godard, 'Epi(pro)logue,' 327
71 Ibid.

72 Daphne Marlatt, *What Matters: Writing 1968–1970* (Toronto: Coach House Press 1980), 54

73 Lola Lemire Tostevin, Afterword, in *Gynotext* (Toronto: Underwhich Editions 1983), n. pag.

74 Lola Lemire Tostevin, *Color of Her Speech* (Toronto: Coach House Press 1982), n. pag.

75 The light effects utilized in bissett's *Pass th Food, Release th Spirit* are especially outstanding: the text there becomes a pure visual surface, a texture for light to play with. The manipulation of white spaces, light, and printed matter seems independent from any semantic code. Similar results may be obtained purely through typing-over techniques, an approach bissett was to use consistently from 1970 on. *Liberating Skies* (Vancouver: Blew Ointment Press 1970) presents the most obvious effort towards a systematization of this technique, where it becomes a typographical metaphor for mood and feeling, a dramatic rendition of a subjective state with no stage directions. See, for instance, Fig. 30, where the intricacy of enmeshed letter-types indicates intense confusion and excitement on the caller's part, until control is regained and the sentence resumes its normal articulation.

76 Linguistic studies have shown that in spite of cause and effect relationships between syntax and semantics, one cannot necessarily deduce the nature and function of one from the other. As F. François notes in *Le Langage*, ed. A. Martinet (Paris: Gallimard 1968), 253: 'Even if there is a statistical link between syntax and semantics ... one cannot use semantics to define syntactical terms ... nevertheless one should discard the idea of a self-evident separation between the two and could turn syntax into a pure form within which semantic elements would then insert themselves' (translation mine).

77 bpNichol, *Love: A Book of Remembrances* (Vancouver: Talonbooks 1974), n. pag.

78 Bissett, *What Fuckan Theory*, n. pag.

79 See his poem 'To-day's Your Big Pubic Reading,' in *What's So Big about Green?* (Toronto: McClelland and Stewart 1973), n. pag., and his novel *Turvey: A Military Picaresque* (Toronto: McClelland and Stewart 1976), which presents an interesting range of idiomatic expressions whose orthography follows phonological expression more than spelling rules.

80 In which case it is difficult to determine whether or not rules have been broken since there may have been none.

81 He sometimes paradoxically reverts to traditional spelling, present participles thus recovering the *ing* endings (see Fig. 46).

82 See Webster's *New International* edition (1975); also M.H. Abrams, *A Glossary of Literary Terms* (New York: Holt, Rinehart and Winston 1971), 93.

83 The full text of 'Clover' is in Nichol, *Love: A Book of Remembrances*, n. pag.

84 Notice the recurrence of present participles in Fig. 44.

85 On the concept of *breakthrough* see Richard Kostelanetz, *Breakthrough Fictionneers* (Barton: Something Else Press 1973). See also Russell, *The Avant-Garde Today*. As Gerald Graff has shown in *Literature against Itself* (Chicago: University of Chicago Press 1979), admittedly with a certain polemical resentment, a number of breakthroughs of post-modernism were already apparent in modernism. Secondly, he maintains that this linear concept of literature is very much dependent upon a naïve conception of progress, of improvement, and contemporary superiority. On the whole issue of the relativity of modernity as an operating concept see David Hayne's paper 'Modern and Modernism in Literary History,' University of Toronto Conference on Postmodernism, March 1987.

86 H. Marcuse, *Essay on Liberation* (Boston: Beacon Press 1969), 38–9

87 In North America other critics, such as Richard Gilman, Richard Poirier, and Leo Bersani, speak on behalf of such choices. See, for instance, Gilman's comment on how 'the cultural revolution speaks for energies which cannot be domesticated within the organized form of politics, for an antinomian self which cannot be tailored to fit the requirements of any society, however ideal' (Richard Gilman, *The Confusion of Realms* [New York: Random House 1969], 264).

88 See Graff, 76.

89 Jay Martin, 'Americans in a Post-American Age,' *The Antioch Review* 33, no. 2 (Summer 1975), 20

90 Bruce Andrews, 'Constitution, Writing, Politics, Language, the Body,' *Open Letter*, 5th ser., no. 1 (Winter 1982), 163 (originally published under a different title in *L-A-N-G-U-A-G-E*, nos. 9–10 [Oct. 1979])

91 Ibid. 164

92 See McCaffery and Nichol, eds., *Sound Poetry: A Catalogue* on the therapeutic effect of sound.

93 The link of each with non-Western mystical traditions is easily retraceable. I have commented often on bissett's and Nichol's use of native Indian teleology. As for dada, both the Zen and Taoist characterizations of the nature of reality were said to have had the most consistent significance for it. See Richard Sheppard, 'Dada and Mysticism: Influences and Affinities,' in *Dada Spectrum: The Dialectics of Revolt*,

ed. Stephen Foster and Rudolf Kuenzli (Madison, Wis.: Coda Press 1979), 100–6, who also refers to the use dadaists made of German thirteenth-century mystical writings and pre-Socratic documents. The ethnological pulsions present in both dada and Canadian concrete reflect this same tension between dynamic chaos and elusive order; in each, nature is conceived of as the secret patterning and co-existence of the two. On the African ties of dadaists with what was then termed 'primitivism,' see: Tristan Tzara, 'Seven Dada Manifestoes,' in *Dada Painters and Poets*, ed. Robert Motherwell (New York: Wittenborn and Schultz 1951), 77; Robert Goldwater, *Primitivism in Modern Art* (New York: Random House 1967), 260; and Dickran Tashjian, 'New York Dada and Primitivism,' in Foster and Kuenzli, eds., *Dada Spectrum*, 123. Destruction of a certain standing order, political and economic, is perceived as one way of working towards a more equit-able society, envisioned here by both dadaists and later ethnologists. Western and European art-forms are perceived as bankrupt by both dadaists and concretists.

94 'Mushy Peas: 6 London Texts,' in Steve McCaffery and bpNichol, *In England Now That Spring* (Toronto: Aya Press 1979), is an interest-ing exception to the rule.

95 Raoul Duguay, *Lapokalipsô* (Montréal: Editions du Jour 1971), 11

96 See Joseph Bonenfant, 'Lapokalipsô,' *Livres et auteurs québécois* (1971), 145–7.

97 Ibid. 147. See also André Bourassa, 'Duguay ou l'envers et l'endroit,' *Lettres Québécoises*, no. 3 (1976), 12.

98 On the concept of the carnivalesque in Québécois fiction, see André Belleau, 'Carnavalisation et roman québécois: mise au point sur l'us-age d'un concept de Bakhtine,' *Etudes Françaises* 3, no. 1 (hiver 1983–4), 51–65. See also Maroussia Ahmed, 'The Relevance of the Carniva-lesque in the Quebec Novel,' *Studies in Twentieth-Century Literature* 9, no. 1 (Fall 1984) [special issue on Mikhail Bakhtin], 119–33, and 'The Unique, Its Double and the Multiple: The Carnivalesque Hero in the Quebecois Novel,' *Yale French Studies*, no. 65 (1983), 139–53.

99 Duguay, *Lapokalipsô*, 99

100 See Normand de Bellefeuille quoting Raoul Vanegeim: 'Those who speak of revolution without explicitly referring themselves to everyday life have a corpse in their mouths' ('Le Corps mineur ou l'impossible lyrisme,' *La Nouvelle Barre du Jour*, no. 58 [sept. 1977], 89).

101 *One + one* (Montréal: Les Herbes Rouges 1971); *4 × 4/4 × 4* (Montréal: Les Herbes Rouges 1974); *Tea for One/No More Tea* (Montréal: Les Herbes Rouges 1983)

102 Patrick Straram, 'Vanier – écriture/procès,' *Les Herbes Rouges*, no. 17 (fév. 1974), n. pag. (translation mine)

103 See André Roy, 'La Verge au beau tarif: la différentiation signifiante généralisée,' *La Nouvelle Barre du Jour*, nos. 118–19 (1982), 113.

104 Ibid. 114 (translation mine)

105 Nicole Brossard, 'Vaseline,' *La Barre du Jour*, nos. 41–2 (automne 1973), 12

106 Nicole Brossard, *Le Centre blanc* (Montréal: L'Hexagone, 1970), 224

107 Nicole Brossard and Roger Soublière, 'De notre écriture,' *La Barre du Jour*, no. 26 (oct. 1970), 3–6

108 Brossard, 'Vaseline,' 14

109 Nicole Brossard, '*e* muet mutant,' *La Barre du Jour*, no. 50 (hiver 1975), 11

110 See Nicole Brossard, 'L'Epreuve ou les preuves de la modernité,' *La Nouvelle Barre du Jour*, nos. 90–1 (mai 1980), 61.

111 Bayard and David, *Out-Posts*, 69 (translation mine)

112 Louise Dupré, 'Les Désordres du privé,' *La Nouvelle Barre du Jour*, no. 98 (1981), 5–40

113 Louise Forsyth, 'Regards, reflets, reflux,' *La Nouvelle Barre du Jour*, nos. 118–19 (1982), 20

114 What has come to be looked upon as the generation of *La Barre du Jour* (the old and the new) has in fact been a much looser, more fluid group than this description might lead one to believe. France Théoret, who was often published by this magazine, also moved in *Les Herbes Rouges'* milieu, while Claude Beausoleil and Yolande Villemaire, who certainly demonstrate affinities with *La Barre du Jour's* writers, explored their own paths with *Cul Q* and *Le Noroît*. This fluidity of loyalties from one publisher to another is indicative of the many facets of *la nouvelle écriture*.

115 See Michèle Saucier, '*L'Amèr, Le Sens apparent, Amantes*,' *La Nouvelle Barre du Jour*, nos. 118–19 (1982), 29.

116 See Barbara Godard, 'Language and Sexual Difference: The Case of Translation,' *Atkinson Review of Canadian Studies* 2, no. 1 (Fall–Winter 1984), 13–20.

117 Brossard, *L'Amèr*, 19

118 'produire son propre lieu de désir' (ibid. 16)

119 See Saucier, 29.

120 See France Théoret, 'Le Sens de la formule,' *La Nouvelle Barre du Jour*, nos. 118–19 (1982), 79: 'faire dire le moins possible'; 'travailler à s'effacer.'

121 Ibid.

122 Normand de Bellefeuille, 'Suite logique: pour une grammaire de la différence,' *La Nouvelle Barre du Jour*, nos. 118–19 (1982), 94

123 Brossard, '*e* muet mutant,' 10

124 Ibid. 14

125 Ibid.

126 Pierre Nepveu, 'Nicole Brossard: Notes sur une écologie,' *La Nouvelle Barre du Jour*, nos. 118–19 (1982), 141

127 Ibid. 143

128 André Beaudet, *Fréquences en l'inscription du roman* (Montréal: L'Aurore 1975), cover page: 'sortir de la représentation c'est avant tout évacuer la salle de ses spectateurs et la scène de ses figurants.'

129 See Bertrand, 'Introduction à l'histoire de la rupture'; Charron and des Roches, 'Notes sur une pratique'; and de Bellefeuille, 'La Gageure du lisible' and 'Le Caca et le lisible.'

130 France Théoret, *Bloody Mary* (Montréal: Les Herbes Rouges 1977), 11

131 Ibid. 9–10

132 Brossard, *Le Centre blanc*, 271

133 'me couler douce l'échine,' ibid. 271

134 See Bayard and David, *Out-Posts*, 67: 'The reader will hear more than one level, more than one pleasure. What pleasure to find that which is not evident. Not the blank which gives the reader a chance but three or four possible reading levels' (translation mine).

135 Carole Massé, *Dieu* (Montréal: Les Herbes Rouges 1979), 114

136 Ibid. 124

137 Nicole Bédard, 'L'Oscillée,' *La Barre du Jour*, no. 50 (hiver 1975), 105–22

138 In this case they are from Liange Sin, *Le Détachement féminin rouge* (Peking 1966). See Charron, *Interventions politiques*, 46. Subsequent references to this work appear in the text.

139 See Gaétan Brulotte's Preface to *Pirouette par hasard poésie* (Montréal: L'Aurore 1975), 7–17.

140 Philippe Haeck, *L'Action restreinte de la littérature* (Montréal: VLB 1975), 61 (translation mine)

141 Haeck, *Naissances: de l'écriture québécoise*, 318: 'Leurs paroles sont pleines de nos halètements.'

142 Ibid. 320

143 Louise Dupré, 'La Peau familière,' *La Nouvelle Barre du Jour*, no. 98 (jan. 1981), 5–11. See also *La Peau familière* (Montréal: Editions Remue Ménage 1983).

144 Madeleine Gagnon, *La Lettre infinie* (Montréal: VLB 1984), 51, 53, 54 (translation mine)

145 Claude Levesque, *L'Etrangeté du texte* (Montréal: VLB 1976), 106–7
146 See Hal Foster, 'The Object of Post-Criticism,' in Foster, ed., *The Anti-Aesthetic: Essays on Postmodern Culture*, 86.

CONCLUSION

1 See Culler, *On Deconstruction*, 186.
2 Ibid.
3 See chapter 1, p. 18.
4 See Baudrillard, *L'Echange symbolique et la mort*, 299.
5 Kroetsch, 'Beyond Nationalism: A Prologue,' 84
6 Suzanne Paradis, 'Les Lettres québécoises en 1968,' *Etudes Littéraires* 2, no. 2 (août 1969), 214–20
7 Nichol, *The Martyrology: Books III and IV*, Book 3, VIII, n. pag.

Bibliography

GENERAL REFERENCE WORKS

Abrams, M.H. *A Glossary of Literary Terms*. New York: Holt, Rinehart and Winston 1971

Agacinski, S., et al. *Mimésis des articulations*. Paris: Flammarion 1975

Angenot, Marc. 'Idéologie, collage, dialogisme.' *Revue d'esthétique*, 1978, 341–51

– *La Parole pamphlétaire*. Paris: Payot 1983

Bakermiller, Jean. *Towards a Psychology of Women*. Boston: Beacon Press 1976

Barthes, Roland. *Le Plaisir du texte*. Paris: Ed. du Seuil 1973

– *Roland Barthes*. Trans. Richard Howard. New York: Hill and Wang 1977

– *To Honour Roman Jakobson*. The Hague: Mouton Press 1967

Baudrillard, Jean. *L'Echange symbolique et la mort*. Paris: Gallimard 1976

– *The Mirror of Production*. Trans. Mark Poster. St Louis: Telos Press 1975

– *Pour une critique de l'économie politique du signe*. Paris: Gallimard 1972

Beardsley, Monroe. *Aesthetics*. New York: Harcourt, Brace and World 1958

Bense, Max. *Zeichen und Design*. Baden-Baden: Hyis Verlag 1971

Benveniste, Emile. *Problèmes de linguistique générale*. 2 Vols. Paris: Gallimard 1977

Bosquet, Alain. *Poésie du Québec*. Paris: Seghers 1968

Bourque, Gilles, and Gilles Dostaler. *Socialisme et indépendance*. Montréal: Boréal Express 1980

Conover, Patrick. *The Alternate Culture and Contemporary Communes*. Monticello: Illinois Council of Planning Librarians 1976

Court de Gebelin. *L'Histoire naturelle de la parole*. Paris 1776

– *Le Monde primitif*. Paris 1776

Crean, Susan, and Marcel Rioux. *Deux Pays pour vivre: un plaidoyer*. Montréal: HMH 1980
- 'Overcoming Dependency: A Plea for Two Nations.' *Canadian Journal of Political and Social Theory/Revue canadienne de théorie politique et sociale* 7, no. 3 (Fall/automne 1983), 50–81
Culler, Jonathan. *Structuralist Poetics*. London: Routledge and Kegan Paul 1975
David, Madeleine. *Les Dieux et le destin en Babylonie*. Paris: PUF 1949
de Brosses, Charles. *Traité de la formation mécanique des langues*. Paris: Saillant 1765
Derrida, Jacques. *La Dissémination*. Paris: Le Seuil 1972
- *L'Ecriture et la différence* Paris: Ed. du Seuil 1967
- *La Grammatologie*. Paris: Minuit 1967
- *Margins of Philosophy*. Trans. Alan Bass. Chicago: University of Chicago Press 1982
- *Positions*. Chicago: University of Chicago Press 1981
- *The Post-card*. Chicago: University of Chicago Press 1983
- *Writing and Difference*. Trans. Alan Bass. Chicago: University of Chicago Press 1978
Drache, Daniel, and Arthur Krocker. 'The Labyrinth of Dependency.' *Canadian Journal of Political and Social Theory/Revue canadienne de théorie politique et sociale* 7, no. 3 (Fall/automne 1983), 5–23
Dubois, J., et al., eds. *Rhétorique générale*. Paris: Larousse 1970
Eagleton, Terry. *Walter Benjamin or Towards a Revolutionary Criticism*. London: NLB 1982
Eco, Umberto. *L'Oeuvre ouverte*. Paris: Le Seuil 1965
- *Theory of Semiotics*. Bloomington: Indiana University Press 1979
Felman, Shoshana. *Literary Speech Acts*. Ithaca: Cornell University Press 1983
Février, James G. *L'Histoire de l'écriture*. Paris: Payot 1959
Foucault, Michel. *Les Mots et les choses: une archéologie des sciences humaines*. Paris: Gallimard 1966
- *The Order of Things*. London: Tavistock Publications 1970
Genette, Gérard. *Figures II*. Paris: Le Seuil 1969
- *Mimologiques*. Paris: Le Seuil 1975
Gilman, Richard. *The Confusion of Realms*. New York: Random House 1969
Goldschmidt, Victor. *Essai sur le Cratyle*. Paris: Champion 1940
Goldwater, R.J. *Primitivism in Modern Art*. New York: Random House 1967
Greenlee, Douglas. *Peirce's Concept of Sign*. The Hague: Mouton 1973
Greimas, A.J. *Du sens*. Paris: Larousse 1970
- *Sémantique structurale*. Paris: Larousse 1966

Hjemslev, L. *Prolegomena to a Theory of Language*. Madison: University of Wisconsin Press 1963

Jameson, Fred. *The Prison-House of Language*. Princeton: Princeton University Press 1972

Jowett, B., trans. *The Dialogues of Plato*. New York: Random House 1937

Kayser, Wolfgang. 'La Doctrine du langage naturel chez Jacob Boehme' *Poétique* 3 (1972), 337–65

Kristeva, Julia. *Essais de sémiotique poétique*. Paris: Larousse 1971

– *Polylogue*. Paris: Le Seuil 1977

– *Révolution du langage poétique*. Paris: Le Seuil 1974

– *Sémiotikè*. Paris: Le Seuil 1969

Leibniz, Gottfried. *New Essays*. Cambridge: Cambridge University Press 1981

Locke, John. *Essays Concerning Human Understanding*. Oxford: Clarendon Press 1950

Lyotard, Jean-François. *Dérive à partir de Marx et de Freud*. Paris: Union Générale d'Editeurs 1973

Marcuse, H. *Counter-Revolution and Revolt*. Boston: Beacon Press 1972

– *Essay on Liberation*. Boston: Beacon Press 1969

Martinet, A. *Le Langage*. Paris: Gallimard 1968

Meschonnic, Henri. *Les Etats de la poétique*. Paris: PUF 1985

Morris, Charles. *Signs, Language and Behaviour*. New York: Prentice Hall 1946

Mukarovsky, Jan. *Structure, Sign and Function*. Trans. John Burbank and Peter Steiner. New Haven: Yale University Press 1977

Olson, Charles. *Projective Verse*. New York: Totem Press 1959

Peirce, Charles. *Collected Papers*. Vol. II. Cambridge: Harvard University Press 1932

Pelletier, Anne-Marie. *Fonctions poétiques*. Paris: Klincksieck 1977

Piaget, Jean. *Le Structuralisme*. Paris: Presses Universitaires de France 1968

Reiss, Timothy. *The Discourse of Modernism*. Baltimore: Johns Hopkins University Press 1986

– 'Peirce and Frege in the Matter of Truth.' *Canadian Journal of Research in Semiotics* 4, no. 2 (Winter 1976), 5–11

Richards, I.A. *The Philosophy of Rhetoric*. Oxford: Oxford University Press 1936

Ricoeur, Paul. *Interpretation Theory: Discourse and the Surplus of Meaning*. Fort Worth, Texas: Texas Christian University Press 1976

– *The Rule of Metaphor*. Toronto: University of Toronto Press 1977

Roszak, Theodore. *The Making of the Counter-Culture*. New York: Doubleday 1968

Sarrazin, Guy, and Luc Racine. *Pour changer la vie*. Montréal: Editions du
   Jour 1973
Schaeffer, Maurice. *La Musique concrète*. Paris: Presses Universitaires de
   France 1967
Shukman, Ann. 'The Dialectics of Change: Culture, Code and the Individual.'
   In Zima, ed., *Semiotics and Dialectics*, 311–29
Sollers, Philippe, et al., eds. *Artaud*. Paris: Union Générale d'Editeurs 1973
Spada, Marcel. *Francis Ponge*. Paris: Seghers 1974
Starobinski, Jean. *The Anagrams of Ferdinand de Saussure*. New Haven:
   Yale University Press 1979
Steiner, George. *After Babel*. New York: Oxford University Press 1975
Todorov, Tzvetan. 'Introduction à la symbolique.' *Poétique* 3 (1972), 273–
   308
– *Les Genres du discours*. Paris: Le Seuil 1978
Vincenthier, George. *Histoire des idées au Québec*. Montréal: VLB 1983
Wallis, John. *Grammatica lingua anglicanae*. Oxford 1673
Warburton, William. *The Divine Legation of Moses*. London 1738
Williams, William Carlos. *Selected Essays*. New York: Random House 1954
Zima, Peter, ed. *Semiotics and Dialectics*. The Hague: Mouton Press 1981
Zumthor, Paul. *Introduction à la poésie orale*. Paris: Le Seuil 1983
– *Langue, texte, énigme*. Paris: Le Seuil 1975

LITERARY HISTORY

Ahmed, Maroussia. 'The Relevance of the Carnivalesque in the Quebec
   Novel.' *Studies in Twentieth-Century Literature* 9, no. 1 (Fall 1984), 119–
   33
– 'The Unique, Its Double and the Multiple: The Carnivalesque Hero in the
   Quebecois Novel.' *Yale French Studies*, no. 65 (1983), 139–53
Arp, Hans. *On My Way*. New York: Wittenborn and Schultz 1948
Beausoleil, Claude. 'Reliefs d'arsenal: une écriture d'avant-garde.' *Cul Q*, nos.
   4–5 (été–automne 1974), 85–91
Belleau, André. 'Carnavalisation et roman québécois: mise au point sur
   l'usage d'un concept de Bakhtine.' *Etudes Françaises* 3, no. 1 (hiver
   1983–4), 51–65
Bojko, Szymon. *New Graphics in Revolutionary Russia*. London: Lund
   Humphries 1972
Brommer, Gerald. *The Art of Collage*. Worcester, Mass.: Davis Publications
   1978
Buchloh, Benjamin H.D. 'Allegorical Procedures: Appropriation and Montage
   in Contemporary Art.' *Open Letter*, 5th ser., nos. 5–6 (Fall 1983), 164–93

Choy, William S. 'Space and Its Relation to Poetry.' *Delta*, no. 19 (Oct. 1961), 21–2

Coupey, Pierre. 'Interview.' *Capilano Review*, no. 13 (1978), 92–115

Davey, Frank. 'Introducing *Tish*.' In Gervais, ed., *The Writing Life*, 150–61

– 'The Present Scene.' *Delta*, no. 19 (Oct. 1961), 1–2

Dostaler, Gilles. 'Québec politique.' *Parti Pris* 5, nos. 8–9 (été 1968), 8

Duberman, Martin. *Black Mountain: An Exploration in Community.* New York: E.P. Dutton 1972

Duchastel, Jules. 'La Contre-Culture: l'exemple de *Main Mise*.' In Pelletier, ed., *L'Avant-garde culturelle et littéraire des années 70 au Québec*, 61–82

– 'La Contre-culture: une idéologie de l'a-politisme.' In *La Transformation du pouvoir au Québec*. Ed. Jacques Godbout et al. Montréal: Albert St-Martin 1980, 253–64

– 'Culture et contre-culture: idéologie et contre-idéologie.' In *Idéologies au Canada français 1940–1976*. Ed. Fernand Dumont et al. Québec: PUL 1961, 173–216

– '*Main Mise*: la nouvelle culture en dehors de la lutte des classes?' *Chroniques*, nos. 18–19 (juin–juillet 1976), 38–58

– 'Milieux culturels: culture et transformation sociale.' In *Cultures populaires et sociétés contemporaines*. Ed. Gilles Pronovost. Québec: PUQ 1982, 141–54

Fenollosa, Ernest. *The Chinese Written Character as a Medium for Poetry.* Ed. Ezra Pound. 1936; rpt. San Francisco: City Lights 1963

Foster, Stephen, and Rudolf Kuenzli, eds. *Dada Spectrum: The Dialectics of Revolt.* Madison, Wis.: Coda Press 1979

Gauvin, Lise. 'Les Revues littéraires québécoises de l'université à la contre-culture.'*Etudes Françaises* 11, no. 2 (mai 1975), 161–89

– '*Parti-Pris' Littéraire*. Montréal: Presses de l'Université Montréal 1975

Gauvreau, Claude. '15 Février 1969.' *Liberté* 2, no. 1 (jan.–fév. 1969), 95–7

Gervais, C.H., ed. *The Writing Life: Historical and Critical Views of the Tish Movement.* Coatsworth, Ont.: Black Moss Press 1976

Gomringer, Eugen. 'The First Years of Concrete Poetry.' Trans. Stephen Bann. *Forum*, no. 4 (15 April 1967), 17–18

– 'From Line to Constellation.' *Image*, Nov.–Dec. 1964, 10–21

Grossman, Manuel. *Dada: Paradox, Mystification and Ambiguity.* New York: Pegasus 1971

Isou, Isodore. 'La Fin des dadaistes falsificateurs de la culture et de la critique universitaire obscurantiste.' *Revue Ô*, no. C (June 1965), 10–21

Lamonde, Yvan, and Esther Trépanier, eds. *L'Avènement de la modernité culturelle au Québec.* Montréal: Institut québécois de la Culture 1986

Lemaître, Maurice. *Le Lettrisme devant Dada et les nécrophages de Dada.* Paris: Centre de créativité 1967

Lodder, Christina. *Russian Constructivism.* New Haven: Yale University Press 1984

Maheu, Pierre. *Un parti pris révolutionaire.* Montréal: Parti Pris 1983

Marcotte, Gilles. *Le Temps des poètes.* Montréal: HMH 1969

Marino, Adrian. 'Essai d'une définition de l'avant-garde.' *Revue de l'Université de Bruxelles* 1 (1975), 64–120

Maugey, Axel. *Poésie et société au Québec (1937–1970).* Québec: Presses de l'Université Laval 1971

Milner, John. *Vladimir Tatlin and the Russian Avant-garde.* New Haven: Yale University Press 1984

Moisan, Clément. *L'Age de la littérature canadienne.* Montréal: L'Hexagone 1969

Motherwell, Robert, ed. *Dada Painters and Poets.* New York: Wittenborn and Schultz 1951

Nichol, bp. 'Interview/bpNichol.' *Capilano Review,* nos. 8–9 (Fall 1975– Spring 1976), 313–46

Norris, Ken. 'An Interview with bpNichol.' *Essays on Canadian Writing,* no. 12 (Fall 1978), 243–50

– *The Little Magazine in Canada 1925–1980.* Toronto: ECW Press 1984

– 'The Role of the Little Magazine in the Development of Modernism and Post-Modernism in Canadian Poetry.' Diss. McGill University 1980

Pelletier, Jacques, ed. *L'Avant-garde culturelle et littéraire des années 70 au Québec.* Montréal: Cahiers du Dept. d'études littéraires, UQAM 1986

Piotte, Jean Marc. *Un parti pris politique.* Montréal: VLB 1979

Reid, Jamie. 'Editorial.' *Tish,* no. 4 (Dec. 1964), 1

Richter, Hans. *Dada, Art, Anti-Art.* New York: McGraw-Hill 1965

Rickey, George. *Constructivism: Origins and Evolution.* New York: G. Braziller 1967

Robillard, Yves, ed. *Quebec Underground 1962–1972.* 2 vols. Montréal: Médiart 1973

St-Denis, Janou. *Gauvreau, le Cygne.* Montréal: Le Noroît 1978

Seaman, David. 'Early French Visual Poetry.' *Precisely* 5, no. 3 (1979), 16–29

Seamon, Roger. 'Open City: Vancouver 1968.' *Far Point* 1, no. 1 (Fall–Winter 1968), 48–59

Sheppard, Richard. 'Dada and Mysticism: Influences and Affinities.' In Foster and Kuenzli, eds., *Dada Spectrum,* 91–114

Tadros, Jean-Pierre. 'Tendances et orientations de la nouvelle littérature' [interview with Raoul Duguay]. *Culture Vivante,* no. 5 (1962), 60–8

Tallman, Warren. 'Poet in Progress: Notes on Frank Davey.' *Canadian Literature*, no. 24 (Spring 1965), 24–5

Tashjian, Dickran. 'New York Dada and Primitivism.' In Foster and Kuenzli, eds., *Dada Spectrum*, 115–44

Tzara, Tristan. 'Seven Dada Manifestoes.' In Motherwell, ed., *Dada Painters and Poets*, 73–97

WORKS ON THEORY: CONCRETE / DECONSTRUCTION / FEMINISM / NOUVELLE ECRITURE / POST-MODERNISM / PERFORMANCE

Books

Abel, E., ed. *Writing and Sexual Difference*. Brighton: Harvester Press 1982

Arac, Jonathan, W. Godzich, and W. Martin, eds. *The Yale Critics: Deconstruction in America*. Minneapolis: University of Minnesota Press 1983

Barker, Francis, ed. *The Politics of Theory*. Colchester: University of Essex Press 1983

Benamou, Michel, and Charles Caramello, eds. *Performance in Postmodern Culture*. Milwaukee: Coda Press 1977

Bense, Max. *Einführung in die Information Theoretische Aesthetics*. Reinbeck bei Hamburg: Rowohlt 1969

– *Zeichen und Design*. Baden-Baden: Hyis Verlag 1971

Bronson, A.A., and Peggy Gale, eds. *Performance by Artists*. Toronto: Art Metropole 1979

Brunt, R., and C. Rowan, eds. *Feminism, Culture and Politics*. London: Lawrence and Wishart 1982

Burger, Peter. *Theory of the Avant Garde*. Trans. Michael Shaw. Minneapolis: University of Minnesota Press 1974

Calinescu, Matei. *Faces of Modernity: Avant-Garde, Decadence, Kitsch*. Bloomington: Indiana University Press 1977

Centre de Cérisy-La Salle. *Les Fins de l'homme: à partir du travail de Jacques Derrida*. Paris: Galilée 1981

Chamberland, Paul. *Le Courage de la poésie*. Montréal: Les Herbes Rouges 1981

– *Un parti pris anthropologique*. Montréal: Parti Pris 1983

– *Le Recommencement du monde*. Longueuil: Editions Le Préambule 1983

– *Terre souveraine*. Montréal: L'Hexagone 1980

Cixous, Hélène, Madeleine Gagnon, and Annie Leclerc. *La Venue à l'écriture*. Paris: Union Générale d'Editeurs 1974

Collette, Jean Yves, and Line McMurray. *La Mort du genre*. Outremont: NBJ 1986

− *Pour une éthique de la métamorphose*. Montréal: NBJ 1986
Cook, David, and Arthur Kroker. *The Postmodern Scene*. Montreal: New World Perspectives 1986
Culler, Jonathan. *On Deconstruction*. London: Routledge and Kegan Paul 1983
− *The Pursuit of Signs*. London: Routledge and Kegan Paul 1981
de Campos, Augusto, et al., eds. *Teoria de Poesia Concreta*. São Paulo: Livraria das Ciudades 1975
de Man, Paul. *Allegories of Reading*. New Haven: Yale University Press 1979
− *Blindness and Insight: Essays in the Rhetoric of Contemporary Criticism*. New York: Oxford University Press 1971
Eisenstein, Hester, and Alice Jardine, eds. *The Future of Difference*. New York: Barnard Women's College Center 1980
Fahlstrom, Oyvind. *Bord-Dikta 1952–1955*. Stockholm: Bonniers 1966
Felman, Shoshana. *Le Scandale du corps parlant*. Paris: Le Seuil 1980
Fokkema, Douwe, ed. *Approaching Postmodernism*. Amsterdam: John Benjamin 1986
Foster, Hal, ed. *The Anti-Aesthetic: Essays on Postmodern Culture*. Port Townsend, Wash.: Bay Press 1983
Fredman, Stephen. *Poet's Prose: The Crisis in American Verse*. Cambridge: Cambridge University Press 1983
Garnier, Pierre. *Spatialisme et poésie concrète*. Paris: Gallimard 1968
Garvin, Harry, ed. *Romanticism, Modernism and Postmodernism*. Lewisburg: Bucknell University Press 1980
Graff, Gerald. *Literature against Itself*. Chicago: University of Chicago Press 1979
Harari, Josué, ed. *Textual Strategies*. London: Methuen 1981
Hartman, Geoffrey. *Saving the Text*. Baltimore: Johns Hopkins University Press 1981
Hassan, Ihab. *The Dismemberment of Orpheus: Towards a Postmodern Literature*. 2nd ed. Madison: University of Wisconsin Press 1982
− *Para-criticisms*. Urbana: University of Illinois Press 1975
Hassan, Ihab, and Susan Hassan, eds. *Innovation/Renovation: New Perspectives on the Humanities*. Madison: University of Wisconsin Press 1983
Irigaray, Luce. *Speculum de l'autre femme*. Paris: Minuit 1974
Jardine, Alice. *Gynesis*. Ithaca: Cornell University Press 1985
Johnson, Barbara. *The Critical Difference*. Baltimore: Johns Hopkins University Press 1980
Kofman, Sarah. *L'Enigme de la femme: la femme dans les textes de Freud*. Paris: Galilée 1980
Kostelanetz, Richard, ed. *Aesthetics Contemporary*. Buffalo: Prometheus Books 1978
Lasch, C. *The Culture of Narcissism*. New York: Norton 1978

Lentricchia, Frank. *After the New Criticism*. Chicago: University of Chicago Press 1980

Levesque, Claude. *L'Etrangeté du texte*. Montréal: VLB 1976

Lyotard, Jean-François. *La Condition postmoderne*. Paris: Minuit 1979

– *Des Dispositifs pulsionnels*. Paris: Minuit 1974

McCaffery, Steve, and bpNichol, eds. *Sound Poetry: A Catalogue*. Toronto: Underwhich Editions 1979

McMurray, Line, ed. *L'Ecriture: lieu théorique et pratique du changement*. Actes du colloque de Charleroi, novembre 1986. Outremont: NBJ 1987

Monteith, Moira, ed. *Women's Writing: A Challenge to Theory*. Brighton: Harvester Press 1986

Neuman, Shirley, and Robert Wilson. *Labyrinths of Voice: Conversations with Robert Kroetsch*. Edmonton: NeWest 1982

Norris, Christopher. *Deconstruction: Theory and Practice*. London: Methuen 1982

– *The Deconstructive Turn: Essays in the Rhetoric of Philosophy*. London: Methuen 1984

Palmer, Richard. *Postmodern Hermeneutics of Performance*. Madison, Wis.: Coda Press 1977

Payant, René, ed. *Vidéo*. Montréal: Artexte 1986

Pontbriand, Chantal, ed. *Performance: textes et documents*. Montréal: Parachute Editions 1981

Russell, Charles. *The Avant-Garde Today*. Chicago: University of Illinois Press 1982

Ryan, Michael. *Marxism and Deconstruction*. Baltimore: Johns Hopkins University Press 1982

Scarpetta, Guy. *Eloge de l'impureté*. Paris: Grasset 1985

Schaeffer, Pierre. *La Musique concrète*. Paris: Presses Universitaires de France 1967

Solt, Mary Ellen. *Concrete Poetry: A World View*. Bloomington: Indiana University Press 1969

Sondheim, Alan. *Individuals, Post-Movement Art in America*. New York: Dulton 1977

Thiher, Allen. *Words in Reflection*. Chicago: University of Chicago Press 1984

Articles

Allen, Carolyn. 'Feminist(s) Reading: A Response to Elaine Showalter.' In Abel, ed., *Writing and Sexual Difference*, 304–7

Altieri, Charles. 'Postmodernism: A Source of Definition.' *Par Rapport Series*, no. 11 (1979), 87–100

Andrews, Bruce. 'Constitution, Writing, Politics, Language, the Body.' *Open Letter*, 5th ser., no. 1 (Winter 1982), 154–65

Baert, Renée. 'La Vidéo au Canada: en quête d'une identité.' In Payant, ed., *Vidéo*, 42–54

Barber, Bruce. 'Appropriation/Expropriation: Convention or Intervention?' *Open Letter*, 5th ser., nos. 4–6 (Summer–Fall 1983), 206–35

– 'The Function of Performance in Postmodern Culture: A Critique.' In Pontbriand, ed. *Performance*, 32–7

– 'Indexing: Conditionalism and Its Heretical Equivalents.' In Bronson and Gale, eds., *Performance by Artists*, 183–204

Barth, John. 'The Literature of Exhaustion.' *The Atlantic* 220, no. 2 (1967), 29–34

– 'The Literature of Replenishment: Postmodernist Fiction.' *The Atlantic* 245, no. 1 (Jan. 1980), 65–71

Bartlett, Lee. 'What Is Language Poetry?' *Critical Inquiry* 12, no. 4 (Summer 1986), 741–53

Beaudet, André. 'L'Etat de choisir entre livre/vie, écriture/révolution, rêve/action.' *La Barre du Jour*, no. 30 (automne 1971), 72–88

– 'L'Imposture généralisée.' *La Nouvelle Barre du Jour*, nos. 90–1 (mai 1980), 101–8

Beausoleil, Claude, 'Du texte et du doute (essai fictionnel).' *La Nouvelle Barre du Jour*, no. 59 (oct. 1977), 57–63

– 'La Forme du mot rupture.' *La Barre du Jour*, hiver 1974, 30–40

– 'Hypothèses.' *Dérives*, no. 8 (1977), 18–26

Beausoleil, Claude, and André Roy. 'Pour une théorie fictive.' *Cul Q*, nos. 4–5 (été–automne 1974), 39–51

Benamou, Michel. 'Presence and Play.' In Benamou and Caramello, eds., *Performance in Postmodern Culture*, 3–10

Bense, Max. 'Konkrete poesie.' *Rot*, no. 21 (1965), 15–21

Bernstein, Charles. 'Whole to Part: The Ends of Ideologies of the Long Poem.' *Open Letter*, 6th ser., nos. 2–3 (Summer–Fall 1985), 177–90

Bertrand, Claude. 'Introduction à l'histoire de la rupture' (suite I). *La Barre du Jour*, juin–juillet 1968, 63–71. Suite II. *La Barre du Jour*, no. 16 (oct.–déc. 1968), 47–52

Bertrand, Claude, Pierre Bertrand, Michel Morin, Jean Stafford, and France Théoret. 'Les Dix Propositions.' *La Presse*, 4 April 1970, 34, cols. 5–8

Bicocchi, Maria Gloria, and Fulvio Salvadori. 'Performances and Communication.' In Bronson and Gale, eds., *Performance by Artists*, 205–16

bissett, bill. 'No tay syun.' *Open Letter*, 5th ser., no. 2 (Spring 1982), 57–84

Bowering, George. 'The End of the Line.' *Open Letter*, 5th ser., no. 3 (Summer 1982), 5–10

Bronson, A.A. 'The Rise and Fall of the Peanut Party.' *Arts Canada*, March–April 1977, 72–97

Brossard, Nicole. 'L'Avenir de la littérature québécoise.' *Etudes françaises* 13, nos. 3–4 (oct. 1977), 373–93

– 'L'Epreuve ou les preuves de la modernité.' *La Nouvelle Barre du Jour*, nos. 90–1 (mai 1980), 55–63

– 'Mais voici venir la fiction ou l'épreuve au féminin.' *La Nouvelle Barre du Jour*, nos. 90–1 (mai 1980), 64–8

Buchloch, Benjamin. 'Allegorical Procedures: Appropriation and Montage in Contemporary Art.' *Open Letter*, 5th ser., nos. 5–6 (Summer–Fall 1983), 164–93

Burger, Peter. 'The Significance of the Avant-Garde for Contemporary Aesthetics: A Reply to Jurgen Habermas.' *New German Critique*, no. 22 (Winter 1981), 19–22

Calinescu, Matei. 'Postmodernism and Some Paradoxes of Periodization.' In Fokkema, ed., *Approaching Postmodernism*, 233–9

– 'Way of Looking at Fiction: Contemporary Postmodern.' In Garvin, ed., *Romanticism, Modernism and Postmodernism*, 155–70

Caramello, Charles. 'On Styles of Postmodern Writing.' In Benamou and Caramello, eds., *Performance in Postmodern Culture*, 221–34

Caruso, Barbara, and Steven Scobie. 'Two Views: A Dialogue.' *Open Letter*, 6th ser., no. 4 (Spring 1986), 49–68

Chamberland, Paul. 'Entretien avec Claude Péloquin.' *Parti Pris* 3, no. 9 (avril 1966), 38–45

– 'Manifeste des enfants libres du Québec.' *Hobo-Québec*, no. 2 (fév. 1972), 8

Charles, Daniel. 'Le Timbre, la voix, le temps.' In Pontbriand, ed., *Performance*, 110–17

Charron, François. 'L'Ecriture commence par un rêve.' *La Nouvelle Barre du Jour*, nos. 90–1 (mai 1980), 11–32

– 'Interventions.' *Dérives*, nos. 20–1 (1979), 73–9

– 'Notes sur l'expérience de la peinture.' *Les Herbes Rouges*, nos. 75–6 (nov. 1979), 5–59

Charron, François, and Roger des Roches. 'Notes sur une pratique.' *La Barre du Jour*, no. 29 (été 1971), 1–6

– 'Transgression et/ou littérature politique.' *La Barre du Jour*, nos. 41–2 (automne 1973), 33–43

Chopin, Henri. 'Why I Am the Author of Sound and Free Poetry.' In Solt, *Concrete Poetry: A World View*, 82

Cixous, Hélène. 'The Laughter of the Medusa.' *Signs* 1, no. 4 (Summer 1976), 875–93

– 'Textes de l'imprévisible: grâce à.' *Les Nouvelles Littéraires*, 26 May 1976

Cloutier, Cécile. 'La Nouvelle Poésie.' *Liberté* 9, no. 4 (juillet–août 1967), 118–27

Cobbing, Bob, and Peter Meyer. 'Concerning Concrete Poetry' [manuscript available from the authors]

Corriveau, Hughes. 'Appellation contrôlée.' *La Nouvelle Barre du Jour*, nos. 90–1 (mai 1980), 119–28

Cotnoir, Louise. 'Figurez vous.' *La Nouvelle Barre du Jour*, No. 172 (mars 1986), 44–6

Coupey, Pierre. 'The Alphabet of Blood.' *Open Letter*, 5th ser., no. 2 (Spring 1982), 5–13

Coutts-Smith, Kenneth. 'Post-Bourgeois Ideology and Visual Culture.' *Open Letter*, 5th ser., nos. 5–6 (Summer–Fall 1983), 106–20

Crimp, Douglas. 'The Photographic Activity in Postmodernism.' In Pontbriand, ed., *Performance*, 70–6

Davies, Alan, and Nick Piombino. 'The Indeterminate Interval: From History to Blur.' *Open Letter*, 5th ser., no. 1 (Winter 1982), 31–9

Davis, Robert Con. 'Psychoanalysis and Deconstruction.' *Genre* 17, nos. 1–2 (Spring–Summer 1984), 135–58

Davis, Robert Con, and Ronald Schleifer. 'Introduction: The Ends of Deconstruction.' *Genre* 17, nos. 1–2 (Spring–Summer 1984), 3–18

de Bellefeuille, Normand. 'Le Caca et le lisible.' *Les Herbes Rouges*, no. 38 (aôut 1976), 1–27

– 'La Gageure du lisible.' *La Nouvelle Barre du Jour*, nos. 90–1 (mai 1980), 145–51

– 'Suite logique: pour une grammaire de la différence.' *La Nouvelle Barre du Jour*, nos. 118–19 (1982), 91–8

de Campos, Augusto. 'Eye and Breath.' *Open Letter*, 5th ser., no. 1 (Winter 1982), 116–18

de Duve, Thierry. 'La Performance hic & nunc.' In Pontbriand, ed., *Performance*, 18–27

Duguay, Raoul. 'The Invisible Child: An Interview with Raoul Duguay by Caroline Bayard.' *Only Paper To-day* 3, no. 1 (Sept.–Oct. 1975), 2–4

– 'On the Vibrant Body.' *Open Letter*, 3rd ser., no. 7 (Summer 1977), 26–36

– 'Or Art (Poésie) total du cri au chant au.' *Quoi* 1, no. 2 (printemps–été 1967), 7–14

– 'Poetry Is Yrteop.' *Ellipse*, no. 17 (1975), 80–97

– 'Le Stéréo-poème-audio-visuel.' *Culture Vivante*, no. 12 (12 fév. 1969), 35–42

– 'La Transe et la Gression.' *La Barre du Jour*, automne 1973, 44–58

Durand, Régis. 'Les Limites de la théâtralité.' In Pontbriand, ed., *Performance*, 48–54

Dutton, Paul. 'Open Journal: Milwaukee.' *Open Letter*, 3rd ser., no. 8 (Spring 1978), 44–51

Felman, Shoshana. 'La Méprise et sa chance.' *L'Arc*, no. 58 (1974), 40–8
- 'Rereading Femininity.' *Yale French Studies*, no. 62 (1981), 19–44
- 'Turning the Screw of Interpretation.' *Yale French Studies*, nos. 55–6 (1977), 94–207
- 'Women and Madness: The Critical Phallacy.' *Diacritics* 5, no. 4 (Winter 1975), 2–10

Féral, Josette. 'The Powers of Difference.' In Eisenstein and Jardine, eds., *The Future of Difference*, 88–94

Foley, Barbara. 'The Politics of Deconstruction.' *Genre* 17, nos. 1–2 (Spring–Summer 1984), 113–34

Foucault, Michel. 'What Is an Author?' In Harari, ed., *Textual Strategies*, 151–60

Frank, Peter. 'Auto-Art: Self-Indulgent and How!' *Art News*, Sept. 1976, 43–9

Gale, Peggy. 'History Lesson.' In Pontbriand, ed., *Performance*, 93–101

Gallop, Jane. 'The Mother-Tongue.' In Barker, ed., *The Politics of Theory*, 49–56

Garnier, Pierre. 'Deuxième Manifeste pour une poésie visuelle.' *Les Lettres*, 8th ser., no. 30 (avril 1963), 15–28
- 'Manifeste pour une poésie nouvelle, visuelle et phonique.' *Les Lettres*, 8th ser., no. 29 (1963), 1–9
- 'Projet de plan pilote, 5 août 1963.' *Les Lettres*, 8th ser., no. 31, 2–3

Goldberg, Rose Lee. 'Performance: A Hidden History or the Avant, Avant Garde.' In Bronson and Gale, eds., *Performance by Artists*, 170–5

Hassan, Ihab. 'Prometheus as Performer: Towards a Posthumanist Culture?' In Benamou and Caramello, eds., *Performance in Postmodern Culture*, 201–20
- 'What Is Postmodernism?' In Hassan and Hassan, eds., *Innovation/ Renovation*, 329–41

Heidsieck, Bernard. 'Sound Poetry How?' *Open Letter*, 5th ser., no. 1 (Winter 1982), 101–5

Higgins, Dick. 'Performance Taken Socially.' *Open Letter*, 5th ser., nos. 5–6 (Summer–Fall 1983), 27–31

Humm, Maggie. 'Feminist Literary Criticism in America and England.' In Montieth, ed., *Women's Writing: A Challenge to Theory*, 90–116

Jameson, Frederic. 'Postmodernism and Consumer Society.' In Foster, ed., *The Anti-Aesthetic*, 111–25
- 'Postmodernism and the Logic of Late Capitalism.' *New Left Review*, no. 146 (July–August 1984), 53–92

Johnson, Barbara. 'Gender Theory and the Yale School.' *Genre* 17, nos. 1–2 (Spring–Summer 1984), 101–12

Johnson, Barbara, Louis Mackay, and J. Hillis Miller. 'Marxism and Deconstruction: A Symposium.' *Genre* 17, nos. 1–2 (Spring–Summer 1984), 73–100

Kohler, Michael. 'Postmodernismus: Ein Begriff Geschichtficher Überlick.' *Amerikastudien* 22 (1977), 8–18 [See also in the same issue articles by Gerhard Hoffman and Alfred Horning, and Rüdiger Kunow, 'Modern, Postmodern and Contemporary as Criteria for Twentieth-Century Literature,' 19–46.]

Kristeva, Julia. 'Féminité et écriture.' *Revue des Sciences Humaines*, no. 168 (1977), 177–88

– 'Questions à Julia Kristeva.' *Revue des Sciences Humaines*, no. 169 (déc. 1977), 497–501

– 'Woman's Time.' *Signs* 7, no. 1 (1981), 13–35

Kroetsch, Robert. 'Beyond Nationalism: A Prologue.' *Open Letter*, 5th ser., no. 4 (Spring 1983), 83–9

– 'For Play and Entrance: The Contemporary Canadian Long Poem.' *Open Letter*, 5th ser., no. 4 (Spring 1983), 91–110

Lapointe, Paul-Marie. 'Ecriture-Poésie, 1977.' *La Barre du Jour*, no. 58 (sept. 1977), 37–8

Lethen, Helmut. 'Modernism Cut in Half: The Exclusion of the Avant-garde and the Debate on Postmodernism.' In Fokkema, ed., *Approaching Postmodernism*, 233–9

Lewis, Philip. 'Revolutionary Semiotics.' *Diacritics* 4, no. 3 (Fall 1974), 28–32

Lovell, Terry. 'Writing like a Woman: A Question of Politics.' In Barker, ed., *The Politics of Theory*, 15–26

Lyotard, Jean-François. 'Réponse à la question: qu'est-ce que le postmoderne?' *Critique*, no. 419 (1982), 357–67

– 'The Unconscious as mise-en-scène.' In Benamou and Caramello, eds., *Performance in Postmodern Culture*, 87–98

McCaffery, Steve. 'Absent Pre-Sences.' *Open Letter*, 3rd ser., no. 9 (Fall 1978), 121–34

– 'The F-Claim to Shape in Patalogomena towards a Zero Reading (for Ihab Hassan).' *Open Letter*, 4th ser., nos. 6–7 (Winter 1980–1), 11–14

– 'Notes on Trope, Text, and Perception.' *Open Letter*, 3rd ser., no. 3 (Fall 1975), 40–53

– 'The Politics of the Referent.' *Open Letter*, 3rd ser., no. 7 (Summer 1977), 60–107

Maclow, Jackson. 'Language-Centered.' *Open Letter*, 5th ser., no. 1 (Winter 1982), 23–37

Makward, Christiane. 'To Be or Not to Be ... a Feminist Speaker.' In Eisenstein and Jardine, eds., *The Future of Difference*, 96–105

Marks, Elaine. 'Women and Literature in France.' *Signs: Journal of Women in Culture and Society* 3, no. 4 (Summer 1978), 832–42

Martin, Jay. 'Americans in a Post-American Age.' *The Antioch Review* 33, no. 2 (Summer 1975), 7–25

Mayer, Peter. 'The Concrete Phenomenon.' *Journal of Typographical Research* 2, no. 4 (1970), 383–90

Miller, J. Hillis. 'Stevens' Rock and Criticism as Cure.' *Georgia Review* 30 (1976), 5–33 (Part I), and 330–48 (Part II)

Moi, Toril. 'Sexual/Textual Politics.' In Barker, ed., *The Politics of Theory*, 1–14

Mon, Franz. 'On the Poetry of Surface.' In Solt, *Concrete Poetry: A World View*, 19–20

Monk, Philip. 'Coming to Speech: The Role of the Viewer in Performance.' In Pontbriand, ed., *Performance*, 145–9

Nichol, bp. 'A Conversation with Fred Wah: TRG Report One: Translation (Part 3).' *Open Letter*, 3rd ser., no. 9 (Fall 1978), 34–52

– 'Some Sentences, Paragraphs and Punctuations on Sentences, Paragraphs and Punctuation.' *Open Letter*, 5th ser., no. 3 (Summer 1982), 17–23

Nichol, bp, and Frank Davey. 'The Prosody of Open Verse.' *Open Letter*, 5th ser., no. 2 (Spring 1982), 5–13

Nichol, bp, and Steve McCaffery. 'A Contributed Editorial.' *Open Letter*, 3rd ser., no. 9 (Fall 1978), 5–6

– 'Discussion.' *Open Letter*, 6th ser., nos. 2–3 (Summer–Fall 1985) [Longliners issue], 290–6

– 'Manifesto II.' *Open Letter*, 2nd ser., no. 4 (Spring 1973), 75

– 'TRG Research Report 2: Narrative Part 1.' *Open Letter*, 2nd ser., no. 6 (Fall 1973) 113–20

– 'TRG Report 2: Narrative (Part 3) – "Charting the Obvious." ' *Open Letter*, 3rd ser., no. 9 (Fall 1978) 64–7

– 'TRG Report 2: Narrative (Part 5) – "Manifesto as Interlude." ' *Open Letter*, 2nd ser., no. 9 (Fall 1974), 70–87

– 'TRG Report 2 (Narrative, Part 5): The Search for Nonnarrative Prose, Part 2.' *Open Letter*, 3rd ser., no. 2 (Spring 1975), 39–58

Norris, Christopher. 'Some Versions of Rhetoric: Empson and de Man.' *Genre* 17, nos. 1–2 (Spring–Summer 1984), 191–214

Owens, Craig. 'The Allegorical Impulse: Towards a Theory of Postmodernism, Part I.' *October* 2:50–75

– 'The Allegorical Impulse: Towards a Theory of Postmodernism, Part II.' *October* 13:29–80

– 'The Allegorical Impulse: Towards a Theory of Postmodernism.' In Pontbriand, ed., *Performance*, 37–42 [reprint of Parts I and II above]

- 'The Discourse of Others: Feminists and Postmodernism.' In Foster, ed., *The Anti-Aesthetic*, 57–82

Palmer, Richard. 'Towards a Postmodern Hermeneutics of Performance.' In Benamou and Caramello, eds., *Performance in Postmodern Culture*, 19–32

Payant, René. 'Le Choc du présent.' In Pontbriand, ed., *Performance*, 127–37

Péloquin, Claude. 'Poèmes, manifestes.' *Parti Pris* 3, no. 9 (avril 1966), 46–56

Pelzer, Birgit. 'La Performance ou l'intégrale des équivoques.' In Pontbriand, ed., *Performance*, 28–31

Pignatari, Decio, and Luiz Pinto. 'Nova linguagem, nova poesia.' *Invencao* 3, no. 4 (1964), 82–3

Piper, Adrian. 'Performance and the Fetishism of the Art Object.' *Open Letter*, 5th ser., nos. 5–6 (Summer–Fall 1983), 7–17

Pontbriand, Chantal. 'The Question in Performance.' *Open Letter*, 5th ser., nos. 5–6 (Summer–Fall 1983), 18–25

- 'La Problématique postmoderne de l'hybride.' *Parachute*, no. 26 (printemps 1982), 4–15

- 'Introduction.' In Pontbriand, ed., *Performance*, 6–9

Racine, Luc. 'La Parole et le chant.' *Quoi* 1, no. 2 (printemps–été 1967), 11–25

Saillant, Francine. 'D'Ecrire ça.' *La Nouvelle Barre du Jour*, nos. 90–1 (mai 1980), 129–36

Scarpetta, Guy. 'Erotique de la performance.' In Pontbriand, ed., *Performance*, 138–44

Schafer, Murray. 'Graphics of Musical Thought.' *Open Letter*, 5th ser., no. 3 (Summer 1982), 34–55

- 'The Theater of Confluence.' *Open Letter*, 4th ser., nos. 4–5 (Fall 1979), 30–47

Scott, Gail. 'Spaces like Stairs.' *La Nouvelle Barre du Jour*, no. 177 (mars 1986), 31–6

Seaman, David. 'Early French Visual Poetry.' *Precisely* 5, no. 3 (1979), 16–29

Silliman, Ron. 'The Political Economy of Poetry.' *Open Letter*, 5th ser., no. 1 (Winter 1982), 52–65

Spivak, Gayatri. 'French Feminism in an International Frame.' *Yale French Studies*, no. 62 (1981), 154–84

- 'Il faut s'y prendre en s'en prenant à elles.' In *Les Fins de l'homme: à partir du travail de Jacques Derrida*. Ed. Philippe Lacoue-Labarthe and Jean-Luc Nancy. Paris: Galilée 1981, 505–15

- 'Revolutions That as Yet Have No Model: Derrida's *Limited Inc.*' *Diacritics* 10, no. 4 (Winter 1980), 29–49

Stanton, Donna. 'Language and Revolution: The Franco-American Disconnection.' In Eisenstein and Jardine, eds., *The Future of Difference*, 73–87

Stoianova, Ivanka. 'De quelques aspects multidisciplinaires des performances artistiques dans les conditions postmodernes.' In Pontbriand, ed., *Performance*, 118–26

Sujir, Leila. 'Comment remplacer la mémoire perdue et comment nous représenter.' *Parallélogramme* 12, no. 2 (déc. 1986–jan. 1987), 32–9

Sulliman, Susan. 'Naming and Difference: Reflections on Modernism versus Postmodernism.' In Fokkema, ed., *Approaching Postmodernism*, 255–69

Szabolcsi, Michael. 'Avant-Garde, Neo-Avant-Garde, Modernism: Questions and Suggestions.' *New Literary History* 3, no. 1 (Autumn 1971), 49–70

Tatham, Campbell. 'Mythotherapy and Postmodern Fictions: Magic Is Afoot.' In Benamou and Caramello, eds., *Performance in Postmodern Culture*, 132–58

Théoret, France. 'L'Implicite et l'explicite de la nouvelle écriture.' *La Nouvelle Barre du Jour*, nos. 90–1 (mai 1980), 163–72

Tostevin, Lola Lemire. 'The Pregnant Pause as Conceptual Space (or gimme a break).' *Open Letter*, 6th ser., no. 7 (Spring 1987), 74–6

Vattimo, Gianni. 'From *On the Way to Silence (Heidegger and the Poetic Word).' Open Letter*, 5th ser., no. 1 (Winter 1982), 47–9

White, A. '*L'éclatement du sujet*: The Theoretical Work of Julia Kristeva.' Stencilled Occasional Paper, University of Birmingham Centre for Contemporary Studies, Birmingham 1977

Young, Earl. 'Notation and the Art of Reading.' *Open Letter*, 5th ser., no. 7 (Spring 1984), 5–32

Zurbrugg, Nicolas. 'Tom Phillips and the Verbal/Visual Avant-Garde.' *Open Letter*, 4th ser., no. 12 (Summer 1978), 212–19

CRITICISM ON CONCRETE / NEW WRITING / POST-MODERN TEXTS

Alpert, Barry. 'Post-Modern Oral Poetry: Buckminster Fuller, John Cage, David Antin.' *Boundary 2* 3, no. 3 (Spring 1975), 665–81

Ballstadt, Carl. 'Rag & Bone Shop.' *The Canadian Forum*, July–Aug. 1971, 36–7

Barbour, Douglas. 'bpNichol: The Life of Letters and the Letters of Life.' *Essays on Canadian Writings*, no. 9 (Winter 1977–8), 97–111

– 'Some Notes in Progress about a Work in Process.' *Open Letter*, 5th ser., nos. 5–6 (Summer–Fall 1986), 215–24

Barreto-Rivera, Rafael. 'Random Walking: *The Martyrology, Book v.' Open Letter*, 5th ser., nos. 5–6 (Summer–Fall 1986), 101–8

Basile, Jean. 'Quand Luor freak sur la poésie.' *Le Devoir*, 25 April 1970, 24, col. 16

– 'Si vous n'aimez pas l'Infonie, L'Infonie vous aime quand même.' *Le Devoir*, 1 Feb. 1970, 11, cols. 3–4; 7 March 1970, 11, col. 1

Bayard, Caroline. 'Bill Bissett: subversion et poésie concrète.' *Etudes littér-aires* 19, no. 2 (automne 1976), 81–108

Bayard, Caroline, and Jack David. *Out-Posts/Avant-Postes*. Erin, Ont.: Press Porcépic 1978

Beausoleil, Claude, and Hughes Corriveau. 'Des Herbes Rouges.' *La Nouvelle Barre du Jour*, no. 70 (oct. 1978), 52–79

– 'Du texte et du doute.' *La Nouvelle Barre du Jour*, no. 59 (oct. 1977), 58–75

– 'Ecritures insoumises.' *La Nouvelle Barre du Jour*, no. 114 (mai 1982), 57–71

– 'Sous la forme.' *Hobo-Québec*, nos. 4–5 (1973), 30–1

Bélair, Michel. 'L'Homme multi-dimensionel.' *Le Devoir*, 24 March 1973, 20, cols. 4–8

Bélanger, Marcel. 'La Lettre contre l'esprit ou quelques points de repère sur la poésie de Claude Gauvreau.' *Etudes littéraires* 3 (déc. 1972), 481–97

Bennett, Donna. 'Their Own Tongue.' *Canadian Literature*, no. 107 (1985), 152–5

Berthiaume, Christiane. 'Raoul Duguay aux prises avec Luor Yaugud.' *La Presse*, 21 April 1973, 2, col. 1

Blodgett, E.D. 'Dickinson's Dash: An Apologia for Poetry.' *Open Letter*, 2nd ser., no. 2 (Spring 1972), 21–34

Bonenfant, Joseph. 'Lakolipsô.' *Livres et auteurs québécois* (1971), 145–7

Boone, Bruce. 'Writing's Current Impasse and the Possibilities for Renewal.' *Open Letter*, 5th ser., no. 1 (Winter 1982), 121–8

Bourassa, André. 'Duguay ou l'envers et l'endroit.' *Lettres Québécoises*, no. 3 (1976), 12–14

Brady, Elisabeth. 'The Martyrology.' *Canadian Book Review Annual 1976*, 194–9

Charron, François. 'Violences, répercussions: Denis Vanier.' *Presqu'Amér-ique* 1, no. 10 (oct.–nov. 1972), 23–4

Cloutier, Cécile. 'L'Avant-garde dans la littérature québécoise.' *Présence francophone*, no. 3 (automne 1971), 60–8

Coffey, Michael. 'Grammatology and Economy.' *Open Letter*, 6th ser., no. 9 (Fall 1987), 27–38

Cogswell, Fred. 'Near the Bone.' *Canadian Literature*, no. 49 (Summer 1971), 96–8

Colombo, John Robert. 'New Wave Nichol.' *The Tamarack Review*, no. 47 (Summer 1967), 100–5

Cooley, Dennis. 'Replacing.' *Essays on Canadian Writing*, nos. 18–19 (Summer–Fall 1980), 9–20

Cooley, Dennis, and Robert Enright. 'Uncovering our Dream World: An Inter-view with Robert Kroetsch.' *Arts Manitoba* 1, no. 1 (Jan.–Feb. 1977), 33–7

Davey, Frank. 'Exegesis/Eggs à Jésus: *The Martyrology* as a Text in Crisis.' *Open Letter*, 5th ser., nos. 5–6 (Summer–Fall 1986), 169–82
– *From There to Here*. Erin, Ont.: Press Porcépic 1974
– 'Nobody Owns the Earth.' *The Canadian Forum*, July–August 1972, 44–5
David, Jack. 'My Mouth's on Fire.' *Quill & Quire* 35, no. 1 (Nov. 1974), 22
– 'Visual Poetry in Canada: Birney, Bissett and bp.' *Studies in Canadian Literature* 2, no. 2 (Summer 1974), 252–60
de Bellefeuille, Normand. 'Le Corps mineur ou l'impossible lyrisme.' *La Nouvelle Barre du Jour*, no. 58 (sept. 1977), 82–91
Dorscht, Susan. 'A Deconstructive Narratology: Reading Robert Kroetsch's *Alibi*.' *Open Letter*, 6th ser., no. 8 (Summer 1987), 78–83
Doyle, Mike. 'Notes on Concrete Poetry.' *Canadian Literature*, no. 46 (Autumn 1970), 51–95
Durand, Régis. 'Etats de la performance.' *Parachute*, no. 18 (printemps 1980), 24
Dutton, Paul. 'Confronting Conventions: The Musical/Dramatic Works of bpNichol.' *Open Letter*, 5th ser., nos. 5–6 (Summer–Fall 1986), 131–50
– 'Open Journal: Milwaukee.' *Open Letter*, 3rd ser., no. 8 (Spring 1978), 44–51
– 'The Sonic Graffitist: Steve McCaffery as Improvisor.' *Open Letter*, 6th ser., no. 9 (Fall 1987), 17–26
Dybikowski, Ann, ed. *In the Feminine*. Edmonton: Longspoon Press 1985 [Proceedings from the 'Women and Words' Conference, Vancouver 1983]
Early, Len. 'Bill Bissett: Poetics, Politics and Vision.' *Essays on Canadian Writing*, no. 5 (Fall 1976), 4–24
Farkas, Andre, and Ken Norris, eds. *Montreal: English Poetry of the Seventies*. Montreal: Véhicule Press 1978
Forsyth, Louise. 'Regards, reflets, reflux.' *La Nouvelle Barre du Jour*, nos. 118–19 (1982), 11–26
Frappier, Roger. 'L'Infonie inachevée: un film portrait' [une entrevue de Jean Pierre Tadros]. *Cinéma Québec* 3, no. 2 (oct. 1973), 20–6
Geddes, Gary. 'An Evening of Concrete: The Cosmic Chef by bpNichol.' *The Globe and Mail*, 10 Oct. 1970, 20
Gibbs, Robert. 'Drifting into War.' *The Fiddlehead*, no. 94 (Summer 1972), 133–5
Giguère, Richard, and André Marquis. 'Les Herbes Rouges 1968–1988: persister et se maintenir' [entrevue avec Normand de Bellefeuille, Carole Massé, André Roy, France Théoret]. *Lettres Québécoises*, no. 51 (automne 1988), 10–17
Godard, Barbara. 'Epi(pro)logue: In Pursuit of the Long Poem.' *Open Letter*, 6th ser., nos. 2–3 (Summer–Fall 1985), 301–35

Greengrass, E.E. 'Nichol's Prose.' *Canadian Literature*, no. 85 (Summer 1980), 142–4

Haeck, Philippe. *Naissances: de l'écriture québécoise*. Montréal: VLB 1979

– *L'Action restreinte de la littérature*. Montréal: VLB 1975

– 'La Poésie en 1975.' *Chroniques*, no. 15 (mars 1976), 39–52

– *La Table d'écriture: poéthique et modernité*. Montréal: VLB 1984

Hall, Chris. 'Two Poems of Place: Williams' *Paterson* and Marlatt's *Steveston*.' *The Canadian Review of American Studies*, no. 15 (1984), 141–57

Harvey, Roderick. 'bpNichol: The Repositioning of Language.' *Essays on Canadian Writing*, no. 4 (Spring 1976), 19–33

Henderson, Brian. 'Beyond Martyrology.' *The Canadian Forum*, Feb. 1980, 36–7

– 'Radical Poetics.' Diss. York University 1982

– 'Soul Rising out of the Body of Language: Presence, Process and Faith in *The Martyrology*.' *Open Letter*, 5th ser., nos. 5–6 (Summer–Fall 1986), 111–28

Johnson, Eileen. 'bp.' *The Vancouver Sun*, 3 April 1979, 7a, cols. 1–2

Kamboureli, Smaro. 'Locality as Writing: A Preface to the Preface of *Out of Place*.' *Open Letter*, 6th ser., nos. 2–3 (Summer–Fall 1985) [Longliners issue], 267–77

Kostelanetz, Richard. 'The New Poetries in North America.' *Open Letter*, 2nd ser., no. 7 (Winter 1974), 18–39

Kroetsch, Robert. 'For Play and Entrance: The Canadian Long Poem.' *Open Letter*, 5th ser., no. 4 (Spring 1983), 91–110

Kröller, Eva Marie. 'Canadian Identity and the Long Poem.' *CRNLE Reviews Journal*, no. 1 (1986), 33–6

Lacroix, Pierre. 'Le Manifeste de l'infonie.' In *Livres et auteurs québécois* (1970), 139–40

Lamy, Suzanne. 'L'Emergence du féminin.' *Le Devoir*, 11 Nov. 1981, 13

Lane, Travis. 'Self-conscious Art.' *The Fiddlehead*, no. 142 (1984), 96–107

Laroche, Maximilien. '*Ruts* de Raoul Duguay.' In *Livres et auteurs canadiens* (1966), 108–11

Lecker, Robert. 'Bordering On: Robert Kroetsch's Aesthetic.' *Journal of Canadian Studies* 17, no. 3 (Fall 1982), 124–33

– 'Daphne Marlatt's Poetry.' *Canadian Literature*, no. 76 (1978), 56–67

– *Robert Kroetsch by Robert Kroetsch*. Boston: Twayne 1986

Leger, Pierrot (le fou). 'Denys Vanier ou la solitude littéraire.' *Main Mise*, no. 33 (mars 1974), 3

Lever, Bernice. 'Horse d'oeuvres.' *Quill & Quire*, Aug. 1975, 16

Lowndes, Joan. 'Artist-Poet Bissett Shows Works of Mystic Mood.' *The Vancouver Sun*, 26 Oct. 1972, 36

– 'Show Embraces New Art Trends.' *The Vancouver Sun*, 15 Sept. 1971, 45

McCaffery, Steve. 'Bill Bissett: A Writing outside Writing.' *Open Letter*, 3rd ser., no. 9 (Fall 1978), 7–23

– '*The Martyrology* as Paragram.' *Open Letter*, 5th ser., nos. 5–6 (Summer–Fall 1986), 191–206

MacKendrick, Louis K. 'Robert Kroetsch and the Modern Canadian Novel of Exhaustion.' *Essays on Canadian Writing*, no. 11 (Summer 1978), 10–27

Maheu, Pierre. 'La Poésie rebelle de Raoul Duguay.' *Parti Pris* 5, no. 6 (mars 1968), 51–3

Makward, Christiane. 'La Critique féministe: éléments d'une problématique.' *Revue des sciences humaines*, no. 168 (1977), 619–24

Manguel, Alberto. 'No Excuses.' *Books in Canada*, Oct. 1983, 22

Marchand, Jacques. *Claude Gauvreau: poète et mythocrate*. Montréal: VLB 1979

Miki, Roy. 'The Cosmology of the Long Poem.' *Open Letter*, 6th ser., nos. 2–3 (Summer–Fall 1985), 71–84

– *Tracing the Paths: Reading/Writing 'The Martyrology.'* Vancouver: Talonbooks 1988

Milot, Louise. 'Nicole Brossard: une influence couteuse.' In *Modernité/Postmodernité du roman contemporain*. Actes du Collogue International de l'Université Libre de Bruxelles, 1985, 77–86

Nepveu, Pierre. 'Nicole Brossard: notes sur une écologie.' *La Nouvelle Barre du Jour*, nos. 118–19 (1982), 139–46

Nichol, bp. 'The Typogeography of bill bissett.' In *We Sleep inside Each Other All*. By bill bissett. Toronto: Ganglia Press 1966, n. pag.

Norris, Ken. 'An Open Letter to David O'Rourke concerning Montreal Poetry.' *CV/II* 5, no. 1, 52–3

– *Talking Poetries*. Montreal: Maker Press 1980

Norris, Ken, and Peter Van Toorn, eds. *The Insecurity of Art: Essays on Poetics*. Montreal: Véhicule Press 1982

Novak, Mary. 'Bissett the Visionary.' *The Vancouver Sun*, 11 April 1975, 43, cols. 1–4

Paradis, Suzanne. 'Les Lettres québécoises en 1968.' *Etudes littéraires* 2, no. 2 (août 1969), 214–20

Pelletier, Jacques. 'L'Itinéraire de François Charron: des lendemains qui chantent au temps des incertitudes.' In Pelletier, ed., *L'Avant-garde culturelle et littéraire des années 70 au Québec*. 99–118

Pilon, Jean-Guy. 'La Poésie selon Duguay.' *Le Devoir*, 20 Jan. 1968, 13, col. 4

– 'La Poésie selon Duguay: évolution ou révolution.' *Le Devoir*, 12 Sept. 1970, 13, cols. 1–8

Pontault, Alain. 'Reprise de Babababellll.' *Montréal Matin*, 10 March 1969, 28

Pourbaix, Joël. 'Paul Chamberland: la posture utopiste.' In Pelletier, ed.,
   L'Avant-garde culturelle et littéraire des années 70 au Québec, 83–92
Reiss, Robert. 'Towards a Language of the Sensibility.' *The Structurist*, no. 12
   (1972–3), 17–21
Roy, André. 'La Verge au beau tarif: la différentiation signifiante généralisée.'
   La Nouvelle Barre du Jour, nos. 118–19 (1982), 113–20
Saucier, Michèle. '*L'Amèr, Le Sens apparent, Amantes.*' *La Nouvelle Barre
   du Jour*, nos. 118–19 (1982), 27–44
Scobie, Stephen. 'A Dash for the Border.' *Canadian Literature*, no. 53 (Sum-
   mer 1972), 89–92
– 'Journal, bpNichol.' *The Fiddlehead*, no. 121 (Spring 1973), 136–9
– 'Look Out, the Saints Are Comin' Through.' *The Fiddlehead*, no. 120
   (Winter 1979), 115–22
– 'Metaphor beyond Language.' *The Structurist*, no. 12 (1972–3), 37–55
– 'Surviving the Paraph-raise.' *Open Letter*, 5th ser., nos. 5–6 (Summer–Fall
   1986), 49–68
– 'Two Authors in Search of a Character.' *Canadian Literature*, no. 54
   (Autumn 1972), 37–55
– 'Vingt ans de poésie concrète.' *Ellipse*, no. 17 (1975), 180–8
– 'The Words You Trust to Take You Thru: An Introduction to bpNichol's
   The Martyrology.' *Precisely*, no. 1 (Nov. 1977), 15–21
Scully, Robert Guy. 'L'Automatisme de Gauvreau et le gazouillis de Duguay.'
   Le Devoir, 11 Jan. 1973, 12, cols. 1–8
Sedgwick, Don. 'Sound Poetry: A Catalogue.' *Quill & Quire*, Feb. 1979, 20
Sherry, James. 'Limits of Grammar.' *Open Letter*, 5th ser., no. 1 (Winter
   1982), 108–12
Shikatani, Gerry. 'Briefly: To Martyr and to Suffer.' *Open Letter*, 5th ser.,
   nos. 5–6 (Summer–Fall 1986), 227–36
Smith, Steven. 'bp Nichol: Sonic Snapshots. Fragmentary Movements.' *Open
   Letter*, 5th ser., nos. 5–6 (Summer–Fall 1986), 69–72
Sondheim, Alan. 'Orange County California and the Economics of Language.'
   Open Letter, 5th ser., no. 1 (Winter 1982), 141–6
Stevens, Peter. 'Canadian Writers as Artists.' *Canadian Literature*, no. 46
   (Fall 1970), 19–34
– 'Experimental Poetry since 1950.' *Laurentian University Review* 2, no. 10
   (Feb. 1978), 47–61
– 'Has bpNichol Lost His Ear?' *The Globe and Mail*, 4 Nov. 1972, 35, cols. 1–2
– 'The Perils of a Majority.' *The University of Windsor Review* 9, no. 2
   (Spring 1974), 100–9
Straram, Patrick. 'Vanier – écriture/procès.' *Les Herbes Rouges*, no. 17 (fév.
   1974), n. pag.

Stratford, Philip. 'Fine, but Will They Make It to the Eighties?' *The Globe and Mail*, 27 Nov. 1971, 33, cols. 1–3

Surette, P.L. 'The Fabula Fiction of Robert Kroetsch.' *Canadian Literature*, no. 77 (Summer 1978), 6–19

Tallman, Warren. 'Wonder Merchants: Modernist Poetry in Vancouver during the 1960's.' In Gervais, ed., *The Writing Life*, 27–69

Théoret, France. 'Le Sens de la formule.' *La Nouvelle Barre du Jour*, nos. 118–19 (1982), 77–82

Thériault, Jacques. 'Un poète oral et bienheureux.' *Le Devoir*, 15 June 1975, 12, cols. 1–4

Thomas, Suzanne. 'La Poésie n'est pas que belle, elle est rebelle.' *La Patrie*, 30 March 1969, 63, cols. 3–4

Tostevin, Lola Lemire. 'Paternal Body as Outlaw.' *Open Letter*, 5th ser., nos. 5–6 (Summer–Fall 1986), 77–80

Townsend, Charlotte. 'Poem-Drawings in Praise of Mysteries.' *The Vancouver Sun*, 1 Aug. 1969, 25, cols. 1–3

Wachtel, Eleanor. 'Why bb into cc Won't Go.' *Books in Canada*, June–July 1979, 3–6

Woodcock, George. 'A Swarming of Poets: An Editorial Reportage.' *Canadian Literature*, no. 50 (Fall 1971), 3–16

– 'Poetry.' In *Literary History of Canada*. 2nd ed. Gen. ed. Carl F. Klinck. Toronto: University of Toronto Press 1976. III, 301–2

Young, Earl, and Kevin Power. 'Between Poetry and Painting: A Preface.' *Open Letter*, 4th ser., nos. 1–2 (Summer 1978), 7–10

ANTHOLOGIES OF CONCRETE

Bann, Stephen, ed. *Concrete Poetry: An International Anthology*. London: London Magazine Editions 1967

Barreto-Rivera, Rafael, Paul Dutton, Steve McCaffery, and bpNichol. *Horse-d'oeuvres: Four Horsemen*. Toronto: General Publishing 1975

Birney, Earle, bill bissett, Judith Copithorne, and Andrew Suknaski. *Four Parts Sand*. Toronto: Oberon Press 1972

Bremmer, Claus, and Daniel Spoerri, eds. *Konkrete poesie international*. Stuttgart: Hansjorg Mayer 1957

Brown, Jim, and David Phillips, eds. *West Coast Seen*. Vancouver: Talonbooks 1969

Colombo, John Robert, ed. *New Directions in Canadian Poetry: An Anthology*. Toronto: Rinehart and Winston 1971

Colombo, John Robert, and bpNichol, eds. *The Cosmic Chef: An Evening of Concrete*. Ottawa: Oberon Press 1970

Solt, Mary Ellen. *Concrete Poetry: A World View*. Bloomington: Indiana University Press 1969

Williams, Emmett, ed. *An Anthology of Concrete Poetry*. New York: Something Else Press 1967

CONCRETE / NEW WRITING / DECONSTRUCTION / POST-MODERN WORKS

Beaudet, André. *Félix Culpa*. Montréal: Les Herbes Rouges 1982
– *Fréquences en l'inscription du roman*. Montréal: L'Aurore 1975
– *Interventions du parlogue*. Montréal: Les Herbes Rouges 1985
– *Littérature l'imposture*. Montréal: Les Herbes Rouges 1984

Beausoleil, Claude. *Avatars du trait*. Montréal: L'Aurore 1974
– *Une certaine fin de siècle*. Montréal: Le Noroît 1983
– *Concrete City: Selected Poems 1972–1982*. Montreal: Guernica 1983
– *Dans la matière rêvant comme d'une émeute*. Trois-Rivières: Ecrit des Forges 1982
– *Dead Line*. Montréal: Danielle Laliberté 1974
– *Journal mobile*. Montréal: Ed. du Jour 1974
– *Motilité*. Montréal: L'Aurore 1975
– *Promenade Modern Style*. Montréal: Cul Q 1975
– *Sens interdit*. Montréal: Cul Q 1976
– *Sirrocco: poème-affiche*. Montréal: Cul Q 1976
– *Le temps Maya*. Montréal: Cul Q 1977

Birney, Earle. *Alphabeings and Other Seasyours*. London, Ont.: Pikadilly Press 1976
– *Collected Poems*. 2 vols. Toronto: McClelland and Stewart 1975
– *Ice, Cod, Bell or Stone*. Toronto: McClelland and Stewart 1962
– *Pnomes, Jukollages and Other Stunzas*. Toronto: Ganglia Press 1969
– *Turvey: A Military Picaresque*. Toronto: McClelland and Stewart 1976
– *What's So Big about Green?* Toronto: McClelland and Stewart 1973

Birney, Earle, and Andrew Suknaski. *Fragments for the Wind*. Vancouver: Wind Press 1969

bissett, bill. *An Allusyun to Macbeth*. Coatsworth, Ont.: Black Moss Press 1976
– *Awake in th Red Desert*. Vancouver: Talonbooks 1968
– *Blew Trewz*. Vancouver: Blew Ointment Press 1971
– *Drawings*. Vancouver: Blew Ointment Press 1974
– *Drifting into War*. Vancouver: Talonbooks 1971
– *Th fifth sun*. Vancouver: Blew Ointment Press 1975
– *Fires in th Tempul*. Vancouver: Very Stone House 1967
– *Th First Snow*. Vancouver: Blew Ointment Press 1979

– *Th Gossamer Bed-Pan*. Vancouver: Blew Ointment Press 1967
– *IBM*. Vancouver: Blew Ointment Press 1972
– *Ice*. Vancouver: Writers Forum 1974
– *Image being*. Vancouver: Blew Ointment Press 1975
– *Th Jinx Ship nd Othur Trips: Pomes – Drawings – Collages*. Vancouver: Very Stone House 1966
– *Living with th Vishyun*. Vancouver: New Star Books 1974
– *Liberating Skies*. Vancouver: Blew Ointment Press 1970
– *Lost Angel Mining Company*. Vancouver: Blew Ointment Press 1969
– *Medicine, My Mouth's on Fire*. Ottawa: Oberon Press 1974
– *Nobody Owns th Earth*. Toronto: Anansi 1970
– *Northern Birds in Color*. Vancouver: Talonbooks 1981
– *Of the Land Divine Service*. Toronto: Weed Flower Press 1968
– *Pass th Food, Release th Spirit*. Vancouver: Blew Ointment Press 1973
– *Pomes for Yoshi*. Vancouver: Blew Ointment Press 1972
– *Pomes for Yoshi*. Vancouver: Talonbooks 1977
– *Plutonium Missing*. Vancouver: Intermedia 1976
– *Sa n His Crystal Ball*. Vancouver: Blew Ointment Press 1981
– *Sa n the Monkey: A Bedtime Coloring Spree Pome Book*. Vancouver: Blew Ointment Press 1980
– *Seagull on Yonge Street*. Vancouver: Talonbooks 1983
– *Selected Poems: Beyond Even Faithful Legends*. Vancouver: Talonbooks 1980
– *So th Story I to*. Vancouver: Blew Ointment Press 1970
– *Soul Arrow*. Vancouver: Blew Ointment Press 1980
– *Stardust*. Vancouver: Blew Ointment Press 1975
– *Sunday Work?* Vancouver: Blew Ointment Press 1967
– *Vancouver Mainland Ice & Cold Storage*. n.p.: Writers Forum 1974
– *Venus*. Vancouver: Blew Ointment Press 1975
– *We Sleep inside Each Other All*. Toronto: Ganglia 1966
– *What*. Vancouver: Blew Ointment Press 1974
– *What Fuckan Theory: A Study uv Language*. Toronto: Gronk Press 1971
– *What Poetiks*. Vancouver: Blew Ointment Press 1976
– *Where is Miss Florence Riddle?* Vancouver: Blew Ointment Press 1973
– *Th Wind Up Tongue*. Vancouver: Blew Ointment Press 1976
– *Words in th Fire*. Vancouver: Blew Ointment Press 1972
– *Yu Can Eatit at th Opening*. Vancouver: Blew Ointment Press 1974
Boisvert, Yves. *Simulacre dictatoriel*. Trois-Rivières: Ecrits des Forges 1979
Boucher, Denise, and Madeleine Gagnon. *Retailles: complaintes politiques*. Montréal: Editions L'Etincelle 1977
Brossard, Nicole. *Amantes*. Montréal: Quinze 1980

- *L'Amèr ou le chapitre effrité*. Montréal: Quinze 1977
- *Le Centre blanc*. Montréal: L'Hexagone 1970
- *Daydream Mechanics*. Trans. Larry Shouldice. Toronto: Coach House Press 1980
- *Double impression: poèmes et textes 1967–1984*. Montréal: L'Hexagone 1984
- *L'Echo bouge beau*. Montréal: Estérel 1968
- *Le Forum des femmes*. Outremont: NBJ 1986
- *French-Kiss*. Montréal: Editions du Jour 1974
- *French Kiss or a Pang's Progress*. Trans. Patricia Claxton. Toronto: Coach House Press 1986
- *Journal intime ou voilà donc un manuscrit*. Montréal: Les Herbes Rouges 1984
- *La Lettre aérienne*. Montréal: Editions Remue Ménage 1985
- *Un livre*. Montréal: Editions du Jour 1970
- *Lovhers*. Montréal: Guernica 1986
- *Mécanique jongleuse*. Paris: Génération 1973
- *Mécanique jongleuse*, suivi de *Masculin grammaticale*. Montréal: L'Hexagone 1974
- *Mordre en sa chair*. Montréal: Estérel 1966
- *La Partie pour le tout*. Montréal: L'Aurore 1975
- *Picture Theory*. Montréal: Nouvelle Optique 1982
- *Le Sens apparent*. Paris: Flammarion 1980
- *Sold-out*. Montréal: Editions du Jour 1973
- *Suite logique*. Montréal: L'Hexagone 1970
- *These Our Mothers; or, The Disintegrating Chapter*. Trans. Barbara Godard. Toronto: Coach House Press 1983

Charlebois, Jean. *La Mour/L'Amort*. Montréal: Le Noroît 1982

Charron, François. *D'où viennent les tableaux?* Montréal: Les Herbes Rouges 1983
- *Feu*. Montréal: Les Herbes Rouges 1981
- *La Fragilité des choses*. Montréal: Les Herbes Rouges 1987
- *Interventions politiques*. Montréal: Les Herbes Rouges 1974
- *Je suis ce que je suis*. Montréal: Les Herbes Rouges 1983
- *1980*. Montréal: Les Herbes Rouges 1980
- *La Passion d'autonomie*. Montréal: Les Herbes Rouges 1982
- *Pirouette par hasard poésie*. Montréal: L'Aurore 1975
- *Projet d'écriture pour l'été 1976*. Montréal: Les Herbes Rouges 1973
- *Le Temps échappé des yeux*. Montréal: Les Herbes Rouges 1979
- *Toute parole m'éblouira*. Montréal: Les Herbes Rouges 1982

Cixous, Hélène. *La Jeune née*. Paris: Union Générale d'Editeurs 1979

Copithorne, Judith. *Heartside*. Vancouver: Community Press 1973
– *Meanderings*. Vancouver: Returning Press 1967
– *Miss Tree's Pillow Book*. Vancouver: Intermedia 1971
– *Rain*. Toronto: Ganglia Press 1969
– *Release: Poem-drawings*. Vancouver: Baux-xi Gallery 1969
– *Returning*. Vancouver: Returning Press 1965
– *Runes*. Toronto: Coach House Press 1970
– *Until Now*. Vancouver: Heshe and it works 1971
Collette, Jean Yves. *A propos du texte/textualisation*. Outremont: NBJ 1985
– *Carré de contrainte*. Outremont: NBJ 1986
Corriveau, Hughes. *A Double sens: échanges sur quelques pratiques modernes*. Montréal: Les Herbes Rouges 1986
– *Les Compléments directs*. Montréal: Les Herbes Rouges 1978
– *Le Grégaire inefficace*. Montréal: Les Herbes Rouges 1979
– *Du masculin singulier*. Montréal: Les Herbes Rouges 1981
– *Revoir le rouge*. Montréal: VLB 1983
– *Les Taches de naissance*. Montréal: Les Herbes Rouges 1982
Dargis, Daniel. *Scénario grammatical*. Trois-Rivières: Ecrits des Forges 1982
de Bellefeuille, Normand. *Pourvu que ça ait mon nom*. Montréal: Les Herbes Rouges 1979
Dedora, Brian. *He Moved*. Toronto: Underwhich Editions 1979
des Roches, Roger. *L'Observatoire romanesque*. Montréal: Les Herbes Rouges 1979
– *Reliefs de l'arsenal*. Montréal: Les Herbes Rouges 1986
Dudek, Louis, and the Véhicule poets. *A Real Good Gossin': Talking Poetics*. Montreal: Maker Press 1980
Duguay, Raoul. *Lapokalipsô*. Montréal: Editions du Jour 1971
– *Le Manifeste de l'infonie*. Montréal: Editions du Jour 1970
Dupré, Louise. *La Peau familière*. Montréal: Editions Remue Ménage 1983
Farkas, Andre. *Face-off*. Montreal: The Muses' Company 1980
– *From Her to Here*. Montreal: The Muses' Company 1982
– *Romantic at Heart and Other Faults*. Montreal: Cross Country Press 1979
Fougues, Paul, and John McAuley. *The Véhicule Poets*. Montreal: Maker Press 1979
Francoeur, Lucien. *Drive-In*. Paris: Seghers 1976
– *Minibrixes réactés*. Montréal: L'Hexagone 1972
– *Néon in the Night*. Trans. S. Harwood. Montreal: Véhicule Press 1981
– *A Propos de l'été du serpent*. Paris: LeCastor Astral 1980
– *Rockeurs sanctifiés*. Montréal: L'Hexagone 1982
– *Snack-bar*. Montréal: Les Herbes Rouges 1973   .
Gagnon, Madeleine. *Au coeur de la lettre*. Montréal: VLB 1981

– *Autographie I: fictions*. Montréal: VLB 1982
– *La Lettre infinie*. Montréal: VLB 1984
– *Pensées du poème*. Montréal: VLB 1983
– *Poélitique*. Montréal: Les Herbes Rouges 1975
– *Pour les femmes et tous les autres*. Montréal: L'Aurore 1974
Gay, Michel. *Mentalité détail*. Montréal: NBJ 1986
Haeck, Philippe. *La Parole Verte*. Montréal: VLB 1981
Konyves, Tom. *Poetry in Performance*. Montreal: The Muses' Company 1982
Kroetsch, Robert. *Field Notes 1–8, a Continuing Poem: The Collected Poetry of Robert Kroetsch*. Don Mills, Ont.: General Publishing 1981
– *The Ledger*. London: Applegarth Follies 1975
– *Seed Catalogue: Poems*. Winnipeg: Turnstone Press 1977
– *The Stone Hammer Poems, 1960–1975*. Nanaimo: Oolichan Books 1975
Labine, Marcel. *La Marche de la dictée*. Montréal: Les Herbes Rouges 1980
Lapointe, Paul-Marie. *Ecritures*. Montréal: L'Obsidienne 1980
Lewis, Ken. *THESE!encampments!* Kingston, Ont.: Quarry Press 1982
McAuley, John. *Hazardous Renaissance: Concrete Poetry*. Montreal: Cross Country 1978
McCaffery, Steve. *Panopticon*. Toronto: Blew Ointment Press 1984
– *A Section from Carnival*. Toronto: Ganglia Press 1969
– *Transitions to the Beast: Post-Semiotic Poems*. Toronto: Ganglia Press 1970
McCaffery, Steve, and bpNichol. *In England Now That Spring*. Toronto: Aya Press 1979
Marlatt, Daphne. *How Hug a Stone*. Winnipeg: Turnstone Press 1982
– *Leaf Is*. Los Angeles: Black Sparrow Press 1969
– *Selected Writing: Net Work*. Vancouver: Talonbooks 1980
– *Steveston: Poems*. Vancouver: Talonbooks 1974
– *Touch to My Tongue*. Edmonton: Longspoon Press 1984
– *What Matters: Writing 1968–1970*. Toronto: Coach House Press 1980
Massé, Carole. *Dieu*. Montréal: Les Herbes Rouges 1979
– *L'Existence*. Montréal: Les Herbes Rouges 1984
– *Je vous aime*. Montréal: Les Herbes Rouges 1986
Morrissey, Stephen. *Divisions*. Toronto: Coach House Press 1983
Nations, Opal L. *Inter-Sleep*. Montreal: Véhicule Press 1978
– *The Strange Case of Inspector Loophole*. Montreal: Véhicule Press 1977
Nichol, bp. *ABC, the Aleph Beth Book*. Ottawa: Oberon Press 1971
– *Alphabet*. Toronto: Seri Press 1978
– *Captain Poetry Poems*. Vancouver: Blew Ointment Press 1970
– *Continental Trance*. Lantzville, BC: Oolichan Books 1982
– *Craft Dinner: Stories & Texts 1966–1976*. Toronto: Aya Press 1978
– *Criss-Cross: A Textbook of Modern Composition*. Toronto: Coach House Press 1977

- *Doors to Oz*. Toronto: Seri Press 1979
- *Grease Ball Comics I*. Toronto: Ganglia Press 1970
- *Journeying and the Returns*. Toronto: Coach House Press 1967
- *Konfessions of an Elizabethan Fan Dancer*. Toronto: Weed Flower Press 1973
- *Love: A Book of Remembrances*. Vancouver: Talonbooks 1974
- *Love Affair*. Toronto: Seri Press 1979
- *The Martyrology: Books I and II*. Toronto: Coach House Press 1972
- *The Martyrology: Books III and IV*. Toronto: Coach House Press 1976
- *The Martyrology: Book V*. Toronto: Coach House Press 1982
- *Monotones*. Vancouver: Talonbooks 1971
- *Moosequakes & Other Disasters*. Windsor: Black Moss Press 1981
- *Mutetations*. Vancouver: Very Stone House 1969
- *Nights on Prose Mountain*. Toronto: Ganglia Press 1969
- *Of Lines: Some Drawings*. Toronto: Underwhich Editions 1981
- *The Other Side of the Room*. Toronto: Weed Flower Press 1972
- *Postcard*. Toronto: Coach House Press 1969
- *Selected Poems: The Arches*. Vancouver: Talonbooks 1980
- *Selected Writing: As Elected*. Vancouver: Talonbooks 1980
- *Still*. Vancouver: Pulp Press 1983
- *Still Water*. Vancouver: Talonbooks 1970
- *The True Eventual Story of Billy the Kid*. Toronto: Weed Flower Press 1970
- *White Sound*. Toronto: Ganglia Press 1976

Norris, Ken, and Peter Van Toorn. *Cross-cut: Contemporary English Quebec Poetry*. Montreal: Véhicule Press 1982

O'Huigin, Sean. *Poe Tree*. Windsor: Black Moss Press 1978
- *The Ink, the Pencils and the Looking Back*. Toronto: Coach House Press 1978

Péloquin, Claude. *Manifeste infra*. Montréal: L'Hexagone 1967
- *Oeuvres complètes: le premier tiers*. Montréal: Beauchemin 1976

Pozier, Bernard, Yves Boisvert, and Gille Lemire. *Code d'oubli*. Trois-Rivières: Ecrits des Forges 1978
- *45 Tours*. Trois-Rivières: Ecrits des Forges 1981
- *Manifeste: Jet, Usage, Résidu*. Trois-Rivières: Ecrits des Forges 1977
- *Têtes de lecture*. Trois-Rivières: Ecrits des Forges 1980

Roy, André. *Les Lits de l'Amérique*. Montréal: Les Herbes Rouges 1983
- *Monsieur Désir*. Montréal: Les Herbes Rouges 1981
- *Petit Supplément aux passions*. Montréal: Les Herbes Rouges 1980

Smith, Steve. *Intervals & Elevations*. Toronto: Phenomenon Press 1979

Sommer, Richard. *Blue Sky Notebook*. Montreal: Delta 1974

Straram, Patrick. *4 × 4/4 × 4*. Montréal: Les Herbes Rouges 1974
- *Irish Coffees au no name bar*. Montréal: L'Hexagone 1972

- *Tea for One / No More Tea*. Montréal: Les Herbes Rouges 1983
Suknaski, Andrew. *Circles*. Wood Mountain, Sask.: Deodar Shadow Press [197?]
- *Montage for an Interstellar Cry*. Winnipeg: Turnstone Press 1982
- *Old Mill*. Vancouver: Blew Ointment Press 1972
Théoret, France. *Bloody Mary*. Montréal: Les Herbes Rouges 1977
- *Nécessairement putain*. Montréal: Les Herbes Rouges 1980
- *Nous parlerons comme on écrit*. Montréal: Les Herbes Rouges 1982
- *Une voix pour Odile*. Montréal: Les Herbes Rouges 1978
- *Vertiges*. Montréal: Les Herbes Rouges 1979
Tostevin, Lola Lemire. *Gynotext*. Toronto: Underwhich Editions 1983
- *Color of Her Speech*. Toronto: Coach House Press 1982
UU, David. *Before the Golden Dawn*. Toronto: Weed Flower Press 1971
- *Motion-Pictures*. Toronto: Ganglia Press 1969
Vanier, Denys. *Pornographic Delicatessen*. Montréal: Estérel 1968
- *Lesbiennes d'acid*. Montréal: Parti Pris 1972
Villemaire, Yolande. *Adrénaline*. Montréal: Le Noroît 1982
- *Du Côté hiéroglyphe de ce qu'on appelle le réel*. Montréal: Les Herbes Rouges 1982
- *Que du stage blood*. Montréal: Editions Cul Q 1977
- *Machine-t-elle*. Montréal: Les Herbes Rouges 1974
- *Terre de mue*. Montréal: Editions Cul Q 1978
- *La vie en prose*. Montréal: Les Herbes Rouges 1980
Young, Karl. *Should Sun Forever Shine*. Toronto: Underwhich Editions 1980
Zend, Robert. *Beyond Labels*. Toronto: Hounslow Press 1982
- *From Zero to Zero*. Mission, BC: Sono Nis Press 1970
- *OAB I*. Toronto: Exile Editions 1983
- *OAB II*. Toronto: Exile Editions 1985

CONCRETE / NEW WRITING / DECONSTRUCTED TEXTS PUBLISHED IN MAGAZINES AND PERIODICALS

Auerbach, George. 'Automat-O-Concrete Poem.' *Elfin Plot*, no. 10 (Winter 1971), n. pag.
Aylward, David. 'Journeys.' *Blew Ointment* 5, no. 1 (Jan. 1967), n. pag.
- 'The War against the Asps.' *Gronk*, 4th ser., no. 4 (1968), n. pag.
Ball, Nelson. 'Force Movements.' *Gronk*, 3rd ser., no. 4 (1969), n. pag.
Beausoleil, Claude. 'Ahuntsic Dream' and 'Now.' *Les Herbes Rouges*, no. 27 (mars 1975), 8–28
Bédard, Nicole. 'L'Oscillée.' *La Barre du Jour*. no. 50 (hiver 1975), 105–22
Bélanger, Yrénée. 'Untitled.' *Co-incidences* 1, no. 2 (avril 1971), 10–14

Bertrand, Pierre. 'Machine à laver.' *La Barre du Jour* 3, no. 2 (juin–juillet 1968), 48–53

Birney, Earle. 'First Aid.' *Capilano Review* 1, no. 1 (Spring 1972), 18

- 'On the Night Jet.' *Elfin Plot*, no. 10 (Winter 1971), n. pag.

- 'Schoolhouse.' *Blew Ointment* 5, no. 1 (Jan. 1967), n. pag.

- 'Universe.' *Elfin Plot*, no. 4 (Summer 1970), n. pag.

bissett, bill. '*August* Long.' *Tuatara*, nos. 8–9 (Fall 1972), 80

- 'The Berbers Are Really Camped Out on the Wires Tonight.' *The Canadian Forum*, Feb. 1966, 247

- 'The Body.' *The Canadian Forum*, March 1965, 278

- 'Brother Soul Meets the Safety Ring.' *Alphabet*, nos. 18–19 (June 1971), 14

- 'Calligraphies.' *Alphabet*, no. 9 (Nov. 1964), 94–5

- 'Chile.' *Blew Ointment: Tantrik Speshul* [no date], 48

- 'Dance Beautiful Lady Dance.' *Blew Ointment* 3, no. 1 (Nov. 1965), n. pag.

- 'A Drawing.' *Vigilante*, no. 1 (May 1970), 35

- 'For Martina.' *IS*, no. 2 [no date], 9

- 'The Golden Dawn.' *Vigilante*, no. 1 (May 1970), 37

- 'The Good Ship Changes.' *Vigilante*, no. 1 (May 1970), 41

- 'Good Tea Is Good Tea Good Tea.' *Blew Ointment: Oil Slick Special* (1970), 16

- 'Heads Turned.' *Alphabet*, nos. 18–19 (June 1971), 16

- 'I Can't Take This Any Longer.' *Blew Ointment* 9, no. 7 (June 1967), n. pag.

- 'Ken Wismer Was Here.' *Alphabet*, nos. 18–19 (June 1971), 15

- 'Lebanon Voices: 1st Phase.' *IS*, no. 4 [no date], n. pag.

- 'Lebanon Voices: 3.' *Ganglia*, 1st ser., no. 7 (Nov. 1966–March 1967), n. pag.

- 'The Magic Lure of Sea Shells.' *Alphabet*, nos. 18–19 (June 1971), 17

- 'Now.' *Blew Ointment* 3, no. 1 (Nov. 1965), n. pag.

- 'Ocean Shiftes Yu.' *The Canadian Forum*, July–August 1971, 4

- 'Peopul Get Ready.' *Vigilante*, no. 1 (May 1970), 40

- 'Peopul Still Drink.' *Vigilante*, no. 1 (May 1970), 38

- 'Perhaps.' *Blew Ointment*, Dec. 1972, n. pag.

- 'Phallas.' *Tish*, no. 7 (March 1962), 4

- 'Poetry Is a Worldly Please.' *Blew Ointment: Poverty isshew*, March 1972, 50–3

- 'The Powr of th Dream Is in Heaven.' *Prism* 5, nos. 3–4 (Winter 1965–Spring 1966), 16–19

- 'Remember.' *Tuatara*, nos. 8–9 (Fall 1972), 81

- 'The Sea Is Calling Yu.' *Tuatara*, nos. 8–9 (Fall 1972), 82

- 'A Small Kraft Warning Is in Effect.' *Blew Ointment*, Feb. 1969, n. pag.

- 'Starting th Fire.' *Vigilante*, no. 3 (April 1970), 20

- 'Stuck on the Way to the Sault.' *Open Letter*, 2nd ser., no. 8 (Summer 1974), 61
- 'Tears Cut Grief.' *Blew Ointment* 3, no. 1 (Nov. 1965), n. pag.
- 'They.' *Evidence*, no. 9 (1965), 106
- 'To Draw Paint.' *Evidence*, no. 9 (1965), 105
- 'Transparencies.' *Tish*, no. 31 (Feb. 1966), 6
- 'Untitled.' *Blew Ointment* 3, no. 1 (Nov. 1965), n. pag.
- 'Untitled.' *The Canadian Forum*, June 1968, 56
- 'Untitled.' *Capilano Review* 1, no. 1 (Spring 1972), 52
- 'Untitled.' *Evidence*, no. 9 (1965), 104
- 'Untitled.' *Prism*, no. 2 (Winter 1972), 48–9
- 'Untitled.' *Vigilante*, no. 1 (May 1970), 36
- 'Untitled.' *Vigilante*, no. 1 (May 1970), 39
- 'Untitled.' *Vigilante*, no. 3 (April 1971), 20
- 'Untitled Collages.' *Blew Ointment* 1, no. 6 (1966), n. pag.
- 'Untitled: Cover and Back Page.' *Tuatara*, no. 11 (Winter 1973)
- 'Urinal, Stage Door, Vancouver Art Gallery.' *The Canadian Forum*, April –May 1971, 32
- 'What It Duz for Her.' *The Canadian Forum*, April–May 1971, 32
- 'White Lightning.' *Alphabet*, nos. 18–19 (June 1971), 16
- 'Why Are They So Many John Bay.' *Evidence*, no. 9 (1965), 106
Blackburn, Paul. 'Changing Faces.' *IS*, no. 10 (Summer 1971), n. pag.
Brossard, Nicole. 'Me couler douce l'échine vulnérable.' *La Barre du Jour*, hiver 1973, 24–35
- '*e* muet mutant.' *La Barre du Jour*, no. 50 (hiver 1975), 10–27
- 'Vaseline.' *La Barre du Jour*, nos. 41–2 (automne 1973), 11–17
Broudy, Hart. 'Cluster: A Pome for Corinne.' *Gronk*, 4th ser., no. 2 [1969?], n. pag.
Chamberland, Paul. 'Je n'ai pas.' *La Barre du Jour*, nos. 31–32 (hiver 1972), 50–66
- 'Métronome aphasie.' *La Barre du Jour*, no. 16 (oct.–déc. 1968), 2–11
- 'Untitled.' *La Barre du Jour*, no. 42 (automne 1973), 18–32
- 'Vers le grand changement.' *Main Mise*, oct. 1974, 21
Chute, Robert. 'Collagraphs.' *West Coast Review* 4, no. 1 (June 1973), 34–6
Cixous, Hélène. 'The Laughter of the Medusa.' Trans. Paula Cohen and Keith Cohen. *Signs* 1, no. 4 (Summer 1976), 875–93
Clinton, Martina. 'A Selection of Poems.' *Ganglia*, 1st ser., no. 6 (Jan. 1966), n. pag.
Collette, Jean-Yves. 'VPSSP-2.' *La Barre du Jour*, no. 28 (mai 1971), 2–11
Copithorne, Judith. 'The City's Servings.' *Blew Ointment* 5, no. 1 (Jan. 1967), n. pag.
- '9 Poem-Drawings.' *Alphabet*, nos. 18–19 (June 1971), 30–8

– 'Two Poem-Drawings.' *IS*, no. 6 [no date], 51–2
– 'Untitled.' *Tish*, no. 30 (June 1965), 10
Corriveau, Hughes. 'Troisième Figure.' *La Nouvelle Barre du Jour*, no. 62 (jan. 1978), 13–28
Coté, Michel. 'L'Absence.' *Ellipse*, no. 17 (1975), 39
– 'Untitled.' *Ellipse*, no. 17 (1975), 37
Coupey, Pierre. 'Terminal Collage Series.' *Capilano Review* 1, no. 1 (Spring 1972), 50
David, Gilbert. 'Mémoire d'o(eil) et d'o(eil).' *La Barre du Jour*, no. 25 (été 1970), 52–5
Day, David. 'Barcelona Gallery.' *Tuatara*, nos. 8–9 (Fall 1972), 37
de Campos, Augusto. 'Sem um numero.' *Invencao*, no. 5 (1967), 7
Dewdney, Keewatin. 'Untitled.' *Alphabet*, no. 12 (Aug. 1966), 67
Dexter, Greg. 'Meditation.' *Blew Ointment: Oil Slick Special* (1970), 15
Duguay, Raoul. 'Allô toulmonde.' *Main Mise*, oct. 1973, 47–50
– 'C'est la vie.' *Main Mise*, nov. 1973, 47–9
– 'D'armour suprême de.' *Parti Pris* 5, no. 6 (mars 1968), 53
– 'Duotude.' *La Barre du Jour* 2, no. 3 (jan.–fév. 1966), 20–2
– 'Et sur un seul accord.' *Main Mise*, jan. 1974, 43–5
– 'La Naissance d'Ora.' *Main Mise*, no. 3 (juillet 1974), 31–9
– 'L'Oeil du silence.' *Main Mise*, avril 1974, 36
– 'OM et FAM.' *Main Mise*, mai 1974, 36
– 'La Poésie n'est pas que belle.' *Parti Pris* 5, no. 6 (mars 1968), 52
– 'Pour la terre.' *Main Mise*, déc. 1973, 45–8
– 'La Transe et la Gression.' *La Barre du Jour*, automne 1973, 44–58
– 'Untitled.' *Main Mise*, juin 1974, 48–50
– 'Le Voyage.' *Main Mise*, sept. 1973, 16–17
Dupré, Louise. 'Les Désordres du privé.' *La Nouvelle Barre du Jour*, no. 98 (1981), 5–40
'Editorial.' *Elfin Plot*, no. 9 (Fall 1971) n. pag.
Etlinger, Amelia. 'The Earth Was without Form.' *Antigonish* 1, no. 3 (Autumn 1970), 88
Gilbert, Gerry. 'Four Untitled Poems.' *IS*, no. 6 [no date], 53–6
– 'Phone Book.' *Gronk*, 3rd ser., no. 3 (1969), n. pag.
Gunther, Peter. 'Concrete Poem.' *Elfin Plot*, no. 10 (Winter 1971), n. pag.
Harris, David W. 'Motion Picture.' *Gronk*, 4th ser., no. 1 (1969), n. pag.
Hébert, Marie-Francine. 'Extraits.' *La Barre du Jour*, no. 25 (été 1970), 42–9
– 'Histoire d'écrire.' *La Nouvelle Barre du Jour*, no. 58 (sept. 1977), 55
– 'Où n'es-tu pas que tu ne me tailles en tranches de pain.' *La Barre du Jour*, no. 24 (mars–avril 1970), 20–5
– 'Ping Pong.' *La Barre du Jour*, no. 27 (nov. 1970–fév. 1971), 48–57

Labbe, Jean Marc. 'Pouce par pouce il se pousse.' *La Barre du Jour* 2, no. 3
(jan.–fév. 1967), 32–8

Lachance, Bertrand. 'Untitled: Cover Page.' *Tuatara*, no. 12 (Summer 1974)

Larche, Marcel. 'Triple on the Rock.' *Co-incidences* 1, no. 2 (April 1971),
40–5

– 'Untitled.' *Co-incidences* 1, no. 2 (April 1971), 10–14

Latta, Richard. 'Vision.' *Elfin Plot*, no. 4 (Summer 1970), n. pag.

Lee, Dennis. 'Talking Graffiti Magnificat.' *Blew Ointment: Tantrik Speshul*
[no date], 61

Levy. D.A. 'The Para-Concrete Manifest.' *Blew Ointment* 5, no. 1 (Jan. 1967),
n. pag.

McCaffery, Steve. 'Narrative.' *Open Letter*, 2nd ser., no. 5 (Summer 1973),
17–22

McFadden, David. 'The Round Poem.' *IS*, no. 4 [no date], n. pag.

McMurray, Line. 'A quel titre se vouer.' *La Nouvelle Barre du Jour*, nos.
127–8 (juin 1983), 13–22

Mongeau, France. 'Croquis d'un texte en suspens.' *La Nouvelle Barre du Jour*,
no. 114 (mai 1982), 27–31

Nichol, bp. 'Book of Common Prayer.' *IS*, no. 9 (Fall 1970), n. pag.

– '(b)y wa(y) of a le(tt)er.' *Black Moss* 1, no. 2 [no date], 10

– 'Chapter 2 from a Novel in Progress.' *Capilano Review* 1, no. 5 (Spring
1974), 5–10

– 'Cycle #36.' *Blew Ointment* 5, no. 1 (Jan. 1967), n. pag.

– 'The Death of the Poem.' *Gronk*, 1st ser., no. 1 (Jan. 1967), n. pag.

– 'Family Poem.' *Blew Ointment* 5, no. 2 (Aug. 1968), n. pag.

– 'Four Ideopomes: King Cobra, Christian Cross, Johnny Ray Pomes, Popular
Song.' *Alphabet*, no. 10 (July 1965), 43–4

– 'A Fragment from a Poem Continually in the Process of Being Written.'
Ganglia, 1st ser., no. 6 [no date], n. pag.

– 'Frames.' *IS*, no. 10 (Summer 1971), n. pag.

– 'Green Soap.' *Blew Ointment* 1, no. 9 [no date], n. pag.

– 'A Little Story.' *Tuatara*, nos. 8–9 (Fall 1972), 18

– 'Mike O.' *Tuatara*, nos. 8–9 (Fall 1972), 20

– 'Movie Bill: The Outrage.' *Blew Ointment* 5, no. 1 (Jan. 1967), n. pag.

– 'Old Friends Told Tale.' *Tuatara*, nos. 8–9 (Fall 1972), 17

– 'Real George.' *Tuatara*, nos. 8–9 (Fall 1972), 19

– 'Scraptures.' *Alphabet*, no. 12 (Aug. 1966), 72–3

– 'To Islands Rowboats to Stand On.' *The Canadian Forum*, March 1966,
288

– 'Untitled.' *Blew Ointment* 4, no. 1 (1966), n. pag.

– 'Untitled.' *Island*, nos. 7–8 (May 1967), 61

– 'Waiting.' *Open Letter*, 2nd ser., no. 5 (Summer 1973), 17–22

Page, P.K. 'Poem, illuminated.' *Alphabet*, nos. 18–19 (June 1971), 10

'Poet-arty.' *Alive* 11, no. 9 (April 1971), 22–4

Riddell, John. 'Criss-Cross.' *Ganglia*, 1st ser., no. 4 [no date], n. pag.

Roy, André. '9 septembre.' *Chroniques*, nos. 29–32 (automne 1977–hiver 1978), 314–16

St-Pierre, Gaétan. 'Untitled.' *Les Herbes Rouges*, no. 2 (déc. 1968–mars 1969), 16–17

Schafer, Murray. 'Loving.' *Open Letter*, 4th ser., nos. 4–5 (Fall 1979), 49–64

Smith, A.J.M. 'Those Are Pearls & C.' *Yes*, no. 14 (Sept. 1965), n. pag.

Stafford, Jean. 'Neige 7.' *La Barre du Jour* 2, no. 3 (jan.–fév. 1967), 32–3

Stevens, Peter. 'The Magic Square.' *Alphabet*, no. 12 (Aug. 1966), 66

Straram, Patrick. 'Interprétations de la vie quotidienne.' *Parti Pris* 3, no. 6 (jan. 1966), 52–7, and 3, no. 8 (mars 1966), 67–71

Suknaski, Andrew. 'Dice.' *Vigilante*, no. 2 (Fall 1970), 40

– 'Purse.' *Vigilante*, no. 2 (Fall 1970), 39

– 'Rose Way in the East.' *Gronk*, 4th ser., no. 7 (1969), n. pag.

– 'Synapsis no. 2.' *Gronk* [Runcible Spoon Special Canadian International Number] 5th ser. [no date], n. pag.

– 'Untitled.' *Connexion* 1, no. 4 (April 1971), n. pag.

– 'Way.' *Vigilante*, no. 2 (Fall 1970), 42

Tanguay, Bernard. 'Extrait de Transe-vie express.' *La Barre du Jour*, no. 25 (été 1970), 36–8

Thibaudeau, Colleen. 'A Tree for S & T.' *Connexion* 1, no. 3 (Nov. 1969), n. pag.

Tremblay, Mitch. 'Amendment.' *Alive* 1, no. 7 (Sept.–Oct. 1970), 15–16

Tubman, Vercutio. 'Untitled.' *Far Point*, no. 1 (1968), 39–40

'Untitled: Cover Page.' *Iron*, no. 5 (1969)

UU, David. 'Concrete Poem.' *Elfin Plot*, no. 10 (Winter 1971), n. pag.

– 'Impressions of Africa.' *Capilano Review* 1, no. 1 (Spring 1972), 49

– 'Love.' *Ganglia Concrete Series*, no. 2 (1967), n. pag.

– 'Pigs Blood.' *Alphabet*, nos. 18–19 (June 1971), 11

Vanier, Denys. 'Le clitoris de la fée des étoiles.' *Les Herbes Rouges*, no. 17 (fév. 1974), n. pag.

Vanier, Denys, and Josée Yvon. 'Transpercées.' *Hobo-Québec*, nos. 21–2 (jan.–fév. 1975), 9

Wagner, Donald R. 'Sprouds and Vigables.' *Gronk*, 3rd ser., no. 7 (1969), n. pag.

Zend, Robert. 'Bouquet to BIP.' *Exile* 1, no. 3 (1972), 93–9

– 'OAB.' *Exile* 1, no. 1 (1972), 79–109

– 'The Time of Our Life.' *Exile* 1, no. 3 (1972), 97

RECORDS OF PHONIC POETRY

Barreto-Rivera, Rafael, Steve McCaffery, Paul Dutton, and bpNichol. *Canadada.* Phonodisc, 12 inch, 33½. Toronto: Griffin House 1971
bissett, bill. *Awake in th Red Desert.* Phonodisc. Vancouver: See/Hear Productions 1968
– *Medicine, My Mouth's on Fire.* Microgroove, 7 inch, 45. Inserted in *Medicine, My Mouth's on Fire.* Ottawa: Oberon Press 1974
Duguay, Raoul. *L'Envol.* LP, 33½. Montreal: Disques Capital Emi 1974
– *L'Infonie.* LP, 33½. Montreal: Disques Capital Emi 1971
Nichol, bp. *Borders.* Phonodisc, 7 inch, 45. Inserted in *Journeying and the Returns.* Toronto: Coach House Press 1967

OTHER LITERARY WORKS

Burroughs, William. *Texts.* Paris: L'Heure 1967
Claudel, Paul. *The East I Know.* New Haven: Yale University Press 1914
– *Oeuvres complètes.* 28 vols. Paris: Gallimard 1950–78
– *Oeuvres en prose.* Paris: Gallimard 1965
Gauvreau, Claude. *Oeuvres créatrices complètes.* Montréal: Parti Pris 1977
Giguère, Roland. *L'Age de la parole: poèmes 1949–1960.* Montréal: L'Hexagone 1965
Mallarmé, Stéphane. *Un coup de dés jamais n'abolira le hasard / A throw of dice will never abolish chance.* Trans. Daisy Aldan. New York: Tiber Press 1956
– *Oeuvres complètes.* Paris: Gallimard 1945
Valéry, Paul. *Oeuvres complètes.* Vol. I. Paris: Gallimard 1957. Vol. II. Paris: Gallimard 1971

BIBLIOGRAPHIES

Bayard, Caroline. 'A Raoul Duguay Bibliography.' *Open Letter*, 3rd ser., no. 8 (Spring 1978), 37–9
Caruso, Barbara, and bpNichol. 'A Seripress Bibliography 1971–1979.' *Open Letter*, 6th ser., no. 4 (Spring 1986), 71–8
Curry, J.W. 'Notes toward a Bleepliography' [on bpNichol]. *Open Letter*, 6th ser., nos. 5–6 (Summer–Fall 1986) 249–70
David, Jack. 'A Published Autopo-pography' [bpNichol]. *Essays on Canadian Writing*, no. 1 (Winter 1974), 39–46
Houle, Ghislaine, and Jacques Lafontaine. *Ecrivains québécois de la nouvelle*

culture. Bibliographies québécoises, no. 2. Québec: Ministère des Affaires Culturelles de Gouvernement du Québec 1975

Nichol, bp. 'The Annotated, Anecdoted, Beginnings of a Critical Checklist of the Published Works of Steve McCaffery.' *Open Letter* , 3rd ser., no. 9 (Fall 1987), 67–92

Index

The numbers in bold face refer to the Figures.